DAVID MAMET

DAVID MAMET

Language as Dramatic Action

Anne Dean

Rutherford • Madison • Teaneck
Fairleigh Dickinson University Press
London and Toronto: Associated University Presses

© 1990 by Associated University Presses, Inc.

Associated University Presses
440 Forsgate Drive
Cranbury, NJ 08512

Associated University Presses
25 Sicilian Avenue
London WC1A 2QH, England

Associated University Presses
P.O. Box 488, Port Credit
Mississauga, Ontario
Canada L5G 4M2

The paper used in this publication meets the requirements of the American National Standard for Permanence of Paper for Printed Library Materials Z39.48-1984.

Library of Congress Cataloging-in-Publication Data

Dean, Anne, 1950–
  David Mamet : language as dramatic action / Anne Dean.
    p.   cm.
  Includes bibliographical references.
  ISBN 0-8386-3367-6 (alk. paper)
  1. Mamet, David—Criticism and interpretation.   2. Mamet, David—Language.   3. Mamet, David—Motion picture plays.   I. Title.
  PS3563.A4345Z66   1990
  812'.54—dc20   89-45405
                                                                                CIP

SECOND PRINTING 1992

PRINTED IN THE UNITED STATES OF AMERICA

140008

For my parents
and
Irene

Contents

Preface

The main subject of this book is David Mamet's celebrated use of language as dramatic action. In order to appreciate fully his linguistic techniques, it is necessary to look at his strategies not only as a playwright but also, to a lesser extent, as a writer of screenplays. In the introductory chapter, therefore, I have utilized extracts from many of Mamet's works in order to give some indication of his range as a dramatic poet.

There then follows a detailed study of the five plays that, I believe, best illustrate his versatility with language. Chronologically, these are: *Sexual Perversity in Chicago, American Buffalo, A Life in the Theatre, Edmond,* and *Glengarry Glen Ross.* Each of these has been produced both in Great Britain and in the United States, and I have included critical reviews from both countries where these add to a thorough understanding of Mamet's drama.

All in-text parenthetical citations of Mamet's plays refer to the editions listed in the Select Bibliography.

Acknowledgments

Space does not permit me to acknowledge all those who have in some way helped in the writing of this book. I must, however, specifically thank the following individuals, the importance of whose contributions cannot be overstated. I would firstly like to express my gratitude to David Mamet for his kind permission to use salient extracts from his works and for his support. Since this book is a revised version of my doctoral thesis on the language in Mamet's drama, I would also like to state my indebtedness to Dr. Richard Allen Cave of Royal Holloway & Bedford New College, University of London, who supervised my initial research and was a source of unceasing inspiration. I must also thank the six actors and actresses interviewed in the course of research. They are: Connie Booth, Freddie Jones, Miranda Richardson, Patrick Ryecart, Jack Shepherd, and Colin Stinton.

I also gratefully acknowledge the use of material from *Writing in Restaurants* by David Mamet. Copyright © 1986 by David Mamet. All rights reserved. Reprinted by permission of Viking Penguin, a division of Penguin Books USA, Inc. Finally, I must stress my incalculable appreciation to Irene Kemp for her intelligent criticism and endless support, and to my dear parents for their unflagging encouragement, now and always.

DAVID MAMET

Introduction

Perhaps more than those of any other American playwright, David Mamet's works constitute a theatre of language: the lines spoken by his characters do not merely contain words that express a particular idea or emotion; they are the idea or emotion itself. A description by Samuel Beckett of James Joyce's *Finnegans Wake* could be equally applied to Mamet's drama. Beckett observed that "Here form *is* content, content *is* form."[1] Similarly, critic Robert Storey considers that "Mamet's characters . . . *are* their language; they exist insofar as—and to the extent that—their language allows them to exist. Their speech is not a smokescreen but a modus vivendi."[2] Jack Kroll calls Mamet "that rare bird, an American playwright who is a *language playwright*."[3] All playwrights are obviously "language playwrights" in one sense, but Mamet's poetic and rhythmic gifts enable the language to become much more than dialogue—it becomes the shape of the play itself. For example, the disjointed and monochromatic language in *Edmond* is reflected in the actual form of the play; the discontinuity of experience felt by its protagonist is echoed in the short blackout scenes in which the drama is written. Thus, the very structure of the play reflects its linguistic strategy. Similarly, the brevity of the scenes in *Sexual Perversity in Chicago* reflects the characters' inability to sustain an interest in anything beyond the present moment. Because of the fear of incipient boredom, their sentences are short and pithy, and so too are the scenes Mamet creates to accommodate them. The play gains its energetic pace not by any overt stage action, but by the speed of the dialogue.

Mamet concentrates not upon cultivated expression, "but upon that apparent wasteland of middle American speech,"[4] which is the language of the lower classes of the United States. He molds their attenuated and brutalized words into some of the most vital and original dialogue that can be heard in the theatre. In spite of their inarticulateness, his characters have a passion for speaking, a desperate energy that permeates all their conversations. As John Lahr observes, through "the hilarious brutal sludge of his characters' speech, Mamet makes us hear exhaustion and panic."[5] Such characters feel an overpowering need to talk, to make a mark in

15

space that confirms their importance and temporarily assuages their fears. Without exception, Mamet's characters yearn for more than they have, and they express their yearning in words that, although often impoverished and debased, authentically—often brilliantly—reflect their predicament. From the bluntest of materials, Mamet carves his dialogue, establishes mood and character, and imbues his work with tension and movement. With apparently so little, he achieves so much.

Mamet utilizes every nuance of dialogue to forward his plots and to depict character. He considers the action of his plays inextricably bound up with the rhythms he creates. To Mamet, "rhythm and action are the same. . . . in the theatre, if you have to use any narration, you're not doing your job."[6] He is fascinated by the way in which language can actually influence action, can impinge upon the subconscious to the extent that *it* motivates behavior, rather than vice versa. The notion of language dominating and prescribing codes of behavior derives from the writer's early training as an actor under the direction of Sanford Meisner, a founding member of The Group Theatre and a staunch advocate of the Stanislavski method of acting. Mamet believes that the teachings of Stanislavski helped him to understand certain crucial aspects of language and that his exposure to them deeply influenced his writing style. Acknowledging his debt to Stanislavski, Mamet states:

> My main emphasis . . . is on the rhythm of language—the way action and rhythm are identical. Our rhythms describe our actions—no, our rhythms *prescribe* our actions. I am fascinated by the way, the way the language we use, its rhythms, actually determines the way we behave, rather than the other way around.[7]

Robert Storey has noted the tendency of Mamet's characters to follow the lead of their language:

> Because so much of the activity of his characters is prescribed by their speech, it is often fruitless to analyse their "psychology"; like the victors of Dos Passos' *USA*, like Jay Gatsby, like the unenlightened of a Hemingway novel, they behave as their language directs them to behave, with unquestioning faith in its values.[8]

This is how Teach, in *American Buffalo*, can talk himself into corners from which there is no escape other than a reliance upon further linguistic invention. Having let his words determine his actions, he has no other choice but to be led on further by them.

Similarly, the sharklike salesmen in *Glengarry Glen Ross* are constantly propelled forward by their language; to them, to talk is to survive. As the words spill out, so their behavior endeavors to match them.

Mamet's characters speak in words that sound absolutely authentic and believable and yet contain the essence of true poetry with all of its compression, rhythm, and artificiality. Mamet's priority as a dramatist is not with a verbatim reproduction of conversation (which would undermine his poetic control in favor of mundane accuracy), but with a stylized evocation of the tonality of discourse. He points out that the language in a play such as *American Buffalo* is far from being a literal transcription from life: "Of course it's not really spoken speech at all; it's dramatic writing that happens to have rhythms similar to those of spoken speech."[9] Christopher Edwards observes how Mamet

> possesses a wonderfully acute ear for the vernacular of Chicago and re-creates it in all its raw poetic vigour, repetitive obscenity and desperate velocity. But the powerful naturalism of the speech is not mere literal transcription of what is heard. Like all naturalism, it only seems so because of the conscious artistry of the author. Mamet's effect is accomplished by way of a stylized formality.[10]

Mamet is less concerned with the narrative thrust of plot than with the retention, in his dialogue, of the cadences and rhythms he has set up. "If it's not poetic on the stage," he has said, "forget it."[11] During a radio interview with Christopher Bigsby, Mamet outlined his primary aim as a dramatist:

> I'm trying to write dramatic poetry. . . . I'm trying to capture primarily through the rhythm and secondarily through the connotation of the word the intention of the character. So when that is successful, what one ends up with is a play in free verse. If people want to say that it sounds just like the people on the bus, that's fine with me, because that's how the people on the bus sound to me.[12]

Mamet, therefore, appreciates the dramatic potential already present in ordinary speech yet, as he has made clear, does not merely record what he hears around him, but manipulates it into free verse. Because of the apparent authenticity of his dialogue, however, he has often been categorized as a naturalistic playwright, writing a kind of "kitchen-sink" drama. He feels frustrated when reviewers miss the poetry in his work and comment only upon its ostensible realism. American theatre in general, Mamet observes,

is obsessed with the concept of realism. "Most American theatrical workers are in thrall to the idea of *realism*. A very real urge
to be truthful, to be *true,* constrains them to judge their efforts
and actions against an inchoate standard of *realism,* which is to
say, against an immutable but *unspecified* standard of reality."[13] He
goes on to say that in any serious discussion of theatre, "that to
which the artist must be *true* is the aesthetic integrity of the
play."[14] Elsewhere, Mamet asserts that "[drama] is not an attempt
to depict something which is real in the external world but rather
an attempt to depict something which is real in an internal
world. . . . It's the difference between being a painter and an
illustrator."[15]

In a short essay entitled "On Being Truthful in Acting,"
Stanislavski writes about the differences between presenting "reality" onstage, and an artistic representation of that reality. His
subject is acting, but the comments are relevant to a study of
Mamet's own creative methods:

> What does it really mean to be truthful on the stage. . . . Does it mean
> that you conduct yourself as you do in ordinary life? Not at all.
> Truthfulness in those terms would be sheer triviality. There is the
> same difference between artistic and inartistic truth as exists between
> a painting and a photograph: the latter reproduces everything, the
> former only what is essential; to put the essential on canvas requires
> the talent of a painter.[16]

Mamet sets out to tell the truth in his plays, but chooses to do so
by means of his artistry and poetry rather than by documentary
devices (which merely record and include every detail). He believes that there is a great need for what he calls "true drama,"[17]
that is, "the drama [which is] based solely on the honest perception of a writer and the honest intention of the actor"[18] and feels
that he can best achieve success in this medium by concentrating
upon the poetic elements in his work. In this way, the depths of
character and nuances of motivation, which could never be communicated by pure realism, will be conveyed. The essential and
the evocative will be separated from the morass of information,
and sensitively manipulated into verse. For Mamet, then, the
poetry is all-important and takes precedence in his work. Even his
celebrated use of "obscene" language is subjected to close scrutiny. "A line's got to scan," he says. "I'm very concerned with the
metric scansion of everything I write, including the rhythmic
emphasis of the word 'fucking.' In rehearsal, I've been known to
be caught counting the beats on my fingers."[19] It is perhaps ironic

that the word "poet" is so frequently applied to a writer whose work includes the roughest usages of the vernacular. Through linguistic devices, often covert or disguised, Mamet employs the resources of metrical scansion to transform the most basic threads of discourse into verse. He utilizes fully the associative and lyrical value of words, their rhythm and cadence, imagistic compounds, and tonal effect. The following short extracts and analyses may illustrate some of the methods Mamet uses to create his poetic drama.

At the end of *Glengarry Glen Ross*, Richard Roma proposes that he and Shelly Levene should form a partnership:

> *Roma:* Okay: Two things, then. One . . . I been thinking about this for a *month*, I said "the Machine . . . There's a fellow I could *work* with," never, isn't that funny? I never did a thing. Now: That shit that you were slinging on the guy today was *very* good, and excuse me it isn't even my *place* to *say* that to you that way; I've been on a hot streak, so big deal. What I'm saying, it was *admirable* and, so was the *deal* that you closed. Now listen: there's things I could *learn* from you— you see, I *knew* we'd work well together—Here's what I was think- ing, we Team Up. We team up, we go out together, we split every- thing right down the middle . . . (act 2, p. 63)

There is an irresistible—although dislocated—rhythm to the character's words here that is set up in the opening of the quote and continues through to its end. Reflecting both Roma's neurotic personality and his too-sincere manner of speaking, it acts not only as rhythmic verse but also as a means of depicting character. Roma begins with monosyllables that have something of the ca- dence of a phrase like "Ready, steady, go!" after which his sen- tences gather momentum and rush breathlessly ahead. The entire speech is written rather like a race from the first word to the last, constantly threatening to get to the point and then back-tracking, or stumbling on its way. After he has (he imagines) gained Levene's attention, Roma builds his words rapidly into what is almost a hymn of praise for his friend's abilities: he launches into a stream of hyperbole and mixed-up syntax, which is stemmed only by the imposition of his carefully placed verbal scaffolding. Amidst the flattery, he moves from the initial "Okay: Two things then. One" to "Now" to "Now listen" to "Here's what I was thinking." At first, Roma implies that he is going to list the "things" he has on his mind, but in his haste forgets to do so, leaving the "One" dangling superfluously in a torrent of speech. To "sell" his idea to Levene, he tries to compress what is essentially a sales pitch into as little time as possible. In his anxiety, Roma's mind works faster than his mouth can form the words. The "never" in "There's a fellow I could *work* with, never, isn't that funny?" intrudes before he can place it in "I never did a thing," the sentence for which it was intended. The underlined words suggest tonal emphasis, as well as sustaining the cadences Roma has set up for himself. The emphases also suggest his shallow sycophancy—how he strains to appear self-effacing and modest. The liberal use of a comma suggests a mind that runs ahead of itself, pausing infrequently and even then not long enough to justify a full stop. With what is an original operation of poetic paradox, Mamet makes Roma's metaphor of the "shit" that Levene was "slinging on the guy" one of admiration rather than denigration. Further, Roma's "I" and "You" only become "We" when he has mentally determined that Levene will concede his request.

In *Reunion,* Bernie begins to tell his daughter a story:

> *Bernie:* . . . So I'd been drunk at the time for several years and was walking down Tremont Street one evening around nine and here's this big van in front of a warehouse and the driver is ringing the bell in the shipping dock trying to get in (which he won't do because they moved a couple of weeks ago and the warehouse is deserted. But he doesn't know that). So I say, "Hey, you looking for Hub City Transport?" And he says yeah, and I tell him they're over in Lechmere. . . . I figured maybe I could make a couple of bucks on the deal.
> And why not.
> So I ride over to Lechmere.
> I find the warehouse.
> You ever been to Lechmere? (P. 14)

Bernie's tale at first takes the form of a stream-of-consciousness ramble, unbroken by punctuation. His mind, like Roma's, works faster than his mouth is able to formulate the words, but the rhythms here are quite different. Bernie is an elderly man, a former alcoholic who is seeing his only daughter after an absence of over twenty years, and his slightly muddled syntax and confusion of tenses reflect both his nervousness and past history. Saying that he had "been drunk at the time for several years" is Bernie's rather unsubtle way of conveying self-pity, but it also affords Mamet the opportunity to use a metaphor that forms an image more common to poetry than to the prose in which it is written. The use of specific names such as "Tremont Street" and

"Lechmere" are included not only for their mellifluous qualities but also to particularize events. This is a familiar Mametian device that serves to personalize the characters, and establish them as living, breathing people with a background in palpable reality. Bernie frequently begins his sentences with the word "so," which lends a subtly hypnotic undercurrent to the rhythm of the story, at the same time echoing the repetitive nature of authentic speech. Indeed, the entire quote has all the hallmarks of everyday discourse although the last few sentences are set out as free verse; the repetition of the melodic "Lechmere" suggests Bernie's pleasure in saying the word aloud and establishes a brief rhyme.

A short sketch entitled *In the Mall* concerns a conversation between a thirteen-year-old boy and a sixty-year-old man. The boy tells the man:

> B: . . . I like to do things, you know, that people say that they can't do. I climbed this fence once that everyone said you can't get over. It had barb wire at the top. They make this stuff it's razors. It's a razor-ribbon you can't climb it. I went up. You hold on to the barb wire you go right over I came down the other side. *They* didn't care. They said that it was stupid. I bought a pair of socks once they had stripes on top I folded 'em down. I thought, "Maybe this is to show us where to fold." (P. 82)

This is perhaps the most obviously poetic of the quotes examined here. The boy refers to the barbed wire on the fence as "barb wire," shortening the word onomatopoeiacally so that it sounds more like what it is meant to suggest: a hard, abrasive metallic image. His poor grammar in the phrase "They make this stuff it's razors" renders the phrase, paradoxically, more powerfully descriptive than if he had spoken it articulately. The metaphor he chooses is purer and more precise than the simile it would have become had his speech been "correct." Mamet then extends the metaphor into the alliterative "razor-ribbon," hyphenated to imbue it with more strength and to emphasize the rough, rolling r at the beginning of each word. In describing his action of actually climbing over the fence, the boy verbally reenacts it. It is significant that, as he imagines the action occurring, he describes it in terms of "you" but when he has actually accomplished his task, he reverts to "I"—he is, after all, the person who has achieved this feat of bravery and he subconsciously takes the credit for it. The first part of his description of the climb therefore takes the form of a kind of instruction—how one would go about accomplishing such a task—whereas the latter part is a statement of achievement. Mamet captures perfectly the impudent, boastful manner of speech enjoyed by adolescent boys but then contrasts his character's apparent toughness with a final show of innocence and naïveté—the boy muses that the stripes on a pair of socks might indicate where he should fold them.

Mamet's ability to produce wonderfully funny dialogue that retains all of the grammatical chaos of ordinary conversation, while functioning brilliantly as a kind of free verse, is illustrated in a scene from *American Buffalo*. In a burst of bathetic exaggeration and self-pity, Teach complains to Don that he has been badly treated by Grace and Ruthie, two women with whom they play poker:

> *Teach:* . . . But to have that shithead turn, in one breath, every fucking sweet roll that I ever ate with them into *ground glass* . . . this hurts me, Don. This hurts me in a way I don't know what the fuck to do. *(Pause.)*
>
> *Don:* You're probably just upset.
>
> *Teach:* You're fuckin' A I'm upset. I am *very* upset, Don. . . . They treat me like an asshole, they are an asshole . . . *(Pause.)* The only way to teach these people is to kill them. (act 1, pp. 10–11)

This manic verbal torrent is, despite its ostensibly anarchic structure, far from slapdash. Mamet paces Teach's words with carefully placed commas and emphases, expressly designed to achieve the maximum impact. The comparison of the "sweet roll" with the alliterative *"ground glass"* is very telling; not only are they syllabically identical, which contributes to the peculiarly mesmeric music of the speech, but they also show the machinations of Teach's mind. A sweet roll probably represents to him the most inoffensive example of something he has shared with the treacherous Grace and Ruthie; it also contains the word *sweet*, which subliminally suggests his own "sweet" nature. In order to contrast the halcyon days of the "sweet roll," when Teach in his innocence shared with and even bought food for his persecutors, he selects a surrealistic and cruel image, *"ground glass"* to underline his torment. His long opening sentence is a poetically brillant and accomplished paean to anger, and its length and rhythm make the short colloquy far more powerful and ironic. Teach's language seems to prescribe its own eccentrically compelling rhythms as he ploughs through words in an effort to assuage his anger. It must be remembered that the remark that sparked off all of this verbal violence was, in fact, a very minor insult.

The syntactical frenzy of a sentence such as "They treat me like an asshole, they are an asshole" suggests Teach's mounting frustration, the repetition simultaneously highlighting his apparent helplessness and desperation. There is here a disconsolate childishness, and a whine is written into the lines, intended to draw sympathy for his cause and to win his audience's support. Don's inane attempts to console Teach add considerably both to the empathetic pulse which underlies the scene and to the dark and sardonic humor. His assertion that Teach is "probably just upset" is as brilliant a model of understatement as one is likely to find.

The preceding extracts are, of course, only a small selection from the many more excellent examples of Mamet's poetic gifts. However, they do give some impression of the playwright's versatility with language, and particularly his skill in writing original and acute dramatic poetry.

Mamet has been called the "Aristophanes of the inarticulate."[20] Like the Greek dramatist, he is a poet and a satirist, an iconoclastic demolisher of contemporary sacred cows. Through the language of his characters, which, although raised into dramatic verse, remains at its base an attenuated and debased form of communication, he exposes what he sees as an iniquitous social system. In order to dramatize the injustices inherent in modern, urban society, he usually draws his characters from the working classes, or from those who live on the fringe of society, the outcasts, misfits, and petty criminals. Much in the same way as Harold Pinter, Mamet creates a kind of drama in which such characters can be placed in the center of a play. Relatively minor—certainly unheroic—characters who converse in ostensibly mundane and unimaginative language are common to the work of both writers. Mamet acknowledges his debt to Pinter, dedicating *Glengarry Glen Ross* to him. In the belief that it is quite impossible for a modern playwright not to be influenced by a writer like Pinter, or, indeed, Beckett, Mamet says, "Beckett and Pinter—of course I am influenced by them. If you're interested in modern dance, how could you not be influenced by Martha Graham?"[21]

During an interview, the actor Jack Shepherd, who has appeared in two National Theatre productions of Mamet's plays, commented upon the similarities and differences between the works of Mamet and Pinter. According to Shepherd,

Mamet's way is very typical of American drama—there are many confrontations and the characters tell each other exactly what they think—or appear to, at least. His work is much more brash than that of Pinter, although there is the same concern for subtlety and nuance.

With English drama of the Pinter type, it is *all* nuance and oblique sense, but with American drama, it appears to the audience to be far more direct.[22]

Like those of Pinter, Mamet's plays often take the form of dramatized conversations that deal in detail with apparently unimportant issues. Every word is, however, absolutely crucial to the overall shape of the work. A good example is *The Duck Variations*, which, on the surface, seems to be nothing more than an extended duologue between two old men in a park, each of them vying for verbal supremacy in a continuing debate about ducks. It is the measure of Mamet's talent for burying layers of meaning into simple discourse that the play takes on a far more serious tone, although without losing any of its humor. This work is actually concerned with fear of change and the terrors of the modern world, the loss of individuality, the constant need for story-telling, and even existential anguish.

Pinter's deceptively simple plays with their "ordinary" characters and apparently banal linguistic style opened Mamet's eyes to the possibilities awaiting a dramatist, particularly one who is primarily interested in language. Mamet explains how "Pinter was probably the most influential when I was young and malleable . . . *The Homecoming, The Basement,* especially his revue sketches. I felt a huge freedom because of Pinter's sketches—to deal in depth and on their own merit with such minutiae."[23] In Mamet's drama, too, the commonplace finds a valid form of dramatic expression; what seems insignificant is filled with meaning and the most prosaic speech is given the kind of attention usually reserved for "great art." Indeed, Mamet's superb rendering of inarticulate speech is one of his major strengths. When even the most trite or obscene language is taken to have more than one level of meaning, it then becomes possible to envisage its vast potential in dramatic form. John Ditsky points out that Mamet's characters' "inarticulateness becomes the direct theatrical representation of interior stress, of psychic missed-connections. . . . the theatre of inarticulation . . . may prove significant because, ironically, it lets us better understand: in other words, because it lets us see the thought there."[24]

When one of Mamet's characters has something of importance to say, his or her abortive attempts at eloquence can paradoxically speak volumes. They *always* have something important to say, even if it is only they themselves who believe it. Often, their lack of fluency actually serves as an aid to audience concentration, since such language enforces alertness and sensitivity to nuance. It is not possible to listen half-attentively to such lines as

> Lookit, sir, if I could get ahold of some of that stuff you were interested in, would you be interested in some of it? (*American Buffalo*, act 1, pp. 27–28)

or

> What are we giving ninety per . . . for *nothing*. For some jerk sit in the office tell you "Get out there and close." "Go win the Cadillac." Graff. He goes out and *buys*. He pays top dollar for the . . . you see? (*Glengarry Glen Ross*, 1. 2, p. 14)

Through his characters' banal and incoherent discourse, Mamet can make transparent their oververbalized as well as their unspoken emotions. Possibly one of his greatest achievements resides in his ability to suggest what lies just beneath the surface of their speech. He is able to draw attention to that which is barely apprehended by the speakers themselves, let alone given the substantiality of language. The tough and gritty dialogue in a play such as *Lakeboat* conceals its characters' desperate loneliness and sense of abandonment; behind their incessant references to sex, gangsters, and gambling there lies emptiness. Rather than admit fear and vulnerability, the men who work on the boat find solace in fictionalizing events, distancing themselves from the reality of their situation. So entrenched have they become in their make-believe world, they hardly remember that it is, in fact, make-believe. Their discourse is freqently blunt to the point of savagery, but this does not prevent Mamet from extracting every possible nuance to convey his dramatic point.

Partly because of his study of the acting techniques of Stanislavski (as modified by Sanford Meisner), Mamet recognizes that it is often not the content of what is said that matters most, but the action that underlies it. For him, communication frequently has less to do with actual language than with the silent empathy that exists between speakers. To Mamet, "rhythm and action are the same . . . words are reduced to the sound and rhythm much more than to the verbal content."[25] An episode occurs in *American Buffalo*, in which the surface chatter belies what is actually taking place. Teach has been trying to persuade Don that Bobby is too inexperienced and risky a proposition to trust with the coin heist they are planning. Bobby has been sent out to get coffee and food for breakfast and, just as Teach reaches a crescendo of rhetoric about the boy's unsuitability, Bobby returns:

> *Teach:* . . . And what if (God forbid) the *guy* walks in? Somebody's nervous, whacks him with a table lamp—you wanna get touchy—and you can take your ninety dollars from the nickel shove it up your ass—the good it did you—and you wanna know *why?* (And I'm not *saying* anything . . .) because you didn't take the time to go first-class.
> *(Bob re-enters with a bag.)*
> Hi, Bob.
> *Bob:* Hi, Teach. (act 1, p. 38)

There follows an exchange about the food between Don and Bobby. Teach remains silent until:

> *Teach: (to Bob.)* How is it out there?
> *Bob:* It's okay.
> *Teach:* Is it going to rain?
> *Bob:* Today?
> *Teach:* Yeah.
> *Bob:* I don't know. *(Pause.)*
> *Teach:* Well, what do you think?
> *Bob:* It might.
> *Teach:* You think so, huh?
> *Don.* Teach . . .
> *Teach:* What? I'm not saying anything.
> *Bob:* What?
> *Teach:* I don't think I'm saying anything here. *(Pause.)*
> *Bob:* It *might* rain. *(Pause.)* I think *later.*
> *Teach:* How's your pie? (act 1, pp. 38–40)

There is here an almost Chekhovian subtext. In the same way that Lopakhin engages Varya in mundane conversation in *The Cherry Orchard* instead of proposing marriage, Teach talks to Bobby about the weather and the suitability of his pie in an effort to convince Don of the extent of the boy's dimness. It is almost possible to visualize Teach's sidelong glances at Don as he demolishes the last vestiges of Bobby's credibility as a potential accomplice. Stanislavski writes that Chekhov "painted pictures from life, not plays for the stage. Therefore he often expressed his thought not in speeches but in pauses or between the lines or in replies consisting of a single word."[26] He goes on to note how "Chekhov's plays are profound in their amorphousness, the characters often feel and think things not expressed in the lines they speak."[27] The works of both Chekhov and Mamet thus allow the audience a glimpse of what lies beneath the superficial words, as well as delineating their characters' motives. Teach's show of friendship and concern is plainly bogus. Even the pathetic Bobby is aware that something is awry, yet he plays along with the chitchat until Don prompts him to become really nervous. He then tries desperately to please Teach by supplying him with the answers he thinks he wants to hear. With wonderful irony, Mamet twice has Teach state: "I don't think I'm saying anything." He most certainly is not, but the tension that he has created has a powerful eloquence of its own. The dramatic effect of this pared-down, sparse dialogue is entirely due to the contradiction between the words spoken and the emotional and psychological action underlying them.

Like Chekhov in works such as *The Seagull* and *The Three Sisters*, Mamet combines symbolism with surface naturalism. The cluttered chaos of Don's junk shop in *American Buffalo* reflects the detritus that Mamet sees clogging up modern America. *The Woods* is set not only in the actual month of September but also in the emotional autumn of its character's relationship—against a backdrop of ominous rain clouds and decaying vegetation, they play out what may be the last days of their love affair. The real-estate office in *Glengarry Glen Ross* is, perhaps a microcosm of capitalist society gone mad, and the subsequent break-in redolent of the collapse of law and order. The plight of the workers in *Lakeboat* is surely intended to reflect a general malaise and boredom, and to underline the metaphysical void in which they find themselves, and in *Edmond* the titular character's lashing out as he murders Glenna is no doubt intended to illustrate the breakdown and violence of the whole of modern society, to symbolize the lack of understanding between people. Miranda Richardson, who played Glenna—as well as the Fortune Teller and the Peep Show Girl—in the Royal Court production of *Edmond* in 1985 observes that the "way in which Edmond murders Glenna is deeply symbolic. Glenna dies, as all of Mamet's characters suffer, because of a profound lack of communication and understanding. Edmond tries to find the truth, believes he has found it, and then has it negated . . . his only reaction is one of panic and to kill what stands in his way."[28] But Mamet's symbolism is never heavy-handed or obvious; each symbolic image can be quite painlessly offset with one of absolute realism. For example, Don's junkshop may represent chaotic America but it is also just another very untidy second-hand store; Ruth and Nick may be symbolic of babes in the wood with the concomitant implications of both innocence and loss, but they are also merely another couple who have decided to spend a weekend in the country. The symbolic aspects of Mamet's other works are similarly unobtrusive; nothing is ever forced or strained for the sake of effect.

All Mametian characters use language creatively, picking up linguistic scraps from one another and reworking and redefining them to suit their own ends. Perhaps the best example, however, occurs in *Glengarry Glen Ross* when Moss tries to entrap his colleague into complicity in a robbery, drawing him into agreement about the unfairness of their present lot:

> *Moss:* We're stuck with *this* fucking shit . . .
> *Aaronow:* . . . *this* shit . . .
> *Moss:* It's too . . .
> *Aaronow:* It is.
> *Moss:* Eh?
> *Aaronow:* It's too . . .
> *Moss:* You get a bad month, all of a . . .
> *Aaronow:* You're on this . . .
> *Moss:* All of, they got you on this 'board' . . .
> *Aaronow:* I, I . . . I . . .
> *Moss:* Some *contest* board . . .
> *Aaronow:* I . . .
> *Moss:* It's not right.
> *Aaronow:* It's not.
> *Moss:* No. (act 1. 1, p. 13)

Mamet capitalizes upon the fact that real-life conversations seldom proceed smoothly and logically from point to point; most dialogue is repetitious or inconsequential, or both. As Moss prompts his colleague into culpability, he need utter only a fragment of a sentence for Aaronow to finish it, or half-finish it for him. Aaronow's insecurity and fear are all too obvious in his stammering and compliant agreement; Moss knows that the moment for his "coup" is not far away; his poor victim is skillfully and ruthlessly led into what amounts to a verbal slaughter.

In 1888, in his Preface to *Miss Julie*, August Strindberg outlined his feelings on the irregularity and lack of form of most speech. He intended that in his play, the characters should appear to speak naturally and without obvious authorial interference; they should not become "catechists who sit asking stupid questions in order to evoke some witty retort."[29] Strindberg was concerned that his characters' speech should sound as lifelike as possible and, in order to give the impression of naturalism, he "allowed their minds to work irregularly, as people's do in real life, when, in conversation, no subject is fully exhausted, but one mind discovers in another a cog which it has a chance to engage."[30] As a result of this, Strindberg's dialogue "wanders, providing itself in the opening scenes with matter which is later taken up, worked upon, repeated, expanded and added to, like the theme in a musical composition."[31]

Mamet strives to create natural-sounding speech in his dialogue, but always within the confines of his dramatic poetry and, as Strindberg does, he uses recurrent motifs, both verbal and purely dramatic. In *Prairie du Chien,* the motif takes the form of the Storyteller repeatedly asking if the child in the carriage is asleep, as he builds up the suspense of his dark, chilling tale; in *American Buffalo,* it is the symbol of Teach's missing hat, which culminates in his construction of a new one out of paper to avoid getting wet—an action very much at odds with one who wishes to pass himself off as a hardened gangster; in *House of Games,* a recurrent theme is established by the "Freudian slips" with which Dr. Ford reveals the truth about her own compulsive personality; and, in *A Life in the Theatre,* the leitmotifs that run throughout are Robert's pretentious references to the theatre as life and his irritating and affected habit of referring to the "fitness" of things.

Film, radio, and television have for several generations brought the verbal textures of American speech to England. As Gareth Lloyd Evans notes, it is not difficult to understand why, on a purely linguistic level, American language should hold such a fascination for the British.

> There is an element of "thrill" in listening to a language which is apparently built of the same materials as one's own but which has strongly unusual features—noises, rhythms, words, phrases, nuances. Without pushing the notion too far, we may perhaps consider that there is an analogy here with the thrill of listening to poetry. It, too, uses the raw materials of our own common stock of speech, but its attractiveness and power come from the unusual usages to which that common stock is put . . . Americans sometimes may use [language] badly, but they rarely use it dully.[32]

Mamet's characters frequently use language "badly;" their syntax becomes garbled or their phrasing perverse but in his hands, such "inferior" diction can be molded, without a hint of condescension or parody, into utterly authentic-sounding poetic cadences. Ross

Wetzsteon remarks upon Mamet's ability to capture what sounds like genuine American discourse.

> The American stage is littered with the language of the lower-middle classes. Every playwright who's ever wandered into a diner seems to think he has an ear for the pungent patois, the idiosyncratic idioms, the colourful cadences of a truly American speech, more diverse, more realistic, more honest than the homogenised vocabulary, rhythms and accents increasingly force-fed into our minds by the relentlessly regionless blandness of national television. What results is almost always a condescending caricature. . . . [This is so unlike Mamet's] careful, gorgeous, loving sense of language . . . he has the most acute ear for dialogue of any American writer since J. D. Salinger.[33]

The language Mamet's characters speak is littered with all kinds of linguistic antecedents suggestive of Jewish, Italian, Spanish, and African-American origin. Harold Clurman once described Clifford Odets's dramatic language as

> an ungrammatical jargon—and constantly lyric. It is composed of words heard on the street, in drugstores, bars, sports arenas, and rough restaurants. . . . It is the speech of New York; half-educated Jews, Italians, Irish, transformed into something new-minted, individual, and unique. . . . His dialogue is moving, even thrilling, and very often hilarious. It is not "English"; in a sense it is not "realistic" at all. It is "Odets."[34]

How easily Clurman's words could be applied to Mamet's work! Indeed, it is instructive to note that Mamet cites Odets as a particular influence upon his own writing.[35] However, Mamet gathers together all the strands and molds them into an idiom peculiar to relatively small areas of the United States: New York and, particularly, Chicago. As John Ditsky points out, Mamet's language "owes nothing to an effete, drawing-room mid-Atlantic tradition, and little to any commercial New York-Los Angeles sort of slanginess."[36] Ross Wetzsteon expresses his admiration for a writer who has a true gift for particular speech patterns, unlike most writers who attempt to reproduce dialogue for the stage and feel that they have " 'captured' Brooklyn by using 'dese' and 'den' and 'dose,' the South with a drawl, Texan with a twang."[37]

One aspect of Mamet's linguistic technique that frequently attracts attention is his knack for incorporating the pace of city life into his dialogue. The world Mamet dramatizes is one in which literally every second counts, and where there may be danger around every corner. Consequently, brevity of expression becomes extremely important. Mamet's characters frequently leave out words they feel to be extraneous or redundant in their sentences: they have something that they wish to convey, and they do so in as little time as possible. In *American Buffalo*, Teach, in his haste, sometimes telescopes his words: "probably" becomes "prolly" (act 1, p. 16). He often utters sentences that seek to communicate their meaning in a kind of telegraphic frenzy: "(He don't got the address the guy?)" (act 2, p. 85); "I'm not the *hotel*, I stepped out for coffee, I'll be back one minute" (act 1, p. 57); and "What's the good keep the stuff in the safe . . ." (act 2, p. 80). Similarly, in *Pint's a Pound the World Around*, "A" states that "The guy should have been in Tuesday, I spect him Friday, if he don't come then" (p. 67) and in *Glengarry Glen Ross*, Roma observes that the policeman who was brought in to solve the burglary " . . . couldn't find his fuckin' couch the *living-room*" (act 2, p. 62).

Jack Barbera comments upon Mamet's use of compressed and abbreviated language in an article that acknowledges Mamet's part in creating a highly stylized dialogue out of everyday speech, but also points out that, in today's frantic city bustle, such language becomes more and more common. People actually *do* speak in this brief, truncated fashion. Barbera recalls an interview given by Mamet on the Dick Cavett Show in which the playwright "mentioned entering an elevator and hearing a woman say: 'Lovely weather, aren't we?' "[38] Thus, the rhythms and syncopations of Mamet's language authentically reflect both the inner pressures of his characters and the pace and confusion of their urban environment, as well as distill the Chicago dialect into precise, idiomatic verse. During an interview, Jack Shepherd spoke about the difficulties of mastering Mamet's authentic Chicago accent. "*American Buffalo*" he said, "very definitely has an accent built into it, but it is different from that in *Glengarry Glen Ross*. The rhythms are similar, but they are more like those in 'Kojak'—sly, idiomatic city talk. Chicago is quite a hard accent—I couldn't really get to grips with it and eventually settled for New York!"[39] Writing about his experiences of working in Mamet's work, Shepherd elaborates:

> In plays by Mamet the actor has to talk much more quickly than is customary in British theatre. . . . The rhythms of the text are breathtaking. . . . Once the actor gets the rhythms right, he starts sounding authentic. He starts talking Chicagoanese. In *American Buffalo*, I was told that my accent sounded authentically American New York. In *Glengarry Glen Ross* I was told that I sounded like I came from

Detroit, which is a good bit further west. By the next production I might make it to Chicago.[40]

It is almost impossible to speak Mamet's texts in a standard English accent—it sounds quite wrong—although Jack Shepherd believes that both *American Buffalo* and *Glengarry Glen Ross* could be successfully performed with Cockney or Northern English accents. This would not appear to be a viable alternative, since Mamet's idiom is totally and uncompromisingly American. His Chicago rhythms imbue every single line, and would, I feel, make an "English" interpretation of any kind seem dangerously contrived and inauthentic.

Mamet's characters speak a language that accurately reflects the cultural abyss into which their country has fallen; they have become emotionally dessicated in their struggle to survive in a society that no longer coheres. It is only through public myths and a life lived according to the dictates of the mass media that they are able to communicate. Indeed, there are now only the most vestigial traces of authentic communion between them. Such characters no longer speak with a genuine voice that can impart what they most need to say; they take on false roles, converse in a superficial and second-rate style, and, eventually, deny their true personalities in favor of an adopted—more socially acceptable—myth. Subsequently, they seem to dissolve into what is expected of them in their (adopted) social roles, but continue to feel the need for something more. It is as if the language they have plundered from already debased sources such as television soap operas and advertising jargon denies them the means of genuine communication. Referring specifically to *American Buffalo*, but with obvious pertinence to his other work, Mamet has commented upon that "essential part of the American consciousness, which is the ability to suspend an ethical sense and adopt instead a popular, accepted mythology and use that to assuage your conscience like everyone else is doing."[41] If this is accepted, it becomes easy to see how Mamet's characters constantly delude both themselves and those around them. It is easier for them to fall in with the myths manufactured in their society than to fight them. Some of the pressures of life are alleviated by such action— the myths, after all, offer a specious form of security—but such relief remains at best superficial. The rot at the core remains unchecked. Their ability to explain away the finer points of the ethics of robbery, cheating, blackmail, overt sexism, and racism allows them to literally "assuage [their] conscience[s] like everyone else is doing." For such characters, self-interest and self-preservation obviate concern for others.

Mamet observes that a genuine, innocent voice has been lost in contemporary America. "What I write about," he notes, "is what I think is missing from our society. And that's communication on a basic level."[42] His characters' reliance upon an artificially created mythology in order to escape reality is reminiscent of the society dramatized by Arthur Miller in *The American Clock*, his satire on the Great Depression. In the play, Miller's characters attempt to escape from the terrible hardships they experience by overindulgence in cinema-going and an obsession with popular music. Priorities become distorted and, at the beginning of act 2, Miller suggests the encroaching stupidity that threatens to descend upon the entire populace. Rose frets about

> the crazy ideas people get. Mr. Warsaw on our block, to make a little money he started a race track in his kitchen, with cockroaches. Keeps them in matchboxes, with their names written on—"Alvin," "Murray," "Irving" . . . They bet nickels, dimes . . . Wherever you look there's a contest; Kellogg's, Post Toasties win five thousand, win ten thousand . . . Sing! *(She sings opening of "Do-do-do What You Done-Done-Done Before.").* . . . I must stop getting so stupid. I don't see anything, I don't hear anything except money, money, money . . . .[43]

Characters like these resort to desperate diversions not through any fault of their own, but through fear. Mamet dramatizes a very similar society, although in his world there is now no major economic Depression, merely a generalized and deeply rooted depression. His characters are aware of the inadequacy and cheapness of their life experience, but are unable—even unwilling—to do anything to rectify matters, despite a gnawing feeling that they should do so. One of the ways in which their frustration is dramatized is through their use of obscenities. Compulsively foul-mouthed, they indulge in expletives that have become almost meaningless through endless repetition, although occasions do remain when their original definitions are powerfully enforced. However, Mamet utilizes this kind of language for a number of dramatic purposes: to maintain rhythm, to express the frustration felt by his characters, to illustrate the bond and understanding that exists between them, and to demonstrate the *ordinariness* and acceptability of such language to certain sectors of society. Mamet makes no apology for recording the harshest street language without censoring any of its rough edges. Indeed, these jagged shards of speech become an important means of depicting character, shaping emotional responses, and creating tension, as well as serving as a perverse vehicle for Mamet's poetic diction. Ross Wetzsteon seizes on this latter aspect, declaring that "not since Celine has obscenity seemed so poetic."[44]

In Mamet's hands, obscenity does become poetic, certainly dramatic. By punctuating his characters' words with language that has seldom, if ever, found itself spoken onstage—at least in such quantity—he creates rhythm and verse out of the most unmelodic sounds and at the same time runs the risk of becoming a target for those who would reduce him to the level of verbal pornographer. Mamet claims that his dialogue is liberally spiced with obscenities because that is indeed the way in which people in certain areas of society speak. Further, he believes that, despite the paucity of such language, there is undoubtedly a level at which it is totally honest and forthright. "You really have to love that kind of talk to write it. . . ." he says, "More than that, you have to need it. The people who speak that way tell the truth. They don't institutionalise thought. They speak from a sense of need."[45] Thus, Mamet suggests that despite all of the negative influnces which serve to render their language spare and inadequate, there is truth to his characters' minimal expression, an honesty that is uncluttered by the bonds of polite conversation.

Colin Stinton, an American actor who has appeared in a number of Mamet's plays, explains some of the reasons why he believes the dramatist includes so much profanity in his work:

> This is how people really do speak, although Mamet does more than merely record. . . . Anyone who has ever worked on a construction crew, or in a real-estate office, or been on a lakeboat will know that this is the way people do converse—especially men—often poetically, often brilliantly in their own kind of perverse way. . . . Men working together tend to get set into certain linguistic patterns; they develop a kind of masculine bond of communication. Mamet builds upon such relationships in his plays. I used to work with some guys who, when they hurt themelves or were annoyed in any way, would chant "Jesus, Jesus, Jesus." There was a certain rhythm in which they had to say this which never varied. Once, however, one of them hit his hand with a hammer and, for the first time, he worked in another "Jesus," which altered the cadence to something like "Jesus, Jesus, *Jesus*, Jesus."[46]

Mamet even rearranges the syllables of a word in order to include an obscenity if it fits in with his rhythms. One example occurs in *American Buffalo* when Don describes a girl he has seen: "The ass on this broad, un-be-fucking-lievable in these bicycling shorts sticking up in the air . . ." (act 1, p. 33). Stinton comments on this particular linguistic effect:

> Mamet's constant inclusion of words such as "fuck" or "fucking" are incorporated for a rhythmic purpose. Sometimes he has a character work in one in the middle of another word, so that it becomes "im-fuckin'-possible" or whatever. They actually break up the syllables to fit in a cussword, so intent are they in (a) gaining the maximum effect from their words and (b) keeping up the cadences they have set themselves.[47]

Stinton feels that the emphasis which is placed upon the writer's use of "bad language" arises partly *because* of his linguistic dexterity rather than through any lack of imagination as a writer of dialogue. "[Mamet] is verbally so dazzling," says Stinton, "that you can sometimes fail to see themes in his plays straight away. All that is apparently on show is a lot of flashy language, and the nature of the flash is often the way in which the characters have pornographic or vulgar elements in their speech. Consequently, these can be the aspects which show up most on a cursory viewing."[48] This idea is a far cry from the view that the obscenities are included only to inflame the sensibilities of the audience or, as Leo Sauvage puts it "to provoke giggling and bursts of hysterical laughter, most often from women."[49]

It would, however, be naïve to suggest that Mamet is totally innocent of the desire to shock his audience; any writer who sets out to evoke, without censorship or apology, the blunt and often savage language of the streets must in some way deliberately court outrage. He frequently sets his plays in the seamy—and seedy—underworld, choosing for his characters low-life villains and misfits, and he does dwell upon their base language. But this is not the action of a verbal pornographer: it is Mamet's way of finding the truth, of offering a picture of society without any prettification of its unpleasant realities. Mamet includes the linguistic violence because only by incorporating such elements into his work can he offer an honest representation of the world he chooses to dramatize. Mamet sets out to grab the attention of the audience by including every oath and, if the audience is offended by such naked exposure to an ugly reality, then Mamet is making no apology for it.

In the same way that Edward Bond writes plays that depict the most appalling violence to emphasize his political point of view, so Mamet utilizes obscene language as a means of pointing to the spiritual malaise that he considers endemic in the United States.

The decline in the quality of spoken language is, to him, symptomatic of a much wider decay. In the preface to *Lear*, Bond writes:

> I write about violence as naturally as Jane Austen wrote about manners. Violence shapes and obsesses our society and if we do not stop being violent we have no future. People who do not want writers to write about violence, want to stop them writing about us and our time. It would be immoral not to write about violence.[50]

Mamet uses another kind of violence to expose what he considers a corrupt and venal culture—a culture that has exchanged the golden vision made possible by the American Dream for the tinselly ostentation of a society of excess. Mamet is dismissive of those who find his language shocking. "Is the language shocking?" he asks, "I guess different people are shocked by different things. I'm shocked at the torture in South America, or how high officials do dastardly crimes and, rather than punishing them, we say they've suffered enough. That stuff's shocking to me."[51] Mamet's plays may be outrageously controversial, but he is concerned not with somehow making obscenity more theatrically valid but with drawing the attention of the audience to the deeper implications of his work—to make them think about why his characters *do* speak in that way, and the kind of society that has created them.

In order to obtain an overall view of Mamet's use of language in his work, it is illuminating to look at his writing techniques and the objectives he sets for himself as a dramatist. Mamet writes with extreme economy of expression. With very few words, he is able to convey a great deal. Because he sets up his theatrical coups with such meticulous precision, he can utilize language very sparingly indeed. Nothing in his drama is redundant; every word is counted and refined until he is satisfied that it does its job succinctly. Mamet is obsessed with the idea of *pattern* in his work. If anything is omitted from or added to the total schema, he believes that it will be glaringly obvious and detract from the sense of the piece. He observes that "every time the author leaves in a piece of non-essential prose (beautiful though it may be) he weakens the structure of the play."[52] Similarly, Harold Pinter, when describing his own structural strategy, says, "I pay a meticulous attention to the shape of things, from the shape of a sentence to the overall structure of the play. This shaping, to put it mildly, is of the first importance. I'm not in favour of diarrohea on the stage."[53] Speaking about the tightness and economy in Mamet's work, Colin Stinton notes how Mamet "is continually on the lookout for things he feels are sentimental or overstated, to see if there is a better—or shorter and clearer—way of putting across what he wants to say. . . . One of his favorite maxims is 'KISS'—Keep it Simple, Stupid."[54] Mamet postulates the theory that the perfect formula for a well-constructed play is that of the dirty joke:

> The model of the perfect play is the dirty joke. "Two guys go into a farmhouse. An old woman is stirring a pot of soup." What does the woman look like? What state is the farmhouse in? Why is she stirring soup? It is absolutely not important. The dirty-joke teller is tending toward a punch line and we know that he or she is only going to tell us the elements which direct our attention *toward* that punch line, so we listen attentively and gratefully.[55]

Edmond is an excellent example of a play in which everything but the absolutely essential has been pared away, leaving only brief, pungent episodes that sting with the power of their "punch line." Remarking upon two scenes in this play that demonstrate, even by Mamet's usual economical standards, extreme brevity and conciseness while simultaneously forwarding the action, Colin Stinton notes "There is an amazing terseness in the very short hotel scene, and in the way Mamet highlights Edmond's wife's real concerns and intentions when she visits him in jail."[56] After Edmond has been mugged and beaten, he goes to a hotel where he hopes to find refuge and comfort. The hotel is only identified as such in the printed text, thus the audience in the theatre has no idea where he is until he asks for a room. Nothing specific has been stated, nor have any obvious clues been given as to the setting for this scene until these words are spoken. The second example cited by Stinton occurs in the scene in which Edmond's wife visits him in prison. Edmond tries to keep the conversation going, his wife offering only monosyllabic and non-commital responses until she asks him: "Did you kill that girl in her apartment?" (scene 19, p. 87). It is not merely that she confronts her husband about the murder—this seems to be of secondary importance when the line is analyzed—but that she asks whether he killed the girl "in her apartment." The real motive of her query is not why Edmond should have committed murder, but to find out if he had been unfaithful to her.

Mamet's recent experience in filmmaking had a direct influence upon his writing of *Edmond*. When he began working on the play, he had just completed the screenplay for Sidney Lumet's film, *The Verdict*, and the extreme economy of means used in *Edmond* reflects his desire to say as much as possible in the briefest of scenes. There is, in *Edmond,* a very filmic interest in moving the action forward with as little hindrance as possible. Stinton remarks upon this as follows:

> *Edmond* and *The Verdict* were written very closely together . . . [Mamet] became more conscious of getting what you want out of a scene as rapidly as possible, of constructing it so that it accomplishes a specific objective and makes the audience want to know what happens next. . . . In *Edmond,* perhaps more than in any of his other plays, [Mamet] tries to accomplish something with each scene, and this makes him more of a storyteller himself. He has always been a storyteller in the sense that his characters tell stories . . . but in *Edmond* he has become more adept at writing scenes which together make stories.[57]

Mamet's plays are frequently so terse and brief that audiences can sometimes miss important aspects, despite their desire to know "what happens next." Stinton considers Mamet's ability to present information in such economical terms both a strength and a flaw:

> there will be those in the audience who will not appreciate his brevity, and the writing will go right past them without their having understood just what is going on. Mamet's plays are so dense . . . so ingenious that they can, unless the audience is extremely well-tuned to his idiom, be misunderstood. Most people are used to having things spelled out for them and [Mamet] doesn't do that . . . it's just straight in. He expects them to fill in the blanks and to follow the clues, the very definite clues, he provides. . . . Possibly one of his shortcomings is that he expects everyone to be as quick and precise as he is in picking up clues and nuances. He is an incredibly perceptive listener. If he has a flaw, then that is it, but it is also one of his greatest virtues, this ability to be so precise and terse.[58]

Brevity and conciseness of expression are, therefore, two principles of playwriting that are constantly on Mamet's mind. "The whole truth lies," he has said, "in what you leave out."[59] Mamet therefore believes that he can best convey the truth by constantly paring down his plays; the less padding he includes, the less distraction there will be from his central objective, that is, to present a theatrical experience that is as honest as possible. In an essay entitled "Semantic Chickens," Mamet sums up what he believes to be the quintessential purpose of theatre: "The purpose of the theatre, as Stanislavski said, is to bring light to the life of the human soul; and the theatre . . . possesses this potential. Alone among community institutions, the theatre possesses the power to differentiate between truth and garbage."[60]

Mamet has gained the reputation of being an "actor's playwright," that is, one who has a deep regard and respect for those who perform his works. As a former actor (albeit an unsuccessful one), he understands the acting process and retains an unwavering sympathy for the actor's lot. Colin Stinton recalls that

> Mamet won't waste time on something which doesn't sound true, or poetic. He trusts his actors to be intelligent and to do their very best with the lines he gives them but, if those lines don't work, he is as likely to cut them completely as to use up valuable rehearsal time in amending them or embellishing them. This is so unlike the practice of so many playwrights who are jealous of every single word they write.[61]

Freddie Jones, who played Robert in the 1979 production of *A Life in the Theatre* at The Open Space, avers that "Mamet desperately loves and respects actors. His heart is with us . . . he really does care about us. You can tell this by the *ease* with which actors take to his texts . . . they are, more so than usual, written *for* actors to perform and thus they invite the best kind of acting."[62] Mamet himself observes that "actors are an important part of the writing process. Good actors are working with controlled consciousness. If they find the words awkward, it's because they probably *are* awkward. There are actors, for example, who can convey an entire speech in a single line."[63]

Mamet's early training still influences him heavily; his characters are so meticulously realized and his plays so densely structured that successful performance in them demands the kind of commitment that comes with Method acting, the "moment to moment" style of exposition. It is essential for an actor to immerse him or herself in the role, to engage in the kind of "groundwork" that Jack Shepherd found necessary in his preparation to perform both *American Buffalo* and *Glengarry Glen Ross*. "The only way to act Mamet" he says, "is to live in the moment, let the other actors take you by surprise, take yourself by surprise! *Prepare* at home, and in rehearsal, in performance—*let go*, take a spontaneous reaction even if it's wrong. Try not to do anything *exactly* the same twice."[64] During an interview, Shepherd spoke about Stanislavski and Mamet's own contributions to rehearsals of *Glengarry Glen Ross*, as both a playwright and former actor:

Mamet's work is perfect for the Method. . . . It immediately concentrates your energy on either the person or the thing you're meant to be addressing and [Mamet] believes very deeply in the benefits of the System. He writes from within; he approaches his texts like an actor. . . . Mamet acts out the part in his head, saying the lines to himself to see if they sound real, or if they sound poetic—ideally, he wants them to sound both. . . . You have to enjoy Mamet's dialogue . . . the actor should endeavor to live in the present when acting his work . . . as Stanislavski said, in the now. Listening to other actors and responding moment by moment. The idea is to produce energy, vivacity, and spontaneity, to be as natural as possible, to be true—this is essential for Mamet's drama.[65]

Mamet's work is expressly written to be performed, rather than merely read. Although it is indeed written as dramatic poetry, its strengths do not emerge until the words are actually spoken aloud. Both Colin Stinton and Jack Shepherd comment on this aspect of his drama, Stinton observing that "[Mamet] does not write 'literature' per se, and so if actors decide to find the 'literariness' of his work at the expense of actually *acting* it, they will be doomed to failure."[66] Similarly, Shepherd notes how "in *American Buffalo* and *Glengarry Glen Ross* the rhythm is fast! . . . To speak the text well you have to speak it fast. . . . Approach it with 'literary' considerations in the back of your mind, and the poetry won't stand a chance."[67]

Both Stinton and Shepherd have found Mamet's scripts surprisingly easy to learn; because they are so precisely designed, there is no room for an odd ad-lib. They are simple to memorize not only because they strongly resemble the patterns of real speech but also because they are so expertly crafted that if a line is read incorrectly, it becomes immediately obvious. The "beat" has been disturbed, and the line sounds false. Stinton recalls how he has "always found it really very easy to remember Mamet's lines . . . his words just seem to work effortlessly. His texts may *look* difficult to remember, so full are they of ellipses and grammatical anomalies, but they are really quite simple because of their rhythm."[68] Shepherd remembers that when he first saw the script for *Glengarry Glen Ross* he thought it was a kind of code, but a code that could be broken. "The text" he remarks, "really does look like code . . . you wonder how you can possibly memorize this sort of language but it's surprisingly simple once you get the rhythms. It becomes difficult to get it *wrong*. There are no spaces in his work, no room for improvization."[69]

In many of his plays, Mamet makes a stylized use of specific areas of dialogue, namely the enclosure of certain excerpts within parentheses. In a footnote to *American Buffalo,* he instructs that such extracts denote "a slight change of outlook on the part of the speaker—perhaps a momentary change to a more introspective regard."[70] In all the plays in which this parenthetical device occurs, characters are able momentarily to look inward, to question motives or to reflect upon recent utterances. It could be said that Mamet's parentheses are similar to Pinter's pauses; they are dramatic opportunities for a character to pause, to switch mood, if only for a few seconds. However, they can also be a source of considerable confusion; it is often difficult to see why certain words should be marked so, and can lead to the feeling that one is missing some vital hidden meaning. It is only when the lines are read aloud that the significance becomes clear. "The first read-through of a Mamet play," Colin Stinton observes, "is always exciting because you suddenly see those things which you didn't quite understand on the printed page now make sense. If you trust him, and give thought to the words within the brackets or above the underlinings, if you 'hit' the words he advises you to 'hit,' the meaning will eventually become clear."[71]

American Buffalo contains more of these parenthetical comments than any of Mamet's other plays. The following brief selection gives some indication of how theatrically effective they can be. In the early scene in which Don chides Bobby for not eating properly, he moves from the specific to the general and there is an indication that this lecture is just another in a long line of pep talks to the boy:

> Don: . . . You know how much nutritive benefits they got in coffee? Zero. Not one thing. The stuff eats *you* up. You can't live on coffee, Bobby. (And I've told you this before.) (act 1, p. 7)

Don muses on the times that he has had the self-same discussion with Bobby. An actor might interpret his parenthetical remark as one to be spoken either in an overtly sincere or world-weary manner, harboring concern for his young friend's welfare or plain impatience. Later, as Teach nears the end of what has been an overwhelmingly violent verbal assault on Grace and Ruthie, he interpolates his vicious denigration with remarks that seem designed to gain him sympathy and concurrence as well as to maintain his reputation as a man "to be reckoned with":

> Teach: . . . Ruthie . . . I mean, *you* see how she fucking plays. . . . (You see what I'm talking about?) . . . I know you like the broad and

> Grace and, Bob, I know he likes 'em too. And I like 'em too. (I know,
> I know.). . . . But all I ever ask (and I would say this to her face) is
> only she remembers who is who and not to go around with *her* or
> Gracie either with this attitude. "The Past is Past, and this is Now, so
> Fuck You." You see? (act 1, pp. 14–15)

Teach is careful not to alienate Don and Bobby; he needs them as
allies. In spite of his viciousness, he ironically makes every effort
to appear fair, to stress his impartiality and even fondness of
those whom he so forcefully condemns. He strives to cast himself
as the much-maligned victim of the piece, a "true pal" who has
been sorely abused. Mamet's use of parentheses here is almost
akin to his repeated use of obscenity; as Colin Stinton has remarked, by continually reverting to a profanity, Mamet's characters bring the conversation back to an area of common ground that
all parties have an interest in and understand. In this case, the
obscenities are replaced by Teach's use of parenthetical asides,
expressly intended to gain him both agreement and sympathy,
but the effect is just the same.

In order to appreciate fully Mamet's meticulous use of language, it is necessary to look not only at his work for the theatre,
but also at his screenwriting techniques and his screenplays: He
has achieved considerable success in both media, winning the
1984 Pulitzer Prize for *Glengarry Glen Ross* and earning an Oscar
nomination for his screenplay of *The Verdict* the same year. Since
then he has also been highly praised for his work on *House of
Games,* a film both written and directed by him.

Writing for the screen is not an occupation Mamet views as
inferior to playwriting, but, rather, equally demanding and pains-
taking. He says, "I think screenwriting is most definitely an art
form; a different art form from the theater, but an art form."[72]
Although there are obvious similarities between playwriting and
screenwriting, such as presentation of dialogue, Mamet feels that
the two occupations differ considerably, and that a separate set of
skills is necessary for each. He explains the prime difference
between the two as follows:

> [Writing is] very different in a movie than in plays. In a movie you're
> trying to show what the characters did and in a play they're trying to
> convey what they want. The only tool they have in a play is what
> they're trying to say. What might be wretched playwriting—describ-
> ing what a character does—may be good screenwriting.[73]

Elaborating upon the differences, Mamet believes that

in a play . . . the only way you have to convey the action of the plot is through the action of the characters, what they say to each other. With a movie, the action has to be advanced narratively. To advance it through the dialogue is just boring; it is not the proper exploitation of the form. It has to be advanced, showing the audience what's happening, narrating to them the state of mind of the protagonist which . . . is the worst kind of playwriting. From what I can see in the writing and directing, film is getting things structured so that it succeeds in spite of itself. . . . You . . . are taking out the elements of feeling and sensitivity, so you're relying absolutely on the structure of the script.[74]

Mamet has long been an admirer of the work of Arthur Miller, and he notes Miller's advice to playwrights who are interested in writing for the screen: "You've got to do both or you'll lose the touch."[75]

Mamet's first job as a screenwriter was for Bob Rafelson's version of the James M. Cain novel, *The Postman Always Rings Twice*. Mamet believes that he achieved a wide and useful knowledge of film technique and—as ever—much enjoyed the discipline of working within a tight framework. He observes how: "It was such a thrill to have a good scene that's five minutes long and get it down to a minute and a half and make it a better scene".[76] Too often, he feels, playwrights leave unnecessary dialogue in their works, and ignore the rules. Having inserted some appealing, though nonessential, lines in a play, the writer might muse:

it's not consistent, but it sure is pretty. Why should I be bound by the rules of dramaturgy when no one knows them but me. . . . The rule in question here is Aristotle's notion of unity of action: in effect, that the play should be about only one thing, and that that thing should be *what the hero is trying to get.* Unstinting application of this rule makes great plays because the only thing we, as audience, care about in the theater is what happens next. All of us writers know this but few of us do it. We don't do it because it is too difficult. It is much easier to write great dialogue (which is a talent and not really very much of an exertion) than to write great plots.[77]

Two of the screenplays to be considered here, *The Postman Always Rings Twice* and *The Verdict*, were both adapted from existing novels. Mamet says that he experienced great difficulties with the former because "it is written as first-person narrative and almost all the incidents are incited by a change in the protagonist's state of mind, which is, at best, boring to express on film. . . . The problem of the screenplay was how to distort an internal psycho-

logical monologue into a visible clash of visible forces."[78] What
Mamet saw as the real challenge was how long he could withhold
vital information from the audience without confusing or disori-
entating them:

> At what point do you give the audience information about the charac-
> ters? And by withholding that information, how do you create sus-
> pense so that it is possible, in most instances, to have revelations on
> the part of the protagonist that are in consonance with the revelations
> of the audience? How do you make that happen for the protagonist at
> the same time you make it happen for the audience, so you're neither
> telling the audience something it already knows nor telling the au-
> dience something it can't appreciate.[79]

Mamet sows the seeds for the highly charged and passionate
relationship that grows between Frank Chambers, the protagonist, and his employer's wife, Cora, at the very beginning of
the work. Frank's first sight of Cora is as tantalizing for the
audience as it is for him. Mamet places Cora in the kitchen with
her back to the camera; she is visible only through a partially open
door. "She is putting dishes in the sink. She wipes sweat off her
brow with her upper arm. Her blouse falls open showing her
breast."[80] Mamet then focuses the audience's attention on Frank,
and on the double entendre that follows:

> Frank looking at Cora . . . Frank is entranced.
> Frank: The food . . . delicious.
> Cora turns to look at Frank . . . She looks . . . for a moment, as if focusing,
>   wondering what he is talking about, then she nods, and goes back to her
>   washing.[81]

This is quite different from Cain's introduction of Cora's character;
Mamet retains the erotically charged atmosphere, but omits at this
point the overtly sadistic tone inferred by the novelist's description: "she had a sulky look to her, and her lips stuck out in a way
that made me want to mash them in for her."[82] Indeed, although
the finished film was one of the most visually erotic pieces of
cinema yet released, Mamet's script tended to veer away from the
rather sadistic and pornographic elements in Cain's novel, while
at the same time remaining faithful to the general impulse of the
plot. Whereas Cain concentrates upon the sadomasochism of
Frank and Cora's relationship, Mamet emphasizes its passion.
There indeed remain sadomasochistic elements in Mamet's version but he has, by virtue of a sensitive script, raised them above

the pornographic and distasteful. The preceding extract is a good example of his ability to infer eroticism through linguistic suggestion rather than via brutalization, and it accords with Mamet's desire to convey information simultaneously to the audience and to the protagonist. The audience's first perception of what might occur is consonant with that of Frank and, typically, the tension has been established with very few words.

Opening the story out at times in order to make more clear the developing relationships, Mamet at other times condenses Cain's tale into extraordinarily brief scenes. One example occurs when Frank and Cora's first attempt to murder Nick (Cora's husband) fails and they try to revive him while waiting for the ambulance to arrive. Mamet condenses nearly three pages of tightly packed narrative into a suspenseful—and almost silent—scene, at the same time depicting Frank's ambiguous attitude toward the man he has tried to kill:

> *Frank:* Nick . . . Nick . . . hey, wake up. Wake up, Nick . . . I'm *talking* to you, Nicholas. Wake *up,* you fuckin' *wheeze.*[83]

At first, Frank seems to show concern for his unfortunate victim, feeling pity for him in the realization that it is only because of his own love for Cora that they are in such a position. Then, as Nick fails to regain consciousness, a mixture of fear and resentment creeps into Frank's voice. He calls Nick "Nicholas" for the first time, perhaps suggesting his contempt for and patronage of a man whose wife no longer loves him. Finally, anger and frustration overtake Frank completely as he begins to curse his victim bitterly. With so very few words, Mamet opens up Frank's character brilliantly, condensing the many elements of his changing personality into this one, short scene.

Similarly, in his screenplay for *The Verdict,* mood and character are established with great economy. The opening scene sets the tone of what follows: it is hypocritical, devious, and tragic. Mamet's theme is corruption, and the lengths to which a failed lawyer will go in order to secure a job on a criminal negligence case. Joe Galvin, the lawyer (and protagonist) is first seen at a funeral service putting "a discreetly folded ten-dollar bill"[84] into the hands of a man who appears to be some sort of official. Galvin is then introduced to the grieving widow:

> *Funeral Director:* Mrs. Dee, this is Joe Galvin . . . a very good friend of ours, and a very fine attorney.

> *Galvin:* It's a shame about your husband, Mrs. Dee . . . I knew him
> vaguely through the Lodge. He was a wonderful man. *(Shakes head
> in sympathy.)* It was a crime what happened to him. A crime. If
> there's *anything* that I could do to help . . .
> *Galvin removes a business card from his jacket pocket and hands it to her as
> if he were giving her money. (i.e.,* "Take it. Really. I *want* you to have
> it . . .") *She takes the card.*[85]

Mamet's script potently underscores the visual subtext; Galvin's
pushing the business card into the woman's hand is an almost
obscene gesture, given the circumstances, and is horribly redolent of the image of his hand giving over money to the funeral
official moments earlier. Galvin's covert hypocrisy and his piety in
front of the widow are nauseating; Mamet's dialogue establishes
the hushed tones of sincerity and, at the same time, points to
Galvin's duplicity. The language succinctly but powerfully com-
plements the visual image; it is a scene of wickedly subtle words
and gestures, in which every sound and movement contributes to
the overall tastelessness of the situation. Galvin's words, though
ostensibly simple and appropriate in such circumstances are, in
fact, chosen with extreme care. He cleverly states that he knew
Mrs. Dee's husband "vaguely" through an establishment such as a
Masonic Lodge, an institution to which women are denied access.
Although he scarcely knew him, he insists that her husband was
"a wonderful man" in the hope of flattering the distraught woman
and gaining her trust. He then repeats the word "crime" to ensure
that it leaves its mark; he does not wish to appear pushy or
insensitive, but leaves the word's resonance in the air, to work
indirectly and covertly. Galvin ends his little speech with a very
general and standard cliché, "If there's *anything* that I could do to
help," which Mamet makes doubly ironic by Galvin's action of
"selflessly" pressing the business card into the woman's hand.

The rigorous economy of expression and understanding of the
cinematic process, which Mamet began with Rafelson's film and
refined in Sidney Lumet's *The Verdict,* is perfected in *House of
Games.* Here, he produces a kind of heightened naturalism; the
deliberate artificiality of the film both comments upon and com-
plements the labyrinthine world it depicts. The screenplay is, as
ever, replete with his harsh, staccato poetry and illustrative of his
concern with language but, on this occasion, the story is told
more through image and gesture than through words. It is this
self-conscious artistry that gives the film its visual power. *House of
Games* has the look and feel of a 1940s film noir, and its darkened
streets, shady gaming rooms, and downtown bars resemble a

series of tableaux painted by Edward Hopper. There is also surely a nod toward the surrealist cinema of Luis Buñuel; his films often lead the viewer to believe that reality is being represented on-screen, and then suddenly fragment that "reality," revealing it as part of a character's dreams. Mamet misdirects not only the audience—it is often difficult to tell who is conning whom—but also the heroine, Margaret Ford. It is around the experiences of this woman, an eminent psychiatrist and writer, that the story revolves. Her initiation into the American underworld moves from her initial suspicion of Mike, the arch con man, to sexual attraction, to hatred and murder. The final irony of a film replete with ironic juxtaposition is Margaret's acknowledgment—with some pleasure, I feel—that she and Mike are basically the same under the skin.

The film charts territory explored elsewhere by Mamet, most notably in *American Buffalo* and *Glengarry Glen Ross*, but here the confidence trick, the "scam" that is performed as much for pleasure as for the ultimate payoff, is raised to almost mythic proportions. Mike is the natural successor to schemers and opportunists like Teach and Richard Roma. Although he is clearly a confidence trickster, conning primarily to make money, there is a sense that his skills are a life-giving source of energy for him, a way to keep "high," to remain in control, and without which he could not function. He explains the basis of his "craft" to Margaret:

> *Mike:* The basic idea is this: it's called a *"confidence"* game. Why? Because you give me your confidence? No. Because I give you *mine.* So what we have here, in addition to "Adventures in Human Misery" is a short course in psychology. (p. 34)

What is fascinating about this short speech is how succinctly Mamet manages to suggest the parallels between Mike and Margaret's life experience; both deal in issues of confidence, and both exercise a profound knowledge of psychology. It is clear that Mike relishes his "profession"; he wants to appear knowledgeable and—apparently ignorant of Margaret's own occupation—strives to lend weight to his words with satirical asides and a reference to psychology. *House of Games* is also notable for illustrating how Mamet plays a double game; neither Margaret nor Mike is cast as the "innocent" party. The audience knows that Margaret is a famous psychiatrist-psychologist, and yet she listens patiently to a man who arrogantly strives to teach her something of this subject. It is in fact Margaret who is "using" Mike at this point, as she learns the tricks of *his* trade. Mike is playing his own game, as we later learn, but the basic ambiguity remains: who is the real "victim" of the piece?

Set on the trail by a so-called compulsive gambler, it is Margaret who turns out to the the true compulsive. As Mike points out to his cronies after the final, superbly realized con, "the broad's an *addict*" (p. 61). Her uncertainty about herself and her role in life leads her to make several Freudian slips throughout the film: at one point she unconsciously substitutes "pressures" for "pleasures," and in the following scene, which involves a discussion with Maria, a colleague at the hospital where she is employed, Margaret "slips" again:

> *Ford:* Why do we listen to their troubles when we can't help them?
> *Maria:* Oh. You have been talking to your murderess again.
> *Ford:* I know why she is in the hospital, she's sick. The question is what am *I* doing there. It's a sham, it's a con game. There's nothing I can do to help her, and there's nothing I can learn from her to help others avoid her mistakes. That poor girl, all her life my father tells her she's a whore, so all her life she seeks out . . .
> *Maria:* "My father . . ."?
> *Ford:* I'm sorry?
> *Maria:* You said, *"My* father says that she's a whore."
> *Ford: My* father . . .? *(Beat.)* I said, *"My"* father . . . ? (p. 30)

Thus Mamet's psychiatrist refers to psychology as a con game and his confidence trickster cites the con game as psychology. In a sense, Mike provides the "help" Margaret craves, an assistance she feels powerless to offer her patients. Her low self-esteem is overwhelmingly obvious, and Mamet suggests a possible reason for the "slip"; it is Margaret who feels like a whore, a worthless woman—the notion possibly stemming from the relationship between herself and her own father.

An excellent example of Mamet's use of image and gesture to progress his story occurs after Margaret has been convinced that she shot and killed a man. Distraught, she goes to the college where Maria is giving a lecture.

> *. . . Ford, outside the lecture room, looking in. A late student moves past Ford to open the door. We hear Maria lecturing as the door opens.*

> *Maria:* Compression, inversion, elaboration, are devices for transforming the latent into the manifest. In the dream, and also, in the . . . ? In the *Joke!*

As she makes her point she points her finger at the class, as if she held a gun. We hear a gunshot.
Angle: Close-up. Ford, recoiling.
Angle: The businessman's face.
Angle: Ford's hand, turning the pages of her notebook, to the page which reads "House of Games."
Angle: The businessman sliding down the wall. A loud bell rings.
Angle: Ford in the hall, stunned. The bell stops. We hear Maria calling "Maggie . . . Maggie, What is it. . . ?"
Angle: The hall. The students, changing classes. Maria, in the classroom door, calling to Ford.

Ford: I have to . . . I have to talk to you. (p. 55)

The rapid cutting between the scene of the "murder" of the businessman and the current realities of the college hall are skilfully interwoven to produce an aura of considerable menace. Margaret's anguish has been established primarily through visual and aural—but not verbal—means, Maria's gesture and the ringing of the bell producing in Margaret a state that verges on collapse.

It is plain that Mamet brings the same subtlety and depth to his screenwriting as he does to his plays. His writing is again spare yet strong, creating tension and depicting character without a wasted syllable. What makes one look forward to his future forays into the cinematic arts is his increasing ability to combine superb verbal technique with powerful visual imagery.

Mamet's plays are undoubtedly fresh and original, but he candidly acknowledges his debt to a number of writers who have exerted a particularly strong influence upon his work. Among the novelists he cites are Willa Cather, Sherwood Anderson, Willard Motley, Ernest Hemingway, Frank Norris, and Saul Bellow,[86] as well as Theodore Dreiser, Sinclair Lewis, and Upton Sinclair.[87] What attracts Mamet to these artists is not only their love of language and their authentic rendering of the linguistic rhythms of urban America but also that they all wrote "a story of possibility . . . the West is beginning and . . . life is capable of being both understood and enjoyed."[88] This optimism is expressed over and over again in Mamet's plays. No matter how low his characters may fall or how base they may become, there still remains in them an almost tangible feeling of hope. It is difficult not to be reminded of Samuel Beckett's "voice" in *The Unnameable*, when it concludes, "I don't know, I'll never know, in the silence you don't know, you must go on, I can't go on, I'll go on."[89]

As far as playwrights are concerned, Mamet is very specific about those who have inspired him. In addition to Harold Pinter and Samuel Beckett, his other greatest influences have been Anton Chekhov, Eugene O'Neill, and Clifford Odets. Mamet states, "I'd like to write a really good play sometime. Like O'Neill, Odets, Chekhov, something the way it really is, capture the action of the way things really go on."[90] He also considers that Tennessee Williams wrote "the greatest dramatic poetry in the American language [and dramatized] a kind people living in a cruel country [who] don't know how to show [their] love."[91]

Mamet takes an amalgam of the styles of all these writers and makes them unmistakably his own. His language is the hard-boiled, abrasive dissonance of contemporary America, thoroughly modern in sound and content. It is constantly enlivened and refreshed by a blisteringly original use of figurative speech and the rhythms of urban life. His use of obscenity and scatalogy somehow enrich what is desperately plain and prosaic. Mamet may set out to demonstrate the awful barrenness he feels now exists in American society but, en route, he offers some truly remarkable writing.

1

Sexual Perversity in Chicago

Like most of Mamet's plays, *Sexual Perversity in Chicago* is set in a desensitized society. The characters inhabit a cheap and fraudulent world in which standards decline daily and sexual intimacy seems to have become public property. Language is often used shoddily and obscenities are commonplace—their sexual connotations have, through overuse, become dulled, rather like their users' consciousnesses. Human relationships have become attenuated to the point at which men and women view each other as little more than media-created stereotypes, and millions of people watch television soap operas sincerely believing that their convoluted plots reflect real life.

In the mid-1970s when the play was written, what Mamet calls the "jejeune super-sophistication"[1] of the American populace was at its height. The "Swinging Sixties" had come and gone and, in their place, was a cynical, rather detached society that plundered the most negative aspects of the previous decade's sexual revolution, emphasizing promiscuity and irresponsibility to the detriment of its emotional sanity. Because of the dominating influence of all things sexual, erotica flourished, pornography boomed, and sex could be found in the unlikeliest of places. It was—indeed, it still is—used to sell clothes, food, cars, books, and toothpaste. Such an emphasis upon the nonemotional aspects of sexuality was bound, sooner or later, to result in a deleterious blunting of the nation's consciousness. This is precisely what has happened to the four young people portrayed in Mamet's play. For them, sex really has become a dirty word, a sniggering pastime for the easily bored. Rather than fulfilling its original function as an integral part of an emotional relationship, sex is for them little more than a cheap thrill, something that men "do" to women and for which women should be grateful.

Mamet's view of such a society is bleak; his characters are alienated in every sense of the word. Alienation, as Marx observed, is descriptive of more than people's sense of estrangement from the result of their labors. Marx wrote, "What is true of man's relationship to his work, to the product of his work, and to himself, is also true of his relationship to other men, to their labor, and to the objects of their labor . . . each man is alienated from others, and . . . each of the others is likewise alienated from human life."[2] As a result of this sense of alienation, human relations come to rest on what Christopher Bigsby describes as "an exploitation that is not necessarily of itself material but is derived from a world in which exchange value is a primary mechanism. One individual approaches another with a tainted bargain, an offer of relationship now corrupted by the values of the market. . . . people become commodites, objects."[3]

The characters in *Sexual Perversity in Chicago* are, in common with many others in Mamet's drama, emotionally adrift in a world where the second-rate has been accepted as the norm. They occasionally glimpse the possibility of something other than the tawdry lives they endure, but these momentary revelations have no chance of taking root in the febrile atmosphere in which they exist. With no real moral base upon which to pin their ideas, their lives are shapeless, distorted, and corrupt. As Richard Eder points out,

> the characters speak as if calling for help out of a deep well. Each is isolated, without real identity. They talk to find it—"I speak, therefore I am"—and the comic and touching involution of their language is the evidence of their isolation and tracklessness. . . . Their world is full of. . . . lessons learned but learned wrong because of the unreasonable ferocity, the lack of shape or instruction of middle American life.[4]

Sexual Perversity in Chicago is replete with dialogue powered by a pulsatingly neurotic energy. Its urban rhythms are merciless and relentless; its movement is conveyed by Mamet's rapid sentence structure and the fast-paced episodes. The frenetic verbal affrays that the characters indulge in are their way of concealing the vacuum that exists at the root of their lives; the abandon with which they bounce wisecracks and platitudes off one another only partially conceals their desperation. So long as they can continue to joke, criticize, and fantasize, they can delude themselves that they are happy.

Structured in swift, short scenes that rise, like dirty jokes, to punchlines, the play examines the void at the heart of contemporary sexual relationships. Life for Mamet's characters is as shallow as the fictional lives of their soap opera heroes and incorporates many aspects of an obscene joke; their exploits are crude, debased, and usually over very quickly. The form and shape of the play are themselves reminiscent of such jokes, and so the very structure of the piece enacts its meaning. The parallel is carried one stage further with Mamet's Bernie constantly spouting his elaborate and ludicrous sexual fantasies. These are reported to Danny as fact, but are little more than routine dirty stories that have been opened out into mini-dramas in which Bernie himself is the chief protagonist. Sex dominates all their conversations, just as work dominates those of the salesmen in *Glengarry Glen Ross*. Such characters have only one subject at their disposal and they must discuss it exhaustively in an effort to conceal their insecurity and loneliness. Their relentless bragging is intended to impress, but underneath the cool bravado lies a desperate vulnerability. Mamet has commented upon this aspect of the work: "Voltaire said words were invented to hide feelings. That's what the play is about."[5]

Bernie is an excellent example of a man who uses language to conceal his insecurity. He urges Danny to view women as he does—as sexual objects that can be picked up and discarded at random. He does his very best to impress his friend with his callous insouciance and contemptuous reductivism but, in fact, he is terrified of women. There is no evidence to suggest that he has ever had a satisfactory relationship, in spite of all his masculine posturing. Bernie is, literally, "all talk." In order to assuage his fears, he constantly reduces women to the most basic physical level. For him, they can be succinctly summed up in the following crude jingle:

Tits and Ass. Tits and Ass. Tits and Ass. Tits and Ass. Blah de Bloo. Blah de Bloo. Blah de Bloo. Blah de Bloo. (*Pause.*) Huh? (scene 30, p. 47)

The opposite sex is thus described in purely sexual terms, which are debased further still by occurring alongside a string of nonsense words designed to convey Bernie's apparent casual contempt. By saying the words aloud, he can wield his spurious power over women. However, his final "Huh?" suggests his weakness and need for approbation and concurrence from an easily swayed friend.

In *Sexual Perversity in Chicago*, Mamet looks at the ways in which language can contribute to the formation of sexist attitudes. His characters employ a kind of subtle linguistic coercion as a means of influencing and persuading their companions to concur with their way of thinking. Consequently, barriers are erected that are then exceedingly difficult to penetrate. Bernie's relentless chauvinism filters through to Danny, who is influenced by and in awe of his ostensibly suave friend. As a result, he eventually becomes as coarse and offensive as his mentor. Mamet points out that the play is much concerned with

> how what we say influences what we think. The words that Bernie Litko says to Danny influence his behavior; you know, that women are broads, that they're there to exploit. And the words that Joan says to her friend Deborah: men are problematical creatures which are necessary to have a relationship with because that's what society says, but it never really works out. It is nothing but a schlep, a misery constantly.[6]

Partly because of the pressures of language exerted by their companions and partly through cultural fiats, any relationship formed between Mamet's male and female characters is doomed to failure. The men are unwilling—or unable—to view women as anything other than sex slaves and receptacles for their pleasure and, not surprisingly, the women regard men as natural enemies and emotional cripples. The reductive and crude exploitative images of women that are daily emblazoned across tabloid newspapers and broadcasted in countless films and television programs have perverted the perception of their audience. In such a society, women have only two choices: they can try to emulate the ideal feminine stereotype pushed forward by the media and craved by unimaginative men like Bernie and Danny, or they can turn to feminism with a vengeance. Those who choose the former are satirized by Tom Wolfe in his essay, "The Woman Who Had Everything." In this work, Wolfe writes of the trouble to which some women will go in an effort to conform to a popular (and desirable) stereotype:

> Women [engage in a ceaseless quest to] make themselves irresistibly attractive to the men of New York . . . coiffeurs . . . The eternal search for better eyelashes! Off to Deirdre's or some such place, on Madison Avenue—moth-cut eyelashes? Square-cut eyelashes? mink eyelashes? . . . Or off to somewhere for the perfect Patti-nail application, $25 for both hands, $2.50 a finger, false fingernails . . . [then] the skin . . . that purple light business at Don Lee's Hair Specialist Studio . . .[7]

Desirability often depends therefore upon as much artificial assistance as can reasonably be applied—and at a price. Wolfe exposes the obsession with public myths of beauty and sexuality for the absurdity it undoubtedly is. Good sense and dignity are overridden by a desperate need to conform.

Although women are without question the most offensively exploited of the sexes, men do not escape the pressures of the media. They, too, must manufacture a false image and endeavor to live up to it in order to attract the equally false objects of their desire. It is little wonder that love should so infrequently enter such relationships; they are superficial in the extreme, with both parties acting out a fantasy ideal of what they imagine the other craves. Mamet blames the mass media for much misery and heartache, observing that *Sexual Perversity in Chicago* is, "unfortunately, tales from my life."[8] He explains,

> My sex life was ruined by the popular media. It took a lot of getting over. There are a lot of people in my situation. The myths around us, destroying our lives, such a great capacity to destroy our lives. . . . You have to sleep with every woman that you see, have a new car every two years—sheer, utter nonsense. Men who never have to deal with it, are never really forced to deal with it, deal with it by getting colitis, anxiety attacks and by killing themselves.[9]

Certainly Bernie seems to be desperately trying to live up to a stereotype; his adopted persona suggests that he is something of a "super-stud." What is so tragic about a man like Bernie is that he is, at base, painfully aware of his own inadequacy and fear, and that is why he must behave in the overtly masculine fashion that has become his trademark.

The "perversity" of the title is not, as one critic ironically observes, "a misprint for perversion"[10] but is entirely intentional. Mamet's characters are indeed perverse, but not in the sense that might be expected—although one of them does observe that "nobody does it normally any more" (scene 1, p. 13). The perversity Mamet has in mind emanates from his characters' diminished perception of each other, their lack of understanding, and the cold, inhumane manner in which they conduct their lives. What is crucially missing is any real sense of value beyond the material, or an awareness of any need unrelated to immediate sexual satisfaction.

Sexual Perversity in Chicago was voted the best Chicago play of 1974 and, in 1975, won an Obie for its off-Broadway production. There have been a number of productions of the work, both in the United States and England and, in 1986, a filmed version was released under the title of *About Last Night*.

The first scene sets the tone for the play: it is fast, funny, and outrageous. In this episode, Bernie lovingly outlines for Danny the details of a ludicrously unlikely story about a recent "erotic" exploit. Bernie's tale is something of a tour-de-force of sexual fantasy, and the longest and most involved of a number of stories he relates throughout the play. What is ironic is that he wants Danny to believe every word he utters. This hymn to sexual excess is hypnotic not only for Danny but for Bernie as well; so involved does he become in the sheer force of his narrative that he appears to believe it himself. This early conversation establishes Bernie as the character with the "knowledge" and Danny as his eager ingénu and is reminiscent of the power plays of language frequently found in the work of Harold Pinter:

> *Danny:* So how'd you do last night?
> *Bernie:* Are you kidding me?
> *Danny:* Yeah?
> *Bernie:* Are you fucking kidding me?
> *Danny:* Yeah?
> *Bernie:* Are you pulling my leg?
> *Danny:* So?
> *Bernie:* So tits out to here so.
> *Danny:* Yeah?
> *Bernie:* Twenty, a couple years old.
> *Danny:* You gotta be fooling.
> *Bernie:* Nope.
> *Danny:* You devil.
> *Bernie:* You think she hadn't been around?
> *Danny:* Yeah?
> *Bernie:* She hadn't gone the route?
> *Danny:* She knew the route, huh?
> *Bernie:* Are you fucking kidding me?
> *Danny:* Yeah?
> *Bernie:* She *wrote* the route. (scene 1, p. 7)

Bernie's responses to Danny's initial questions are intended by him to be rhetorical; answering a question with another question is his way of emphasizing just how incredible a time he actually enjoyed the previous evening. He works Danny up into a kind of verbal frenzy merely by refusing to give him anything other than strongly implied hints of sexual success. Mamet captures perfectly the grammatical anarchy of idiomatic conversation in the repetition of "building" words like "so" and "yeah" and the abbreviation of a sentence such as "Twenty, a couple years old." The age of the girl is left totally ambiguous, which is just as well since, shortly after its initial mention, it moves from about eighteen to over twenty-five, depending upon whether Bernie currently favors the idea of corrupted naïveté or well-seasoned maturity. Bernie encourages Danny's lasciviousness through his carefully constructed routine; Danny's breathless "Yeah?" increases in intensity until one can almost hear his jaw drop open in erotic anticipation. Exactly why Danny finds it difficult to believe that the girl should have been "Twenty, a couple years old" is unclear. His incredulity is possibly due to the fact that Bernie's success with such a young woman seems unlikely; although Bernie's age is unstated, it is clear that he is considerably older than his friend. Perhaps the woman's age, referred to by Bernie, most potently symbolizes female sexual rapacity for the two men. Or perhaps Danny's incredulity is his way of encouraging Bernie into new areas of excess.

In an effort to make his fantasy sound as realistic as possible, Bernie takes pains to establish the correct location and timing. Danny enjoys the detail, no matter how irrelevant, and incites his friend's erotic imagination still further by uttering neat, monosyllabic asides that will not interrupt the flow of things too much:

Danny: So tell me.
Bernie: So okay, so where am I?
Danny: When?
Bernie: Last night, two-thirty.
Danny: So two-thirty, you're probably over at Yak-Zies.
Bernie: Left Yak-zies at one.
Danny: So you're probably over at Grunts.
Bernie: They only got a two o'clock license.
Danny: So you're probably over at the Commonwealth.
Bernie: So, okay, so I'm over at the Commonwealth, in the pancake house off the lobby, and I'm working on a stack of those raisin and nut jobs . . .
Danny: They're good.
Bernie: . . . and I'm reading the paper, and I'm reading, and I'm casing the pancake house, and the usual shot, am I right?
Danny: Right.
Bernie: So who walks in over to the cash register but this chick.
Danny: Right.
Bernie: Nineteen, twenty-year old chick . . .
Danny: Who we're talking about.
Bernie: . . . and she wants a pack of Viceroys.
Danny: I can believe that. . . . Was she a pro? (scene 1, pp. 8–9)

Bernie still plays cat and mouse, keeping Danny in suspense until the last possible moment. He wants to paint a picture of the events that will accurately reflect his "experience" in all its glory and he makes Danny work for the trifles he offers. Bernie creates an atmosphere of Yuppie-style establishments, where neon lights and potted palms endeavor to give some class to what are, essentially, late-night pickup joints. The slightly sleazy sounding bar and restaurant names add to the aura of Bernie's sexual adventure: "Yak-Zies" and, especially, the onomatapoeiac "Grunts." Danny's responses to the more prosaic aspects of Bernie's tale add immeasurably both to the humor of the scene and to our understanding of him. The banality of his reactions is absolutely hilarious. Despite Bernie's linguistic game of suspense and titillation, which both men clearly relish, Danny unfathomably wishes to hear even mundane details. Whatever the input, he exhibits no impatience and enjoys the opportunity to comment on (and become vicariously involved in?) Bernie's "adventure."

Danny is also obsessed with establishing if the girl was, in fact, "a pro" (pp. 9–10 and 14), that is, a prostitute. At regular intervals, he repeats the question: "Was she a pro?" as if this fact would somehow add to the spiciness of Bernie's tale. As far as Bernie's fantasy is concerned, this information is—at least for his present purposes—irrelevant. He has not yet made up his mind whether she should be a sexually voracious virgin who has been deranged by his charms, or a hard-nosed trouper to whom such exploits are routine. He stalls Danny's tireless questions by responding with variations on the theme of "Well, at this point we don't know" and "So, at this point, we don't know. Pro, semi-pro, Betty Co-Ed from College, regular young broad, it's anybody's ballgame" (scene 1, p. 9).

As Bernie's story progresses to the ridiculous point at which the girl dons a World War II flak suit before allowing him to make love to her, so Danny's ingenuousness similarly reaches new heights:

Bernie: . . . From under the bed she pulls this suitcase, and from out of the suitcase comes this World War Two Flak suit.
Danny: They're hard to find.
Bernie: Zip, zip, zip, and she gets into the Flak suit and we get down on the bed.
Danny: What are you doing?
Bernie: Fucking.
Danny: She's in the Flak suit?
Bernie: Right.
Danny: How do you get in?

Bernie: How do you think I get in? She leaves the zipper open. (scene
   1, pp. 11–12)

Bernie is clearly getting carried away with his fantasy. He no
longer wishes to hear Danny's questions and inane remarks, but
wants to get on with the action. As Bernie moves further and
further into the ecstasies of libidinous fantasy, Danny remains
down-to-earth, questioning details that had at first acted as spurs
to give the story depth and realism, but now serve only as interruptions and irritations.
   The fantasy eventually ends with Bernie's "recollection" that the
girl telephoned her friend during their lovemaking, asking her to
make "airplane noises" over the telephone, and then set fire to the
hotel room in an orgy of abandon:

   Bernie: . . . Humping and bumping, and she's screaming "Red dog
      One to Red dog Squadron" . . . all of a sudden she screams "Wait."
      She wriggles out, leans under the bed, and she pulls out this five-
      gallon jerrycan. . . . she splashes the mother all over the walls,
      whips a fuckin' Zippo out of the Flak suit, and WHOOSH, the
      whole room is in flames. So the whole fuckin' joint is going up in
      smoke, the telephone is going "Rat Tat Tat," the broad jumps back
      on the bed and yells "Now, give it to me *now* for the Love of Christ."
      (Pause.) So I look at the broad . . . and I figure . . . fuck this
      nonsense. I grab my clothes, I peel a saw-buck off my wad, as I
      make the door I fling it at her. "For cabfare," I yell. . . . Whole
      fucking hall is full of smoke, above the flames I just make out my
      broad (she's singing "Off we go into the Wild Blue Yonder"). . . .
   Danny: Nobody does it normally anymore.
   Bernie: It's these young broads. They don't know what the fuck they
      want. (scene 1, p. 13)

Bernie concludes his imaginary exploit without his having
reached orgasm: it is as if, even within the realms of a dream, to
submit to such an action is to acknowledge some form of commitment. As he imagines his "lover" lying amidst the smoke and
flames, his fear of and sheer contempt for women become the
uppermost emotions in his mind. Rather than complete the sexual
act he has begun, he prefers to turn on the girl, flinging money in
her face as if to suggest that she is nothing more than a common
prostitute and he a disgusted client. For such deep-seated contempt to manifest itself within the safety of a sexual fantasy
suggests Bernie's very real sexual problems. He tells Danny that,
having set the room aflame and produced her quota of sound

effects, the girl begged him to bring her to orgasm. By denying her that satisfaction, Bernie likewise denies himself. His language takes on the coldness of a character like Mickey Spillane's Mike Hammer; his terminology owes more to fictional cops and robbers than to real life. He evidently sees himself as the cool-headed, although rather misogynistic, stud who has been represented by countless film and television heroes. Bernie has been acting all the time, but perhaps nowhere so purposefully as here; he strives to give Danny the impression of his supreme control over the situation and, in so doing, verbally reenacts what has never taken place. By saying the words aloud, Bernie enjoys a frisson of excitement over an event that had only ever existed in his mind.

Bernie's contempt for women is consolidated as he blames the imaginary girl for her perversion: "It's these young broads. They don't know what the fuck they want." This is patently untrue since, if nothing else, the girl in his dream exploit knew *exactly* what she wanted. Symbolically, Mamet has suggested Bernie's inability to have a satisfactory sexual relationship with a woman, and does so within the first few minutes of the play. Finally, Danny finds out if Bernie's "lover" was indeed "a pro":

> *Bernie:* A pro, Dan . . . is how you think about yourself. You see my point? . . . I'll tell you one thing . . . she knew all the pro moves. (scene 1, p. 14)

Sexual Perversity in Chicago has much in common with Jules Feiffer's *Carnal Knowledge,* which was filmed in 1971 by Mike Nichols. In fact, Mamet's play has been directly compared with Feiffer's work: in his book, *The Literature of the U.S.A.,* Marshall Walker observes that it is "a set of clever variations on material . . . treated in Jules Feiffer's screenplay for Mike Nichols's *Carnal Knowledge,*"[11] and John Elsom likens it to "Feiffer's cartoons, but less acid and more human."[12] *Carnal Knowledge* concerns the changing fortunes of two young men from their college days through to their early forties. The film version was a great success; Jack Nicholson starred as the sexually predatory Jonathan and Art Garfunkel as his more reserved friend, Sandy. Like Bernie, Jonathan spends his time trying to convey a sense of knowing sexual expertise to his eager, and sexually curious, younger friend. Also like Bernie, Jonathan is unable to sustain a satisfactory sexual relationship. At first, in an effort to retain a feeling of superiority over Sandy, he steals Susan, Sandy's girlfriend, and later becomes involved in a love affair with a stereotypical "dumb blonde" who wants to be loved for more than her body. Jonathan is capable of being aroused only by the most buxom—and passive—of women, is incapable of treating them as individuals, and refers to them always in demotic terms that relate to their physical characteristics. Early in the screenplay, Jonathan and Sandy discuss the ideal woman. Like Bernie and Danny, the two men at first differ from one another in their crassness:

Sandy: You want perfection.
Jonathan: What do you want, wise guy?
Sandy: She just has to be nice. That's all.
Jonathan: You don't want her beautiful?
Sandy: She doesn't have to be beautiful. I'd like her built, though.
Jonathan: I'd want mine sexy-looking.
Sandy: I wouldn't want her to look like a tramp.
Jonathan: Sexy doesn't mean she has to look like a tramp. There's a middle ground. . . . Big tits.
Sandy: Yeah. But still a virgin.
Jonathan: I don't care about that. . . . I wouldn't mind if she was just a little ahead of me—with those big tits—and knew hundreds of different ways . . .[13]

Just as Danny is the character in Mamet's play who actually manages to sustain some kind of sexual relationship, however, brief, so it is the naïve Sandy who first attracts the beautiful—and sexually experimental—Susan. Like Bernie, Jonathan resents the relationship and ignores any emotional involvement that may exist, reducing it always to a sexual level. The truth of the matter is that Jonathan feels excluded. In an effort to put his own "stamp" on the proceedings, he notes how Susan's "tits were too small," how "her legs were great" and (with great generosity!) declares that he "wouldn't kick her out of bed."[14] Bernie, too, realizes that he may be losing his hold over Danny and so tries to influence (and diminish) Danny's view of Deborah:

Bernie: So what are we doing tomorrow, we going to the beach?
Danny: I'm seeing Deborah.
Bernie: Yeah? You getting serious? I mean she seemed like a hell of a girl, huh? The little I saw of her. Not too this, not too that . . . very kind of . . . what? (*Pause.*) Well, what the fuck. I only saw her for a minute. I mean first impressions of this kind are often misleading, huh? So what can you tell from seeing a broad one, two, ten times? You're seeing a lot of this broad. . . . I mean, what the fuck, a guy wants to get it on with some broad on a more or less stable basis, who is to say him no. (*Pause.*) Alot of these broads, you know, you

just don't know. You know? I mean what with where they've been
and all. I mean a young woman in today's society . . . time she's
twenty two-three, you don't know *where* the fuck she's been.
(Pause.) I'm just *talking* to you, you understand. (scene 14, pp. 30–
31)

Bernie includes Danny in his plans for "the beach" without hesita-
tion; to admit the possibility that there may be other parties who
have a claim on his friend's time is unthinkable for him. His
reaction to the news that Danny is "seeing Deborah" is to try to
diminish Deborah's importance in the scheme of things while
carefully avoiding outright criticism—at least at first. Lest Danny
suspect his motives, Bernie must take care not to appear too
jealous or resentful so he begins by praising Deborah. However,
he then moves rapidly into another phase wherein she becomes
just another "broad" who might have a very dubious sexual history. After his initial statement, "she seemed like a hell of a girl,"
he undermines his approach by adding, "The little I saw of her"
and "first impressions . . . are . . . misleading." He goes on to
infer that men can never know women, even if they meet them on
numerous occasions, thus suggesting that Danny's relationship
with Deborah must be of the most shallow kind. He acknowledges that his friend is "seeing a lot" of the woman but infers that
whatever may be between them can only be sexual. Bernie gradually moves toward the final phase of his verbal destruction of
Deborah; almost imperceptibly, she has become just another
"broad." He takes on the attitude of an older brother, an experienced and trusted giver of advice to one who needs assistance;
"Alot of these broads, you know, you just don't know. You know?"
He brings Danny, unwillingly or otherwise, into the conversation,
involving him, making him collude with him, never pausing to
allow time for any response. He begins to talk about Deborah as if
she were something dirty, or diseased: "where [she's] been and
all." Double standards are rife here. It is perfectly acceptable for
Bernie and Danny to have had numerous sexual encounters—
indeed, they believe this makes them attractive catches—but
women are not allowed similar experiences.

Bernie's repetition of "what the fuck" also adds to the coarse-
ness of his innuendo and serves as a means of grounding the
conversation at the most basic sexual level. By now, there is the
suggestion that Deborah is unworthy of any serious consideration, and is probably not unlike the "pro" in his initial fantasy.
This latter insinuation is given further weight by Bernie's echo of

the indeterminate age of his "pro"; Deborah, like the fantasy girl, is aged about "twenty two-three." His concluding assertion that he is merely *"talking"* to Danny about Deborah anticipates Moss and Aaronow's notable linguistic distinction between "talking" and "speaking" in *Glengarry Glen Ross*.

Bernie and Jonathan are excellent examples of what Colin Stinton calls the "Teach-like character";[15] both men are, essentially, full of hot air and have very little genuine knowledge to impart, but they nonetheless see themselves as instructors and mentors. Stinton comments upon the specific type of "teaching" that occurs in *Sexual Perversity in Chicago*. He notes that Bernie's "Teach-like quality is really bullshitting . . . sexual bullshitting of the type that men usually engage in most. The whole idea of the conquest—this is one of the things that identifies such men in their pathetic little way. The likes of Bernie use this built-in tendency to influence and persuade those around them."[16]

Because of the extremely coarse, sexist language used in the play, Mamet has sometimes been accused of being deliberately outrageous and misogynistic. Although there may be some truth to criticism that the playwright courts outrage, Mamet does not do so in order to score cheap laughs out of obscenity and sexism. Connie Booth, who has appeared in two of Mamet's plays, speaks specifically about the playwright's use of obscene and scatalogical language: "He is anything but arbitrary. . . . It would be interesting for those who believe his work to be obscene to take out all those words and see just how much their absence would affect both the sense and rhythm of the piece."[17]

As far as accusations of misogyny are concerned, *Sexual Perversity in Chicago* could, in some ways, be viewed as a feminist play in that it is so very critical of its male characters; Mamet examines what he sees as the deplorable state of sexual morality in modern urban America and, in so doing, illuminates inadequacy and ignorance. His female characters are so disenchanted with the men they meet, and so resentful of the pressures put upon them to form heterosexual relationships, that they appear to have retreated into lesbianism!

Colin Stinton asserts that, although Mamet portrays chauvinistic, sexist, or violent men in his plays, it does not mean that he is in some way advocating their behavior:

A lot of criticism of [Mamet's] work—especially from women—emanates from the rather incredible notion that he is somehow advocating sexist men! If anything, he is calling attention to the fact that there *are*

sexist men and this is why they are that way, this is how their minds
work. He then subjects these characters to some scrutiny. . . . Perhaps more than other writers, he takes to heart the maxim that you
should only write about what you personally have experienced, and
[Mamet's] experience is definitely not having been a woman! . . . He
feels happier writing from the male viewpoint, but the male viewpoint doesn't have to be a sexist viewpoint. One of the things that is
always illuminating is to talk to [Mamet] and to see him in action with
his family and you realize what a caring kind of person he is. You
begin to see that his plays always deal with the obstacles to the kind of
care, kind of love and affection he wishes were there. Some people
feel that because he has portrayed the world in this negative, tragic
way he is somehow saying that this is how it should be. This is really
ridiculous. In fact, what he does is to bemoan the fact that there is not
a better world . . . he is in fact a feminist writer in that sense because
he is very, very critical of males. . . . He depicts such characters to
show up their fragile egos, to show them struggling to find out who
they are. He tries to provide some insight into how their minds
work.[18]

Similarly, Miranda Richardson believes that

Mamet is documenting what he has heard other men say. The fact that
he *does* it is instructive. He is not suggesting that this is the right way
to behave. . . . He might be writing from his own experiences, but I
still enjoy what his experience is. I certainly don't think he's a sexist
writer . . . he still manages to spark one's imagination, even if there
are only ten lines to go on in his script. There's a deep sensitivity in
his writing.[19]

Of the allegations of sexism in *Sexual Perversity in Chicago,* Mamet
says: "There's a lot of vicious language in the play. . . . The real
vicious language is the insidious thing, calling somebody a little
girl or this girl. That's a lot more insidious than calling somebody
a vicious whore—which is also insidious but you can deal with
it."[20] C. Gerald Fraser notes that Mamet's play is about "the myths
that men go through"[21] and that Mamet "credited the Women's
Liberation movement with 'turning [his] head around a lot.' He
added: 'Women have babies, have the menstrual period, for God's
sake, they have something to do with the universe.' "[22]

The women's roles in *Sexual Perversity in Chicago* are quite substantial but, again, it is the male characters who enjoy many of the
best lines. Mamet is only too aware of this imbalance and is
anxious to correct it and thus alleviate some of the criticism. While
writing the play, he remarked, "I kept getting huutzed by the

director and the women in the cast, you know, to write parts for women. I said I don't know anything about women, they said 'Well, you better find out, you're getting too old'—so I tried. The fleshier parts are the male parts. I am more around men; I listen to more men being candid than women being candid. It is something I have been trying to do more of."[23]

Colin Stinton feels that those who urge Mamet to write more parts for women are, in some respects, asking for the wrong thing; he believes that the writer goes to such pains to be truthful in his work that if he should begin to try, self-consciously, to write in a woman's voice, he may be doomed to falsity and failure. Mamet is concerned about the imbalance of male/female roles in his plays to the extent that during the writing of *The Woods*, Stinton was told (albeit apocryphally) that Mamet had given some of Nick's lines over to Ruth to make their dialogue more even in terms of volume. Stinton said that this was exactly the sort of thing that Mamet would do and that the story is probably absolutely genuine. Similarly, the role of John, the clairvoyant in *The Shawl* was obviously written for a male actor, but since the play has been performed, Mamet has considered changing the homosexual pair at the center of the work to a heterosexual couple. Thus, John could, without much hindrance, become Joanne! Mamet retains some doubts, but it is a mark of his desire to appease criticism that he has considered the transition at all.

From my own reading of Mamet's plays and from comments made by him concerning women, I feel that the school of opinion that brands him sexist is completely wrongheaded. Quite clearly, many of Mamet's male characters are hardly admirable or self-assured; there is little in them to suggest that the writer is in some way condoning their behavior. His female characters, on the other hand, often seem to represent Mamet's own wish that the world were a nicer and more caring place. In *The Woods*, Ruth and Nick try to come to terms with their rather precarious love affair. Their propinquity in the weekend cottage serves to underline Ruth's need for love and affection and Nick's reticence and anxiety. Ruth's main concerns are romance and love, whereas Nick's are far more sexually oriented. For Ruth, sex is important only when it is a part of love; for Nick, love can often be an obstruction to good sex. In *Speed the Plow*, it is the temporary secretary who comes to work for Gould, the film producer, who injects compassion and warmth into a sterile and ruthless environment. Whatever Karen's ultimate motives prove to be, she brings a peculiarly feminine vigor and energy to the proceedings, causing the mercenary Gould to reevaluate (at least temporarily) his opinions on what is worthy and what is not. Her idealism and fecund creativity leave their mark on an otherwise barren and arid play.

Deborah and Joan in *Sexual Perversity in Chicago* also appear to be idealistic but, as the play progresses, their disappointment with what they are offered becomes almost tangible. By the end of the work they seem to have concluded that affection is often more genuine and freely forthcoming from members of their own sex, and that the whole fabric of heterosexual pairing is something of a confidence trick. Indeed, Joan laments:

> Joan: . . . and, of course, there exists the very real possibility that the whole thing is nothing other than a mistake of *rather* large magnitude, and that it never *was* supposed to work out. . . . Well, look at your divorce rate. Look at the incidence of homosexuality . . . the number of violent, sex-connected crimes . . . all the anti-social behavior that chooses sex as its form of expression, eh? . . . physical and mental mutilations we perpetrate on each other, day in, day out . . . trying to fit ourselves to a pattern we can neither *understand* (although we pretend to) nor truly afford to *investigate* (although we pretend to). . . . It's a dirty joke . . . the whole godforsaken business. (scene 20, pp. 37–38)

Joan's sentiments are explored further in a short play Mamet wrote in 1977 entitled *All Men Are Whores: An Inquiry;* the female character in that play muses:

> . . . What if this undignified and headlong thrusting toward each other's sex is nothing but an oversight or physical malformity? *(Pause.)* Should we not, perhaps, retrain ourselves to revel in the sexual act not as the consummation of pre-destined and regenerate desire, but rather as a two-part affirmation of our need for solace in extremis. . . . In a world where nothing works. (scene 17, p. 199)

Exactly how seriously we are meant to take all this is left deliberately unclear. Certainly in Joan's case, Mamet has her spout her ideas as she and Deborah have lunch; Joan frequently undercuts the sobriety of the situation by casual interruptions such as "Are you going to eat your roll? . . . This roll is excellent" (scene 20, p. 38) and so on. Deborah responds only intermittently and monosyllabically, twice announcing "I disagree with you" and stating that she is "moving in with Danny." Mamet therefore makes Joan's grave sentiments psychologically questionable; could not there be a suggestion that she is, in fact, jealous of her friend's success with Danny and that her denigration of heterosexuality is little more than resentment? Deborah's disagreement with her friend's ideas is also based on rather ambiguous premises; she has just decided to live with Danny, and so Joan's criticism of the basis of sexual relationships between men and women could be seen as a threat. Her friend's castigation undermines Deborah's security and the reasons for her decision to move in with her lover. It is not, therefore, altogether surprising that she should repeat that she disagrees with Joan—in her present situation, she cannot really afford to do otherwise. There remains the possibility that she secretly agrees with Joan; her silence as her friend rambles on could indicate either concurrence or disapproval. Mamet deliberately leaves the sexual psychology of his female characters ambiguous—and somewhat ambivalent.

In *Sexual Perversity in Chicago*, the characters can conceive of themselves only as sexual beings; the world in which they live forces them to do so. Theirs is a much harsher world than that portrayed in Edward Zwick's cinematic version of the play, *About Last Night* (1986). In the film the director chose to concentrate almost exclusively upon the "romantic" aspects of Danny and Deborah's affair, which completely distorted the meaning and altered the balance of the work. Bernie and Joan were reduced to wise-cracking cyphers who existed on the sidelines of the protagonists' lives. What is intended by Mamet to be a bitterly perceptive satire on contemporary sexual mores became, in the film, little more than a routine Hollywood teenage romance, albeit with a slightly harder edge and a rather more brittle script.

In Mamet's play, the characters' sexual experimentation and hard-edged aggression function as their principal means of expressing their urban neuroses. There is little time for romance or sweet words. Moments of self-perception, or a brief, fleeting acknowledgment of life outside of sex, are undercut by the relentless pragmatics of everyday life. An earlier bout of Joan's lamentations is interrupted by that unavoidable aspect of modern life, the telephone:

> Joan: It's a puzzle. Our efforts at coming to grips with ourselves . . . in an attempt to become "more human" (which, in itself is an interesting concept). It has to do with an increased ability to recognize *clues* . . . and the control of energy in the form of *lust* . . . and *desire* . . . (And also in the form of hope). But a *finite* puzzle. Whose true solution lies, perhaps, in transcending the rules themselves . . . and pounding of the fucking pieces into place where they DO NOT

FIT AT ALL. . . . Some things persist. "Loss" is always possible . . .
(Pause. Phone rings.)
Deb: I'll take it in the other room. (scene 13, pp. 29–30)

When Mamet's characters indulge in philosophical theory, their language inevitably takes on a heightened, linguistically more sophisticated tone. It is as though they have moved beyond their usual limited range of discourse into another sphere of understanding; there is a "textbook" literalness in what they have to say. Joan speaks as she seldom does at such times—her streetwise banter is suddenly replaced by careful phrasing and elevated terminology—and only once does a familiar obscenity intrude. But this speech is unnatural; it is contrived, pretentious, and didactic. Joan tries to sound authoritative, impressive, and in command of what she avers but there remains a sense that Mamet is also satirizing this level of awareness. Like the rest of his characters' conversation, Joan's is artificial—although in a more educated way. That Mamet constantly undercuts high-flown sentiments with crass banalities or ringing telephones is perhaps his way of suggesting that *nothing* these people can say is truly authentic; it is all the manufacture of a false society.

Joan and Deborah share an apartment and are, apparently, close friends. Whether their relationship is of a platonic or a sexual nature is unclear, but Mamet does drop the occasional hint that their friendship may be at least partly lesbian. For example, when Deborah first meets Danny, she announces that she is "a Lesbian" (scene 5, p. 18), although later she refutes this claim, choosing to imply that although she has had "some Lesbianic experiences. . . . and . . . enjoyed them" (scene 7, pp. 20–21) she is, in fact, happily heterosexual. In any case, the friendship between Joan and Deborah seems to be warm and genuine, if a little overpossessive on Joan's part. What is noticeable, both about Joan in her reaction to Danny, and Bernie in his opinion of Deborah is that both parties are jealous of any outside involvement. As Christopher Bigsby notes, they "value only the apparently simple, undemanding and essentially adolescent camaraderie of the same sex,"[24] viewing members of the opposite sex as an intrusion upon their privacy. On both sides, each appears to possess an element of protective concern for his or her friend's welfare; each sees sexual involvement leading inevitably to pain and unhappiness and as something to be avoided on anything other than the most casual basis. The following exchange takes place between Deborah and Joan when the former has been seeing rather a lot of her new boyfriend:

Joan: So what's he like?

Deb: Who?

Joan: Whoever you haven't been home, I haven't seen you in two days that you've been seeing.

Deb: Did you miss me?

Joan: No. Your plants died. *(Pause.)* I'm kidding. What's his name?

Deb: Danny.

Joan: What's he do?

Deb: He works in the Loop.

Joan: How wonderful for him.

Deb: He's an assistant Office Manager.

Joan: That's nice, a job with a little upward mobility.

Deb: Don't be like that, Joan.

Joan: I'm sorry. I don't know what got into me.

Deb: How are things at school?

Joan: Swell. Life in the Primary Grades is a real picnic. (scene 8, pp. 21–22)

From her opening question, it is clear that Joan will in no way be persuaded that the intrusive Danny could possibly be a worthy lover for her friend. In that initial query is an aggressive hard-boiled bitterness, which is not concealed by the question's commonplaceness. The tone of the question is one that invites a response of denigration rather than approval and Joan's edginess and barely suppressed sarcasm establish her mood for the rest of the scene. An actress playing Joan's part could interpret her mood in several ways: she could be hurt, bitter, resentful, aggressive, chiding, or even playful. As always with Mamet's work, great sensitivity to the text is required if all the nuances and subtleties are to be exploited. It would be only too easy to portray Joan as an unsympathetic harpy who is intent upon destroying her friend's relationships. This would, indeed, be a great shame since Mamet has written the part with sensitivity and understanding for the character's emotional position. Although Joan *does* resent Danny's involvement with Deborah, it is important to be aware of her vulnerability and the reasons for her resentment. Joan has found a good and kind friend in Deborah and is understandably loath to lose her to someone who might be a harmful influence.

Joan's convoluted but brilliantly authentic sentence: "Whoever you haven't been home, I haven't seen you in two days that you've been seeing" has been described by Ross Wetzsteon as "the utter clarity of total grammatical chaos."[25] Such language owes something to that heard in Woody Allen films, particularly those that chronicle the increasing incidence of urban neurosis such as *Play it Again, Sam, Annie Hall,* and *Manhattan.* The idiom is purely American, with no concessions made toward "good" English. As Jack Shepherd has observed, Mamet "is so in touch with the way American people talk that he often doesn't use any discernible English grammar."[26] Thus, sentences are relentlessly broken up midway, tenses are confused, and grammatical accuracy is the least priority. It is all ostensibly very naturalistic but, as Shepherd has also observed, "in [Mamet's] text . . . everything that is written is *intended* . . . it is never just there for the sake of it."[27]

Through Joan's convolutions and inconsistencies, Mamet suggests so much about her state of mind. His inspired use of anarchic rhythms is another way in which he extracts every ounce of humor from a situation. Joan's defensive sarcasm—"Your plants died" immediately followed by "I'm kidding"—serves to illustrate her adopted veneer of urban toughness, which can be so easily shattered when she finds herself cornered and in a vulnerable position. Despite her assertion that she is "kidding," she goes on to denigrate Danny's job as a pathetic one for a man to hold and, finally, having failed to elicit any criticism from Deborah, seems to blame her for the fact that "Life in the Primary Grades is a real picnic." It is clear from the tone that it is anything *but!* Joan suggests that her life is tormented and fraught with problems enough as a kindergarten teacher, without Deborah adding to her misery by keeping away from home. Cleverly and insidiously, Joan manages to make Deborah feel guilty for her actions. In Joan's eyes, the selfishness is not her own but that of her gadabout friend.

Bernie is as wounded as Joan by his friend's love affair. As he tells imaginary "buddies" at the gym all about Danny's relationship (about which, presumably, Danny had told him in confidence), Bernie takes on once again the role of seasoned mentor and advisor:

> *Bernie:* So the kid asks me "Bernie, Blah, blah, blah, blah, blah, blah, blah, blah, blah. The broad *this,* the broad *that,* blah, blah, blah." Right? So I tell him, "Dan, Dan, you think I don't know what you're feeling, I don't know what you're going through? You think about the broad, you *this,* you *that,* you think I don't know that?" So he tells me, "Bernie," he says, "I think I love her." *(Pause.)* Twenty eight years old. So I tell him, "Dan, Dan, I can *advise,* I can *counsel,* I can speak to you out of my *experience* . . . but in the final analysis, you are on your own. *(Pause.)* If you want my *opinion,* however, you are pussy-whipped." (I call 'em like I see 'em. I wouldn't say it if it wasn't so.) So what does he know at that age, huh? Sell his soul for a

little eating pussy, and who can blame him: But mark my words.
One, two more weeks, he'll do the right thing by the broad *(Pause.)*
And drop her like a fucking hot potato. (scene 19, p. 37)

Bernie establishes the avuncular tone that he will use to denigrate
Danny's relationship with Deborah in the opening words of this
speech: he calls Danny "the kid" and suggests that Danny's reliance upon his advice is far from unusual. Bernie's dismissal of
the seriousness of Danny's affair moves from his claim that he,
too, has felt exactly the same way to his contention that Danny is
"pussy-whipped." En route, he has condescendingly sneered that
a mere boy (of twenty-eight!) could entertain such feelings and
has wasted no time in repeating, over and over, that Deborah is
nothing more than a broad. There is something pathetic in Bernie's assumption that Danny could not know he was in love "at
that age"; after all, twenty-eight is an age by which many men are
already married with a family. Bernie tries to make Danny sound
like a lovelorn child—"Bernie . . . I think I love her"—and negates
Danny's sentimental outburst by once again reducing the relationship to the crudest level. He implies that Danny is ready to
"sell his soul for a little eating pussy," rushing his words and
abbreviating his sentence in an effort to emphasize the absurdity
of Danny being "in love." He immediately follows this coarse
statement with a phrase that accurately sums up his phony "macho" bonhomie: "and who can blame him". With studied, casual
conceit, Bernie implies that he has, himself, been similarly misguided; the folly of youth is rejected in knowing maturity. The
underlinings emphasize those words that Bernie feels are most
relevant and important to his argument. For him, they are the
essence of friendship but, as he pointedly remarks, "in the final
analysis"—a sly dig by Mamet at a dreadful Yuppie-type cliché—
Danny must make his own decisions. The false effort Bernie
makes to sound fair and reasonable and, above all, *sympathetic* to
his friend's plight, is both appalling and irresistibly funny.

At the end of his speech, Bernie suddenly changes tack. He
announces that Danny will "do the right thing by the broad" by
dropping her like "a fucking hot potato." In his mind, this is
precisely what Danny will do; all he needs is some careful prod-
ding and manipulation. Subtlety is not one of Bernie's strong
points. After he has rid his and Danny's relationship of the offensive Deborah, things can be the same again between the two
friends. There has been no mention that Deborah is being somehow exploited or used by Danny—quite the opposite. However,

in order to give his story a well-rounded and equitable conclusion, Bernie chooses to imply that she would, in fact, be far
better off without Danny, who will soon see the error of his ways.

It is significant that Bernie should begin his destruction of his
friend's affair with a string of nonsense words. Again and again,
Mamet's frightened characters lapse into nonsense language
when under pressure, and Bernie is no exception. He chooses to
forsake normal speech on more than one occasion in the play and
each time he does so he undermines the seriousness of his subject. His reductive chant, already quoted elsewhere, takes its
rhythms from nonsense words: "Blah de Bloo. Blah de Bloo. Blah
de Bloo. Blah de Bloo" (scene 30, p. 47). The "Tits and Ass," which
makes up the rest of the litany is, therefore, reduced to similar
meaninglessness. In *Glengarry Glen Ross*, Richard Roma refers to
the couple to whom Levene has just sold $82,000 worth of land as
"Harriett and blah blah Nyborg" (act 2, p. 38) and in *American
Buffalo*, Teach pretends that he is not angry with Grace and Ruthie
because he has lost a large sum of money at cards, choosing to
affect a world-weary tone of selfless resignation:

> *Teach:* These things happen, I'm not saying that they don't . . . and
> yeah, yeah, yeah, I know I lost a bundle at the game and blah blah
> blah. (act 1, p. 15)

In *The Squirrels*, Arthur responds to Edmond's question about the
sense of a particular passage in one of the plays they are writing
with a stream of repetition, making gibberish of the words he
speaks:

> *Edmond:* What does this mean?
> *Arthur:* Meaning? Meaning?
> *Edmond:* Yes.
> *Arthur:* Ah, meaning! Meaning meaning meaning meaning meaning.
> Meaning meaning meaning. You ask me about meaning and I
> respond with gibberish . . . (episode 1, p. 23)

Roma's description of Mr. Nyborg as "blah blah" suggests his
contempt for and sheer disinterest in the unfortunate man; as far
as the ruthless salesman is concerned, Mr. Nyborg is now completely irrelevant. Teach's concluding "blah blah blah" takes up
the rhythm he sets up in the preceding "yeah yeah yeah" and is
intended to convey his detached emotional stance in the matter. It
fails miserably. Arthur's repetition of "meaning" is a desperate
attempt at ironic humor; both men are supposedly creative writers

but are struggling with a banal story. To conceal his very real sense of impotence, Arthur chooses to joke about it, masking his loss of control in self-deprecating irony in an effort to appear self-effacing and sardonic. It is clear from these random examples that gibberish can be utilized in a most versatile manner; in Mamet's drama, even nonsense can speak volumes.

A number of scenes in *Sexual Perversity in Chicago* are set in night clubs and bars; the one-night stand and casual barroom encounter are obviously familiar occurrences for the individuals dramatized here. In particular, the frequenting of singles bars—those peculiarly horrible inventions of the fake friendly American culture of excess—has become a way of life. In a book that among other things, outlines the contemporary sexual mores of New Yorkers, Stephen Brook recalls a visit to "Rascals," a singles bar on First Avenue:

> This is real singles territory, and lone wolves scour this stretch of the East Side for prey. . . . Opposite the crowded bar, a . . . gutsy-voiced female lead belted out old Stones and Motown numbers. I bought a drink and stood about feeling foolish, then left.[28]

Early in *Sexual Perversity in Chicago*, Mamet satirizes the kind of encounter that can take place in such establishments. Bernie tries to pick up Joan as she sits alone in the bar, and he becomes very hostile indeed when she makes it clear to him that she is not interested:

> *Bernie:* How would you like some company. *(Pause.)* What if I was to sit down here? What would that do for you, huh?
> *Joan:* No, I don't think so, no . . . .
> *Bernie:* . . . So here I am. I'm just in town for a one-day layover, and I happen to find myself in this bar. So, so far so good. What am I going to do? I could lounge alone and lonely and stare into my drink, or I could take the bull by the horn and make an effort to enjoy myself . . .
> *Joan:* Are you making this up?
> *Bernie:* So hold on. So I see you seated at this table and I say to myself, "Doug McKenzie, there is a young woman," I say to myself, "What is she doing here?", and I think she is here for the same reasons as I. To enjoy herself, and, perhaps to meet provocative people. *(Pause.)* I'm a meteorologist for T.W.A. . . . (scene 3, pp. 14–15)

Bernie carries on in this vein for some time, lying about his name and his job, trying to make his life sound romantic and thrilling until, finally, Joan has heard enough:

Joan: Can I tell you something?
Bernie: You bet.
Joan: Forgive me if I'm being too personal . . . but I do not find you
  sexually attractive. *(Pause.)*
Bernie: What is that, some new kind of line? Huh, I mean, not that I
  mind what you think, if that's what you think . . . but . . . that's a
  fucking rotten thing to say.
Joan: I'll live.
Bernie: All kidding aside . . . lookit, I'm a fucking professional, huh?
  My life is a bunch of having to make split-second decisions. . . .
  You think I don't have better things to do. . . . nowhere cunt. . . .
  You're a grown woman, behave like it for chrissakes. . . . I mean
  what the fuck do you think society is, just a bunch of rules strung
  together for your personal pleasure? Cockteaser. . . . You got a lot
  of fuckin' nerve. (scene 3, pp. 16–17)

Bernie completely ignores Joan's assertion that she would not, in
fact, be interested in his company, preferring to launch into his
elaborate, supposedly sexy routine. His line is an extraordinary
amalgam of lies, patronage, and soap-opera bravado. It is interesting to note that he uses a typical WASP name, rather than admit to
his own very ethnic name, Bernie Litko. In his fantasy projection
of himself, Bernie not only takes on another man's job but also
another man's name—one that may be more acceptable to a
woman who might, just possibly, be class conscious or even anti-
Semitic. He also emphasizes the temporariness of his "fling" by
stating that he is "just in town for a one-day layover." Mamet's use
of the term "layover" rather than "stopover" adds a suggestive
subtext to Bernie's opening gambit, as does his statement that he
acted on impulse when he saw her, taking the "bull by the horn."
The use of the word "horn" in the singular, rather than in the
more familiar plural, is surely intended as a phallic quip.

Bernie cannot allow even the smallest detail of his story to slip;
even when Joan wounds his ego with the news that she doesn't
find him "sexually attractive," he stubbornly hangs on to his
fantasy about being a high-flying meteorologist. This, like the rest
of his spiel, is an integral part of the act. Cut to the quick by her
remark, his rhetoric becomes more and more vicious. He alter-
nates obscenities with biting sarcasm until, finally, he resorts to
something that Mamet's characters often rely upon when under
pressure: he cites civic rules of conduct. Bernie appears to be
under the impression that the "bunch of rules" that apply to his
own "personal pleasure" should in no way extend to Joan.

Just as the salesmen in *Glengarry Glen Ross* see themselves only in terms of their jobs, so Bernie views himself purely in terms of a sexual athlete, no matter how absurd this may seem. He has built up for himself a fantasy world that is quite as powerful as that invented by George and Martha in Edward Albee's *Who's Afraid of Virginia Woolf?* or by Susan in Alan Ayckbourn's *Woman in Mind.* Joan's remark that Bernie is not sexually inviting to her is more than a mere insult to such a man; it is tantamount to negating his existence. She has punctured his dream and devastated his self-image. Bernie's violent reaction and frightening aggression is, therefore, understandable. His predicament is reminiscent of that of the Vicomte de Valmont in Christopher Hampton's adaptation of de Laclos's *Les Liaisons Dangereuses;* when the Vicomte's sexual reputation and vanity are threatened, he crumbles. He has become so much a part of his assumed persona that the real man beneath the sophisticated exterior hardly exists. Rather than risk exposure of his essential vulnerability, he decides to give up the love of his life and to accept death. So it is with Bernie, although his dilemma is dramatized in considerably less romantic and expansive terms. As the abuse tumbles out and his grammar collapses, Bernie's agony is almost tangible; he does all he can to crush the woman who has, in a sense, murdered him with words.

After his singular lack of success with Joan, Bernie's first reaction is to advise Danny to behave in exactly the same way! His manner of speaking is infused with the nonchalance of one who has just enjoyed runaway success with his quarry:

> *Bernie:* The main thing, Dan. . . . The main thing about *broads.* . . . Is two things: One: The Way to Get Laid is to Treat 'Em Like Shit. . . . and Two: Nothing . . . *nothing* makes you so attractive to the opposite sex as getting your rocks off on a regular basis. (scene 4, pp. 17–18)

Bernie's linguistic slip in the first two lines suggests his haste to communicate his great knowledge to Danny. At first, it is enough to suggest the "main thing" but then he recalls that there are, in fact, "two things." Bernie has clearly learned little from his encounter with Joan—in fact, the whole incident seems to have receded to the back of his mind or been hastily reconstituted into a success story of which he can be proud. His dictum for success with women is echoed in *Lakeboat.* In that play, too, the men are lonely and ignorant, spending most of their time talking about encounters that have probably never taken place. In a moment of pedagogic fervour, Fred tells Dale how to succeed sexually with women, and exactly reproduces Bernie's advice:

> *Fred:* . . . my uncle, who is over, is conversing with me one night and
> as men will do, we start talking about sex. He tells a story. I tell *My*
> story. This takes him aback. "What?" he says, "The way to get laid is
> to treat them like shit." Now you just stop for a moment and think
> on that. You've heard it before and you'll hear it again but there is
> more to it than meets the eye. Listen: THE WAY TO GET LAID IS
> TO TREAT THEM LIKE SHIT. Truer words have never been spoken.
> And this has been tested by better men than you or me. (scene 10,
> pp. 54–55)

Fred's recipe for success is lamentable. To give it further weight,
he imbues his speech with a number of well-worn, risible clichés
and platitudes, which he fondly believes will consolidate its truth.
Lakeboat is a play without a single female character; there is certainly more than a suggestion that all the fantasizing and bragging
is little more than a means of disguising latent homosexuality—or,
at least, the kind of homosexuality that can develop in an all-male
environment. In a short work written by Mamet to be performed
as a companion piece to the 1979 revival of *Sexual Perversity in
Chicago*, the following, very telling, line is included: "Our most
cherished illusions—what are they but hastily constructed coffer-
dams restraining homosexual panic?" (*Sermon*, p. 157).

A number of critics have commented upon the distinct possibility that Bernie could be homosexual. Certainly, his insistent
and overemphatic displays of masculinity seem to suggest this.
When questioned on the topic, he reacts in a rather panicky way,
at first stating that an early childhood experience with a pervert in
a cinema could have ruined him for life and, moments later,
countering this with, "A kid laughs these things off. You forget,
you go on living" (scene 17, p. 36). The level of hatred he displays
toward such men also has a touch too much hysteria about it; he
viciously decries a homosexual sales assistant as "a fucking fruit"
(scene 17, p. 33) and the man in the cinema as a "faggot queer"
(ibid., p. 35).

Underneath their sardonic acceptance of the world as it is, and
their rare insights into the cause of their anxiety, Mamet's characters are achingly lonely. Without exception, they seek affection
but are unable to sustain relationships based upon emotion. Deborah and Danny enjoy some moments of tenderness but outside
pressures eventually force them to declare their love affair null
and void, and to negate the experience as a waste. Neither of
them has a good word for the other once the relationship has been
dissolved; perhaps to acknowledge that genuine feelings were

ever present is somehow to admit weakness. However, the need for love and the expression of love persist.

A character in *All Men Are Whores: An Inquiry* sums up the overwhelming feeling of powerlessness and abandonment felt by so many of Mamet's individuals:

> Our concept of time is predicated upon our understanding of death.
> Time pases solely because death ends time. Our understanding of death is arrived at, in the main, because of the nature of sexual reproduction.
> Organisms which reproduce through fission do not "die."
> The stream of life, the continuation of the germ plasm, is unbroken.
> Clearly.
> Just as it is in the case of man.
> But much less apparently so in our case. For we are sentient.
> We are conscious of ourselves, and conscious of the schism in our sexuality.
> And so we perceive time. *(Pause.)* And so we will do anything for some affection. (scene 1, p. 185)

Later in the play, the same character laments the lack of true affection in the world:

> Where are our mothers, now? Where are they?
> . . . . In cities where we kill for comfort—for a moment of reprieve from our adulterated lives—for fellow-feeling *(Pause.)* (I have eyelashes, too . . .)
> . . . . One moment of release.
> . . . . We have no connection.
> . . . . Our life is garbage.
> We take comfort in our work and cruelty. We love the manicurist and the nurse for they hold hands with us. Where is our mother now? We woo with condoms and a ferry ride; the world around us crumples into chemicals, we stand intractable, and wait for someone competent to take us 'cross the street. (scene 16, p. 197)

The need for affection is sensitively spelled out in *Sexual Perversity in Chicago* when Danny, unsure of his position with Deborah in the latter stages of their relationship, presses for a response to his questions in the middle of the night:

> *Danny:* Deborah. Deb? Deb? You up? *(Pause.)* You sleeping? *(Pause.)* I can't sleep. *(Pause.)* You asleep? *(Pause.)* Huh? *(Pause.)* You sleeping, Deb? *(Pause.)* What are you thinking about? *(Pause.)* Deb? *(Pause.)* Did I wake you up? (scene 26, p. 43)

Although it is plain that Deborah is sleeping, Danny childishly insists upon awakening her. The short, simple sentences are indicative of the insecurity he feels; their brevity and repetition bring some form of comfort to one who craves assurance. Merely by hearing the words spoken aloud, Danny is afforded some solace; Deborah's stillness must, at all costs, be broken.

A little earlier in the play, Danny defends Bernie to "an imaginary co-worker" who has presumably criticized his friend. Aware that his love affair may soon be over, Danny holds on steadfastly to the reality of his friendship with Bernie:

> Danny: . . . I know what you're saying, and I'm telling you I don't like you badmouthing the guy, who happens to be a friend of mine. So just let me tell my story, okay? So the other day we're up on six and it's past five and I'm late, and I'm having some troubles with my chick . . . and I push the button and the elevator doesn't come, and it doesn't come, and it doesn't come, so I lean back and I kick the shit out of it three or four times. . . . And *he*, he puts his arm around my shoulder and he calms me down and he says, "Dan, Dan . . . don't go looking for affection from inanimate objects." *(Pause.)* Huh? So I don't want to hear you badmouthing Bernie Litko. (scene 25, p. 43)

Mamet manages to incorporate a great deal of urban despair into this one, short speech. Danny's defense of Bernie is quite ludicrous, given the set of circumstances he describes. At first glance, it is difficult to understand why Bernie's advice should have inspired such loyalty—especially to the extent that it is cited as a shining example of friendship—but if the language is analyzed, various aspects emerge. In the loveless world he inhabits, *any* constant, unswerving, *steady* manifestation of kindness is lifeblood to Danny; it is immaterial how this kindness presents itself. As he viciously attacks the elevator door (probably fantasizing that it is, in fact, Deborah) Bernie calms him down by suggesting that he should not seek affection from "inanimate objects." This is a strange statement, but one that nevertheless communicates affection to the wretched Danny. There are two ways of looking at Bernie's advice. The first—and less interesting—is that one must not expect elevators to work upon command. The society in which Bernie and Danny live is a mechanized and complex one, and mechanical objects often malfunction. It is, therefore, futile to expect "affection" (or cooperation) from such objects. The second—and most likely—possibility is that Bernie

somehow regards Deborah as just such an "inanimate object" and
suspects that deep down, Danny probably agrees with him. She
doesn't "function" properly; she has caused great difficulties for
both men; she has interrupted the natural, easy flow of their lives
and is, therefore, less than human. As a good, caring friend,
Bernie endeavors to convince Danny that he, alone, is worthy of
Danny's love and trust; Deborah is a very poor substitute indeed.
This information appears to be subliminally communicated to
Danny because his defense of Bernie exceeds any other display of
affection that can be found in the work.

As Danny and Deborah's affair crumbles, each vies for the last
word during their many arguments. It is their growing impatience
with and lack of tolerance for their partner's position that prompts
them into endless verbal sparring. They both use black, sardonic
humor and cruel remarks to upstage one another and their quick-
fire dialogue temporarily disguises the emptiness that lies just
beyond their words:

> *Danny:* . . . You know very well if there's any shampoo or not. You're
> making me be ridiculous about this. *(Pause.)* You wash yourself too
> much anyway. If you really *used* all that shit they tell you in *Cos-*
> *mopolitan* (And you *do*) you'd be washing yourself from morning til
> night. Pouring derivatives on yourself all day long.
> *Deb:* Will you love me when I'm old?
> *Danny:* If you can manage to look eighteen, yes.
> *Deb:* Now, that's very telling. (scene 23, p. 41)

The sheer pettiness of this is a well-observed and painfully accurate reflection of the absurdity of many arguments between the
sexes. Danny blames Deborah for making him "be ridiculous"
about the existence of shampoo; in a neat jump, he shifts the
responsibility. His sarcasm is meant to chasten, but its only effect
is to further enrage Deborah, who responds with cynical and
platitudinous remarks. Danny ridicules her need to keep up with
all the beauty hints in *Cosmopolitan*, at the same time requiring her
to "look eighteen" even when she's old. Since this is both unrealistic and absurd, it compounds the superficiality of their love and
underlines the all-embracing obsession with physical attractiveness to the exclusion of all else.

The couple's linguistic battle for supremacy continues in a similar vein:

> *Danny:* I love your breasts.
> *Deb:* "Thank you" *(Pause.)* Is that right?
> *Danny:* Fuck you. (scene 23, p. 42)

Deborah's parody of the stereotyped response expected from a docile woman prompts Danny to lash back with a coarse expletive. When the pair eventually does break up, the verbal recriminations reach an almost frightening level of intensity:

> *Danny:* Cunt.
> *Deb:* That's very good. "Cunt", good. Get it out. Let it all out.
> *Danny:* You cunt.
> *Deb:* We've established that.
> *Danny:* I try.
> *Deb:* You try and try. . . . You're trying to understand women and I'm confusing you with information. "Cunt" won't do it. "Fuck" won't do it. No more magic. (scene 28, p. 46)

A desperate sarcasm pervades these lines. Deborah's assertion that Danny is trying to understand feminine psychology by way of means that in no way *involve* him is at once brilliantly funny and painfully true. As Colin Stinton remarks, "Mamet captures so accurately the tension which builds up in situations like this; Danny pretends that he wants to understand Deborah but, deep inside, he can't really be bothered. He wants to learn painlessly, by a kind of osmosis, not by having to make any effort!"[29] Danny now seems to be as insensitive as his influential friend; although he must be aware that Deborah is deeply hurt by their arguments, the only way he can respond to her self-defense is to call her a "cunt." Communication between them having reached such a nadir, it is little wonder that Deborah should reflect that there is simply "no more magic." Nothing either of them can say could inject life into what is now moribund and wretched. Whatever romance once existed has dissolved, and the sexual attraction that once passed for true love has been reconstituted into something fetid and obscene.

Throughout the play, Bernie and Danny reduce the women they encounter to purely physical dimensions, but this activity reaches its apotheosis in the final scene when they lie on the beach, admiring or deriding the women who pass by them. This episode, more forcefully than any other, underscores their sheer inability to perceive women as people. It is vulgar, tragic, and very funny. Bernie draws Danny's attention to what is presumably a well-endowed woman:

> *Bernie:* Hey! Don't look behind you.
> *Danny:* Yeah?
> *Bernie:* Whatever you do, don't look behind you.

Danny: Where?
Bernie: Right behind you, about ten feet behind you to your right.
Danny: Yeah?
Bernie: I'm telling you.
Danny: (Looks.) Get the fuck *outta* here!
Bernie: Can I pick 'em?
Danny: Bernie . . .
Bernie: Is the radar in fine shape?
Danny: . . . I gotta say . . .
Bernie: . . . *Oh* yeah . . .
Danny: . . . that you can *pick* 'em. (scene 34, p. 51)

This echoes the rhythms of the opening scene, in which Bernie and Danny feed on each other's enthusiasm, but there has been a definite change. Danny is less the eager pupil to Bernie's teacher than a wised-up accomplice in lechery. Bernie may still be the man with "the radar," but Danny is rapidly catching up to him. Mamet utilizes the mock-irony of remarks like, "Whatever you do, don't look behind you," to suggest the renewed camaraderie between the two men. As the words are uttered, it is clear that Bernie wants Danny to do exactly the opposite! It is *essential* for Danny to "look behind" to see the object of Bernie's disbelief. He even issues exact directions. Both men use humor as a means of boosting morale and confirming their macho bravado—thoroughly enjoying their "game." This idyllic pastime is suddenly shattered, however, when Bernie's behavior takes a strange and unnerving turn. As they criticize the women around them, he notices one whom he denounces as "something of a pig" (scene 34, p. 54). The presence of this woman on the beach seems to spark something in Bernie and he begins to blame her and the rest of the women for flaunting their assets, beautiful or ugly:

> *Bernie:* . . . I mean who the fuck do they think they are . . . coming out here and just flaunting their bodies all over? . . . I come to the beach with a friend to get some sun and watch the action and . . . I mean a fellow comes to the beach to sit out in the fucking sun, am I wrong? . . . I mean we're talking about recreational fucking space, huh? (scene 34, p. 54)

As Bernie castigates and villifies the women in his midst, his words take on a rather hysterical note. His sentiments are reminiscent of those who would defend an act of rape by suggesting that the victim, after all, "asked for it" by the clothes she wore or by her provocative behavior. Bernie's (low) opinion of women arises, he suggests, through their cheapness and brazenness. He repeats that the only reason for his and Danny's presence on the beach is "to get some sun." This is so blatantly untrue that it becomes a pathetic plea for understanding. That he should refer to the beach as "recreational fucking space" is also deeply telling; Bernie presumably uses the obscenity as an expletive but there is, surely, a sense that he wishes it were a verb instead!

Eventually, Bernie realizes that he has said too much for his own good—and for the good of his image as a suave womanizer. Danny's perplexed question prompts Bernie into defensive action:

> *Danny:* Are you feeling alright?
> *Bernie:* Well, how do I look, do I look alright?
> *Danny:* Sure.
> *Bernie:* Well, than let's assume that I feel alright, okay. . . . I mean, how could you feel anything *but* alright, for chrissakes. Will you look at that body? *(Pause.)* What a pair of tits. *(Pause.)* With tits like that, who needs . . . anything. (scene 34, pp. 54–55)

Within seconds, Bernie has reverted back to his old routine. He simply cannot afford to let down his "front" in this uncharacteristic way, and his aggression in the phrase, "how do I look, do I look alright?" is a warning to Danny not to probe any further. It is, however, clear that all this bluster and bravado is no more than that; we have briefly seen beneath the surface brittleness into a morass of insecurity and fear.

Bernie's final words, ignorant as they are, manage to speak volumes about the tragic state of his sexuality: "With tits like that, who needs . . . anything." By once again diminishing the importance of women to their sexual anatomy, Bernie demonstrates his supreme lack of imagination and his need for fantasy. He plainly requires much more than "tits," but it is highly unlikely that he will ever attain it. Behind the arrogant façade lies a fearful naïveté. Both men hatch plans and exchange ideas about the best ways in which to bed the women they ogle, but their potential success is questionable, to say the least. On a beach full of people, Bernie and Danny remain isolated, solitary. Perhaps more so now than ever, they are on the outside looking in. More bruised by life experience than they had been at the beginning of the play, they appear overwhelmed by a deep-seated bitterness. This is borne out by the final words in the work, which manage to combine arrogance, cruelty, and sarcasm. When a woman passes them, she ignores their greetings:

Bernie: Hi.
Danny: Hello there. *(Pause. She walks by.)*
Bernie: She's probably deaf.
Danny: She did *look* deaf, didn't she?
Bernie: Yeah. *(Pause.)*
Danny: Deaf *bitch.* (scene 34, p. 55)

Bernie's misogyny has apparently influenced Danny to a fatal degree; perhaps he has become a more dangerous type of sexist than his friend. The absurdity of his observation that the girl "did *look* deaf" and his need for corroboration from Bernie—"didn't she?"—suggest that the veil of ignorance and insecurity has, at least partially, been transferred from Bernie to Danny. Until now, Danny has been portrayed as a fairly normal, if unimaginative young man, but one who was largely without real malice. For him to utter the final, brutal words in a brutal play is Mamet's way of dramatising how fatally Danny has come under Bernie's spell and how he has absorbed the deadening influence of an artificial and sterile society.

Sexual Perversity in Chicago is a very fast—and very black—comedy. The sheer exuberance of the dialogue is compelling, although its vitality is essentially illusory. The characters end the play as they began—confused and vulnerable, and perhaps even more lonely. Friedrich Hebbel once wrote, "Drama shouldn't present new stories but new relationships."[30] In this work, Mamet certainly seems to have fulfilled this requirement. With an accurate ear for the cadences of supposedly sophisticated urban speech and with an acute observation of contemporary sexual mores, he has produced a work that is wholly original and that dramatizes the emptiness of relationships in an empty society. Mamet has devised a play that is absolutely contemporary in its verbal style; the text is a bubbling amalgam of slang, clichés, and what the characters take to be wit, and he invents a linguistic personality for each character that is totally believable. Bernie's false shield of confidence is superbly exposed in the subtext to his aggressive linguistic forays, which have been described as "a combination of whiplash and theatrical swoops"[31] and Danny's ingenuousness and growing dependence on his friend reveals itself in his employment of certain phrases favored by his mentor. Deborah's speech has about it a vitality and innocence that is squashed as the play progresses; she finds only disappointment and frustration in a relationship she believed to be truly loving.

Joan is a woman who longs for love but is afraid of it; her language may be cynical and hard but Mamet is able to suggest that under Joan's brittle, sassy linguistic bravado, a subtext of vulnerability and fear remains.

A sharp satire on contemporary sexual mores in the urban America of the 1970s, *Sexual Perversity in Chicago* is also an exposé of what a media-dominated, capitalist-structured society can produce. But finally, Mamet's greatest strength lies not in his persuasiveness as a social critic, nor even in his sensitivity to the plight of human relations: it resides in his superb timing and peerless control over language.

2

American Buffalo

American Buffalo is prefaced by the following lines:

> Mine eyes have seen the glory of the coming of the Lord.
> He is peeling down the alley in a black and yellow Ford.[1]

Mamet no doubt chose this extract from an old "folk tune" because it very neatly conveys the essence of his play; its central image is at once funny and profane, and it evokes a culture that has sacrificed spirituality to materialism. In the godless world he dramatizes, success and prosperity have become a kind of religion in themselves in that they offer his lost, deracinated characters some illusion of comfort. Theirs is a violent and entropic society in which everything is uncertain, adrift, and frightening, and the possession of material goods and money at least affords the appearance of stability and power.

Mamet peoples his play with what he describes as "fringe characters,"[2] that is, those who live at the very edges of society, because he feels it is through these characters that he can best illustrate what he sees as a corrupt and venal culture. He observes that when one is "looking at a large picture, you don't go to the top of the foodchain to the King but to the little people,"[3] and he believes that "that which best expresses an integrated idea of the nation is not only those who are in power."[4] Apart from the amassing of material possessions, the only other defense Mamet's characters have against a destructive and threatening environment lies in their use of language; they must cultivate the rapid response and spurious survival skills that will set them apart from their more naïve—and exploitable—neighbors. Life for Mamet's characters is one that must be lived literally from moment to moment, and their language reflects their paranoid neuroses.

Linguistic dexterity is important to them not only as a means through which they can cajole, intimidate, and trick their audience into complicity, but also as a way of convincing themselves of their fantasies. Having lost all control over their lives, they seek security in the adoption of "acceptable" social roles. For Teach and his colleagues, this necessitates an evolution into a shallow embodiment of what they most wish to be—half-achieving their dream of becoming businessmen. At the bottom of the social ladder, they absurdly aspire to the heights of the most prestigious boardroom. As a result, they live their lives as ersatz "executives" constantly—often hilariously—justifying their appalling behavior as being a necessary consequence of business.

It seems that by using terminology more commonly heard in offices and at business lunches, Teach and his cronies can convince themselves of the legitimacy of what they are doing; they see themselves as professional men, caught up in high-level negotiations and important activities. So long as they are able to convince themselves of this fantasy, they can temper their feelings of inadequacy and revel in the soothing escapism of a dream.

Mamet's characters exist in a debased wilderness in which morals and metaphysics seem to have no place. Their sense of morality is derived from the false standards by which they live and, consequently, friendship, loyalty, and even love must take second place to the relentless pursuit of an already tarnished El Dorado. But *American Buffalo* is not, finally, a bleak cry of despair that offers no hope. There *is* hope in the play and it resides in the relationship between Don and Bobby. It has been observed that Don is "father in the surrogate family he and Bobby have formed"[5] and his displays of paternalistic care are indeed profoundly touching. Bobby, too, plays his own part as the rather wayward "son." Don really does care about the boy, expressing his concern in gruffly hesitant, though palpably sincere, verbal sallies. He sees himself as a hard man, not given to sentimentality, but there are enough hints of his true affection for Bobby to make us look beyond the surface bluster. The mere existence of their relationship suggests optimism and compassion. Mamet does not offer concrete answers to all the problems he presents, but nevertheless feels that, in his work, essential and fundamental issues have been seriously broached:

> Looking at the America in which I live and which you have to be left with at the end of the play . . . I would hope [I am offering] courage to look at the world around you and say I don't know what the hell the answer is but I'm willing to reduce all of my perspectives of the world around me to the proper place. After everything is said and done, we're human beings, and if we really want to we can find a way to get on with each other, to have the great, almost immeasurable, courage it takes . . . [we must] be honest about . . . our desires and not . . . institutionalise or abstract our relationships with each other.[6]

That genuine and worthwhile relations between people, in Mamet's opinion, remain only a vague possibility suggests the bleakness of the society he dramatizes but, as Christopher Bigsby points out, "that he continues to assert it with such conviction is a testament to his belief that the theatre has a central role to play in social, moral and metaphysical terms."[7] For all their immorality and weakness—or perhaps even because of it—Mamet feels affection for his characters; his compassion for them is as vital a fact in his work as is the contempt he expresses for their values and the corrupt culture they represent. He never patronizes them, nor uses them to score a cheap laugh. He has said, "I don't write plays to dump on people. I write plays about people whom I love and am fascinated by."[8] He has also stated that the writing of *American Buffalo* was "very heartfelt."[9] Much of the strength in Mamet's work emanates from his unswerving compassion and sensitivity; the humor may spring from the characters' sheer vulnerability and humanity but it is never employed as a means of scorning them. We may not wish to have such people as Teach and his colleagues as friends, but it is difficult not to detect something of ourselves in them as we watch their antics in pursuit of an almost certainly unattainable dream.

American Buffalo was premiered in Chicago in November 1975 at the Goodman Theatre. It won an Obie in 1976, and the New York Drama Critics Award of 1977 for the Best Play of the Year. Since then, it has enjoyed a number of revivals, both in the United States and in England.

The America that forms the background of the work is one that is deeply troubled and divided. It had just witnessed the exposure of lies of its military establishments over the Vietnam crisis and its President's increasingly futile attempts to extricate himself from the Watergate fiasco. During a television interview, Mamet designated America as "this wonderfully unhappy country of ours [which] has never decided what is a crime and what is not."[10] He described Nixon as a "petty crook" and Henry Kissinger as a "liar and a cheat" who got the "Nobel Peace Prize even as he was bombing Cambodia."[11] He has also observed, "We have watched our constitutional government suborned by petty hateful men and women sworn to obey the law, and we have heard them characterize their crimes as actions taken in the public interest. Consequently, we have come to doubt that it is possible to act in the public interest."[12]

The moral standards and ideas of propriety reflected in Mamet's desperate and incompetent crooks are hardly surprising given this background; even those who should be considered above corruption have been exposed as base criminals. Quite apart from the political hiatus that was taking place, popular culture seemed to have reached an unprecedented level of decadence. For example, one of the number-one box office films of the 1970s was *The Godfather*, a movie in which the characters constantly speak of "business" when referring to murder, and do so in tones of what is at once a chilling and absurd politeness. Their veiled manner of expressing violence and hostility is frequently echoed in Mamet's characters; their sentiments are often at odds with the underlying viciousness and duplicity of their discussions. There are obvious links between the language in *American Buffalo* and that heard in films such as *On the Waterfront* and, especially, *The Godfather*. A good example occurs after an intensely violent verbal exposition of hatred when Teach indulges in the following exchange with Bobby as the latter prepares to fetch breakfast.

> *Teach:* And tell him he shouldn't say anything to Ruthie.
> *Don:* He wouldn't.
> *Teach:* No? No, you're right. I'm sorry, Bob.
> *Bob:* It's okay.
> *Teach:* I'm upset.
> *Bob:* It's okay, Teach. *(Pause.)*
> *Teach:* Thank you.
> *Bob:* You're welcome. (Act 1, p. 13)

Similarly, there is a bizarre display of Teach's—and especially Don's— duplicity when Bobby has been "paid off" and will no longer take part in the robbery:

> *Bob:* You said you were giving me fifty.
> *Don:* I'm sorry, I'm sorry, Bob, you're absolutely right . . .
> *(Pause.)*
> *Bob:* Thank you. *(Pause.)* I'll see you later, huh, Teach?
> *Teach:* I'll see you later, Bobby.
> *Don:* I'll see you later, Bob.
> *Bob:* I'll come back later.
> *Don:* Okay. *(Bob starts to exit.)*
> *Teach:* See you. (Act 1, p. 45)

Bobby is prompted into nervousness by Don's overcompensatory apologies and Teach's somewhat forced friendliness. Such an exhibition of bonhomie to Bobby, who is usually regarded as a nuisance and a mere child, is bound to disorient the wretched boy. In this scene, Mamet conveys something of the psychological machinations of each character: under the thin guise of elaborate good manners he variously depicts insecurity, fear, guilt, dishonesty, unscrupulousness, and perfidy.

The coolly murderous ambience of films like *The Godfather* has, it seems, permanently invaded the lives of Mamet's characters, inspiring them to adopt as their own the tones of Mafiosi "arrangements." The violence of such films was somewhat stripped of its glamour and reconstituted into the melodrama of soap opera in another kind of cinematic entertainment popular in the 1970s: the "group jeopardy" or "disaster" movie. Here, ordinary people are caught up in horrors beyond their wildest imagination: vast floods, earthquakes, infernos, and even the invasion of killer bees, haunt them. If the darkened sitting rooms of *The Godfather* provided one way to escape from reality and afforded the means of adopting the fantasy as one's own, the disaster movie provided another, quite different, way out. Mamet explains that "we are so ruled by magic. We have ceased to believe in logic. The cause to which we attribute so many effects is, thinly masked, our own inadequacy. We take refuge in mumbo-jumbo, in the Snake Oil of the Seventies, in escapism."[13] To escape the realities of everyday violence, audiences sought to appease their fears by projecting them onto ever-larger canvases, wallowing in representations of disaster so terrifying that they made their own fears bearable by comparison. Additionally, Mamet observes how

> in our motion picture theaters big black scary monsters interfere with white starlets [the remake of *King Kong*]. Huge and persistent sharks devour tugboats [*Jaws*]. Things burn [*Towering Inferno*], crumble [*Earthquake*] or are inundated with unpleasant amounts of water [*The Poseidon Adventure*]. These are our world destruction dreams. There is in our dreamlife, no certainty. We objectify our insecurity and self-loathing in the form of outside forces endeavoring to punish us.[14]

Mamet wrote *American Buffalo* in order to express his unhappiness at the way in which his society was evolving; decent moral standards no longer appeared to have any place and genuine emotions were being insidiously corrupted. His inspiration for the kind of characters he uses in the work derives from his association with those who live on the borders of society. W. H. Macy, an actor friend of Mamet, has noted that "He's played cards with some guys you'd never wish to meet."[15] In fact, Mamet himself used to be known as "Teach" on his visits to a "North Side junkshop"[16] where he used to play poker and where, he notes, "some very interesting people came in and out."[17] Bill Bryden, who directed both *American Buffalo* and *Glengarry Glen Ross* for the National Theatre, likens Mamet's use of language in *American Buffalo* to that which can be heard during high-stakes card games. For him, the world that Mamet creates "is a world of all-night poker games."[18] The speakers contrive to appear candid and forthright, but underneath their apparent candor their language is tentative, sly, and manipulative, interspersed with long pauses. What is ironic about this state of affairs is that all parties present are completely aware of the linguistic games that they and their partners play, but carry on as if oblivious to any subtext. Bryden goes on to note how in such circumstances "a pause is a check . . . on the pause you check what you have in your hand . . . what the next move should be,"[19] and, in an article about the game of poker, Mamet states that "playing poker is a masculine ritual [and that] a good poker player knows that there is a time to push your luck and a time to retire gracefully, that all roads have a turning."[20] This, and a judicious use of pauses, is translated into linguistic terms when Teach begins to question Don about the proposed heist. When it becomes apparent that Don will not willingly tell him any details, Teach realizes that he must use a different strategy. In order to demonostrate how hurt and offended he is, he affects a wounded tone:

> *Teach:* . . . Who am I, a po*lice*man . . . I'm making conversation, huh?. . . . *(Pause.)*. 'Cause you know I'm just asking for talk. . . . And I can live without this. (act 1, p. 27)

Don finally relents and Teach adopts a manner of righteous indignation designed to make his friend feel as guilty as possible:

> *Teach:* Tell me if you *want* to, Don.
> *Don:* I want to, Teach.
> *Teach:* Yeah?
> *Don:* Yeah. *(Pause.)*
> *Teach:* Well, I'd fucking *hope* so. Am I wrong?
> *Don:* No. No. You're right.
> *Teach:* I *hope* so. (ibid.)

Teach metaphorically plays his ace with this last remark. He has managed to turn the tables, and to make Don feel like a naughty child. Furthermore, he has raised Don's reluctance to include him in his plans into an issue about the importance of trust and friendship, two aspects that he himself will abandon with alacrity in the not-too-distant future.

A specific target for Mamet's satire in the play is what he considers to be the corrupting and dangerous influence of the American business ethic; by relating bad behavior to a business context, almost anything can be excused. Indeed, Christopher Bigsby quotes a Mafia leader as saying "it was business, just business"[21] after strangling a member of his own "family." Mamet is appalled at the way in which business considerations have insidiously found their way into personal relations; he echoes the sentiments of *Herzog* in Saul Bellow's novel of that name who feels that "the life of every citizen is becoming a business. This, it seems to me, is one of the worst interpretations of the meaning of human life history has ever seen. Man's life is not a business."[22] Mamet explains that

> the play is about the American ethic of business . . . how we excuse all sorts of great and small betrayals and ethical compromises called business. I felt angry about business when I wrote the play. I used to stand at the back of the theater and watch the audience as they left. Women had a much easier time with the play. Businessmen left it muttering vehemently about its inadequacies and pointlessness. But they weren't really mad because the play was pointless—no-one can be forced to sit through an hour-and-a-half of meaningless dialogue— they were angry because the play was about *them*.[23]

Elsewhere, he adds pointedly, "Although you see a play about thieves . . . it is not [only] about that particular section of society but about ourselves."[24]

Teach and his colleagues constantly converse in the language of business while planning to commit robberies, but Mamet sees them as no more corrupt than those in the very highest echelons of power. He states, "There's really no difference between the lumpenproletariat and stockbrokers or corporate lawyers who are the lackeys of business [although] part of the American myth is that a difference exists, that at a certain point vicious behavior becomes laudable."[25] Questioned about the use of such "low-life" characters as a representation of the business world as a whole, Mamet defends his play. "The question is, he says, "here are people who are engaged in theft, and [it is said] that they are absurd because they failed. The question is would they become more laudable if they succeed?"[26]

Does the fact that Teach, Don, and Bobby are inarticulate and

incompetent make them more culpable than if they were at the
head of a multinational organization or government? Mamet was
inspired to write of this kind of ethical corruption by the American sociologist and economist, Thorstein Veblen (1857–1929) and
confirmed him as his source in a letter to Jack V. Barbera.[27] Veblen
saw at the turn of the century what Mamet believes is happening
today—that the corrupting influence of the evolving economic
system will eventually destroy civilization. Veblen notes how, in
such a society, "the obtaining of goods by other methods than
seizing comes to be accounted unworthy of man. . . . The performance of productive work, or employment in personal service,
falls under the same odium for the same reason."[28] Don therefore
feels he has failed as a shopkeeper unless he has been able to
cheat his customers. He refuses to acknowledge that the function
of a salesman is to serve his clients, and to offer them a fair deal.
He tells Teach about the coin collector and how he believes the
man slighted him by his very presence:

> *Don:* He comes in here like I'm his fucking doorman. . . . Doing me
> this favor just by coming in my shop. . . . Like he has done me this
> big favor just by coming in my shop. (act 1, p. 32)

A simple business transaction has thus been distorted by Don's
logic; he sees it not as a mutually beneficial financial contract but
as proof that the customer has in some way taken advantage of
him. His words are childish and self-justifying, and the repetition
of "my shop" underscores his (misplaced) sense of importance as
the owner of such a derelict establishment. The fact that he had
been paid a large sum of money for an item he had previously
considered to be worthless has become irrelevant; Don feels that
he has been cheated, that the coin was probably worth a great deal
more than he was paid and that he has, therefore, been ridiculed.
Consequently, the robbery to steal the buyer's entire coin collection is justified in the name of business. Theft is legitimized in
Don's eyes because one deceit deserves another.
      Earlier, Bobby's assertion that Fletch had "jewed Ruthie out of
[some] pig iron" (act 1, p. 6) is countered by Don's avowal that the
deal was totally legitimate, even though it is likely that the pig iron
was indeed stolen. This is corroborated by Teach later in the play
when he tells Don that Fletch "stole some pig iron off Ruth" (act 2,
p. 77). However, when Bobby raises the issue, Don will not hear
any criticism of Fletch:

Don: She was mad at him?
Bob: Yeah. That he stole her pig iron.
Don: He didn't steal it, Bob.
Bob: No?
Don: No.
Bob: She was *mad* at him . . .
Don: Well, that very well may be, Bob, but the fact remains that it was *business*. That's what business is.
Bob: What?
Don: People taking *care* of themselves. (act 1, pp. 6–7)

In Don's last line there is an essential truth: in the world he and his cronies inhabit, selfishness and one's own interests obliterate all other considerations. To extend this kind of logic even further, any game of cards in which Teach has lost money is automatically assumed to have been fixed; if Fletch won when Teach did not, the only conclusion possible is that Teach has been cheated. This assumption, in turn, validates Teach's subsequent betrayal of Fletch. Teach urges Don to quickly enlist his help with the job or he will "turn around to find [Fletch has] took the joint off by himself" (act 2, p. 77), an action that he himself has just proposed.

Don, Teach, and Bobby repeatedly confuse friendship with business and engage in all kinds of treachery in its name. Friendship for them has become synonymous with business utility. Teach sees himself as a businessman who won't allow business to impinge upon his personal relationships, but he is in fact the least capable of the three men of separating the two. Speaking of a card game in which he has lost a great deal of money to Fletch and Ruthie, he pretends that his "business" mentality has not influenced his thinking:

> *Teach:* We're talking about money for chrissake, huh? We're talking about cards. Friendship is friendship, and a wonderful thing, and I am all for it. I have never said different. . . . But let's just keep it *separate* huh? . . . and maybe we can deal with each other like some human beings. (act 1, p. 15)

Later, the priority that both Teach and Don give to their business deals is mercilessly exposed. Teach has brutally beaten Bobby for apparently ruining their plans, and Don has allowed it to happen: "You brought it on yourself," he tells Bobby (act 2, p. 98). Thus, even the tenuous love that exists between Don and Bobby can be stretched to the breaking point when business interests are at stake—although, Don's subsequent display of affection and atonement for his complicity in the beating somewhat sweetens his role in the proceedings.

Bobby is himself infected with the business instinct, although Mamet ensures that we view his particular fall into this abyss with sadness and irony. Forced into an impossible position through his own incompetence, he resorts to desperate measures. Bobby believes that he has ruined Don's plans and so tries to reestablish the love he believes may have been lost. He purchases a buffalo nickel (with money incidentally borrowed from Don) and offers it as a token of friendship: "For Donny" (act 2, p. 103). It is significant that the only way that Bobby feels he can atone for his sin is through indulgence in a little "business" of his own. Don is touched, but Teach's reaction to this display of what he sees as mawkish affection is only to say "You people make my flesh crawl" (ibid.) and to fling Don's paternalism in his face:

> Teach: You *fake*. You fucking *fake*. You fuck your friends. You *have* no friends. No *wonder* that you fuck this kid around. . . . You seek your friends with *junkies*. You're a joke on this street, you and him. (act 2, p. 104)

What amounts to the only noble and selfless act in the whole play is thus rejected. Kindness is seen as a betrayal of business and, since neither Teach nor Don are capable of separating personal relations from their money-market mentalities, this results in Bobby's hospitalization, and Teach's affirmation that Don is an object of derision who befriends drug addicts. The violence of Teach's denunciation of Don and Bobby is most forcefully conveyed in the alliterative use of the letter *f* as Teach contemptuously spits out his abuse. In this context, the word *fuck* becomes only one of the obscenities; *all* words beginning with *f* become, by association, obscene. Poor Bobby does not seem to have learned the lesson that Don tried to teach him early in the play, that "there's business and there's friendship" (act 1, p. 7) and that "You don't have *friends* this life" (ibid.), although, as we have seen, there is at least some confusion in Don's mind about the two. This confusion is, in effect, his salvation and a testament to his compassion and innate decency—although, it is very sad that he keeps these attributes so well-disguised.

The world Mamet creates is charged with terror; his characters can barely articulate their rage or sense of impotence and so they often react in the only way known to them—by indulging in deception, betrayal, and violence. Even a man like Teach, although seriously disturbed and profoundly affected by the lack of stability in his society, remains at base a sad and desperate character; he is not a psychopath or a fundamentally evil man, but one who uses his manipulative powers to buy affection and respect. Mamet draws Teach as a particularly vulnerable and child-like person. He is anxious to retain the fragile ties of friendship he has managed to make with Don and Bobby yet his lack of loyalty and his casual cruelty are at odds with this desire. A mass of contradictions, Teach arms himself as a deterrent against "the path of some crazed lunatic [i.e., the owner of the house he plans to rob, who might irrationally see him] as an invasion of his personal domain" (act 2, p. 87). He does not seem to understand that *he* would be the intruder—one whose presence might initiate such violence. As he preaches the virtues of peace and amity, he casually loads his gun in case "God forbid, something inevitable occurs" (ibid.). That he sees a violent attack as not only likely but inevitable points both to his paranoia and his own sadistic propensities. The oxymoron within the sentence again underscores the many contradictions that make up Teach's personality. He goes on: "something inevitable occurs and the choice is (And I'm *saying* "God forbid") it's either him or us" (ibid.). Teach invokes "God" to protect himself and to convince Don that he is the last person who seeks violence. As a reasonable man, he must put his case for the necessity of the gun. As he tells Don, "it could be either him or us." The plural "us" instead of the singular "me" is indicative both of Teach's mounting excitement as he warms to his theme and his wish to personalize the sentence by including Don as a possible victim. To compound further the necessity for arms, Teach describes how the householder might try to defend himself by taking "a cleaver from one of those magnetic *boards* . . . with the two *strips*. . . . And *whack,* and somebody is bleeding to death" (ibid.). Teach's vivid imagination runs on ahead of him; he clearly envisages the meat cleaver and even the kind of magnetic board on which it will be hung. Just as he had tried to personalize his earlier statement, so he now invokes the abstract "somebody" to describe the person who is "bleeding to death." In order to make Don see that he must, by necessity, be armed with a gun, he brings him right into his story, making Don *see* through his words what would happen. Mamet makes Teach's demotic and laughable language serve as an ironic oral version of Joseph Conrad's dictum for written success. The writer must be able to "make you hear, to make you feel . . . before all . . . to make you *see*."[29]

It is instructive to note Teach's frequent use of religious terminology; he uses the phrase "God forbid" twice within a few moments and states that "I pray we don't [need a gun]." As he muses over the safe combination he hopes the proposed victim has written down, he absurdly underscores his wish "in the event that (God forbid) he somehow *forgets* it" (act 2, p. 80). In a spiritually desolate universe, the evocation of God seems necessary only as a kind of good-luck incantation—it has certainly lost all of its deeper resonance. Thus, as Teach calls upon God to defend him while he plans to commit a potentially violent crime, he arms himself against the violence on the streets. He is terrified of violence and yet he, as a violent man, has become what he most fears—*he* is one of the people he tries to avoid! Because of his terror of urban violence, Teach paradoxically admires the police force. As he loads his gun, he speaks of the police.

> *Teach:* They have the right idea. Armed to the hilt. Sticks, Mace, knives
> . . . who knows *what* the fuck they got. They have the right idea.
> Social customs break down, next thing *everybody's* lying in the
> gutter. (act 2, p. 88)

Teach and his colleagues are, of course, instrumental in creating exactly the kind of anarchic environment they dread. Like the real-estate salesmen in *Glengarry Glen Ross* and the protagonist in *Edmond*, they themselves have become part of the problematical society they fear and distrust. They break the law and yet depend on it for protection; they deplore violence and yet are quite prepared to engage in it for their own purposes. The irony of such logic is taken one step further when Fletch, their proposed accomplice, is mugged on the way to the rendezvous.

Not only does Teach value and admire the police force, he is also quick to champion other civic values. Without "free enterprise," the basic right of all American citizens, "we're just savage shitheads in the wilderness. . . . Sitting around some vicious campfire" (act 2, pp. 74–75). When Teach believes that the final betrayal has been perpetrated, he does not merely explode in another tirade of obscenity, but chooses instead to list what he feels are the fundamental elements that must be observed in a civilized society:

> *Teach:* The Whole Entire World.
> There is No Law.
> There is No Right and Wrong.
> The World is Lies.
> There Is No Friendship.

Every Fucking Thing. *(Pause.)*
Every God-forsaken Thing. . . .
We all live like the cavemen. (act 2, p. 107)

The progression from "savage shitheads" to "cavemen" shows Teach's continuity of thought from mere musing about the subject to deeply impassioned crying for order amidst the chaos. Even the much-invoked God has taken his leave of this particular society. Teach derides a world in which there is no "Right and Wrong," although he frequently indulges in acts that are more than a little questionable in their legitimacy; he cites a lack of friendship as he prepares to physically abuse a boy whose display of affection he interprets as betrayal; he observes that nothing in this world can be taken as truthful, although he has been seen to lie and deceive his way out of several corners in the course of the play. Mamet compounds the irony of all this by having Teach cite "law" as yet another essential component in his view of a civilized world.

If, however, one disregards the absurdity of a criminal holding reverence for the law, it is not difficult to understand why Teach should, like the majority of citizens, rely upon the comforting thought of an all-protective blanket like the police force to assuage his anxieties. Mamet notes how the media responded in the 1970s to the ever-increasing twitchiness and paranoia of the American populace; they created more and more cops and robbers television programs intended to work as a kind of soothing balm, a panacea that would send viewers to bed at least a little consoled. He observes how "we turn on our television and we see one show after another glorifying our law-enforcement agencies. We are an open book. Here we propitiate those forces we elect to stave off those who would take our electronic ranges from out of our kitchenette. . . . Surely we must be safe from terrors both of corporeal and social malefactors. The Cop on the Beat . . . protect[s] us."[30]

The notion of a crook maintaining a high regard for law and order even as he commits crimes is one of the subjects of Caryl Churchill's play, *Softcops*. This was in turn inspired by Michel Foucault's *Surveiller et Punir*. In Churchill's play, the arch-criminal Vidocq is actually made Chief of Police while another, Lacenaire, is executed at his own request as an act of profane martyrdom. Churchill sees the boundaries between the activities of the police and those of the criminal fraternity as somewhat blurred. She notes how "there is a constant attempt by governments to depoliticise criminal acts, to make criminals a separate class from the rest of society so that subversion will not be general, and part of this process is the invention of the detective and the criminal, the cop and the robber."[31] In the same way that the media seeks to console the public with happy endings in television crime thrillers, so the government attempts to keep police order and criminal activity separate; although law enforcement methods do seem to be moving closer toward the violence they seek to control. This is further borne out in cult film heroes like *Dirty Harry*, whose viciousness and callousness in the name of the law raises serious doubts about the exact role of the police.

Teach, the criminal, views the police as good men with a job to do and, thankfully, the means to do it. He needs his gun for "protection of me and my partner. Protection, deterrence" (act 2, p. 88). Since protection and deterrence are the reasons for the existence of the police force, it is clear that Teach considers himself spiritually akin to such an institution. However, he still freezes when he catches a glimpse of them "cruising" the streets (act 1, p. 30 and act 2, p. 88), holding his breath until they are no longer visible.

The profound paradoxes and deep dislocations of perspective that exist generally in Mamet's characters are given their sharpest outline in Teach. Jack Shepherd found the role a particularly difficult one to interpret for that reason.

> I had a real struggle with Teach's character. Early on, I based him a bit on "The Fonz"—the accent seemed right, North American working class. . . . I was accused of trying to copy [Robert] DeNiro's style in *Taxi Driver* but this had not crossed my mind. It could have been unconscious as I had indeed seen this film; the protagonist, Travis Bickle, is an unhinged character in a similar vein to Teach. Both men are prone to profound disruptions of logic and speech which are at odds with their general behavior. Teach will say things to Don that last two or three minutes, and which seem totally irrelevant, but the entire speech is a nuance, a means of establishing mood. . . . It's very hard to act this kind of scene, to make the words and actions believable.[32]

Shepherd gives the following examples of what he means by the disproportion between word and deed in Teach: "I am calm. I'm just upset" (act 2, p. 70) and "the odds are he's not there, so when he answers" (act 2, p. 72). Such blatant contradictions are difficult to convey theatrically, although Shepherd believes that by the end of the run he had found how to give an authentic performance, full of "darting movements and quick speech which suggested the contradictions within his personality . . . lots of physical tics and jerkiness."[33]

However, *American Buffalo* is a play that is essentially concerned with language rather than deed, and Mamet advances the action almost entirely through that medium. Because of this concentration on the power of language rather than upon overt stage action, some critics have denounced the play as tedious and static. I am reminded of an article by Thornton Wilder that recalls Maeterlinck's thoughts on movement in drama. He observed that

> Maeterlinck said that there was more drama in the spectacle of an old man seated by a table than in the majority of plays offered to the public. He was juggling with the various meanings in the word "drama." In the sense whereby drama means the intensified concentration of life's diversity and significance he may well have been right; if he meant drama as a theatrical representation before an audience he was wrong. Drama on the stage is inseparable from forward movement, from action.[34]

I would argue that Wilder is incorrect in his assertion that "Drama . . . is inseparable from . . . action." Many of Mamet's plays have been criticized for their stasis or lack of plot, but they nonetheless remain powerfully dramatic. The "spectacle of an old man seated by a table" envisaged by Maeterlinck could easily anticipate Beckett's monologue, *Krapp's Last Tape*, a work that was not actually written until 1958. Similarly, another short play by Beckett entitled *Happy Days* is even more static, in that its heroine is completely immobilized throughout the work in a grassy mound. With such works, it is surely the quality of the text that is all-important, which gives the pieces movement and interest, and has very little to do with how much physical action is actually taking place. Mamet has expressed his frustration at the frequent accusations of his writing plotless, actionless, and amorphously structured plays: "One critic in Chicago . . . says I write the kind of plays where a character wakes up in Act One and finally gets around to putting on his bath robe in Act Three,"[35] and elsewhere has noted how "even after Beckett and Pinter, there are people . . . who think that three men talking for two acts about a break-in which they do not commit does not constitute plot."[36] However, Eugene O'Neill—an avowed influence on Mamet—once observed how, in *The Iceman Cometh*, he had used "no plot in the ordinary sense . . . I didn't need plot; the people are enough."[37]

Teach, Don, and Bobby are almost enough for Mamet in *American Buffalo*; it is certainly a play that concentrates upon character exposition and language rather than plot mechanics although it clearly has a discernible plot and, despite criticism, considerable pace and movement. It is therefore quite understandable that Mamet should feel irritated at critics who declare in frustration: "I'm not asking for unity of action. I'm asking for any bloody kind of action whatsoever."[38] It is difficult to understand why such emphasis should be placed on physical action, when Mamet's language is so vibrant and rich with movement. For example, Teach can apparently conduct all the affairs in his life by means of speech alone; he can coerce and intimidate, wheedle and confuse. Indeed, he is linguistically so versatile that he constantly enmeshes others into his fantasies.

One of the methods he uses to influence and entrap is his construction of what Christopher Bigsby calls an "alternative reality."[39] The intention is that this "reality" should subsume the listener and sweep him or her along with it as if it were indeed the truth, and not merely a bizarre substitute existing only in Teach's mind. It is not quite clear if he believes in the veracity of his fabrications himself—he probably does once he gets into his stride—and this would, therefore, be a good example of Mamet's claim that language prescribes action rather than the other way around. As he talks himself into verbal culs-de-sac, Teach must go on and on inventing in order to extricate himself unharmed from the encounter or to ensure that his linguistic web is of the requisite tautness and immutability.

Teach gathers up what he sees as the essence of disparate incidents and binds them together into a workable narrative. Out of half-formulated ideas and conveniently vague events he creates new truths that can be molded, changed, and developed as he so wishes. Thus, having lent credibility to the notion that Bobby is a villain, the agent of an obscure conspiracy who could threaten Teach's and Don's affairs, Teach vents his anger in a terrifying display. He viciously beats the boy, callously ignoring Bobby's pleas for mercy. The situation that Teach has created has been given weight and veracity by sheer language rather than by any palpable evidence. When his story is weakened by subsequent events and proves to have been totally misguided, he immediately begins to construct another. He never takes responsibility for the chaos he creates. When Ruthie rings to confirm Bobby's story that Fletch is indeed in the hospital—albeit not the one originally cited by Bobby—Teach switches his contempt to her: "*She's* got a lot of nerve" (act 2, p. 99) and, as the truth becomes overwhelmingly obvious, he changes the subject completely and attempts to bring things back to normal, incidentally implying Bobby's indebtedness to him: "And you owe me twenty bucks" (act 2, p. 100). After he has wrecked Don's shop, he is embarrassed by his actions and so complains of the mess that *he* has created, suggesting that Don should "clean this place up" (act 2, p. 110). Teach thus has the ability to use language to disorientate and confuse: merely by listening to and becoming involved in his fabrications, Don forfeits his own interpretation of events. His junk shop is now completely wrecked, his young friend is lying prostrate and bleeding on the floor, and Don hardly knows how it has all happened. With the blackest of irony, Mamet suggests the power of language to infect and corrupt. Teach has many other linguistic tricks available to him. Earlier in the play, Don flies to Bobby's defense when Teach criticizes him for being a drug addict:

Don: . . . I don't want that talk, only, Teach. *(Pause.)* You understand?
Teach: I more than understand, and I apologize. *(Pause.)* I'm sorry.
Don: That's the only thing.
Teach: All right. But I tell you. I'm glad I said it.
Don: Why?
Teach: 'Cause it's best for these things to be out in the open.
Don: But I don't want it in the open.
Teach: Which is why I apologized. (act 1, pp. 35–36)

This kind of linguistic circularity is so typical of Teach; finding himself in a corner, he flatters and then lets fall what he believes to be his trump card. Should this prove ineffectual, he deftly moves the conversation around to confuse his audience into believing that they have no cause for complaint. After a long harangue, during which he questions the advisability of including Fletch in the heist, Teach realizes that he is losing ground. To counter this, he suddenly turns the situation around as though it had been Don who had expressed doubts:

Teach: . . . you think it's good business call Fletch in? To help us.
Don: Yes.
Teach: Well then okay. *(Pause.)* Are you sure?
Don: Yeah.
Teach: All right, if you're *sure* . . .
Don: I'm sure, Teach.
Teach: Then, all right, then. That's all I worry about. (act 1, pp. 54–55)

Similarly, once it has been agreed that Fletch will be included in the deal after all, Teach needs to confirm if Don is angry with him for his virulent opposition. He plaintively asks: "Are you mad at me?" (act 1, p. 56) only to reverse the situation moments later by stating "I want to make one thing plain before I go, Don. I am not mad at you" (ibid., p. 58).

Perhaps the most bizarre examples of Teach's ability to conjure up an entirely fictional reality occur when he and Don are mulling over the finer points of the robbery. Saying the words aloud seems, to Teach, to make them true:

> *Teach:* The man hides his coin collection, we're probably looking the guy has a *study* . . . I mean, he's not the kind of guy to keep it in the *basement.* . . . So we're looking for a study. . . . And we're looking, for, he hasn't got a *safe* . . . he's probably going to keep 'em . . . where? *(Pause.)*
> *Don:* I don't know. His desk drawer.
> *Teach:* (You open the middle, the rest of 'em pop out?)
> *Don:* (Yeah.) (act 1, p. 48)

Eventually, Don raises the possibility that the victim may well have a safe. Teach loses no time in eradicating any worries his colleague may have:

> *Teach:* What you do, a safe . . . you find the combination.
> *Don:* Where he wrote it down.
> *Teach:* Yes.
> *Don:* What if he didn't write it down?
> *Teach:* He wrote it down. He's *gotta* write it down. What happens he forgets it?
> *Don:* What happens he doesn't forget it?
> *Teach:* He's gotta forget it, Don. Human nature. The point being, even he *doesn't* forget it, *why* does he not forget it?
> *Don:* Why?
> *Teach:* 'Cause he got it *wrote down.* (act 2, pp. 79–80)

Teach continues to bamboozle Don with this kind of inverse logic until the whole ludicrous episode is concluded with wonderful irony:

> *Don:* What if he didn't write it down?
> *Teach:* He wrote it down.
> *Don:* I know he did. But just, I'm saying, from *another* instance. Some made-up guy from my imagination.
> *Teach:* You're saying in the instance of some guy . . . he didn't write it down? . . . Well, this is another thing. . . . It's another matter. The

guy, he's got the shit in the safe, he didn't write it *down*. . . . How do you know he didn't write it down?
Don: (I'm, you know, making it up.)
Teach: Well, then, this is not based on *fact*. (act 2, p. 81)

It is clear that Don retains doubts about the validity of Teach's argument, but dares not confront him directly. Don's words are tentative, unsure and his hesitancy betrays a fear of antagonizing his dominant friend. So worried is he of offending Teach's thesis that he suggests "some made-up guy" who may not comply with their wishes. That Teach ends the discussion asserting that Don's postulation is not based on fact and cannot be taken seriously, is surely evidence that he has convinced himself of the authenticity of his case. One can almost hear his mind working as he stalls for time to form an adequate response to Don's all-too-reasonable doubts and then, with what is by now predictable behavior, turns the doubts around and blames Don for making assertions that have no basis in reality!

The language favored by the characters in *American Buffalo* has been culled not only from countless crime films, but also from consumer advertising. A sentence such as Teach's "I mean, the guy's got you're taking his high-speed blender and a Magnavox" (act 1, p. 35) highlights his abrupt change of grammar midsentence as his mind races ahead of his words and includes a domestic trade name like "Magnavox." This is a crucial linguistic ploy of Mamet's and is certainly not included merely to fill up space. These characters use words they have picked up from commercials and consumer magazines to lend weight to their speeches, to impress and to demonstrate what they believe to be their savoir faire. In the same way that teenage boys delight in the ability to name obscure makes of automobile or to brag about their arcane knowledge of music, mechanics, or even sex, Mamet's characters utilize the language of advertising similarly to impress. The "Magnavox" has to be precisely named to give it both substance and veracity whereas, in fact, it might not even exist. Again, by saying such words aloud, Teach somehow believes that this will make them a reality.

Advertising jargon and trade names lead on quite naturally to the use of slang, an indulgence that is widely spread throughout the play. As G. L. Brook observes, the intrusion of slang into a language is neither wholly good nor bad, though it "tends to remove delicate shades of meaning in existing words and leads to over-emphasis and a straining after effect."[40] Chicago poet Carl

Sandburg once wrote that he believed that "slang is English with its sleeves rolled up"[41] and it is undoubtedly this muscular quality of slang that led Mamet to include so much of it in his work. In a survey, many American students said that they used slang for the sake of conciseness and emphasis, to make their speech sound lively rather than stodgy, and to express a desire for intimacy with their friends. They also expressed "discontent with hackneyed words and phrases"[42] that could no longer convey what they most wished to communicate. The need to develop slang usage between friends as an expression of intimacy seems to exist for Mamet's characters. The following exchange is littered with slang words that have obviously been gleaned from the television and/ or film world, and are used here to bind the speakers together in understanding:

> *Don:* So . . . we kept a lookout on his place, and that's the shot. . . . We *think* he's married. They got two names on the bell . . . Anyway he's living with this chick, *you* know . . .
> *Teach:* What the hell.
> *Don:* . . . and you should see this chick.
> *Teach:* Yeah, huh?
> *Don:* She is a knockout. I mean, she is *real* nice-lookin', Teach. (act 1, p. 33)

The use of terms such as "that's the shot," "lookout," and even "chick" is a clear indication of the insidious nature of the criminal terminology gleaned from films and television. These are terms that can be heard in programs like *Miami Vice, Hill Street Blues,* and *Hunter,* although it is again interesting to note the blurred boundaries that exist between criminal and policeman; all of these shows have police heroes—it is not only the crooks who use such underworld argot.

Sexual camaraderie between Don and Teach seems to be very high, and Teach's liberal-minded dismissal of the notion that the couple in question may not be married is meant to illustrate his broad-mindedness. His "yeah, huh?" is a succinct expression of eagerness, of his desire to know more details about "the chick." In those two words, Mamet hints at Teach's salacious and lecherous nature. They can also be seen as the first hints of his sexual jealousy of the "mark." His resentment at the man's success with women can only fuel his desire to harm him in some way.

The indulgence in a casual use of slang leads to an equally casual use of cliché. As Milton Shulman has observed, in the world of *American Buffalo*, "the cliché is a way of life."[43] Indeed, American language in general seems to have a peculiar propensity for slang and cliché, and Raymond Chandler once noted how his native tongue is much "more alive to clichés."[44] Teach often uses the most hackneyed phrases as a means of expressing his own strangely convoluted philosophies; his ideas again derive from television, particularly the impossibly tortuous world of television soap operas. The common parlance in such programs is contrived and artificial and usually reflects a completely immoral world in which truth is prostituted as the most banal cliché. Here, as nowhere else, the cliché rules; the world is seen only in black and white. Emotional responses are minimized or exaggerated to fit in with plot lines, extremely traumatic events are given similar weight to minor problems, and an ordinary set of moral values does not seem to exist. The world portrayed is one dominated by big business, oil deals, broken marriages, and illegitimate children. To exist in such a world, one must either succumb to pressure or fight back; Teach has internalized the values championed by these shows and chosen the latter course of action. He evidently sees himself as one of the heroes: hard, remorseless, and determined. His mental picture of himself is very different from that perceived by the audience.

A highly sensitive individual in some ways, Teach has been dulled emotionally over the years by constant media battering; he selects his words not because they serve as genuine communication but because his thoughts are guided by artificial standards. Sometimes, his use of clichés is entirely inappropriate and ridiculous—as when he remarks of a man he has never met, "some people never change" (act 1, p. 32)—and sometimes superfluous: holding up the dead pig–leg spreader, he asks Bob what he thinks it is. He finally informs him, in tones reminiscent of John Wayne: "Things are what they are" (act 1, p. 40). Clichés are scattered throughout the play, relentless and absurd: "nobody's perfect" (act 1, p. 52) and "can't take the truth" (act 2, p. 83) are merely two random examples. As Archie Rice in Osborne's *The Entertainer* would have it, in this play, clichés have a habit of "dropping like bats from the ceiling."[45]

Teach seriously considers himself a philosopher but Mamet continually deflates Teach's spurious ontological speculations with a deadly irony.

Teach: . . . Man is a creature of habits. Man does not change his habits

> overnight. This is not like him. (And if he does, he has a very good
> reason) . . . (act 2, p. 80)

Mamet milks Teach's grave tone for all it's worth. First, he gets the
cliché all wrong by adding an *s* to "habit" and then, to ensure that
he cannot lose this particular argument, he qualifies his statement
with a parenthetical aside that (unintentionally) negates what he
has just said. Don catches some of Teach's philosophical pretension. When he and Bob are discussing the cost of valuable coins,
Don declares that they are "oddities, Bob. Freak oddities of
nature" (act 2, p. 63). This bizarre statement reveals Don to be as
much an ignorant braggart as Teach. Since a coin is a manmade
object, it cannot at the same time be a freak of nature! Don's
attempt to impress Bob with his knowledge of numismatics probably succeeds, however, because Bob is even more ignorant than
Don and no doubt believes he is hearing the important opinions
of a coin expert. When Teach has looked at a book on coin
identification for less than a minute, he similarly declares himself
something of an expert:

> *Teach:* . . . One thing. Makes all the difference in the world.
> *Don:* What?
> *Teach:* Knowing what the fuck you're talking about. And it's so rare,
>   Don. So rare. (act 1, p. 50)

Minutes later, when he realizes that he cannot possibly learn
anything of value in so short a time—indeed, that the learning of
something takes application and skill—Teach becomes derisive,
completely negating what he has just said:

> *Teach:* . . . *fuck* the book. What am I going to do, leaf through the book
>   for hours on end? The important thing is to have the *idea* . . . (ibid.,
>   p. 51)

Studying seriously is too much like real work to a man like Teach;
if he cannot learn by a kind of invisible osmosis, he is not interested.
   Teach is the model for what have been referred to as Mamet's
"Teach-like characters."[46] Colin Stinton talks about Mamet's use of
this particular type of character:

> The Teach-like character—in both the sense of Teach in *American
> Buffalo* and in the instructor sense of the phrase—is one which recurs
> . . . in Mamet's work. He is a man who pretends to know something

of importance when, more often than not, he knows very little. What he does not know, he makes up . . . this is usually a great deal . . . Mamet's characters are all trying to assert who they are, continually trying to identify themselves and, in so doing, part of the theory behind the Teach-mentality is revealed. Their thoughts run along the following lines: if I can teach knowledge, therefore it must be true. If it can be passed along, therefore it must exist. I teach therefore I am! The imparting of knowledge, true or false, gives some sense of substantiality to their lives. By adopting the role of instructor, they give themselves status and importance which at least lasts as long as they "teach." There are many, many people like this in [Mamet's] work; obviously Teach in *American Buffalo* but also Robert in *A Life in the Theatre*, Bernie in *Sexual Perversity in Chicago* and, after a while, Edmond.[47]

In an article concerning Mamet's style and the "Teach-like" character, Richard Eder almost echoes Stinton's words by asserting that the maxim and governing motto of such characters is "I speak, therefore I am."[48]

American Buffalo has become known as a classic in American theatre. It is a sobering thought that when it was premiered, it was seen by some critics as little more than a foul-mouthed exposé of the criminal underworld, well-rendered but fundamentally meaningless. Indeed, some subsequent productions were similarly described. When he first saw the play in 1977, John Beaufort considered that "the playwright's observations (psychological, sociological, etc) [were] too superficial to waste time upon. . . . [it is] a very thin slice of low life."[49] Edwin Wilson observed that "the play is as limited in its vocabulary as it is in its plot,"[50] while Brendan Gill described it as "a curiously offensive piece of writing . . . street language attempting in vain to perform the office of eloquence."[51] Christopher Porterfield felt that Mamet "revels a bit too much in . . . scatalogy and blasphemy"[52] and believed that if one was to "delete the most common four-letter Anglo-Saxonism from the script . . his drama might last only one hour instead of two."[53]

These misunderstandings and misinterpretations are instructive. For these critics, the play represents only simple naturalism, poorly plotted and cast with inarticulate characters who indulge in tiresome and disgusting small talk to no apparent end. Mamet believes that the initially poor critical response was due both to these kind of misunderstandings and to the unwillingness of the reviewers to grant the work metaphorical status. He feels that it touched an uncomfortable nerve. "In this country [America]" he says, "we only understand plays as dope, whose purpose is anaesthetic, meant to blot out consciousness. . . . A play which does not soothe or reinforce certain preconceived notions in an audience . . . simply baffles them."[54] He also muses on how it was acceptable "in the fifties to do plays about junkies and long-shoremen who were understood as a metaphor for ourselves; and in the seventies to present plays about people who were dying of cancer [but the criminal subclass] was not at that time a generally accepted metaphor, so that it was difficult for a lot of people to accept it as a play about ourselves, because the convention wasn't current."[55]

American Buffalo is, in fact, a deeply symbolic play. Not only does the junk shop reflect what Mamet sees as the detritus of modern America but June Schlueter and Elizabeth Forsyth note an earlier echo of this image in Nathanael West's *Miss Lonelyhearts*. They observe that

> the America of Nathanael's West's *Miss Lonelyhearts* is a spiritual wasteland, the suffering of its people chronicled in the doleful letters received by "Miss Lonelyhearts," the newspaper advice columnist. Psychologically exhausted by the pleas of his readers, Miss Lonelyhearts imagines himself gazing at the "paraphernalia of suffering" through a pawnshop window, seeing among its accumulated objects the remnants of America's broken dreams.[56]

Mamet surely had this work in mind when he wrote *American Buffalo* and also *Mr. Happiness*, a short play that deals with a radio equivalent of Miss Lonelyhearts who similarly dispenses clichéd wisdom and platitudes to his desperate listeners. Significantly, however, Mr. Happiness does not appear to suffer the same pangs of agony endured by West's creation; he has become part of the show business enterprise, which airs the problems of its pathetic audience as a form of entertainment. To carry the junkshop metaphor further, Christopher Porterfield notes how Don and Bobby draw together at the conclusion of the play in "a fragile bond of shared futility, human castoffs alongside the inanimate ones."[57]

The very title of *American Buffalo* is symbolic. In a review of the play, Harold Clurman writes: "Look at the face of the coin . . . the buffalo looks stunned, baffled, dejected, ready for slaughter. The animal is antiquated, and the would-be robbers are a mess. The combination is symbolic."[58] The coin of the title is symbolic because of the fact that it is of monetary value; the characters are guided by the rules of the business world and their whole fantasy robbery revolves around the sale of what was once considered worthless. Further, it has been observed that "Mamet's choice of the buffalo coin offers a further irony, for the buffalo, which once roamed the American plains in abundance . . . has declined to near extinction [and is now] reduced to a relief on the back of a coin, its value as a powerful presence in the expansion of the American West and the attainment of the American dream transformed into money."[59] Perhaps another level of symbolism is intended by Mamet in that the American slang word for intimidation is to "buffalo" someone: there is certainly a good deal of intimidation in the work, most notably on the part of Teach.

Happily, there were a number of reviewers who, when the play was premiered, recognized it as a serious and important work, and many more who came to similar conclusions at subsequent performances of the piece. Robert Storey considers that *American Buffalo* is "arguably Mamet's best play. . . . Perhaps because he is working within a continuous two-act structure, perhaps also because he is not insisting self-consciously upon the comedy in his material . . . he makes his characters behave with a consistency and economy of function."[60] Frank Rich opines that it is "one of the best American plays of the last decade. . . . with such terse means, Mr. Mamet has created a combustible and sympathetic portrait of inarticulate American underclass dreamers."[61] Of the play, Clive Barnes writes "It really is a lovely play—if you twist my arm, a meaningful play. Mamet has caught a moment in our Judeo-Christian civilization. It is not flattering—but I fear it is accurate."[62]

Many critics commented upon the brilliance of the dialogue and referred especially to the solecisms, truisms, tautologies, vagaries, and misapplied homilies scattered throughout the work. When Clive Barnes first saw the play in 1981 he described its language as a "poetic, almost choral use of words"[63] and by the time he saw *Glengarry Glen Ross* in 1983, he claimed that "Mamet . . . makes poetry out of common usage. [The speech he uses] is not ordinary speech . . . it is more ordinary than that, it is ordinary speech raised to its basic potential."[64] It is instructive to analyze Barnes's use of "raised" in the phrase "raised to its basic potential" as opposed to the more obvious "lowered." This suggests Mamet's ability to move mundane and banal language onto a higher level where it perhaps becomes suggestive of the subtext beneath, or where its rhythms are so seductive that the listener is carried away with them despite the actual *meaning* of the words. It is also interesting to note how often Mamet's work is given a musical analogy: for Robert Cushman, *American Buffalo* "is a Chicago jazz opera";[65] for Howard Kissel, it is a "jam session, in which the music (here often cacophonously vulgar language) is tossed off with spontaneity and verve."[66] For Dennis Cunningham, it is "very like intricate music, a wonderfully profane fugue . . . a song"[67] and David Skerritt describes the play as "A Fugue for Three Voices in a Junk Shop."[68]

American Buffalo is not the only play of Mamet's that has been likened to a musical score. Peter Stothard, writing about *The Duck Variations,* notes how "Mamet's two old men . . . spin out rhythmic exchanges like the interlocking themes of a symphony, neither sticking to the same tune for long but passing it between themselves for extension and development."[69] Jack Shepherd feels that the dialogue in *Glengarry Glen Ross* is "like a drum solo by Philly Joe Jones."[70] Connie Booth recalls that when she saw *Glengarry Glen Ross* for the first time, she was struck as to the musicality of the piece; to her it was "like an unfinished symphony in the way that it suddenly stopped."[71] She also noted that the dialogue in *Edmond* called for "octave leaps"[72] from the actor involved in order to find the rhythm and sense of the text. Ross Wetzsteon has described *Sexual Perversity in Chicago* as "a series of fugue-like vignettes"[73] and Jack Kroll called the same play "a sleazy sonata of seduction."[74]

The critics who decry Mamet's talent for using obscenity for no apparent reason have not, it seems, looked very closely at the play. An excellent example of the use of such language to depict far more than a deliberately shocking scenario occurs when Teach has been incensed by a mildly sarcastic remark made by Ruthie. This scene, I believe, completely demolishes the views of those who aver that Mamet's text is arbitrarily and unnecessarily foulmouthed. Teach appears in the doorway of Don's shop and walks around for a while muttering "Fuckin' Ruthie" six times in succession (act 1, p. 9). He then sets out to describe the circumstances that have led to this abuse, and, after a cursory explanation, lets fall the following:

> *Teach:* Only (and I tell you this, Don). Only, and I'm not, I don't think, casting anything on anyone: from the mouth of a Southern bulldyke asshole ingrate of a vicious nowhere cunt can this trash come. (ibid., p. 10)

Teach has been onstage a very short time when this tirade is unleashed. With marvelous economy, Mamet tells the audience a great deal about this character's paranoid, highly neurotic personality, as well as hinting at his sexism, cunning, childishness, and easily ruffled sensitivity. Teach begins the attack in a politely diffident way, slowing down his words with commas and parenthetical asides before building rapidly into what is nearly a stream-of-consciousness crescendo of hatred. He is most anxious for Don to agree that he has been sorely slighted; he struggles to appear reasonable and kind, to convey the fact that he is a good, sensitive soul who has been cruelly exploited. A trifle such as Ruthie's remark has caused him extreme pain, for he has interpreted it as a callous blow to what he considers his own pristine and exemplary friendship. As the play progresses, the audience becomes cognizant of how easily this "friendship" he supposedly cherishes, can become corrupted, particularly when any business interests are involved. At this stage, however, the only clues are Teach's overly solemn manner and contrasting offensive language. It is absurd that he should be so angry about a throw-away remark and his behavior merely points to insecurity and fear; Teach is terrified that his friends may not, after all, really be his friends. He fully intends to destroy Ruthie for raising such doubts in his mind, and the effect of his speech is both funny and frightening. With his careful syntactical construction, Mamet manipulates Teach's words to achieve the right tone of self-righteousness and violence, two aspects of Teach's personality that are further explored throughout the play. It is enlightening to look closely at the most abusive part of the speech to see how Mamet builds disgust into Teach's words.

At first, Ruthie is refered to as a "Southern bulldyke." The word "Southern" implies the supposed ignorance of the southern population of the United States, the "rednecks" to whom Northerners traditionally feel superior. The crass name "bulldyke" infers not only gross ugliness but also masculinity—"dyke" being a familiar slang term for lesbian. Ruthie has become for Teach an alien creature. She is no longer a woman who deserves respect and some delicacy of description, but a manly freak. Having established her as less than normal, he goes on to describe her in words that become more savage with every breath. Ruthie then becomes an "asshole," paradoxically the most common and certainly least cruel of Teach's descriptions of her; this word is used so much in daily discourse in urban America that it has practically lost its meaning altogether. It is included here, perhaps, as a substitute word, a random obscenity dragged out by Teach to fall in with his rhythm, to fill a gap he cannot for the moment satisfy with a more fitting, more bestial word. The choice of "ingrate" is strange, yet believable. It has a weird, archaic sound to it and yet somehow fits in perfectly with the rest. Mamet's characters frequently interject learned, "big" words into their otherwise demotic conversations in order to impress, deceive, and/or disorient. Teach's use of "ingrate" is another example of this, although there remains a sense of his disgust at Ruthie's profound ingratitude for all his help and friendship over the years. Teach later reminds Don how unfairly he has been treated.

> *Teach:* . . . (I'm wondering were they eating . . . and thinking "This guy's an idiot to blow a fucking *quarter* on his friends" . . .) (act 1, p. 10)

With this in mind, it is little wonder that Teach should refer to Ruthie as "vicious" at the next stage in his verbal destruction. As his anger mounts, his language increases in ferocity. Although the word "nowhere" is not in itself an obscenity, it becomes one within this context. Ruthie is placed right out of existence: by so insulting Teach, she has forfeited her right to live. Whatever this unfortunate woman may have been or done in the past, she has lost her credibility as a human being. As if to compound this, she finally becomes no more than a crude word for the female sexual organ, a "cunt." Since this is probably the most chauvinistic insult a man can express, it acts as a fitting addition to this aria of hatred. Ruthie is now deprived of all identity except that of a sexual orifice, in this context an object of contempt so vile and loathsome that the very sound of the word as it is spat out—the hard *c* adding a choking, gutteral dimension—suggests its meaning as something obscene. That this term is commonly held to be the worst of all insults speaks volumes about a society that so designates it; it is testimony to the fear and ignorance of women in those who choose to use it.

After his demolition of Ruthie as a person, Teach then turns to the issue that has caused all this ire—her mildly chiding and probably teasing remark. Her comment is termed "trash." Ruthie is not only all of the terrible things Teach has thus far labeled her, but her very speech is mere rubbish and unworthy of consideration. In this short but bitterly effective scene, Mamet has established the strange sense of priorities that Teach and his associates hold. Cheating and deception turn out to be quite admissable, even admirable, when utilized in the name of business; violent injury can be excused if there are sufficient grounds—or at least, the suspicion that such grounds exist—but a chance remark like Ruthie's is truly unforgiveable.

Although the setting for *American Buffalo* is given only as "Don's Resale Shop" (act 1, p. 2), there are enough clues, verbal and otherwise, to set the action very precisely in Chicago. Near the beginning of the play, Mamet includes a favorite allusion: the Century of Progress Chicago Exposition of 1933—held in an era that at once represented hope and progress for America and embodied all that Mamet finds ironic about Chicago's grip on history. He explores the irony of the sheer lack of any real progress in American society further in *The Water Engine,* a play set in 1933, which deals with one man's attempts to patent a machine that runs on water. Although his machine really does work, it never sees the light of day because of the vested interests of corrupt big businessmen whose profit margins would be threatened by the device.

The characters in *American Buffalo* exclude history from their lives; they live in a marginal subculture that does not recognize its importance other than as the source of a few clichéd expressions occasionally dragged out to make a spurious point. It is significant that the characters refer to the exhibition as "the thing" (act 1, p. 17). This indicates both their apathy and their sense of dispossession; the "progress" that the event symbolized has completely passed them by and so the exhibition is not even dignified with a proper name. Once again, Mamet makes a point that proves to be more substantial than a mere illustration of his characters' inability to speak properly.

Jack V. Barbera points to a number of purely verbal clues that place the action firmly in Chicago. He notes how Teach refers to a "sweet roll"[75] instead of a bun and the reference to "Lake Shore Drive" (act 1, p. 42), a well-to-do and desirable neighborhood in Chicago would also suggest, to anyone familiar with that city, a particular social milieu. Chicago has been called America's most American city, and the poet Carl Sandburg's epithets "Stormy, husky, brawling, / City of the big shoulders"[76] suit it perfectly. It is loud, vulgar and working-class. Everything is constantly on the move in Chicago, and everyone is engaged in a quest for success. Mamet's petty criminals also seek that success; they also want to be the "excellent men"[77] of whom Mamet has spoken but, as Mamet told the director of a recent production of the play, "society hasn't offered them any context to be excellent in."[78]

Living in a big city affects not only the personalities of Mamet's characters but also their language. One of the reasons for the playwright's elliptical stylization is to suggest pace and bustle, and Teach, in his haste to convey meaning, continually leaves out words. When Bobby is thought to have betrayed his and Don's scheme, Teach declares: "Loyalty does not mean *shit* a situation like this" (act 2, p. 97); as he begins to describe the incident at the Riverside Cafe, he explains: "I sit down at the table Grace and Ruthie" (act 1, p. 9); as he stalls for time when attempting to eliminate Fletch from their deal, he asks "(He don't got the address the guy?)" (act 2, p. 85); and as Don questions his abilities as a robber, he cries: "What the fuck they live in Fort Knox?" (act 2, p. 79). With these clipped sentences, Mamet infers the tension and paranoia of Teach. Paradoxically, Bobby's language is slow and painfully self-conscious. He, too, has been infected by big city life, but his exposure has led him to use drugs as a means of escape. Although Bobby's sentences, like those of Teach, are often fragmented, Mamet writes them in such a way that to speak them quickly and neurotically would be to lose their flavor. Bobby's mind has been damaged by narcotics in much the same way that Aston's has in Pinter's *The Caretaker.* When Bobby comes to tell Don and Teach that Fletch has been mugged, he chooses his words carefully and nervously; he is clearly frightened of the effect this news will have upon his two colleagues:

> *Bobby:* Grace and Ruthie . . . he's in the hospital, Fletch. *(Pause.)* I only wanted to, like *come* here. I know you guys are only playing *cards* this . . . now. I didn't want to disturb you like *up,* but they just I found out he was in the hospital and I came over here to . . . tell you. . . . He got mugged. (act 2, p. 90)

Bobby mixes up his words and offers information that is not required before he finally gets to the point. His tone is apologetic, stalling; he tries to buy time to express himself more successfully but his sloth enrages Teach to the point of violence. It is of some interest to note how Mamet uses both very rapid, paranoiac speech and slow, stumbling words to convey fear and trepidation. Both are most convincing, particularly in the breakdown of grammar and syntax.

Of the three men, Don seems to be the most relaxed. He only becomes edgy when confronted with Teach, which is hardly surprising. When he is alone with Bobby, he speaks mostly in paternal, kindly rhythms, which seem designed to put the boy at ease although, as John Ditsky points out, there is still a kind of Pinteresque power play going on here, which also exists elsewhere in Mamet's drama. Of *Sexual Perversity in Chicago,* he notes how

> one character constantly defines himself as dependent, inferior, questioning, eager to learn—even going to the point of asking questions or

making repetitions that merely continue the rhythm of the scene. . . . [In *American Buffalo* he notes how] the power-posture apparent in language distinguishes Bob and Don from the first words of the play—"So?"—onward. As in the military, discipline is insured by making the inferior character "recite."[79]

The following exchange is a good example of this:

> *Don:* . . . Now: What do you see me eat when I come in here every day?
> *Bob:* Coffee.
> *Don:* Come on, Bob, don't fuck with me. I *drink* a little coffee . . . but what do I *eat?*
> *Bob:* Yogurt.
> *Don:* Why?
> *Bob:* Because it's good for you. (act 1, pp. 7–8)

Don's treatment of Bobby here certainly appears to corroborate Ditsky's observations about inferior and superior "power-postures." Don's paternal yet (he would like to think) unsentimental concern for Bobby is revealed very strongly when he tries to get the boy to eat properly and to take vitamins to improve his health:

> *Don:* . . . And it wouldn't kill you to take a vitamin.
> *Bob:* They're too expensive.
> *Don:* Don't worry about it. You should just take 'em.
> *Bob:* I can't afford 'em.
> *Don:* Don't worry about it.
> *Bob:* You'll buy some for me?
> *Don:* Do you need 'em?
> *Bob:* Yeah.
> *Don:* Well, then, I'll get you some. What do you *think?*
> *Bob:* Thanks, Donny.
> *Don:* It's for your own good. Don't thank *me* . . .
> *Bob:* Okay.
> *Don:* I just can't use you in here like a zombie. (act 1, p. 8)

Don *is* seriously worried about Bobby's health—and not just because of his poor performance as a "gopher" in his store—yet he carefully manipulates the conversation around to a point at which he can elicit the request for vitamins from Bobby himself. This way it will seem as if Don is merely doing Bobby a favor because Bobby asked him to, rather than admit the truth: that it was his own idea to buy the vitamins. Bobby plays his part of the dependent, childlike sycophant as he emphasizes his wish to have the vitamins: *"Yeah."* Likewise, Don plays the reluctant father, only doing what is right and deserving of no thanks. The reference to work in the last line underscores Don's need to distance himself emotionally from the boy—he does not wish to appear too "soft"—but his affection is rather movingly demonstrated anyway in the patience he displays as he repeats at least three times that Bobby should "get something to eat" (act 1, pp. 11–12) and also by his willingness to repeat what the vague Bobby has been unable to assimilate: Don tells him Fletch won four hundred dollars at the card game and, seconds later, Bobby asks how much he won (act 1, p. 4).

Writing about the work of Anton Chekhov, Robert Brustein notes that "while [Chekhov's] characters seem to exist in isolated pockets of vacancy, they are all integral parts of a close network of interlocking motives and effects. Thus, while the dialogue seems to wander aimlessly . . . it is economically performing a great number of essential dramatic functions."[80] Mamet's dialogue may sometimes seem arbitrary and pointless, but there are always reasons for everything he writes. He imbues his work with recurrent leitmotifs that serve to comment upon the action currently taking place as well as to remind the audience of past events that may have a bearing on it. Teach simply cannot forget the insult he received at the Riverside Cafe, and, throughout the play, he makes little paranoid digs regardless of the context but always when he feels insecure or threatened. In a conversation with Don about the poker game they had played the night before, Teach cites Ruthie as a cheat and Grace as her probable accomplice. Don tries to defend Ruthie—"She's a good card player" (act 1, p. 14)—but Teach will not listen:

> *Teach:* She is *not* a good card player, Don. She is a mooch and she is a locksmith and she plays like a woman. (ibid.)

The absurdity of accusing Ruthie of playing "like a woman" apparently escapes Teach. Later, while trying to convince Don that Fletch also cheats at the game, Teach invokes the women's names again, this time in frustration: "(All day long. Grace and Ruthie Christ.)" (act 2, p. 82). The women are not in any way involved in this particular conversation, but the association of cheating and lack of trust brings them again to Teach's mind. As he prepares to attack Bobby, Teach cites the women again, this time in a mental association with those who, like Bobby, deserve to suffer: ". . .

fuck around with Grace and Ruthie, and you come in here." (act 2, p. 96).

Another recurrent motif is the disappearance of Teach's hat. In act 1, he tries to ascertain its whereabouts, and at the play's conclusion, the subject resurfaces amidst all the chaos: "You got a hat?" he asks, "Do you have a piece of paper?" (act 2, p. 109). Since Don does not have Teach's hat nor another he can lend him, "*Teach walks to the counter, takes a piece of newspaper and starts making himself a paper hat*" (ibid.). As he looks at his reflection in the shop's window, he observes: "I look like a sissy" (ibid.). Teach's missing hat has served several distinctly different dramatic purposes. To begin with, it provides an early illustration of his neurotic and untrusting nature and, secondly, it acts as an anchor subject during a conversation that has nothing whatever to do with it— Teach's thought associations, however, *make* it something of relevance. In the last scene, the missing hat is used to diffuse the tension and to inject humor into a tragic situation. It also points to Teach's self-consciousness as he realizes that he has been mistaken. His "I look like a sissy" is both a truthful comment and a half-hearted attempt at reconciliation by making himself seem faintly ridiculous. The sight of Teach in his homemade paper hat renders him a patently absurd figure trying both to hold on to his dignity and to buy the sympathy of Bob and Don.

The humor in *American Buffalo*, often emanating from recognition, arises from the simplicity of the language itself. A very amusing—and true—scene occurs at the conclusion of act 1 when Teach is about to leave Don's shop to take a nap:

Teach: And I'll see you around eleven.
Don: O'clock.
Teach: Here.
Don: Right.
Teach: And don't worry about anything.
Don: I won't.
Teach: I don't want to hear you're worrying about a goddamned thing.
Don: You won't, Teach.
Teach: You're sure you want Fletch coming with us?
Don: Yes.
Teach: All right, then, so long as you're sure.
Don: I'm sure, Teach.
Teach: Then I'm going to see you tonight.
Don: Goddamn right you are.
Teach: I am seeing you later.

Don: I know.
Teach: Good-bye.
Don: Good-bye. (act 1, pp. 57–58)

Mamet told Ross Wetzsteon that he was really pleased with this scene:

> Some of my favorite writing is at the end of Act I . . . that "See you later" scene. . . . I'm so glad you liked that. That is exactly the kind of thing I am trying to capture in my plays. Have you ever listened to two people trying to say goodbye on the phone? Especially in a business situation. They just cannot say goodbye. And their language is so revealing of their relationship. All those quid pro quos. Who owes what to whom? They can end up saying "okay, okay, okay" for half an hour. I think I have a gift for that kind of attentuated scene.[81]

American Buffalo is a brilliant play that can be viewed on a number of different levels: as a satire on modern America, as a critique of the American business ethic, and as an exposé of the decline of communication in urban society. When asked what he hopes to achieve with his work, Mamet replied: "I hope what I'm arguing for, finally and lately, has been an *a priori* spirituality. Let's look at the things that finally matter."[82] If there is little space within his plays where such spirituality can thrive, there remains a faint possibility of redemption. Like Tennessee Williams, Arthur Miller, and Edward Albee before him, Mamet laments the debasement of the American Dream into something cheap and worthless. For him, his country has lost an essential innocence, which is very forcefully dramatized in the convoluted immorality of *American Buffalo*. Christopher Bigsby observes how "the America his characters inhabit is shapeless. Its animating principles survive only as a collection of rhetorical pieties drained of all meaning and moral content."[83] However, Mamet tenaciously holds on to the hope that, by confronting the immense problems head-on, he can inspire a sense of purpose, a need to create order in a depressing confusion.

At the end of the play, the audience is left with a wrecked junk shop and an injured and bleeding boy. However, that boy is being taken to the hospital by one man who sincerely cares about him, and another who needs love as much as he.

3

A Life in the Theatre

Without exception, all of Mamet's characters are storytellers or performers—or both. They are somewhat like O'Neill's gallery of misfits in *The Iceman Cometh;* rather than face the realities of an uncertain, often threatening world, they rely upon illusion and the performance of a comforting role to get by. Actors all, they prefer the relative security and coherence of their fictional "pipe dreams" to the incompleteness and ambiguousness of cold experience.

In Mamet's world, to act is also to exist, to make a mark in space. His characters take on their myriad roles to create meaning in their lives, and to give themselves importance and substance. That these roles are sometimes as unsatisfactory as the reality they are designed to conceal is one of the recurring ironies of his work. In *A Life in the Theatre*, Mamet's characters are literally actors, professional players who perform in public as a career. However, Robert and John do not restrict their acting abilities to the stage— they are actors both in and out of the theatre. They put on the costumes and makeup for the drama they must perform as actors, but Mamet makes it very clear that the roles they perform onstage are but a small part of their mimetic gifts. They never stop acting; from the moment they awake to the moment they go to sleep, Robert and John are each performing a role for the benefit of the other. They strive to reinforce their own self-images as they quibble, bicker, and generally try to upstage one another. Their "real-life" performances become hopelessly confused and merge with the characters they represent.

When Mel Gussow first saw the play, he described it as "a comedy about the artifice of acting"[1] but when, some months later, he saw a revival, he felt that "it was about the artifice of living."[2] The very title of the work gives a clue to Mamet's intentions: it is at once a parody of Stanislavski's autobiography, *My Life in Art* and an indication of the analogy he intends to make between life and drama. It also points to the pastiche he will use affectionately throughout the play and subtly suggests the serious elements that both offset and contribute to its humor.

A Life in the Theatre is primarily a comedy, but one that is not without pathos. Mamet describes the work as a "comedy about actors"[3] but goes on to say that

> as such it must be, and is, slightly sad. It is, I think, the essential and by no means unfortunate nature of the theater that it is always dying: and the great strength and beauty of actors is their bravery and generosity in this least stable of environments. They are generous and brave not through constraint of circumstances, but by choice. They give their time in training, in rehearsal, in constant thought about their instrument and their art and the characters which they portray.[4]

In an essay about the play, Mamet quotes Camus as saying that the actor's task "is a prime example of the Sisyphean nature of life."[5] Even as that metaphorical rock begins to roll backward, the actor doggedly continues with the struggle. Further he notes how "a life in the theater need not be an analogue to 'life.' It *is* life."[6] For example, Robert is terrified of losing his touch, of growing old and becoming obsolete in the modern world, hence his insistence upon the necessity for actors to grow and accept change—although change is, in fact, the last thing he can accept. At the beginning of the play, John is full of the insecurities of youth: he is naïve, eager to please, and most reverential of his older colleague. As the work progresses, however, his reverence turns to contempt and irritation as he comes to believe—perhaps erroneously—in his own star quality.

Mamet recalls Sanford Meisner humorously remembering a certain kind of actor, whom it is wise to avoid: "When you go into the professional world, at a stock theatre somewhere, backstage, you will meet an older actor—someone who has been around a while. . . . Ignore this man."[7] Freddie Jones, who played Robert in the 1979 Open Space production agrees that this character can be exasperating, but also points out that he fulfills an important function in the work: "The play is an allegory about death and rebirth—Robert is on the wane and the young actor is on the way up."[8]

Evanescence is a fundamental concern in *A Life in the Theatre;* an actor's life is, of necessity, evanescent; there is nothing fixed about a stage performance. At the end of the evening, the player's exploits live on only in the imagination of the audience. As a result, Mamet believes that "this is why theatrical still photographs are many times stiff and uninteresting—the player in them is not *acting* . . . but *posing—indicating feelings.*"[9]

Actors constantly tell each other stories because "the only real history of the ephemeral art is an oral history; everything fades very quickly, and the only surety is the word of someone who was there, who *talked* to someone who was there, who vouches for the fact that someone told him she had spoken to a woman who knew someone who was there. It all goes very quickly, too."[10] As Mamet notes, Robert relies upon ephemera and nostalgia to capture important memories, recall past glories, and reflect upon his career. In spite of his assertions that he is "modern" in outlook, Robert's speech is florid, hyperbolic—sometimes positively Victorian in nature. In an ecstasy of theatrical self-indulgence, he speaks of

> A life spent in the theatre. . . . Backstage. . . . The bars, the House, the drafty halls. The pencilled scripts . . . Stories. Ah, the stories that you hear. (scene 26, p. 55)

This is not the speech of everyday conversation: it is studied, pretentious, and melodramatic. Robert is not acting a part here, but merely making random observations about his experience of theatrical life. It is clear that the often overripe diction of certain melodramas has influenced him to the extent that even the most ordinary discourse is imbued with theatricality and exaggeration. Thus, Robert clings to the past because it comforts him to do so. Old-fashioned diction lends him a specious sense of security as he battles to fend off fears of impending obsolescence—in and out of the theatre.

The main metaphor of the play is, as the title suggests, that all life is a kind of theatre. Here, as elsewhere in his drama, Mamet seems to be saying that the kind of life his characters are forced to endure is a second-hand affair, full of clichés and desperate pretensions. Not only this, but their metaphysical position is unclear. In *A Life in the Theatre*, perhaps more obviously than in his other works, Mamet depicts the absurdity of the human condition. In the image of the solitary actor speaking out into an empty space, he conveys not merely the egoistic need for posturing center-stage by an affected narcissist, but the futility and desperation of man's uncertainty of his place in the universe. The potency of the image is clearly intended to extend far beyond the theatre into a question concerning the very existence of God. In *Rosencrantz and Guildenstern are Dead*, Tom Stoppard touches upon a similar theme. The Player cries out in alarm that his one purpose in life as an actor has been seriously undermined—he suddenly realizes that he is performing without an audience:

You don't understand the humiliation of it—to be tricked out of the single assumption which makes our existence viable—that somebody is *watching*."[11]

Similarly, in Arthur Miller's *The Archbishop's Ceiling*, the characters' uncertainty as to whether the seraphically decorated ceiling is bugged or not is surely intended to carry resonances beyond their immediate situation. They conduct their lives as though unseen eyes are indeed watching, but neither they nor the audience are ever able to verify this fact.

The language used by Mamet to convey the ambiguities of life both in front of and away from the footlights seems once again to be effortless and completely authentic. It is, of course, far from effortless but as carefully wrought and constructed as that found in any of his plays. Nothing is included without a reason, every word forwards the plot or comments upon a previous action or emotion. It is true that the text resembles a number of conversations that have been faithfully captured and rendered verbatim. Mamet does indeed include all the ellipses and idiosyncrasies of ordinary conversation but, as John Ditsky has noted, although the dialogue may *appear* banal or merely naturalistic, it is "a deliberately bland language [that] is used to mask action of only apparent simplicity."[12] Mamet allows us to cut through the excesses of Robert's hyperbole and see beneath the brevity of much of John's dialogue by his careful manipulation of every word they utter. He provides a fascinating glimpse into the personalities of men who do all they can to hide their true feelings. Emotions may often run riot in this play, but it would be difficult without Mamet's linguistic virtuosity to ascertain those that are genuine and those that constitute yet another aspect of an unceasing performance. Patrick Ryecart, who played John in the Open Space production considers that

> what Mamet achieves with so little is . . . quite incredible. With so few words, he can tell us all we need to know about Robert and John. He achieves amazing economy. He must write a great deal in the beginning and then set about bringing it right down, paring and paring, getting the words down to the narrative bone. The text of *A Life in the Theatre* is not only supremely funny, but also brilliant in its conciseness.[13]

A Life in the Theatre is a kind of love letter to everything Mamet holds dear about the stage and its performers. The lines of the text are imbued with a sweetness and affection that are not wholly negated by the often critical stance adopted by the playwright. Like Chekhov, Mamet has the ability to like and even admire his characters at the same time as exposing their weaknesses and faults. Mamet's own summary of the play is that it is "an attempt to look with love at an institution we all love, The Theater, and at the only component of that institution (about whom our feelings are less simple), the men and women of the theater—the world's heartiest mayflies, whom we elect and appoint to live out our dreams upon the stage."[14]

The work was first staged in 1975 at the Goodman Theatre, Chicago and was then produced in 1977 at the off-Broadway Theatre-de-Lys in New York City. Since then, it has enjoyed a number of revivals, the most recent of which was at the Open Space Theatre, London in 1979. The play has been described by Michael Coveney as being "rather like Terence Rattigan's *Harlequinade*, with a nod in the direction of Molnar [*Play at the Castle*] and Pirandello [*Six Characters in Search of an Author*]."[15] Although Mamet has expressed his admiration for Rattigan's work, and there is certainly more than a hint of Molnar's verbal trickery in the play, the presiding genius of *A Life in the Theatre* is undoubtedly Luigi Pirandello. In both his dramas and his fiction, Pirandello, like Mamet, creates works that explore the many faces of reality. He examines the relationships between actor and character, self and persona, and face and mask, and was a precursor of the work of writers such as Anouilh (*Dear Antoine*), Giraudoux (*Intermezzo*), Genet (*The Balcony* and *The Maids*), and Stoppard (*Rosencrantz and Guildenstern are Dead*), all of which explore the possibilities inherent in such a concept. Pirandello wrote:

> Your reality is a mere transitory and fleeting illusion, taking this form today and that tomorrow, according to the conditions, according to your will, your sentiments, which in turn are controlled by an intellect that shows them to you today in one manner and tomorrow . . . who knows how? Illusions of reality, represented in this fatuous comedy of life that never ends, nor can ever end.[16]

In *Six Characters in Search of an Author,* a company of actors rehearses a play, which is itself an illusion of reality. As the rehearsals progress, six created characters—other aspects of illusion—enter and interrupt the proceedings. Raymond Williams describes how "the resulting contrast between these various stages in the process of dramatic illusion, and the relation of the process to its context of reality, is the material of Pirandello's play."[17] Michael Billington notes how Mamet demonstrates that "the theatre [is] a place that both imitates life and devours it. . . . where . . . actors begin to feel trapped inside their stage roles. . . . one gets so occupied with representing life one ceases to notice it passing one by."[18]

Certainly Robert's life has been "spent" in the theatre in every sense of the word. He explains to John how his life as an actor cannot be separated from that which he lives when not onstage—the time spent somehow merging and becoming one:

> Robert: . . . the theatre is of course, a *part* of life. . . . I'm saying, as in a grocery store that you cannot separate the *time* one spends . . . that is it's all part of one's *life*. (*Pause.*) In addition to the fact that what's happening on *stage* is life . . . (scene 23, p. 48)

Robert has become so much a creature of the theatre that his own identity is unclear. Robert, the man, puts on the mask of Robert, the actor; that Robert is himself a character played by a real actor merely adds to the metadramatic ironies. Where does reality end and fantasy begin? A mock-prayer spoken by Guildenstern in Stoppard's play accurately sums up the fantasy life into which it is all too easy for actors to retreat when he intones "Give us this day our daily mask."[19]

In *A Life in the Theatre,* Mamet constantly blurs the boundaries between life and art, and the work has been described by Mel Gussow as "a triple Pirandello." He observes how "the actors play to [an] imaginary audience, while we, behind the scenes, see and hear the artifice—the asides, whispers and blunders."[20] The real theatre audience watches two actors playing another two actors, who in turn perform to an unseen audience apparently located at the opposite end of the stage. We see Robert and John perform to their audience with their backs toward us, whereas when Mamet's play proper is in progress, they play facing outward into the stalls. This is the way in which the first American production was staged, and Mamet has called this staging "a beautiful solution."[21] He goes on to explain how it operates in practice:

> . . . Gregory Mosher and Michael Merritt, the play's first director and designer, respectively. . . . decided that it might be provocative if, a *second* curtain were installed—this one on the *upstage* portion of the stage. It is behind this curtain that the audience for the "plays" in which John and Robert play sits. This curtain is opened when John and Robert are onstage, which is to say, playing in a "play." Thus we

see the actors' backs during the *onstage* scenes, and we get a full-face view of them during their moments *backstage*.[22]

The theatre audience therefore listens to the characters' backstage gossip, witnesses the ambiguity between the roles they inhabit onstage and their real selves, follows the inexorable shifts in power, and learns to detect the reality behind what looks artificial and the speciousness of what is presented as truth. Patrick Ryecart speaks about the metadramatic ironies within the work:

> The kind of play which constantly reminds the audience that it *is* indeed a play can become very tedious and rather patronizing. However, Mamet is very good with this in *A Life in the Theatre*. In our production, we had a mirror at the back of the set which enclosed the audience even more within the piece, making them really feel a part of it . . . they were thus brought right into the action in a very unselfconscious way. Not only this, but Mamet brings them into the action in another, brilliant way: on the first page of the text you have a direct reference to them. John says, "They were very bright" and goes on to flatter them further. They were "an intelligent house," he says, "attentive," and so on. Mamet includes at least five instances of direct audience flattery within the first few moments of the play![23]

The playwright therefore incorporates the outside world into the work, fusing theatre and reality in a memorable dramatic form. Robert's benediction at the conclusion of the play, addressed to a supposedly absent audience but in fact spoken to the real stalls, similarly identifies a gesture of incorporation. Robert stands alone center-stage as he delivers his farewell speech:

> *Robert:* . . . The lights dim. Each to his own home. Goodnight. Goodnight. Goodnight. (scene 26, p. 56)

Much of the humor in the play derives from Robert's pompous efforts to link life and drama. Whereas Mamet is in no doubt whatever that direct connections do exist, he invests Robert's linguistic forays on this topic with an undercutting irony and wit. Robert has a certain idea of himself as a consummate professional, what has been called "a flamboyant actor of the old school,"[24] an "old Wolfitian barnstormer,"[25] as well as "an ageing, histrionic bombast."[26] Patrick Ryecart comments upon Robert's self-importance and hilarious egotism, and marvels "at his ability to be such a huge fish in such a tiny, insignificant building . . . such as the third-rate rep theatre in which he obviously works."[27] Because of Robert's many years in the theatre, he feels perfectly justified to act as John's mentor and guide, endlessly pointing out the ambiguities of and the connections between life and art. He strives to maintain his sense of superiority and worldliness by prattling on incessantly about the importance of the theatre. He grandly avers:

> *Robert:* Our history goes back as far as Man's. Our aspirations in the Theatre are much the *same* as man's. *(Pause.)* Don't you think? . . . We are explorers of the *soul.* (scene 5, p. 23)

and later

> *Robert:* About the theatre, and this is a wondrous thing about the theatre, and John, one of the ways in which it's most like life. . . . in the *theatre,* as in life—and the theatre is . . . a *part* of life. . . . of one's *life.* . . . what's happening on *stage* is life . . . of a sort . . . I mean, it's part of your *life.* (scene 23, p. 48)

The way in which Robert emphatically underscores the words "theatre," "stage," and "life" suggests the urgency he feels in communicating some of what he believes to be his profound insight. Mamet breaks up his sentences, making him begin again and again without finishing and inserting phrases such as "of course," "of a sort," and "I mean." All this serves to undercut the portentousness—and pretentiousness—of the tone. Robert believes he has a truly important task to perform; however, he is constantly shown to be full of self-delusion and evasion and his hyperbolic remarks are therefore somewhat diminished in the light of our knowledge of his true state of mind. He struggles to find meaning in banality because to admit the frailty of his position as a third-rate actor struggling to make a living on the very fringe of the profession would be to invite terror and despair. Tennessee Williams once wrote that "fear and evasion are the two little beasts that chase each other's tails in the revolving wire cage of our nervous world. They distract us from feeling too much about things."[28] Fear and evasion are certainly present behind Robert's false bluster and phony air of confidence. So long as he can keep on talking, inventing, and pontificating, he can convince himself—and, hopefully, others—of his importance as an actor.

Robert has become the kind of performer who gives his all to plays that do not warrant such devotion; nagging doubts about his worth force him to struggle to find depth where none exists and to give performances of almost Shakespearian profundity in scenes that are little more than badly-scripted soap operas. Certainly, none of the scenes we witness bear any scrutiny whatsoever: they are laughable because of their in-built pretentiousness. Watching Robert and John flinging themselves wholeheartedly into such poorly-crafted episodes is a source of much humor and reminds the audience that the two men are very far from the center of American theatrical excellence. Indeed, they spend their time playing to half-hearted provincial audiences who are probably among the "bloody boors," "bloody shits," and "boring lunatics" (scene 10, pp. 31–32) whom Robert decries in a fit of rage.

Although both players seem to be dedicated to the work they are given to perform, it is Robert who works doggedly to invest their dreadful scripts with some sort of artistic credibility and, amazingly, finds it! As he and John discuss the "Lifeboat" scene, Robert waxes lyrical about the script's 'profundity':

> *Robert;* . . . I'm just thinking. "Salt. Saltwater." Eh? The thought. He lets you see the thought there. . . . Salt! Sweat. His life flows out. . . . Then salt*water!* Eh? . . . "Kid, we haven't got a chance in hell.". . . . "We're never getting out of this alive." *(Pause.)* Eh? He sets it on the sea, we are marooned, he tells us that the sea is life, and that we're never getting out of it alive. *(Pause.).* . . . The man could write. . . . Alright. Alright. (scene 13, pp. 34–35)

Mamet invests a scene like this with just enough evidence of the sheer tawdriness of the material Robert and John are given, and then goes on to show the older actor in ecstasy at the quality of the text. All his pretensions fritter away before us while he remains gloriously unaware of the absurdity of his position. The heavy significance of his words act as a hilarious correlative to the tackiness of the script. He sounds like a particularly anxious— although naïve—undergraduate faced with his first essay in literary criticism—his frequent use of "Eh?" acts as an indication of a need for approbation and a shared opinion. Mamet ends the discussion of this particular slice of dialogue with Robert's assertion that "the man could write. . . . Alright. Alright." The repetition suggests a mind mulling over what it considers to be first-class literature, pondering on the brilliance of one who could garner so much meaning, so much *life* into a metaphor about the sea. Robert's previous experience as an actor has apparently taught him little about quality writing; it is quite absurd that he should admire that which is so blatantly hackneyed and risible.

Elsewhere, Robert talks about the trite legal drama in which he and John are about to perform. John asks him how he is feeling as they prepare to go onstage:

John: . . . How do you feel this evening?
Robert: Tight. I feel a little tight. It's going to be a vibrant show tonight.
   I feel coiled up.
John: Mmm.
Robert: But I don't feel tense. . . . Never feel tense. I almost never feel
   tense on stage. I feel ready to act. (scene 8, p. 25)

The repetition of the words "tight" and "tense" indicate the extent
of Robert's nervousness, despite his denials. The way he almost
spits out his response to John's initial query suggests the reaction
of one who is not merely "coiled up" but rather pitched on the
edge of nervous collapse. The alliterative sound of the repeated *t*
adds to the tension and demonstrates all too clearly Robert's
deep-rooted anxiety. That he should refer to the show as "vibrant"
and declaim in the manner of an Olivier or a Gielgud that he is
"ready to act" is quickly shown to be an absurd pretension given
the vacuity of the scene that follows in which stage props refuse to
work properly, cues are missed, and both actors go completely to
pieces with a script that would shame a troupe of amateur players.

   Robert may elevate the theatre into a kind of holy shrine for the
worship of moral values and all that is laudable and pure, but he is
all too capable of indulging in spiteful and cruel denigrations of
his fellow performers. Life in the theatre and life outside have
merged for Robert and become hopelessly confused. When he
speaks of an actress whom he despises for her unnecessary "mug-
ging" and "mincing," he mixes up moral standards and theatrical
technique. He avers that the woman has "No soul . . . no human-
ism. . . . No fellow-feeling. . . . No formal training. . . . No sense
of right and wrong" (scene 1, pp. 13–14). Thus "soul" and "formal
training" are inextricably linked in Robert's mind. What the
actress *is* probably guilty of is daring to upstage him and what we
are witnessing is little more than petulant jealousy.

   In a mistaken effort to side with Robert against the woman,
John comments that she relies on her looks to get by:

John: She capitalizes on her beauty. *(Pause.)*
Robert: What beauty?
John: Her attractiveness.
Robert: Yes.
John: It isn't really beauty.
Robert: No.
John: Beauty comes from within.
Robert: Yes, I feel it does. (scene 1, p. 14)

Patrick Ryecart comments on this scene:

> At this stage, John hangs onto every word Robert utters. He wants to establish a bond, a trust, a feeling that they are in league together and plunges ahead rather recklessly. He thinks he will be pleasing Robert but actually succeeds in rather annoying him. This sort of conversation is so true, so superbly caught . . . people getting themselves into corners whilst trying to flatter or please and then having to eat their words.[29]

Despite his irritation, Robert knows that John is trying to please him and feels smugly secure in the knowledge that he has the young man on his side. He even lets John lead the conversation, a rare event indeed. It is very infrequently that Robert responds to a remark with only a monosyllabic "yes" or "no," but on this occasion he feels confident enough to restrict his comments. His complacency is momentarily rattled, but John qualifies his statement about beauty by offering, by way of atonement, the assertion that the woman's charm "isn't really beauty." He is anxious not to upset what he currently sees as the fine sensibilities of his companion. Once Robert's responses have assured him that all is still well and that they are friends, John even chances a platitude: "Beauty comes from within." It could almost be Robert speaking here, clichés to the fore.

Robert may lecture John about the importance of good behavior, sensitivity, and the evolution of theatrical "etiquette," but such sentiments are easily jettisoned when his own security is threatened. Far from behaving in a gentlemanly fashion, he calls the actress a "cunt" and announces that he would willingly murder her if he thought he could get away with it (ibid., p. 13). Later, he swears at John, calling him a "fucking twit" (scene 22, p. 47); Mamet utilizes the irony in John's overly polite reply, "I beg your pardon" to consolidate further our doubts about Robert's claims that he embodies all things fine and elevated in the theatre.

To make quite certain that the audience should not even momentarily take Robert a little too seriously, Mamet deflates his pomposity by having him use the most hackneyed clichés ("the show goes on", scene 1, p. 13 and "good things for good folk," scene 14, p. 37) or, more frequently, by setting his speeches in contexts that by their very nature undermine their seriousness. For example, he rambles on about the necessity to *"grow"* as artists while John is practicing at the barre: the latter is more concerned with looking at his own reflection in the rehearsal room mirror than with listening to Robert's platitudes yet again. Consequently, he responds infrequently and appears to practice selective deafness, not really taking in what is being said. The scene ends with his prosaic question, "Is my back straight?" to which Robert can only reply, "no" (scene 5, p. 24). Elsewhere, John interrupts his colleague's speeches with such demotic remarks as, "Please pass the bread" (scene 14, p. 36), "How's your duck?" (ibid.), and "May I use your brush?" (scene 17, p. 40). He also frequently responds to Robert's speechifying with an "mmm," a linguistic tic Robert himself adopts toward the end of the play, signifying the level of influence the younger man gradually exerts over him.

Mamet describes one of the play's intentions as a means of delineating a turning point in the acting careers of the two players. However, the actual moment of change is ambiguous. Mamet notes how "the event we have decided on as the turning point . . . was, looking back, quite probably not it at all."[30] Nevertheless, it is clear that Robert views *any* change with caution and trepidation. He tells John that the process of life is "a little like a play" (scene 5, p. 23) in which "you start from the beginning and go through the middle and wind up at the end" (ibid.). As Robert speaks airily about his favorite analogy, Mamet imbues his words with fear. That acting, like life, has a beginning, a middle, and an end is a sobering thought for Robert. As he speaks, the logic of his narrative pulls him inexorably into dangerous and frightening areas. Like those of Emil and George in *The Duck Variations*, Robert's speeches have a habit of wandering into territory he would rather not explore.

Patrick Ryecart describes as "those terrible scenes"[31] the episodes in which Robert pathetically lingers backstage to hear the voice of the new generation as it practices onstage and where, tragically, he attempts to cut his wrists. Robert is a genuinely tragic figure, but one who is drawn without sentimentality or condescension. Freddie Jones notes how "The character of Robert is drawn with great powers of observation and is completely without sentimentality. The writing is witty, observant, but never sentimental. What's sentimental about getting old? . . . Mamet's writing is astute and compassionate, not sloppy."[32] Patrick Ryecart believes the work is wholly without cloying sentimentality:

I don't think it is at all sentimental. On the contrary, it is often very harsh. Even in those terrible scenes where Robert stays behind and the young actor catches him watching and listening with great sadness . . . and where he tries to slash his wrists . . . these are totally unsentimental. It would have been easy for Mamet to veer over the edge but he does not. . . . There is nothing remotely excessive or cloying in the play. Each situation arises quite naturally out of the text.[33]

This is a view which is not shared by Milton Shulman who avers that "there is a hollow and artificial ring to this sentimentalised portrayal of the life-style of actors."[34] Mamet walks a fine line between genuine pathos and overt sentimentality, and mostly succeeds in avoiding the latter. Colin Stinton has observed how the playwright is constantly—even pathologically—aware of and on the lookout for "creeping sentimentality"[35] in his work and will go to great lengths to excise all traces of it. In *A Life in the Theatre*, Mamet wishes to demonstrate the generosity and bravery of actors but, in so doing, realizes that he must temper any potential sentimental incursions with irony. Perhaps he goes a little too far. He is at such pains to show up the pretentiousness of Robert and the rampant ambition of John that, although we still regard them with affection, we also see them diminished as representatives of their profession. However, in spite of his characters' inadequacies—perhaps even because of them—we do enjoy Mamet's representation of their experiences and attitudes. There is also an often unstated but nonetheless tacit expression of friendship in the play; despite Mamet's ironic deflations, the bond that exists between Robert and John ensures that we regard them with warmth and empathy.

The depiction of character through language is wonderfully accurate in this play. Each actor's speech changes subtly throughout to indicate his present mood and John's move from gauche naïveté at the beginning of the work to unnerving self-reliance by the end is superbly controlled. John has less showy dialogue than Robert but this is no way detracts from the power of his presence. Of this aspect of Mamet's writing, Patrick Ryecart says:

> It all comes down to reaction to Robert's words . . . John "speaks" just as much as if he had three pages of dialogue—You can make or break an entire speech just by your reaction . . . If reaction is not catered for in the writing then it is a different thing . . . but in a good play with good writing (as this has) it doesn't matter if a character has ten minutes of silence—if its relevance is there, then it is fully justified.[36]

There *is* a bond that unites Robert and John, but its strength is sometimes weakened, as in the latter's eventual move away from his colleague. John no longer feels he need tolerate Robert's end-less rhetoric and this is shown through the almost monosyllabic quality of most of his lines, a brevity that demonstrates all too clearly his impatience and exasperation. However, Patrick Ryecart insists that John's behavior is perfectly understandable; he does not see him as a cold and callous individual, but merely one who is quite naturally trying to get on with his own career and avoid the proselytizing excesses of his garrulous friend. Ryecart sug-gests John does not mean to be cruel and his gradual rejection of Robert is entirely legitimate.

> You cannot have a relationship that goes beyond working with every-one. . . . Robert has been such a bloody old bore that, frankly, you can't blame John for his coolness, if that is what it is. I *know* these types like Robert; they sit in their dressing rooms with a little tin of sardines and they drone on and on and they are so *boring*. . . . It isn't necessarily coldness or cruelty . . . I would argue that it is not callous for John to want to get away from such a person.[37]

However, in spite of such assertions in defense of John's character, Mamet's play does hint at his dismissive nature and his brash, ambitious manner. His language is terse, even curt, and his re-sponses to Robert's verbal forays take on a rather brutal impa-tience. He becomes patronizing and sarcastic, apparently absorbing the very worst aspects of Robert's personality. This is clearly *not* the kind of education that Robert had in mind! Where once John was eager to please, in the later stages of the play he becomes arrogant and rude. His actions may be understandable, given the often trying circumstances he has to endure, but Mamet ensures that he is, nonetheless, seen as rather cool and calcu-lating.

A good example of the gradual change in the actors' rela-tionship occurs when John tries to rehearse alone onstage. Sud-denly Robert appears and launches into a long speech that is both dubiously flattering and coolly critical of the younger man's work. John is irritated enough to indulge in a little sarcasm; he decides to mock Robert by echoing one of his favorite theatrical terms, "fitting":

> *Robert:* . . . It's good. It's *quite* good. I was watching you for a while. I hope you don't mind. Do you mind?
> *John:* I've only been here a minute or so.
> *Robert:* And I've watched you all that time. It seemed so long. It was so full. You're very good, John. Have I told you that lately? You are

becoming a very fine actor. The flaws of youth are the perquisite of the young. It is the perquisite of the Young to possess the flaws of youth.

John: It's fitting, yes . . .

Robert: Ah, don't mock me, John. You shouldn't mock me. It's too easy. (scene 23, p. 48)

John can perceive the edge to Robert's "flattering" remarks; Robert observes that he had watched John "all that time"—a period that was apparently only a minute or two. The implication is surely not that John is mesmerizing in his ability to fit so much power and meaning into his acting but that he is laboring the point, spinning out what should be brief and succinct. To counteract this inference and to play it safe, Robert immediately states that John is becoming "a very fine actor." However, he then deflates this by mentioning "the flaws of youth" and then, in another verbal swerve, reverts to complimentary remarks about John's abilities—although he is almost certainly insincere. His use of the rather archaic word "perquisite"—twice—is another indication of his fussy and pedantic nature; it is no doubt intended to demonstrate his learning and superior command over language, but probably only succeeds in irritating rather than impressing John. There is in this exchange a sour sense of the alienation that is gradually developing between the two men; they no longer speak to one another as they once did and now expend their energies trying to falsely flatter or deflate egos. Robert's habit of referring to the "fitness" of things has obviously rankled John to the extent that he now nastily throws a mocking echo of it into Robert's face.

Robert's last remark, "You shouldn't mock me. It's too easy," can be interpreted in two contrasting ways. His plain and simple diction is in marked contrast to his usual verbose style and could be intended to indicate that this is indeed the real Robert. The mask of pretense has been momentarily cast aside and the true identity of the man is revealed. A bitter, self-deprecating irony can be detected in the words and, for the first time in the play, Robert is perhaps acknowledging his own absurdity and egotism. On the other hand, he may be simply admonishing John for using sarcasm to demonstrate his irritation; as a professional, John should be able to counter any attack by means more worthy than parody.

The reversal in dependence that occurs in Robert and John's relationship in fact begins much earlier. One of the most powerful aspects of the work is the peerlessly executed role delineation and subsequent role reversal that begins on the first page of the script and is concluded, neatly and succinctly, on the last. Patrick Ryecart observes how

> there are two little instances of dialogue, right at the beginning and right at the end, which convey what the whole play is about. At the beginning, Robert says to John: "I thought the bedroom scene tonight was brilliant"—or words to that effect—to which John eagerly replies, "Did you?" He is at this stage delighted to have the praise of a respected and revered colleague. In the last scene, Robert says: "I loved the staircase scene tonight" to which John now replies: "You did?" It's so subtle but the effect of the two is totally different. The nuance is entirely changed. John's new-found confidence and maturity just shines out . . . so Mamet, with those four little words, two at the start and two at the finish, conveys the essence of the piece. . . . The role reversal happens throughout the play but is set off by the opening words. . . . There are probably examples on every page in which you can see how Mamet builds up the sense of changing attitudes.[38]

A further hint of irony is injected in that Robert's first compliment concerns the "bedroom scene" whereas at the end it is the "execution scene" that is discussed. Robert's professional "death" is thus carefully made ready by Mamet. It *is* tempting to read significance into the choice of bedroom scene—with its suggestions of intimacy and even regeneration—and the execution scene, which carries its own obvious implications.

Another good example of reversal in dependency occurs after an audition at which John believes he has done very well. He has received some good notices from the critics and these have, perhaps not surprisingly, made him a little conceited:

> *Robert:* They've praised you too much. I do not mean to detract from your reviews, you deserve praise, John, much praise. . . . Not, however, for those things which they have praised you for.
> *John:* In your opinion. (scene 22, p. 46)

Robert continues to advise John not to take what the critics have to say too seriously, until John is moved to respond:

> *John:* I thought that they were rather to the point.
> *Robert:* You did.
> *John:* Yes.
> *Robert:* Your reviews.
> *John:* Yes.
> *Robert:* All false modesty aside.
> *John:* Yes.

Robert: Oh, the Young, the Young, the Young, the Young.
John: The Farmer in the Dell. (ibid., pp. 46–47)

Mamet captures the slightly bitchy, though ostentatiously sincere diction of an actor like Robert. There is more than a touch of effeminate spite in his remarks and Mamet picks up on his linguistic slip in the line, "Not, however, for those things which they have praised you for," undercutting the words of Robert, a man who believes he has a superior command over language. As John defends his position, Robert half-smilingly patronizes him with short statements intended to annoy him. In case John should somehow miss the subtle deflation of all this, Robert then flounces off into what he wishes to convey as an affectionate scoff at the charming pretensions of youth. John remains quite unamused, responding only with the sardonic: "The Farmer in the Dell" with its echoes of nursery rhymes and childhood, perhaps intended to suggest Robert's incipient senility and imbecilic childishness.

Rival recriminations notwithstanding, both men know that they are engaged in something of an uphill battle to survive and this knowledge unites them. There are a number of overtly affectionate scenes scattered throughout the work, but perhaps the most touching of these occurs when John removes a smear of greasepaint from behind Robert's ear:

John: Here. I'll get it. . . . No. Wait, We'll get it off. . . . There.
Robert: Did we get it off?
John: Yes. (scene 1, p. 17)

John's language is paternalistic, even down to the plurality of, "We'll get it off." He changes from the singular pronoun to the plural in order to render the sentence more intimate, something that Robert immediately notices and to which he responds,—in fact, he then uses the same style of speech. Moments later, *he* takes on the parental role; John throws the crumpled tissue toward the wastebasket but misses. Robert picks it up *"and deposits it in the appropriate receptacle"* murmuring: "Alright. All gone. Let's go. *(Pause.)* Eh?" (ibid.).

There is, in this scene—and elsewhere in the play—the suggestion that there may be some latent homosexual feelings between the two men, although neither Patrick Ryecart nor Freddie Jones agree that any such implication exists. It is difficult to completely reject this inference, particularly when considering the scene in which Robert's fly breaks and John tries to fix it. Robert's exhortations for John to hurry up surely suggest more than a mere plea for speed; the double entendres practically collide as they spill out. The scene begins innocently enough:

> *Robert:* My zipper's broken.
> *John:* Do you want a safety pin?
> *Robert:* I have one. *(Looking for safety pin.)*
> *John: (Rising, starting to leave.)* Do you want me to send the woman in?
> *Robert:* No. No. I'll manage. Shit. Oh, shit. (scene 8, p. 27)

Even here there are subliminal suggestions of what may follow. Having refused the attentions of the "woman," Robert struggles with the pin until John is moved to offer his assistance:

> *John:* Oh, come on. I'll do it. Come on. *(Pulls out chair.)* Get up here. Come on. Get up. *(Robert gets up on the chair.)* Give me the pin. Come on . . . (ibid., p. 28)

They lose the safety pin, but John finally sees it and begins again:

> *John:* Stand still now.
> *Robert:* Come on, come on. *(John puts his face up against Robert's crotch.)* Put it in.
> *John:* Just hold still for a moment.
> *Robert:* Come *on*, for God's sake.
> *John:* Alright. Alright. You know I think you're gaining weight . . .
> *Robert:* Oh, fuck you. Will you stick it in.
> *John:* Hold still. There. (scene 8, pp. 27–28)

Apart from being hilariously "naturalistic" dialogue that conveys Robert's desperation as he tries to get ready in time for his cue, Mamet's dialogue imbues both actors' speech with a subtly suggestive harmony. The repetition of pseudosexual phrases, such as "Come on" and "Hold still," deftly contributes to the flirtatious undercurrent of the scene. As it moves towards its conclusion, and John is placed with *"his face up against Robert's crotch,"* the scene provides John with a deliciously cheeky quip, which is at once an acknowledgment of the physical intimacy of the moment and a mildly sarcastic observation of the kind that might be frequently utilized by homosexual or effeminate men. The tone is quite different from that of the first scene, when Robert comments upon his weight problem and John replies: "You're having trouble with your weight? . . . But you're trim enough" (scene 1, p. 16).

John may not be absolutely sincere in his flattery, but there is at this stage no trace in his tone of the impertinent and rather effeminate stance he later adopts. Robert's response to John's later saucy remark is itself suggestive and almost equally flirtatious; he responds with an obscenity (which may even be a half-conscious wish!) and an exhortation that it is difficult to ignore as yet another double entendre. Such a reading of certain scenes should not, however, be viewed as the mainspring of Mamet's intention in the play. Homosexuality may well be a subtext in specific instances, but *A Life in the Theatre* is not a work wholly concerned with the subject. To view it in this manner is to seriously diminish its impact and to lessen the subtlety of Mamet's characterization. It is enough to be aware that such an element probably exists and to leave it at that.

By the last scene in the play, the roles have reversed. It is Robert who is nervous and slightly uneasy in John's company; it is now Robert who accepts John's compliments about his performance with what seems to be excessive gratitude:

John: I thought the execution scene worked beautifully.
Robert: No. You *didn't* . . .
John: Yes. I did. *(Pause.)*
Robert: Thank you . . . (scene 26, p. 54)

It is now Robert who is "not eating too well these days" because he is "not hungry" (ibid., p. 55), as opposed to John who, in the opening scene spoke of not having "had an appetite for several days" (scene 1, p. 10), and it is now Robert who addresses the empty auditorium with a pathos that was not evident in John's earlier solitary speech.

In *A Life in the Theatre*, Mamet's dialogue is, once again, taut with invention. Milton Shulman notes how Mamet "cleverly reproduces those exchanges of hesitant compliments and sly insults that actors use when they discuss each other's performances."[39] Mel Gussow feels that the language in the play "glistens. . . . [it] is a cross between the elegant and the vernacular. . . . [his] timing is as exact as Accutron. . . . he is an eloquent master of two-part harmony."[40] As Robert and John's linguistic battle for supremacy gathers momentum, it is easy to see why Gussow feels that their language "glistens" and why he compares Mamet's timing to "Accutron." In the following scene, the playwright's command over rhythm and subtle inflection reaches its zenith. Robert feels that John is unfairly upstaging him during one of their scenes together and suggests that he should "do less":

Robert: (Pause.) In our scene tonight . . .
John: Yes?
Robert: Mmmm . . .
John: What?
Robert: Could you . . . perhaps . . . *do* less.
John: Do less?
Robert: Yes.
John: Do less???
Robert: Yes . . . *(Pause.)*
John: Do less *what???*
Robert: You know.
John: You mean . . . what do you mean?
Robert: (Pause.) You know.
John: Do you mean I'm walking on your scene? *(Pause.)* What do you
    mean?
Robert: Nothing. It's a thought I had. An aesthetic consideration.
John: Mmm.
Robert: I thought may be if you *did* less . . .
John: Yes?
Robert: You know . . .
John: If I *did* less.
Robert: Yes.
John: Well, thank you for the thought.
Robert: I don't think you have to be like that. (scene 8, pp. 26–27)

Freddie Jones has observed that Mamet's writing in such scenes is "fluid, musical. We really do speak in an iambic pentameter and Mamet's work is never rhythmically erroneous."[41] Patrick Ryecart believes that examples like this scene consolidate Mamet's position as "a superb dramatic poet. There is a strong and true rhythm in the lines which propel the actors along."[42]

The timing here is as acute as that to be found in any music-hall patter; it is reminiscent of the verbal bantering that occurs between many of Beckett's aging burlesques as they bicker and prod one another into responsive action. Robert begins politely and even deferentially, delaying the moment by pauses and contemplative noises, until he feels he can safely make his request. His nervousness and uncertainty as to the exact moment to choose is cleverly conveyed; he is perhaps a little unnerved by the curtness of John's responses, and believes that it may be prudent to wait a moment before stating his case. In the exchange that follows, "Could you . . . perhaps . . . *do* less" to "Do less *what???*" Mamet uses rhyme as well as rhythm. The phrasing is as tight and measured as jazz. Indeed, Patrick Ryecart comments upon Mamet's use of rhythm and rhyme. " 'Do less', 'do less,' 'do less what' . . . the words are so musical. It's like jazz. The rhymes have the rhythms of the purest forms of jazz. I am sure Mamet listens to his texts as music . . . counting the beats, working in the pauses."[43]

John is both outraged and indignant that he should be asked to modify his acting technique. He becomes coldly angry and his tone takes on a hint of menace. Certainly Robert senses the potential danger and negates the request by pretending it was an "aesthetic consideration." When John merely responds with a less threatening "Mmmm," erroneously conveying to Robert a lull in his anger but probably intending contemptuous resignation, Robert decides to take on another tone. In an effort to buy back any lost sympathy, he tries to convey meek insecurity; the use of the uncertain "thought" and "maybe" are clearly intended to deflate the seriousness of his request and to show the unnecessarily ruffled John that it was merely a casual suggestion. When John counters his groveling with sarcasm, Robert again changes his tone, this time to indignation. He tries to impress upon John that his response to mild criticism is unprofessional and childish, wholly improper for a man of his "calling." Thus, Robert tries to stabilize an inflammatory situation by reverting to familiar sentiments—the need for a mature approach to acting in which one eschews minor and selfish considerations and embraces criticism in an endless quest for perfection.

Such high-minded sentiments are obviously something that Robert himself cannot adopt since, later in the play, he responds with almost hysterical venom to what can only be seen as poor critical response to his work:

> Robert: The motherfucking leeches. The sots. (Pause.) The bloody boors. All of them . . . All of them. . . . Why can they not leave us alone . . . (scene 10, pp. 31–32)

Elsewhere in the work, he describes critics as "Fucking leeches. . . . [who will] praise you for the things you never did and pan you for a split second of godliness. What do they know? They create nothing. . . . They don't even buy a ticket" (scene 22, pp. 45–46). To Robert, critics are ignorant philistines who lead a parasitic existence, living off professionals like him. Unlike actors, "they create nothing" and do not even contribute financially to the theatrical arts.

Critical response to *A Life in the Theatre* has been largely favorable, although some reviewers have criticized the lengthy pauses

that exist between some scenes due to costume changes, position-
ing of props, and so on. However, as both Patrick Ryecart and
Freddie Jones point out, these "longeurs" are crucial to the whole
structure of the play. It is precisely *because* the audience is permit-
ted a glimpse into a backstage world that is usually denied them
that the play is so fascinating. Freddie Jones considers these
moments as essential to the overall structure of the piece as the
dialogue:

> The most important thing in a work like this is not to rush. Part of the
> fascination of it is the drama of watching people at work. The way they
> put sight-holes in hoardings so that you can watch people digging a
> hole sixty feet below suggests the spell of watching—it is almost
> voyeuristic. You see bowler-hatted businessmen in the city avidly
> watching the laborers. The psychology of *A Life in the Theatre* is identi-
> cal to that. If you rush it, it makes it look like a bottleneck, a failure in
> the script. If you trust it, do it leisurely, the only way you really can, it
> works . . . by moving more slowly, you are smoothing the action,
> making it fluent. . . . But as actors, you are always sorely tempted to
> rush, the pressure is so great. This must be avoided![44]

Similarly, Ryecart believes that "for a member of the audience, the
hold-ups would not be seen as hold-ups at all, but as an integral
part of the action which, of course, they are . . . they are what
Mamet wants and are deliberately written into the play."[45] Although there is a degree of sadness in *A Life in the Theatre*, there is
also a great deal of humor, the majority of which undoubtedly
stems from the brief scenes from the "plays" within the work.
Ryecart recalls how

> these scenes were very difficult to act because the writing is so deliber-
> ately bad, whereas the backstage scenes are easy due to the superb
> characterization . . . it is important to do the little scenes awfully well
> because if there are any areas in the play where one might lose the
> attention of an audience, it is there. They have to be *very* funny and
> the acting style quite different to the (most important) backstage
> scenes.[46]

Freddie Jones stresses the importance of "a judicious use of 'ham'
in the playlet scenes,"[47] to get the very best theatrical effect.

The structure of *A Life in the Theatre* is quite similar to that of
Clifford Odets' *Waiting for Lefty* in that realistic action is coupled
with brief scenes within scenes, which both comment upon and
forward the action of the whole. However, the playlet scenes in

Mamet's work forward the action only insofar as they contribute to the sense of inexorable decay on Robert's part and the increase of confidence on John's. This becomes more evident in the later scenes when lines are fluffed, cues are missed, and off-stage irritations intrude.

The first of these scenes is set *"in the trenches."* John and Robert are dressed as Doughboys and sit in a trench, *"smoking the last cigarette."* Mamet has obviously seen a great many films that contain scenes of just this banal and clichéd type. The dialogue is appallingly—and hilariously—stilted and is redolent of B-films popular in the 1940s and 1950s in which actors like John Wayne and Audie Murphy conversed with a sincerity that only emphasized the dire quality of their scripts. Mamet captures perfectly the phony gritty dialogue spoken in such films—language only considered realistic by writers without any experience on which to base their fantasies and with "tin" ears for naturalistic cadences:

> *John:* They left him up there on the wire.
> *Robert:* Calm down.
> *John:* Those bastards.
> *Robert:* Yeah.
> *John:* My God. They stuck him on the wire and left him there for target practice. . . . Those dirty, dirty bastards. (scene 3, p. 19)

This is followed by a supposedly sophisticated scene in which two lawyers struggle to maintain their dignity. From the outset, Mamet ensures that the audience is unable to take this seriously since it has been preceded by the episode in which Robert's zipper breaks and must be held together by a safety pin. Robert plays an urbane attorney, a successful individual at the peak of his career; a broken fly zipper hardly goes along with this image. Consequently, Robert must try to conceal his embarrassment and adopt an air of sobriety and authority. John, playing a lawyer, confronts Robert's character with the news of his wife's pregnancy:

> *John:* Gillian's going to have a baby.
> *Robert:* Why, this is marvellous. How long have you known?
> *John:* Since this morning.
> *Robert:* How marvellous!
> *John:* It isn't mine.
> *Robert:* It's not.
> *John:* No.
> *Robert:* Oh. *(Pause.)* I always supposed there was something one said in these situations . . . but I find . . . Do you know, that is, have you been told who the father is?

John: Yes.
Robert: Really. Who is it, David?
John: It's you, John.
Robert: Me!
John: You!
Robert: No.
John: Yes.
Robert: How preposterous. (scene 9, p. 30)

This is purely the language of soap opera, right down to the way in which both men pointedly call each other by name. There is also the additional joke of having John call Robert "John". This somehow adds to the idiocy of what the two men are doing in a play such as this. The short, almost monosyllabic sentences, quickly following one another add to the artificiality of the text, although the "writer's" intention is undoubtedly that it should be seen as realistic, serious dialogue.

The next playlet is written in a "Chekhovian" style. Here, Mamet manages to invoke aspects of several Chekhov plays while retaining a dialogue that is stultifying—even stupefying—in its boredom and banality. Robert is wheeled onstage in a bath chair by John—a sight that is in itself bound to cause tittering in the audience. Robert asks for his robe:

John: Oh, the autumn. . . . Oh, for the sun . . .
Robert: Will you pass me my robe, please?
John: Your laprobe. (scene 11, p. 32)

In these lines, Mamet manages to suggest echoes of at least two of Chekhov's plays—*The Three Sisters* and *Uncle Vanya*. The specific, and rather clumsy, reference to a "laprobe" is no accident since Serebryakov's laprobe falls about his ankles while he sleeps in act 2 of *Uncle Vanya*. Not only does Robert and John's script suggest not even an inkling of Chekhovian subtext (although the references to seasonal and meteorological topics are clearly intended to suggest one), it is also quite useless as naturalistic dialogue:

John: Maman says just one more day, one more day, yet another week.
Robert: Mmm.
John: One more week.
Robert: Would you please close the window?
John: What? I'm sorry?
Robert: Do you feel a draft?
John: A slight draft, yes. *(Pause.)* Shall I close the window?

Robert: Would you mind?
John: No, not at all. I love this window . . . (ibid., pp. 32–33)

The puerile repetitions and blatantly contrived questions render any hint of naturalism null and void. Mamet demonstrates how a poorly understood Chekhovian style can very easily turn into farcical absurdity. The script strains toward a Russian feel, but fails at every turn. John's assertion that he loves the window is a weak and clichéd reference to Gayev's affectionate speech to the bookcase in act 1 of *The Cherry Orchard*. Both are sentimental, but the difference is that Chekhov knew how to make sentimentality work as a means of character delineation whereas Mamet's imaginary dramatist does not. The scene drags on interminably; far from suggesting Chekhovian emotions such as apathy, frustration, and resignation, the fictional author achieves only a drawn-out—and unintentionally hilarious—melodrama in which, literally, nothing happens. If the piece had genuine humor (apart from Mamet's wickedly ironic comedy), it could almost be Beckettian!

In the French Revolution scene, Robert's lengthy soliloquy reads a little like a scene from an inferior version of Büchner's *Danton's Death* or Sardou's *Robespierre*, the play commissioned by Irving to provide him with a truly "dramatic" role. There is definitely something of the Irving school of acting about Robert's part here. The "dramatist" clearly believes he can display a linguistic flourish in bombastic rhetoric and overwhelm through the power of words alone. Alas, the rhetoric is fatuous and frequently downright silly:

> *Robert:* . . . The heart cries out: the memory says man has always lived in chains . . . has always lived in chains . . . *(Pause.)* Bread, bread, bread, the people scream . . . we drown their screaming with our head in cups, in books . . . in newspapers . . . between the breasts of women . . . in our work . . . enough. (scene 16, p. 38)

Robert must relish the opportunity of playing such parts. He can strut about displaying his self-importance and enjoy the excitement of having the stage completely to himself. He has nothing to worry about, other than that he must give his best performance; the increasingly threatening presence of John is not even there to distract him. At this half-way stage of the play, Robert *is* still mostly in control, but there are already hints of John's lessening dependence upon him, and Robert's sad realization of this fact.

The vacuity of the piece Robert so lovingly performs bears little scrutiny. The "manliness" and robust nature of the speaker is meant to be conveyed in lines such as, "our head in cups . . . between the breasts of women," and similar bathetic exclamations. What is actually conveyed is the very limited imagination of the author. Whether the repetition of "has always lived in chains," in the first part of the speech is intentional or is an indication of Robert simply forgetting his lines is unclear. When, at the conclusion of the extract, he utters, "enough," it is difficult not to agree with him. Robert's character goes on to list the causes to which it is necessary to swear allegiance in the interests of the Revolution:

> Robert: . . . Our heads between the breasts of women, plight our troth to that security far greater than protection of mere rank or fortune. Now: we must dedicate ourselves to spirit: to the spirit of humanity; to life: (Pause.) to the barricades. (Pause.) Bread, bread, bread. (ibid.)

This part of the soliloquy appears to lean toward Shakespearian rhythms, rhythms that are plainly ill-suited to the sheer vacancy of the words. Robert separates the "causes" by means of emphatic colons. Unfortunately for the grandeur of the speech, the final "cause" is "the barricades," which necessitates a change in tone and meaning. The call is surely to march *to* the barricades themselves, but the speech is so badly written that it could appear to be merely another in the speaker's list of worthy causes. The concluding, "Bread, bread, bread," serves to emphasize the true lack of passion in the writing, calling to mind, if anything, a musical moment from *Oliver*.

The scene about the barricades is not only noteworthy because of its accurate verbal humor, it also contains the visual debacle of Robert flinging back his head in a grandiose gesture and consequently losing his wig. The next time we see Robert's thespian skills is in the famous lifeboat scene. It should be recalled that this is the episode to which he had given so much thought in an earlier scene, finding meaning where little existed and lauding the author to the skies. The dialogue is, once again, trite and risible but is here rendered totally ludicrous by the actors' obligatory "*English accents*" (scene 18, p. 41). This is one occasion when an American actor's voice is most definitely called for:

> Robert: Rain . . .? What do *you* know about it? (Pause.) I've spent my whole life on the sea, and all that I know is the length of my ignorance. Which is *complete*, Sonny. (Pause.) My ignorance is complete.

John: It's gotta rain.
Robert: Tell it to the marines.
John: It doesn't rain, I'm going off my nut.
Robert: Just take it easy, kid . . . What you don't wanna do now is sweat. *(Pause.)* Believe me. *(Pause.)*
John: We're never getting out of this alive. *(Pause.)* Are we?
Robert: How do you want it?
John: Give it to me straight.
Robert: Kid, we haven't got a chance in hell . . . (scene 18, p. 41)

The fictional dramatist is evidently attempting dialogue that is a hybrid of Steinbeck and Hemingway, the latter in his *The Old Man and the Sea* period. What he actually achieves is an inane and mannered version of such classic works. The "author" has a stab at metrical scansion: "the length of my ignorance" and so on. Such serious speculation is then mercilessly rejected in favor of phrases like, "It's gotta rain" and, even worse, "Tell it to the marines." The so-called sea-dog experience of the elder man is suggested in a series of clichés that would probably seem overdone in a children's adventure serial but that, as we have seen, Robert considers inspired writing. This truly dreadful piece of work probably *is* the best the actors have to perform, which is saying very little.

The final playlet takes place in an operating room; it is here that Robert's professional expertise is seriously called into question and where he refuses to take notice of John's desperate attempts to prompt him. The scene begins well enough: Robert, though in character, is momentarily back in his paternal role as an older surgeon doling out advice to his junior colleague. Offstage, his authority may be crumbling, but here it is he who teaches the novice the ropes and it is he who knows the tricks of the trade, just as Robert the actor knows well the tricks of his own profession. However, it soon becomes clear that Robert has mixed up his lines and is confusing the action here with that of another scene:

John: (Pointing.) What's that!!!?
Robert: What is what? Eh?
John: What's that near his spleen? *(A pause.)* A curious growth near his spleen?
Robert: What?
John: A Curious Growth Near His Spleen? *(Pause.)* Is that one, there?
Robert: No, I think not. I think you cannot see a growth near his spleen for some *time* yet. So would you, as this man's in shock . . . would you get me, please, give me a reading on his vital statements? Uh, Functions . . .? Would you do that one thing for me, please?
John: (Sotto.) We've done that one, Robert.

> *Robert:* I fear I must disagree with you, Doctor. Would you give me a
> reading on his vital things, if you please? Would you? *(Pause.)* For
> the love of God?
> *John: (Sotto.)* That's in the other part. (scene 24, pp. 51–52)

It is illuminating to look at this scene in some detail in order to
glean how Mamet builds up the comedy. Robert is incensed that
John should think he has forgotten what to do and persists with
the wrong lines despite John's efforts to save the situation from
disaster. Robert improvizes frantically; he begins to flounder.
Panicking, he fishes around in his mind for any medical-sounding
terms that might cover up John's "error." Eventually, he runs out
of even remotely suitable "medical" words and requests "a reading on [the patient's] vital things." Patrick Ryecart recalls how this
particular section always induced near hysteria in the audience
and often led to considerable "corpsing" between Freddie Jones
and him: "We often played the scene absolutely shaking with
laughter,"[48] he says. Robert's intransigence unnerves John. He too
begins to panic, and this is suggested by his pointed remark,
highlighted by capital letters for full effect: "A Curious Growth
Near His Spleen." As the scene limps weakly to its conclusion,
John seems deflated and completely devoid of energy. He mut-
ters: "We've done that one, Robert," calling his colleague by name
to let him know that it is *he* who is at fault. Robert ignores this; he
is adamant and carries on frantically like a man possessed, the
professional to the end. To keep up the charade, he refers to John
as "Doctor" even when all credibility has plainly been sacrificed.
    A final mix of reality and artifice occurs in the next few lines
when Robert berates John for a lack of feeling, which, it seems, is
not only intended for his partner's onstage character:

> *Robert:* . . . He's in shock. He's in shock, and I'm becoming miffed
> with you. Now: if you desire to work in this business again will you
> give me a reading? If you wish to continue here inside the hospital?
> *(Pause.)* Must I call a *policeman!!?* Have you no feeling? This man's in
> deepest shock!!! (ibid., p. 52)

Is Robert telling John the actor that he must cooperate if he wishes
to "work in this business again"? Is it John the actor with whom
Robert is "miffed?" Robert tries to make his "lines" sound as if
they were written for him, while at the same time criticizing John
for what he feels is his total incompetence and refusal to cover up
his gaffe. However, when Robert mentions the *"hospital"* rather
than the reality of the stage on which they both stand, he betrays

his nervousness and fear of the younger man. He realizes that John is aware of his direct criticism and so, to be safe, once more moves into the relative security of fantasy. His final words, "This man's in deepest shock!!!" underlines the ambiguity. Which man is in shock? The imaginary patient or Robert himself?

Mamet prefixes his play with a short quotation from Rudyard Kipling's poem, *Actors:*

> We counterfeited once for your disport,
> Men's joy and sorrow; but our day has passed.
> We pray you pardon all where we fell short—
> Seeing we were your servants to this last.[49]

This appears to be a comment on the decline of Robert but it could also be viewed as a worried reminder of the declining importance of theatre to the general public, a state of affairs Mamet is most anxious to prevent. *A Life in the Theatre* has been called "a wary hymn to the theatre"[50] and so it is. It celebrates the fleeting joys of a satisfying performance and it dramatizes most touchingly the bond that exists between those who dedicate their lives to the stage. On the other hand, it offers a far from glamorous picture of theatrical life. For the audience, such a play is somewhat akin to watching a third-rate conjurer whose magic tricks all come to nought. We see behind the artifice into the sometimes painful areas that usually remain concealed; as Robert rather grandly avers of one of the fictional authors in the play, the writer "lets you see the thought there" (scene 13, p. 34). The work may be a play about two actors and their particularly specialized lives in the theatre, but it is universal in its theme. It may be about acting, but it is also about the conflicts of age and youth, rites of passage, and simple human nature. Mel Gussow believes that *A Life in the Theatre* is a play in which "the author spoofs actors' insecurities, pretensions [and] illusions—the pretensions and ignominies of the profession."[51] One might add to this that Mamet additionally deals with the "insecurities, pretensions [and] illusions" of life itself, the "ignominies of the profession" standing for the ignominies of human existence.

4

Edmond

Edmond is perhaps Mamet's most personal play to date, in that it truthfully and alarmingly reflects his darkest fears about modern America and its damaging effect upon the ordinary citizen. Through the picaresque experiences of his (anti) hero, he dramatizes the confusion and panic of life in a bustling metropolis. Edmond is the archetypal "alienated" individual; he feels cut from his history, his traditions, and his sexuality. Schizophrenically separated out into various roles, split into a series of sexual, social, and economic functions that make impossible a fully harmonious existence, he has lost his sense of uniqueness. Since there is no cohesion in Edmond's life, there can be no real belonging. Mamet has stated that there is a lot of himself in the character of Edmond, an ordinary man who tries to escape the mediocrity of his life for a more enriching, vital existence, and he notes how, in his own adolescence, he felt deracinated and adrift: "My grandparents were Russian-Jewish immigrants. My father grew up poor but subsequently made a good living. My life was expunged of any tradition at all. Nothing old in the house. No color in the house. The virtues expounded were not creative but remedial; let's stop being Jewish, let's stop being poor."[1] This colorless existence is echoed in *Edmond,* and Connie Booth notes that "Other than a 'marriage' we don't know the history of, Edmond and his wife are unknown to us. . . . As they speak with a table between them, she complaining of a broken lamp, things seem to have taken the place of roots in their relationship."[2] Apart from a general feeling of rootlessness, there are at least three other elements in the play that link Mamet's identity with that of his character. Edmond chooses to break away from the norm, to be unconventional, and Mamet has stated that, as a young man, "I had to invent my own life and my own fun. Anything that wasn't official, I knew that's where I wanted to be."[3] At base, Edmond simply wants to find happiness and peace; he cries out for a world that is "full of *life.* And *air.* Where people are *kind* to each other, and there's *work* to do. Where we grow up in *love,* and in security we're *wanted*" (scene 21, p. 96). How similar these sentiments are to Mamet's own ideas for a life of joy and contentment: "We need to be loved; we need to be secure; we need to help each other; we need to work."4

Edmond's first action in the play is to visit a Fortune-Teller who might give him direction and purpose and, although there is no evidence of Mamet being similarly motivated, he has written a play that is specifically concerned with the powers of clairvoyance, *The Shawl*. Carl Jung has noted how, in modern society "it is chiefly in times of physical, political, economic, and spiritual distress that men's eyes turn with anxious hope to the future, and when anticipations, utopias, and apocalyptic visions multiply."5 Lacking confidence in his own ability to make decisions, Edmond seeks guidance from one who claims future knowledge. The banality of his life has forced him to seek a means of escape, and a glimpse into a better future is one way to achieve such liberation. A natural egotist, he seizes hungrily at the Fortune-Teller's suggestion that he is in some way "special" and with this, and the advice of a stranger that he should "get laid," in mind, Edmond sets himself adrift on a vertiginous downward spiral from which it is impossible to retreat. There is no going back and no going forward; he is trapped in a fragmented existence in which none of the components fully cohere and, therefore, can offer him little solace. As Jack Kroll observes, "Edmond is the rock-bottom man, the man who's dried up, who can't be either happy or unhappy, only enraged at his own emptiness."6

Edmond leaves behind a loveless and joyless marriage, rejecting former friends and job ties to plunge headlong into a search for sensation and satisfaction. It is his tragedy that he can no more be a part of the chaotic and somewhat anarchic subculture toward which he flees than the mundane and routine domestic situation he leaves behind. He is too much a product of his upbringing, taking with him an excess of the constraints of a bourgeois life. Temperamentally unsuited to disorder and unscrupulousness, he cannot deal with the opportunism he finds to be rampant. However, Edmond does lack one crucial bourgeois requirement—the ability to take responsibility for one's actions. He acts without thinking of the consequences and is, ultimately, destroyed. Whether this lack is Edmond's own deficiency as an individual is a moot point; in an industrialized and depersonalized society, Jung notes how "the individual is increasingly deprived of the moral decision as to how he should live his own life, and instead is ruled, fed, clothed, and educated as a social unit, accommodated in the appropriate housing unit, and amused in accordance with the standards that give pleasure and satisfaction to the masses."[7] Mamet seems to suggest that Edmond is not necessarily to blame for his deficiencies as a moral being, but is the victim of the inadequacy and coldness of a brutal society.

The plight of the individual in a complex urban labyrinth is not, of course, a subject new to writers and philosophers. Many of the issues raised in *Edmond* have been discussed, dramatized, and postulated elsewhere. Mamet's *specific* concerns, however—a sense of uncertainty and lack of tradition, metaphysical confusion, and man's sense of himself as a deracinated, depersonalized being searching for a way out of a mazelike confusion— are touched on by Saul Bellow, Erich Fromm, and Norman Mailer. In his novel *Herzog*, Bellow's protagonist muses on the predicament of modern man: "Individual character [is] cut off at times both from facts and from values. But modern character is inconstant, divided, vacillating, lacking the stone-like certitude of archaic man."[8] Similarly, Fromm considers that "post-modern man is more profoundly perplexed about the nature of man than his ancestors were. He is now on the verge of spiritual and moral insanity. He does not know who he is. And having lost the sense of who and what he is, he fails to grasp the meaning of his fellow man, of his vocation and of the nature and purpose of knowledge itself."[9] This sense of fundamental uncertainty and moral deterioration is echoed by Norman Mailer:

> You don't have to put people in a concentration camp to dehumanise them; you can dehumanise them right down on the street—and we do. And not just in America, in all the countries in the world. The 20th century is going through the most peculiar period of men's dehumanisation, and it's too easy to say the fault is all American capitalism. In fact, it's something deeper than that. It's almost as if there's a titanic battle going on about the nature of the continuance of man.[10]

Mamet sets his play in New York, a city that to him represents everything that is wrong with modern society: it is vast, impersonal, vulgar, corrupt, and hopelessly violent. He has described New York variously as an "inferno [that is] infested by hustlers and thugs"[11] and "a vision of hell."[12] He sees its lack of moral standards, the high level of crime, its burgeoning vice industry, and virulent drug culture as portents of the creeping decay that threatens every corner of his country. But New York is only the most extreme symptom of a general malaise that, Mamet believes, is sweeping over the entire continent: "America," he says, "is a very violent country full of a lot of hate. You can't put a Band-Aid on a suppurating wound."[13] He opines that the fabric holding his country together is falling apart because it no longer subscribes to values that ensure the continuity of stability and order. He notes how "it is falling away from *all* values . . . the terrible thing about America is the terrible disdain people have had for the Constitution. The document has been subverted—at least it represented the continuity of a unified nation based on fair laws."[14] Talking specifically about *Edmond*, Mamet explains how the protagonist

> precipitates himself into an individual period of destruction—into a downward slide so that he can find rest. Which is what is going to happen in society . . . it is inevitable. If you take an overall view you can see that any place you care to look, whether it is destruction of the environment by economics, or destruction of the earth by nuclear weapons; we are like a child spilling its milk . . . we are trying to solve something by destruction [in the hope of finding] a phase of rest.[15]

Mamet believes that contemporary culture—especially in cities like New York—is based on anarchic and destructive principles: "Part of the modern culture in New York has to do with destruction: graffiti art, punk music and punk styles. Performance art has to do with destruction."[16] In an essay entitled "The Undiscovered Self," Jung observes that "the development of modern art with its seemingly nihilistic trend towards disintegration must be understood as the symptom and symbol of a mood of universal destruction and renewal that has set its mark on our age. This mood makes itself felt everywhere, politically, socially, and philosophically."[17] Mamet believes that people are only too aware of the fact that their hold on a stable, safe society is disintegrating before their eyes and they live in constant terror because of this. Their only chance of surviving mentally intact is to subscribe to the "intellectual idea that if we keep going, things will continue as they are."[18] Consequently, the populace represses its fears and engages in a frantic covering up of the real issues. The pressures are, Mamet says, quite simply "driving people nuts."[19] It is little wonder then that Edmond should go so tragically off the rails; he rejects the notion that he should "keep going" and opts instead to "drop out" of his respectable, middle-class life to look for peace elsewhere.

The language Mamet uses to illustrate the world Edmond inhabits is as vitiated and colorless as the emotional lives of the characters. Edmond and his wife are unable to communicate; it is only when they are planning divorce after Edmond's arrest for murder that he observes:

> *Edmond:* I know at certain times we wished we could be . . . closer to each other. I can say that now. I'm sure this is the way you feel when someone near you dies. You never said the things you wanted desperately to say. It would have been so simple to say them. *(Pause.)* But you never did. (scene 19, p. 88)

Edmond's confusion over his use of "I" and "You" suggests the lack of intimacy on both sides; his final statement can be seen either as a declaration of his own inadequacy, or as a sad recollection of his wife's silence. If his relations with his wife are strained and almost monosyllabic, his encounters in the seedy underworld of downtown New York are barely human. Almost without exception, those he meets try to exploit him or to take advantage of his naïveté. Their language is slick, oily, but strangely flat: what remains of a lively street language, which must once have been thrilling, exists now only in brief fragments. The majority of the discourse in these scenes consists merely of the debased slang and obscene ramblings of those whose lives absolutely lack any sense of hope. The street hustlers Edmond meets utter words that are totally devoid of emotional content; their speech patterns follow those of transactional language—bleak, functional, and stark. When there are occasional moments of lyricism, such as in the musicality of the Three Card Monte, these are quickly negated as the banter turns from verbal seduction to a call for physical violence.

Mamet's use of language in *Edmond* is as skilful and subtle as ever, although some critics assert that he has gone "tone deaf"[20] and that the language is "stiff and unnatural."[21] The language may be toneless and flat, but this is precisely the effect the dramatist is trying to attain. In *Edmond,* the episodic nature both of the play and its language reflects the discontinuity, disjunction, and incoherence of modern America. *Edmond* is more expressionistic than realistic, although Mamet once again demonstrates his mastery of authentic-sounding dialogue.

Edmond is a symbol of innocence and naïveté who is eventually destroyed as he kicks and shoves against the barriers that prevent his finding happiness. He may be foolish and rash, violent and selfish but he is also recognizably human and vulnerable. He goes about seeking his salvation in the wrong way, but at least he tries, rather than wallowing in the apathy of a mediocre existence. The play is not meant to be realistic, but fabulistic, an allegory intended to enlighten and inform. Critics like Susie Mackenzie miss so much of what Mamet is trying to achieve when they observe that the play is "an excuse for almost any kind of depraved and anti-social behaviour."[22] As might be expected, Mamet responds to such criticism by stating, "I think it could be taken as an apology. But not by anyone who has read the words."[23] Colin Stinton, who created the role of Edmond in the United States and has also played it in England, defends Mamet's play by emphasizing Edmond's courage in making the first, essential break:

> People misunderstand Edmond. There are so many misconceptions about him . . . that he is cheap, or just trying to get laid, etc., but what he is *trying* to do is to take positive action. He fails but he tries. He just wants to get OUT, and the path he follows seems to him to be the right one. Edmond *knows* that the Three Card Monte sharper will try to "take" him but decides to try and beat him anyway. In that critical little scene as to how to beat the game—how to beat the game of life, if you like—Edmond is advised to pick up the one you would not pick, to do the perverse thing. Throughout the play, he chooses to do something perverse. There was a section at the beginning of the Glenna scene which was subsequently cut . . . Edmond says to her: "You got to stay up late, you got to do something you would *not* do." He is telling her what he believes to be the truth; he feels he has found that one thing necessary which will bring him alive, to beat fate, to be unconventional for once, to do the thing that isn't expected but, by doing it, it makes him alive, it makes him feel real. He wants to pass on this information to Glenna so that she, too, can share in his wonderful discovery. Edmond is trying to seek out, rather heroically, I feel, that way of breaking free from those he feels would inhibit him. He is naïve, he is imperfect, doesn't know the rules . . . but at least he has the courage to *try* . . .[24]

Edmond was written between 1981 and 1982 and was premiered at the Goodman Theatre in Chicago in June 1982. It has also been produced in New York and in November 1985 received its British premiere in Newcastle-upon-Tyne. It then transferred to the Royal Court Theatre in London for a short season. *Edmond* is a short, episodic play made up of twenty-three rapid, pungent scenes depicting its protagonist's downfall. The subject of the work is reflected both in its linguistic and theatrical structure. The sounds and visions of Edmond's world are bleakly jarring and dissonant, and are as cold and functional as the black iron fire escapes and tawdry neon signs that littered the stage in Richard Eyre's Royal

Court production. The play is a vision of hell, of confinement, of a hermetically sealed subculture peopled with desperate and ruthless survivors.

Edmond himself can be viewed in a number of different ways: as a brave adventurer, as the dupe of a manipulative and uncaring society, as a pathetic and helpless victim of fate, as a repressed and violent man who acts out his darkest fantasies, or as an all-too-willing pawn drawn into a world of limitless depravity. Each of these elements is present in the play alongside Mamet's broader philosophical canvas that pictures the gradual disintegration of civilization. What makes it an exceptional piece of theatre is the playwright's ability to work on all of these levels simultaneously.

Edmond's suffering recalls the plight of Saul Bellow's *Herzog* as he muses on his destiny: "when will we civilized beings become really serious? said Kierkegaard. Only when we have known hell through and through. Without this, hedonism and frivolity will diffuse hell through all our days."[25] Edmond appears to be drawn to the seediness and violence he encounters in the same way that Joseph Conrad wrote about "the fascination of the abomination";[26] it attracts and repels him in equal measure. T. E. Kalem feels that Edmond's flight to the underworld "is the quest for identity based on Joseph Conrad's admonition: 'In the destructive element immerse. That is the way.' The way to what? Quite probably, the way to understand and absorb the dark tenor and temper of the age."[27] Francis King believes that Edmond's downfall is at least partly self-motivated: "For almost 40 years, Edmond has lived the life of a respectable, white American, the most recent of them with a wife whom he has long since ceased to love. Through all those years, he has both feared and secretly wished for squalor, promiscuity and violence."[28]

A key sentence in the play is undoubtedly, "Every fear hides a wish" (scene 20, p. 89). When he has been arrested for Glenna's murder, Edmond tells his cellmate that for the first time in his life, he feels no fear. It is as if he had wished for degradation and horror so that, having lived through all his darkest fears, there could be no more suffering, only peace and tranquility:

> *Edmond:* We . . . when we *fear* things I think that we *wish* for them. . . . Every fear hides a wish. . . . I always knew that I would end up here. . . . What I *know* I think that all this fear, this fucking *fear* we feel must hide a wish. 'Cause I don't feel it since I'm here. (scene 20, pp. 89–90)

Although Edmond is indeed a product of his society—a confused and bitter man, a bourgeois, an egocentric chauvinist—he is also, unswervingly, an innocent. In literature there have always been innocents who endure terrible hardships and torments, experiencing the basest cruelty humanity can devise in a quest to find some meaning to life. Two obvious examples are Voltaire's *Candide* and Cervantes' *Don Quixote*. Their hardships are, like of those Edmond, often offset by a grimly ironic humor, black and caustic, but irresistibly funny. Two examples of Mamet's ability to invest an almost tragic situation with sardonic humor occur in Edmond's visits to the Peep Show and the whorehouse. At the Peep Show, "A girl in a spangled leotard" flatly intones the following profane little litany with palpable boredom:

> *Girl:* Take your dick out. *(Pause.)*
>   Take your dick out. *(Pause.)*
>   Come on. Take your dick out.
> *Edmond:* I'm not a cop.
> *Girl:* I know you're not a cop. Take your dick out. I'm gonna give you a good time. (scene 5, p. 31)

What seems certain from this exchange is that Edmond is *not* going to have "a good time." He is separated from the girl by a plexiglass partition that negates any possibility of direct contact, other than via a small hole through which money can be shoved. Miranda Richardson, who played this role as well as that of the Fortune-Teller and of Glenna in the Royal Court production, comments on the scene:

> I had some problems with the Peep-Show girl—it was all voice with her. My interpretation owed more to the [Wim Wenders] film, *Paris, Texas* than to any of the research I did in Soho peep-show joints. I did visit one or two but they weren't really helpful. This girl is totally bored, so fed up with it all and I think Mamet captures this in the tonelessness he writes into the lines. It really is black humor, emphasized by the repetitions, etc. She's thinking: can he hear me? what's he doing? why isn't he responding? . . . this guy's a complete *idiot*.[29]

When Edmond visits the "health club"—a euphemism for brothel—the Whore comes straight to the point despite his pointedly polite manner of speaking to her:

> *Whore:* What shall we do?
> *Edmond:* I'd like to have intercourse with you.
> *Whore:* That sounds very nice. I'd like that, too.

Edmond: You would?
Whore: Yes.
Edmond: How much would that be?
Whore: For a straight fuck, that would be a hundred fifty. (scene 9, p. 42)

On both occasions, the language of sex has been drained of all emotional content—all that remains is the basic act. At this stage, Edmond is unsure how to behave with such girls; he speaks to the Whore as if she were his girlfriend or even his wife. That he should use the term "intercourse" humorously reflects his stuffy and straight-laced mentality, as well as indicating his desire to be regarded as a "nice" person. His tone certainly clashes with the Whore's bluntly prosaic response; she has undoubtedly parroted these words many times and the phrasing comes as easily and as naturally as if she were ordering tea. Her abbreviation of "a hundred fifty" is another indication of her casual attitude and of her desire to get the monetary aspects of the negotiation quickly out of the way. Edmond seems rather surprised when she agrees that she would enjoy having sex with him: "I'd like that, too." In this phrase is conveyed to Edmond the appealing notion that there may be something more in their relationship than a simple sexual and fiscal exchange, although he must be well aware that there is not. It is all a new and exciting game to him, but it is a game with rules he does not yet understand and with speech patterns he has not yet absorbed. He is trusting of those he encounters, and always respectful: it is little wonder that he should be so abused. Without fail, he remembers to say "please" and "thank you" in the most inappropriate circumstances, a very telling testimony to his years of social conditioning.

At the beginning of the play, the Fortune-Teller informs him that he is in some way "special" and that his true destiny lies elsewhere. As a "special" person, Edmond believes he is entitled to pleasure and a better life and he sets off on his grueling journey in order to find happiness. The great irony is that he is far from special; Mamet ensures that he is completely unexceptional, blandly and blatantly ordinary. What happens to Edmond could happen to anyone, given the circumstances and a few unlucky quirks of fate. He is presented as an ironic, modern-day Everyman, moving doggedly through life in search of his salvation, and a number of critics have compared him with the sixteenth-century traveler. Milton Shulman describes him as facing "almost every horror and indignity with the bland resignation of an American Everyman,"[30] and Michael Coveney believes that Mamet imbues

Edmond with "a remarkable sense of a character wanting to break free. . . . In his Everyman normality, Edmond is transformed into a tragic victim."[31] Steve Grant cites *Candide* as the innocent abroad: "Don't be fooled by the 'Candide'-like simplicity of the piece . . . we have *all* been here. Well, almost."[32] In a lengthy review of the play, Jack Kroll muses on the theme of universality:

> We're not really nice. We let bad things happen. Maybe there's murder in our hearts. We're told there are millions of nice people. But statistics aren't the answer. Shakespeare didn't make a survey to find out how many Iagos there were in England. So, watching David Mamet's dark, stark *Edmond,* we can escape the implication by mumbling "That's not me. It's not any of my friends. Edmond's just a guy I read about in the papers." . . . Edmond is neither good nor evil; he's modern man as a bundle of behavioral spasms that turn into a destructive epilepsy when the rotting social-psychological structure finally collapses.[33]

Colin Stinton has remarked on the accuracy of Kroll's reading of the play: "Kroll wrote a very sympathetic review; he got it right, I think. He understood what Mamet was trying to do, but others did not. Kroll understood that Edmond is ordinary, just you or me down on our luck . . . others wanted to make him into a psychopath or something."[34]

The very fact that Edmond *is* so ordinary—an apparently normal citizen—is tremendously effective. It is rather like a thriller in which a scene of absolute calm or scenic beauty is suddenly shattered by a cataclysmic event. Alfred Hitchcock knew how to extricate the maximum shock value out of an ordinary situation; in *Edmond,* Mamet does something similar with his rather boring, "normal" hero. It is not surprising that the suspense and "thriller" elements in *Edmond* should be reminiscent of the films of Hitchcock: it is a very cinematic kind of play. It's short, sharp scenes, which end in blackness, move rapidly from one scenario to another, creating tension with a deft and sure touch. Such scenes have been described as a series of "black-out sketches written in a kind of staccato poetry, like Feiffer cartoons printed in blood and acid."[35] Frank Rich likens the play to "selected screenplays by Paul Schrader (notably *Taxi Driver, Hardcore*) as they might have been rewritten by a Samuel Beckett parodist."[36] The play does indeed resemble many of the films of directors like Martin Scorsese and screenwriters like Paul Schrader. *Taxi Driver* is a film that combines the talents of both men and that is very much like *Edmond* both in its visual and verbal style. In this film, the psychotic misfit

Travis Bickle, loses his grasp on sanity and reason and sets out to
rid the New York streets of what he sees as their living scum.
Mamet himself has cited this film as "exceptional."[37] When, however, Travis displays the full extent of his violent nature in the
gratuitously bloody climax of the film, the audience is scarcely
surprised since he has seemed decidedly unhinged from the
outset. The shockwaves that reverberate throughout the auditorium when such a mild-mannered and apparently normal
man as Edmond suddenly lashes out are almost tangible.

Mamet's extraordinary gift for using language as an integral
part of his drama, as opposed to employing it merely as a means
of rendering dialogue, is once again evident in this play. The very
structure of *Edmond* reflects its verbal style. Sexual gratification
and the means of achieving it are the mainspring of the work and
thus Mamet ensures that both the text and the structure are
suggestive of this. The early scenes are extremely short, breathy,
and impatient; by their form and elliptical text they imply the
preliminaries to sexual congress. As the work progresses, and
Edmond becomes increasingly sexually frustrated, so too the
scenes and the dialogue take on an almost orgasmic—though
fractured—tone. At its conclusion, once Edmond has literally
"spent" his passion, the scenes are slightly longer, more verbally
languorous, and the final scene has a quietness and sense of
peace that even suggests postcoital fulfillment.

The "blackout" formula derives from Mamet's experience of
working at Second City Improvisations. The quick-fire comedy
routines and blackout sketches that he watched during his time
there deeply influenced his writing style and the structure of his
plays, particularly the early ones, but *Edmond* indicates that, as
late as 1982, Mamet was able to utilize profitably this method.
Mamet admits that "for the next 10 years [after working at Second
City] none of my scenes lasted more than eight minutes."[38]
Mamet liked the way the scenes at Second City went straight to
the point, without bringing in unnecessary characters or extraneous plot devices. He explains exactly what is implied by "blackouts": "The blackout format . . . five or seven minutes [with a]
punchline at the end . . . that is blackout. This goes back to music
hall. It is also like American TV which is interrupted by commercials. There's got to be a good payoff since there is no time for
narration, only time left for drama."[39] In Richard Eyre's production of *Edmond*, William Dudley's sets were visual counterpoints
to the "blackouts"; the bleak monochrome of dark and dirty
streets and subways was suddenly and unexpectedly invaded by a

flash of color. This gave an impression of extreme modernism, of an almost stylized stage picture from the pages of a pop art catalogue. The tableaux of colorless individuals leading debased and meaningless lives and speaking a corrupt language were momentarily highlighted or offset by a beam of fluorescent light, flickering neon, or a vibrantly colored hat or dress.

As he moves from one debilitating experience to another, Edmond's speech changes from his early polite chattiness to a raw, violent—almost primal—scream. As he is slowly but inexorably drawn into the hellish underworld of downtown New York, years of anger and frustration begin to rise to the surface in a poisonous surge. Perhaps the turning point for Edmond comes after he has been cheated and beaten by the Three Card Monte and his cohorts. He goes *"torn and battered"* (scene 2, p. 50) to a hotel to seek help. His wallet has been stolen and he has no cash to pay for a room; the hotel clerk will not help him, despite the fact that Edmond is obviously in deep distress:

> *Edmond:* I lost my wallet.
> *Clerk:* Go to the police.
> *Edmond:* You can call up American Express.
> *Clerk:* Go to the police. *(Pause.) I don't want to hear it.* (ibid.)

Edmond tries to bargain with what he believes to be his unimpeachable respectability—he mentions his American Express card. However, the clerk is decidedly unimpressed; he has heard it all before. He refuses to be drawn into Edmond's problems and become involved. Once he realizes that Edmond will persist, he suggests that he call "the credit card people" himself:

> *Edmond:* I have no money.
> *Clerk:* I'm sure it's a free call.
> *Edmond:* Do those phones require a dime?
> *Clerk: (Pause.)* I'm sure I don't know.
> *Edmond:* You know if they need a *dime* or not. To get a *dial* tone . . . You know if they need a *dime,* for chrissake. Do you want to live in this kind of world? Do you want to live in a *world* like that? I've been *hurt*? Are you *blind*? Would you appreciate it if I acted this way to *you*? *(Pause.)* I *asked* you one simple thing. Do they need a *dime*?
> *Clerk:* No. They don't need a dime. Now, you make your call, and you go somewhere else. (ibid. p. 51)

The clerk's cold and unsympathetic manner enrages Edmond; he is simply not used to being treated this way. He is, after all, a man who can rely on the services of American Express to get him out of difficulties. What Edmond fails to realize is that he is no longer the man he was; he has no wallet and therefore no identity. He is as much a product of the tawdry streets as the man whom he asks for help. He is now just another battered individual, possibly drunk and disreputable, with whom it would be a mistake to become involved.

The clerk's tone is one of barely concealed contempt; Mamet builds a sigh of frustration and impatience into a simple phrase like, "I'm sure I don't know," which follows immediately on a pause. The boredom is almost tangible. What moves Edmond to anger is his innate sense of justice, which he finds all too frequently threatened. He demands to know if the unmoved clerk would appreciate being treated in this fashion; he pleads for a world in which people help one another, where individuals trust their neighbors, and treat each other as they themselves would be treated. Such a state of affairs is scarcely characteristic of the world he has left behind with its cutthroat capitalism and loveless marriage. It is even less likely to be an aspect of the world he has chosen to enter. Later in the play, Edmond again utters a similar plea, but it is then addressed to the Prison Chaplain, in whom he confides following his murder of Glenna. If one is aware of this later scene, it is impossible not to feel a frisson of macabre foreboding as Edmond pleads for a better, kinder world.

Shortly after his experience in the hotel, Edmond finds himself on the subway. He attempts a seemingly harmless and friendly conversation with a woman who is standing on the same platform:

> *Edmond: (Pause.)* My mother had a hat like that. *(Pause.)* My mother had a hat like that. *(Pause.)* I . . . I'm not making conversation. She wore it for years. She had it when I was a child. (scene 13, p. 58)

The woman is unnerved by him and begins to move away, but Edmond grabs her:

> *Edmond:* I wasn't just making it "up." It *happened.* . . . who the fuck do you think you *are*? . . . I'm *talking* to you . . . What am I? A *stone*? . . . Did I say, "I want to lick your pussy? . . ." I said, "My mother had that same hat . . ." You *cunt* . . . What am I? A *dog*? I'd like to slash your fucking *face* . . . I'd like to slash your motherfucking *face* apart . . . (ibid.)

Edmond's maniacal outburst is shocking and frightening, but is rendered more understandable if his recent experiences are analyzed. He has been unable to find a woman with whom to have sex, despite visiting a singles bar, a peep show, and a whorehouse; he has been financially abused and emotionally violated; he has even been beaten up by men who have stolen his wallet and treated like an outcast by a mere hotel clerk. He can take no more. Although it is quite natural that the woman should avoid conversing with an unknown—and somewhat dishev-elled—man, Mamet does far more with this scene than state the obvious terrors of rape and assault. The very fact that she is afraid even to speak to Edmond, or indeed acknowledge his existence, is indicative of the paranoia and fear that are rampant in the city. There is very good cause for her to feel fear, but Mamet seems to be commenting upon a wider and more terrible malaise. The barriers here are as palpable and real as those that Edmond had asked to be removed at the Peep Show: "How can we get this barrier to come down?," he asks; "How does this thing come down?" (scene 5, pp. 32–33). The sad fact is that the barrier cannot come down in such a society; it is forever erected to eliminate the possibility of real communication.

To speak to someone is to enter into a sort of liaison with them; it implies an element of trust. In fact, when Edmond is arrested, it is for "speaking" to the woman in a certain way that "is construed as assault" (scene 18, p. 83). Edmond tries to elicit a friendly response from the woman by beginning his conversation with the most innocent-sounding statement possible: that her hat resem-bles one his mother used to have. He even goes so far as to include the safe, secure—and revered—image of "mother." Ed-mond is desperate for some comforting word; he almost begs for a response, even a mere acknowledgment. He grows nervous of the silence that forms between them and tells the woman, absurdly, that he is "not making conversation." In this world, to speak to a woman probably implies a sexual advance and Edmond is anxious that the woman in the hat should not feel this to be the case. He goes on to try to give his story even more human depth and warmth, mentioning the fact that his mother had the hat "for years" when he was a child. His efforts are ignored, and the woman edges nervously away. Despite Edmond's efforts to make innocent conversation, his words have indeed been misin-terpreted as a veiled sexual advance. As she physically moves away from him—an action akin to shunning a leper in Edmond's present hypersensitive state—he is completely overwhelmed by the injustice of the situation. In a long line of bitter insults, the unfortunate woman has just added another. To punish her, Edmond's anger knows no bounds; his speech is dangerous with a deadly, hysterical sarcasm. He plagues her with exactly the sort of sexual jibes she most fears and concludes with an appallingly cruel threat of facial disfigurement. There is a terrible childish revenge evident here; Edmond spits his venom at the woman as if to say "If that's what you *think* I'm implying, then so be it."

The entire scene in the subway is reminiscent of a short play written by Mamet in 1981 entitled *Cold*. In this work, one man—designated as "A"—strikes up a conversation with another, called "B," as they both wait on the platform for a train. At first the conversation is tentative, unsure, and concerned with totally innocuous topics such as the weather, the habits of commuters, and so on. However, as A gets into his stride, he begins to ask rather personal questions that B has no desire to answer. They are personal only insofar as they concern the general whereabouts of B's home and are not intended as an impertinence. When the conversation has taken this turn, B becomes cooler and less amenable to his companion, and the edginess of their brief relationship concludes in the following way:

> *A:* Are you going home now?
> *B:* Yes. *(Looks at sound of subway in the distance.)*
> *A:* That's the other track. *(They watch the train passing.)* Do you live
>   alone?
> *B:* No. *(Pause.)*
> *A:* You live with someone?
> *B:* Yes.
> *A.* Are you happy? *(Pause.)*
> *B:* Yes.
> *A:* Are they there now?
> *B:* *(Pause.)* I think so. *(Pause.)*
> *A:* What are they called?
> *B:* Hey, look, what business is it of yours what they're called. *(Pause.)*
>   You understand? *(Pause.)* (p. 152)

Again, Mamet is surely making a statement about more than the irritation that may be caused when strangers strike up unwanted conversations. A wants only to talk, to communicate with someone but, like Edmond, he does not know—or chooses to ignore—the rules and goes too far. His innocent questioning is construed as sinister prying and he is finally shouted down by B and cast out of his life.

Some critics have seen Edmond's encounter with the woman in the subway as indicative of his pent-up sexism; although there may be some truth in this, sexism is not the mainspring of his anger. However, it is rather more difficult to say the same about the vehemence of his racism in his attack on the Pimp. The Pimp has just promised him a meeting with a prostitute but suddenly turns on the gullible Edmond and demands his money. Although Edmond is momentarily stunned by this, he quickly turns the tables and physically attacks the man. As he beats and kicks him, he screams:

> *Edmond:* YOU MOTHERFUCKING NIGGER! . . . you *jungle*bunny. . . . You *coon,* you *cunt,* you *cock*sucker. . . . You shit. . . . You fucking *nigger.* . . . Don't fuck with *me,* you *coon.* . . . I hope you're *dead.* . . . *(Pause. Edmond spits on him.)* (scene 14, pp. 64–65)

Again, Edmond's trust has been betrayed and his courtesy and sense of fair play violated, but on this occasion, there appear to be more dubious forces at work. It is as if a spring of violence has been uncoiled that can only be staunched by viciousness (both verbal and physical) of the most extreme kind. It could be argued that his actions are purely those of an hysterical man seeking out the worst possible insults to assuage his anger, or that his outburst is another instance of language prescribing one's actions rather than vice versa. As the words spill out, so Edmond must carry out the deed to accompany them. However, this argument is somewhat weakened when, later in the play, he confides in Glenna:

> *Edmond:* . . . I wanted to KILL him. *(Pause.)* In that *moment* thirty years of prejudice came out of me. *(Pause.)* Thirty *years.* (scene 16, p. 69)

The words he chooses to denounce his victim are a curious mixture of childish insult and coruscating obscenity. Edmond not only spits on the Pimp, he spits out his words. The contemptuous, alliterative *c* of "*coon* . . . *cunt* . . . *cock*sucker," with the underlining stress on the first syllable is as much an ejection of bile as the beginning of a word. The content of the tirade is very telling: he repeatedly reduces the man to the most base levels. He even seems to use the word "nigger" as a true obscenity, rather than as an ignorant, racist insult. There is some irony in Edmond's denigration of the man as a "cocksucker"—fellatio is precisely the service he had wished for and had paid for prior to the Pimp's attempt to mug him. The term is interesting for another reason: when Edmond relates the episode to Glenna and she remarks upon a particular group of people she despises—"faggots"—he quickly agrees:

> Edmond: . . . I hate them, too. And you know *why*?
> Glenna: Why?
> Edmond: They suck cock. *(Pause.)* And that's the truest thing you'll ever hear. (scene 16, p. 70)

Edmond reduces the prostrate Pimp to a term of abuse frequently applied to homosexuals. Edmond has, for the first time in living memory, carried out a deed that has made him feel like a real man. It follows then that such an insult is not merely another in a long line of oaths, but is selected to make a particular point; Edmond is now the man—the Pimp, the feared black man, is now a mere "faggot." Edmond tells Glenna:

> Edmond: . . . Something *spoke* to me . . . and I spoke *back* to him. "Up your *ass*, you *coon* . . . you want to fight, *I'll* fight you, I'll cut out your fuckin' *heart*, eh, *I* don't give a fuck. . . . *I* got some warlike blood in *my* veins, too, you fucking *spade*, you coon . . ." The *blood* ran down his neck. . . . if there is a *god* he may love the weak, Glenna, *(Pause.)* but he respects the strong. *(Pause.)* And if you are a *man* you should be feared. *(Pause.)* You should be *feared* . . . (scene 16, pp. 68–69, 71)

Edmond has changed from a mild-mannered liberal into a violent reactionary. It has been noted that he "reveals not just a vast suppressed racism, but also the fact that only in violence does he feel fully alive."[40] Edmond now eschews what he has come to see as the stultifying liberalism, which has long oppressed him and made him feel guilty and afraid. Mamet conveys Edmond's sense of liberation through a striking change in his speech patterns. His tentative, insecure verbal style is now replaced by one of confidence and arrogance. Sitting in the Coffeehouse after the incident with the Pimp, Edmond is a changed man; his tone is clear and decisive and completely in keeping with his new positive image:

> Edmond: I want a cup of coffee. No. A beer. Beer chaser. Irish whiskey.
> Glenna: Irish whiskey.
> Edmond: Yes. A double. Huh.
> Glenna: You're in a peppy mood today.
> Edmond: You're goddamn right I am, and you want me to tell you *why*? Because I am *alive*. You know how much of our life we're alive, you and me? *Nothing*. Two minutes out of the year. . . . Sit down . . .

Glenna: I can't. I'm working.

Edmond: . . . you can do anything you *want* to do, you don't sit down because you're *"working,"* the reason you don't sit down is you don't *want* to sit down, because it's more comfortable to *accept* a law than question it and live your life. All of us. *All* of us. We've bred the life out of ourselves. And we live in a fog. We live in a dream. Our life is a *school*-house, and we're dead. (scene 15, pp. 66–67)

In his new-found masculinity, Edmond rejects his first thought that he should order a coffee; instead, he moves up the scale through the acceptable, "macho" beverages that are available until he reaches Irish Whiskey and orders "a double." His manner is sufficiently buoyant to prompt Glenna to comment on his "peppy mood," which encourages him to launch into a diatribe about the need to break free from life's banal restrictions. His sentences now run on effortlessly, articulately, and with complete confidence. He continually asks rhetorical questions, which he loses no time in answering himself. He wants to pass on some of his joyous discovery to Glenna, to make her accept what he has come to accept: the need to take action and move out of mediocrity into truthful experience. He equates his past with a *"school*-house," suggesting he was a mere child before his discovery, and even goes so far as to observe that, until this moment, he had been dead.

Edmond becomes Glenna's advisor and teacher. He is enlivened by his subject, illuminated from within. It is hardly surprising that Glenna should find this vital, enthusiastic man interesting and attractive. His air of authority is seductive to her, and she listens attentively as he spells out his philosophy.

In complete contrast to his earlier overpolite manner, Edmond now comes straight to the point:

Edmond: . . . I want to go home with you tonight.
Glenna: Why?
Edmond: Why do you think? I want to fuck you. *(Pause.)* It's as simple as that. What's your name?
Glenna: Glenna. *(Pause.)* What's yours?
Edmond: Edmond. (ibid., p. 67)

In the announcement of his name, articulated for the first time in the play, Edmond establishes his new identity. What had earlier been referred to as "intercourse" is now described as his desire to "fuck" Glenna. Judging by the pause that follows this declaration, Edmond's straightforward, no-nonsense manner almost seems to surprise him. Life is now simple, without hindrance and without inhibition. As Edmond says, "It's as simple as that."

Edmond's sudden "breakthrough" into a sense of psychic well-being and superiority is a kind of parody of the self-awareness and personal liberation philosophy that flourished in the late 1960s and early 1970s. This was a period of personal discovery for many people, particularly in America where the media screamed "self-improvement" and "self-awareness" from every corner. In his book, *The Culture of Narcissism—American Life in an Age of Diminishing Expectations* (a telling title indeed), Christopher Lasch notes how "the culture of competitive individualism, which in its decadence has carried the logic of individualism to the extreme of a war against all [has resulted in] the pursuit of happiness to the dead end of a narcissistic preoccupation with the self."[41] It was not for nothing that Tom Wolfe described the 1970s as the "me decade."[42] A renaissance of individualism took place, along with a turning away from social issues, politics, and anything that did not offer an immediate resolution. The preoccupation with the self became all-important. In the screenplay for the film, *Manhattan,* Woody Allen's character muses on "an idea for a short story . . . about . . . people in Manhattan who, uh, who are constantly creating these real, uh, unnecessary neurotic problems for themselves 'cause it keeps them from dealing with, uh, more unsolvable, terrifying problems about, uh, the universe."[43]

What results from such "neurotic problems" and self-obsession is the cult of self-realization, of the search for self-knowledge, and an all-consuming concern with physical and spiritual well-being. Like Woody Allen, Mamet believes that fear of the universe can result in a turning in upon oneself; because of the terrible pressures of outside forces, the individual looks to himself for comfort. Mamet observes how "there is no surety. . . . in a world where anything can happen."[44] Thus, many turned away from the ugliness of society, nuclear threat and relentless violence toward a concern with beauty of both mind and body. A rather public "private" image became crucial and there was a massive increase in the sales of self-help goods such as health foods, exercise regimes of the Jane Fonda/Raquel Welch variety, and books on yoga, meditation, and personal astrology. Lasch calls this trend "the culture of narcissism."[45] He notes how people craved "a more vigorous instinctual existence. . . . more vivid experiences . . . [and tried to] revive jaded appetites."[46]

Edmond is both Mamet's terrified citizen and Lasch's cultural narcissist. When the Whore at the brothel tells him that he has a good body, he proudly replies: "I jog" (scene 9, p. 41). Edmond's assertion may not even be true but it speaks volumes. He has internalized all the "body beautiful" propaganda that proliferates; it is now necessary to jog or, at least, pretend to participate in an activity designed to demonstrate publicly one's good health and vitality. An essentially private occupation such as physical exercise has been taken out into the streets and turned image-conscious.

The permissive sexuality that thrived during the 1960s was seen in the decade that followed as a natural form of self-actualization; an obsessive interest in sex detracted from outside issues. It would probably have been unthinkable for Edmond to consider "dropping out" of respectable society were it not for the precedents set by the alternative culture of the 1970s and the lure of freedom they implied.

In the amoral world Edmond enters, quantity and intensity of experience become values in their own right; it matters very little how these are attained since selfishness overrides all other considerations. Mamet has expressed his distaste for the modern-day views that "the whole universe is created just for you . . . no one is accountable for anything [and that] sexuality is fine"[47] no matter what the circumstances. Edmond's adventures repeatedly confirm both his innate ignorance and selfishness. When Glenna refuses to take part in his "declaration of truth" game, he cannot cope. He believes he has seen the light and, therefore, so should everyone else. Glenna becomes very nervous when he pushes her to admit that she is nothing more than a waitress, despite her insistence that she is an actress:

Glenna: I think that you better go.
Edmond: If you want me to go I'll go. Say it with me. Say what you are. And I'll say what *I* am.
Glenna: . . . What *you* are . . .
Edmond: I've *made* that discovery. Now: I want you to change your life with me. *Right* now, for what*ever* that we can be. *I* don't know what that is, *you* don't know. Speak with me. Right now. Say it. . . .
(She takes out a vial of pills.)
Glenna: I have this tendency to get anxious.
Edmond: (Knocks them from her hand.) Don't take them. Go *through* it. Go *through* with me.
Glenna: You're scaring me.

>*Edmond:* I am not. I know when I'm scaring you. *Be*lieve me. (scene 16,
>   p. 76)

Edmond simply refuses to listen to the distraught woman. He
claims that *he* knows better than she what she really wants: "I
know when I'm scaring you." He lies that he will go if she wishes
and then carries on as if he had not spoken those words at all. He
speaks with all the enthusiasm and fervor of a born-again Christian; indeed, his language resembles that of the Preacher in the
next scene. Edmond denies Glenna any rights at all—he forces
her to speak the "truth"; she must confess to him that she is
merely a waitress and eschew her fantasy of being an actress.
Glenna refuses to acknowledge that she is "just" a waitress; an
elaborate curtain of self-defense and self-confidence would collapse should she admit this. Miranda Richardson notes Glenna's
desperate vulnerability:

>Glenna is trying very, very hard to be an actress—or at least to
>convince herself that she has a chance. It could all be a pose. . . . She
>is attracted to Edmond because he's older than she is—again, it's the
>pupil/teacher relationship which runs throughout Mamet's works . . .
>she thinks she can learn something from him. Girls like her are
>desperate for love, for any affection; if someone comes into their lives
>who looks even half-decent, they clutch at them. Maybe he can get
>her work, help her along, or even become emotionally involved with
>her. Poor Glenna has surrounded herself with this awful brightness,
>this falseness, to get by. I think she has probably had numerous bad
>experiences with men, a lot of one-night stands. She has thought they
>may lead somewhere but has been constantly let down . . . Glenna
>tries to get by in a very fast-moving city with neon lights flashing all
>night and about two cubic feet of space to herself. No wonder she is
>on tranquilizers and no wonder she takes Edmond home, hoping he
>might be her salvation. Unless you are very strong, how *do* you get
>by? A woman alone is in such an insecure and dangerous position.[48]

Edmond is too wrapped up in his own crusading excitement to
notice how terrified Glenna is:

>*Glenna:* Get out! GET OUT GET OUT! LEAVE ME THE FUCK
>   ALONE!!! WHAT DID I DO, PLEDGE MY LIFE TO YOU? I LET
>   YOU FUCK ME. GO AWAY.
>*Edmond:* Listen to me: You know what madness is?
>*Glenna:* I told you to go away. *(Goes to phone. Dials.)*
>*Edmond:* I'm lonely too. I know what it is, too. Believe me. Do you
>   know what madness is? . . . It's self-indulgence. (scene 16, p. 77)

Despite her hysteria, Edmond presses ahead. He even turns on her and brings up the subject of madness, presumably in an effort to make her see her "irrationality." It is by the repeated use of the words "I" and "me" that Mamet conveys Edmond's self-obsession. He blames Glenna for her panic, although he is palpably its cause.

Glenna is murdered because Edmond cannot tolerate that she does not share his visionary zeal and, perhaps more importantly, because in her fear, she turns everything he has come to believe is good into evil. She cries out in panic:

> *Glenna:* Will somebody help you are the get *away* from me! You are the *devil*. I know who you are. I know what you want me to do. Get *away* from me I curse *you*, you can't kill me, get away from me I'm *good*. (ibid., p. 78)

Glenna's hysteria is powerfully suggested in the way her syntax and grammar become fragmented into shards of speech. She begins one sentence and veers wildly away from it, only to return moments later in the middle of another. Mamet builds the action of the scene into the lines: as Edmond moves towards Glenna, her panic mounts and leads her to equate him with the devil and all that is evil. Of this scene, Colin Stinton comments:

> In trying to pass on his new sense of liberation to Glenna, Edmond comes up against not only a rejection of all he now holds to be good and true but also an identification of this with evil . . . I think this is the answer to the much-asked question of why he kills her . . . "You are the devil," she tells him and he just cannot cope. His solution to the problems of life, so painfully won, have been decried as evil. All he aspires to is called horrible. To have someone graphically identify his sense of achievement with evil makes him white with rage and, in a moment of impetuosity and turmoil, he stabs her.[49]

Miranda Richardson has a similar interpretation of the events: "I saw it as his need to shut her up. . . . He does intend to shut her up but he doesn't intend to kill her. He is saying 'I don't want it, it's not happening, take it away, it's not real' and the only way he can stop her is by striking her. By silencing her, he can momentarily carry on with his 'liberating' belief, unsullied by accusations of evil."[50] That Edmond should have come to commit such a brutal crime has been due to his inexorable descent into a literal hell and his absorption of some of its horrors. As Clive Barnes notes, he has been "like Dante without a Virgil to guide him [he is alone in] New York's special inferno."[51]

The murder itself is very rapid and brutal. Glenna is by now almost unintelligible through her terror:

> Glenna: I . . . No. Help! Help.
> Edmond: . . . You're being . . .
> Glenna: . . . HELP!
> Edmond: . . . are you *insane*? What the fuck are you trying to *do*, for godsake. . . . You want to wake the *neighbors*? . . . .Shut up shut up! . . . You fucking *bitch*. You're *nuts* . . . (*He stabs her with the knife.*) (ibid., p. 78)

Edmond's old concerns momentarily intrude; he exhorts Glenna to stop making a noise or she will awaken the neighbors! Her panic is, to Edmond, totally incomprehensible; he can see no valid reason for her behavior and again mentions insanity. Even when he has, albeit unintentionally, stabbed and killed her, he switches the blame from himself, rather like Teach in *American Buffalo* after he has destroyed Don's shop with the pig-iron. Edmond's last words in this scene illustrate both his astonishment at what he has done, and his automatic shifting of the responsibility:

> Edmond: . . . You stupid fucking *bitch* . . . You stupid fucking . . . *now* look what you've done. (*Pause.*) Now look what you've bloody fucking done. (ibid., p. 78)

In his "*now* look what you've done" is an echo of a parent admonishing a child for a wrongdoing; the phrase doesn't carry the weight the circumstances demand and is indicative of Edmond's complete confusion and terror. His use of the word "bloody" in such a situation carries its own implications; it is, after all, a rather unusual oath for an American to use.

Miranda Richardson believes that the tragedy is, essentially, due to a complete lack of communication between the lovers:

> The murder scene is symbolic—the lashing out is symbolic . . . again, as in so much of Mamet's work, the subject is lack of communication. All the way through it is the same thing . . . Edmond and Glenna could have had a good relationship, it could all have been so different. Things could have gone this way instead of that, a word here might have prevented a calamity there. It is so random. The real misunderstandings begin when they start talking about Glenna's acting . . . they keep missing each other by inches all the way through but there is a real sense of danger at this point.[52]

Michael Billington points to the same moment when a stomach-churning sense of foreboding enters the proceedings. He notes Mamet's ability to pinpoint "the way conversations . . . can lurch into unpredictable violence."[53] During their postcoital chat, Glenna tells Edmond that she once played the part of Juliet:

> *Glenna:* In college I played Juliet.
> *Edmond:* In Shakespeare?
> *Glenna:* Yes. In Shakespeare. What do you think? (scene 16, p. 73)

The edginess of Glenna's response, pregnant with indignation that Edmond may not believe her claim, ignites the spark of misunderstanding. Miranda Richardson notes that "Glenna is 'acting' all the time, playing a part, and Edmond suddenly challenges something important about this role. There are shifts in understanding at every line . . . the sad thing is that they *think* they are truly communicating, but they never really do."[54] She goes on to note how "one little word and she has had it. Her doom is imminent—it is a mistake to get into such a potentially touchy (and personal) area after a brief acquaintance but in the 'reveal-all' atmosphere prevailing at the time, it is easy to see how it happens."[55] Edmond worsens matters by refusing to acknowledge the stupidity of his question, and goes on to say, arrogantly:

> *Edmond:* Well, I meant there's *plays* named Juliet.
> *Glenna:* There are?
> *Edmond:* Yes.
> *Glenna:* I don't think so. (ibid., pp. 73–74)

There is a slight hint of sarcasm in Glenna's, "There are?". Edmond is irritated by her reaction and insists that such plays exist but Glenna is equally persistent in what she feels is her superior knowledge of the theatre. Edmond has challenged Glenna on a subject she feels she knows something about, even though she has only ever done "scenes" for her "peers" (ibid., p. 73). Everything was fine as long as they both continued to agree with one another, bolstering egos and opinions with concurrence. Whether their talk led to an admission of hatred for "faggots" or to the joys of standing up for one's rights against a mugger in the Charles Bronson/*Death Wish* type of situation, all was well in happy agreement:

> *Glenna:* Did you kill him?
> *Edmond:* Did I kill him?

Glenna: Yes.
Edmond: I don't care. *(Pause.)*
Glenna: That's wonderful. (ibid., p. 69)

Edmond's admission of brutality is somehow seductive for Glenna. As a frightened, lonely woman living alone in New York City, it is perhaps not difficult to understand why she would express admiration for someone who has "fought back." Edmond's new-found courage is very reminiscent of the state of affairs discussed by Wallace Shawn in an essay written about his play, *Aunt Dan and Lemon.* Shawn observes how easily morality can become totally inverted and how even one act of violence or hostility perpetrated in an atmosphere of self-justification can radically alter an individual's outlook. Suddenly, this new way of life is the *only* way to live and all previous considerations are summarily discounted. Shawn writes about those friends of his who have made the "choice" to act in a new, "immoral" way:

> The amazing thing I've noticed about those friends of mine who've made that choice is that as soon as they've made it, they begin to blossom, to flower, because they are no longer hiding, from themselves or anyone else, the true facts about their own lives. They become very frank about human nature. They freely admit that man is a predatory creature, a hunter and a fighter, and they admit that it can warm a human's heart to trick an enemy, to make him cry, to make him do what he doesn't want to do, and even to make him crawl in the mud and die in agony. . . . They admit that there's a skill involved in playing life's game, and they admit that it's exciting to bully and threaten and outwit the defeat all the other people who are playing against you. And as they learn to admit these things, and they lose the habit of looking over their shoulder in fear at what exists in their own souls, they develop the charm and grace which shine out from all people who are truly comfortable with themselves, who are not worried, who are not ashamed of their own actions.[56]

It is interesting to note that Wallace Shawn is one of the dedicatees to whom Mamet inscribes *Edmond*; it is fairly obvious to see why, in reading the above words. Shawn could be referring to Edmond's confused and unfocused morality and his sense of joy and achievement once he has made an irrevocable move in an alien direction.

The anarchy that would result from an entire society's decision to ignore the constraints of morality is something that clearly terrifies Mamet. He is a staunch supporter of old-fashioned, middle-class values: good education, a home, and a job as rewards for hard work, money in the bank, a comfortable standard of living, and so on. He says "I'd like to think that [in a few years' time] my money will still be in the bank and my daughter can still get a job, etc."[57] In *Edmond,* he explores the crisis and potential destruction of all that was worthy in America's past by an unthinking, immoral culture. Edmond is named after Edmund Burke, the eighteenth-century English conservative writer and political philosopher. In scene 18, Mamet's protagonist declares his name to be "Edmond Burke" and later refers to himself as "Eddie Burke" (scene 22, p. 98) as he writes to the mother of a childhood sweetheart. There is little doubt that a direct connection is intended, despite the fact that Mamet's Edmond spells his Christian name with an *o* instead of a *u*. Since Mamet has made it clear that he fears the descent of his country into a kind of chaotic anarchy, it is not really surprising that he should ironically name his hero after a man who pleaded throughout his life for order and stability. Edmond is a product of an age that has found neither order nor peace; he foolishly and naïvely believes that he can find these by moving out of a mundane, business-oriented world into one that is exciting and unknown. What he finds there however is pain and misery. Edmond's freedom becomes so negligible, long before he is incarcerated for murder, as to exist hardly at all. Perhaps Mamet had in mind the following quotation of Edmund Burke's when he conceived of his character: "The extreme of liberty obtains nowhere; nor ought it to obtain anywhere; because extremes, as we all know . . . are destructive both to virtue and enjoyment. Liberty, too, must be limited in order to be possessed."[58] He could also have been inspired by Burke's observation, "Good order is the foundation of all things."[59] Both these quotations speak plainly to the need for order and restraint, two elements Mamet feels are sadly lacking in modern America.

Burke also wrote a great deal about the United States and his comments upon that country seem curiously apposite when applied to the world Mamet evokes in *Edmond*. Burke observed that "America, at this day serves for little more than to amuse you with stories of savage men and uncouth manners."[60] Edmond certainly mixes with savage men and, tragically, becomes one of them himself. *Edmond* has frequently been called a kind of morality play—or, as Michael Coveney would have it, an "amorality play."[61] Mamet shows up what Burke so quaintly calls "uncouth manners" for all they are worth, and proves that a life without emotional or moral content is really no life at all.

It has been suggested that Edmond is merely acting out in reality the fantasies he has always enjoyed in secret; again Burke is relevant in his observation that "all men that are ruined are ruined on the side of their natural propensities"[62] and it is quite possible that Edmond has always harbored desires for seedy sexuality and gratuitous violence. Burke's quotations provide a kind of framework for Mamet's play: they concern a need for order and stability, the necessity for some limits to freedom (without which there would be nothing short of anarchy), the possibility that a man like Edmond seeks his own doom due to his "natural propensities," and the airing of an opinion that America is both "savage" and "uncouth." It becomes quite clear why Mamet should have so entitled his play, and leaves none of the mystery felt by Clive Barnes when he writes "there are nuggets of puzzlement here; why is the simple hero called Edmond Burke, with all the historical suggestions that implies."[63]

Edmond's dissatisfaction with his life reaches an intolerable level, and his frustrations become actualized when he leaves the Fortune-Teller's establishment for his own boring home. Her opinion of him as "special" is very seductive; it enables him to justify his subordination of the interests of others and to concentrate fully on his own self-fulfillment, irrespective of the effect it may have upon those who share his life. As Michael Coveney observes, "there is here a remarkable sense of a character wanting to break free and going about doing so with rare indelicacy and inefficiency."[64] With a few, bald words, he seals his fate:

> *Edmond:* I'm going, and I'm not going to come back. *(Pause)*.
> *Wife:* You're not *ever* coming back?
> *Edmond:* No.
> *Wife:* Why not? *(Pause.)*
> *Edmond:* I don't want to live this kind of life.
> *Wife:* What does that mean?
> *Edmond:* That I can't live this life. (scene 2, p. 18)

Edmond's language is simplistic. These are not the words of a man who has long deliberated on his future. Rather, they have a ring of spontaneity to them, an immediacy that must come as much of a surprise to Edmond as to his dumbfounded wife. Her feelings are not even considered; what is all-important to Edmond at this moment is to state his case succinctly and positively, to say the words aloud and thereby make them a reality. It is as if he takes his cues for action from his audible thoughts; the more he says, the deeper his psyche is ploughed.

At first he states that he no longer *wants* to live this life and then, moments later, bolsters his case by stressing the impossibility of continuance. His wife is incredulous; she had thought he was going out for a few minutes and had even asked him to bring "back some cigarettes." It is with total disbelief that she continues the conversation:

> *Wife:* "You can't live this life" so you're leaving me.
> *Edmond:* Yes.
> *Wife:* Ah. Ah. Ah.
>   And what about ME?
>   Don't you *love* me anymore? (ibid., pp. 18–19)

The astonished woman is so shocked and outraged that she verbally swerves between stunned disbelief and cutting sarcasm. Her bitter parody of a line one might hear in a soap opera, "Don't you *love* me anymore?" points to her wish to belittle the infuriatingly calm Edmond and make him feel ridiculous. Connie Booth, who played the role in the Royal Court production, had great difficulty with its interpretation since Mamet gives so very little guidance:

> For me, Edmond's wife was a struggle, the problem being that a marriage of some years is being drawn to its conclusion in a space of the lines covering approximately two pages. That Mamet achieves the power he does with such economy speaks for him as a writer. But it presents one hell of a challenge to the actor. Richard Eyre (the director) seemed to have an instinctive as well as an intellectual understanding of this particular play and was a great help to me in working on it.[65]

When Edmond tells his wife that he has long since stopped loving her, and that she does not interest him "spiritually or sexually," she is crushed, devastated. She is so outraged by his cool behavior that it is *she* who leaves the room, despite her following final admonition:

> *Wife:* . . . Good-bye. Thank you. Good-bye. (*Pause.*) Good-bye. (*Pause.*) Get *out*. Get *out* of here. And don't you *ever* come back. Do you hear me? (*Wife exits. Closing the door on him.*) (ibid., p. 21)

She begins her dismissal of Edmond almost as if she were taking leave of a salesman; the tight, sarcastic politeness of her words is sharply contrasted with the heartbroken sob that Mamet writes into the lines. It is as if she does not trust herself with sentences longer than two or three words; it is only after pauses for breath, which allow her an opportunity to bolster her strength, that she dares to say more. The lines are set out like verse, indicating to the actress that the rhythm is all-important. The Wife's distress rises as the timbre of her voice is elevated to a cry of despair, which is stemmed only as she quickly leaves the stage, closing the door that, for her husband, symbolizes the severance of "normal" ties.

Colin Stinton interprets the events leading up to the Wife closing the door on Edmond as yet another example of Mamet's device of preceding the deed with the word. By *saying* something, by making it audible, the speaker then has to act upon it. Stinton believes that Edmond's initial idea was probably not to leave his wife then and there, but that her hostile manner and pettiness over the broken lamp made up his mind. He states that he is leaving, and the inexorable logic of his words forces him to adhere to them. There is no going back. Colin Stinton observes that, "by having the Wife do the actual physical leaving, Edmond is left almost as a victim of circumstances rather than someone who has left his wife. The comical extreme of this would be to give the impression that Edmond is left thinking "Gee . . . was it something I said?"—but it's not far from the truth."[66]

Things happen very quickly in *Edmond*, and Connie Booth likens Mamet's pacy dialogue—indeed the entire play—to the movement of an on-rushing train: "*Prairie du Chien* is actually set on board a train, the Storyteller's tale gaining impetus from the movement of the journey . . . *Edmond*, too, has a similar compulsion, an inexorable feeling of onward movement. I have a feeling that both the text and the content of Mamet's work are like a relentless train journey."[67] Edmond rejects all past ties and sets out, like an uncerebral version of Dostoyevsky's Raskolnikov, to prove to himself his worth and existence through the extremes of experience. Because he does not care to confront the problems in his life head-on, he merely leaves them all behind. Life for him has become both tedious and worthless; instead of trying to find a way out by relating his problems and frustrations to a wider perspective or, perhaps, by confiding in friends, he chooses to retreat into self-obsession. Evasion is the only antidote to suffering for such a man.

In turning his back upon the competitive world of business and domestic life, Edmond becomes exactly like Lasch's narcissist: "Acquisitive in the sense that his cravings have no limits, he does not accumulate goods and provisions against the future . . . but demands immediate gratification, and lives in a state of restless, perpetually unsatisfied desire."[68]

Mamet has written a series of short plays and monologues entitled *The Blue Hour: City Sketches,* which deal with alienation and loneliness in big cities. Finding himself in a sleazy bar in what Bill Bryden has termed "the blue hour . . . when people get the blues."[69] Edmond is drawn into a conversation with a stranger that closely reflects the kind of dialogue found in Mamet's *City Sketches*:

> *Edmond:* What do you do?. . . . What do you do to get out? . . .
> *Man:* What are the things to do. What are the things *anyone* does? . . .
>   *(Pause.) Pussy* . . . I don't know . . . *Pussy* . . . *Power* . . . *Money* . . .
>   uh . . . *adventure* . . . *(Pause.)* I think that's it . . . uh, self-*destruction*
>   . . . I think that that's it . . . don't you?
> *Edmond:* Yes.
> *Man:* . . .uh, *religion* . . . I suppose that's it, uh, *release,* uh, ratifica-
>   tion. . . (scene 3, pp. 23–24)

The alliteration serves to highlight the Man's "seen-it-all" attitude; the words roll off his tongue with a well-worn rhythm. He initially suggests that Edmond seek sex as the means to liberation. He uses the vulgar and demotic term, "pussy," which underscores his advice that sex, not love or emotional attachment, is the key to Edmond's problems. Since Edmond *is* probably sexually frustrated, bearing in mind his recent conversation with his wife, the idea of sexual adventure is appealing; it implies impulsive action, a sense of control, and allows a personal expression of selfhood. For these reasons, Edmond seizes on sexual expression as his way of making an imprint on society but, as Colin Stinton has observed, he could have followed any number of other roads; sex is merely an easy option at this vulnerable time. Stinton believes it is a mistake to take too seriously the notion that Edmond is motivated only by sex: "the challenge could just have easily been to get a good price on tomatoes. To get hung up on Edmond being sex crazy, or even misogynistic, is to totally miss the point. What he wants is *experience*, excitement, to *play the game*. The name of the game doesn't matter; whether it is sex or money or whatever; it's the *playing* that counts."[70]

What is remarkable about the Man's short speech is that it succinctly and acidly delineates the concerns of the entire play. "Power" is something Edmond feels he must attain and, tragically, when he does, it is over the pathetic Glenna. Since money is the stumbling block for so many of Edmond's attempted "adventures," it is ironic that Mamet should include these escapes just prior to "self-destruction." An even deeper irony occurs in "religion" since it is on his way to a revivalist mission that Edmond is finally arrested. Quite what his "ratification" amounts to is unclear; perhaps it is merely that at the end of the play he no longer has any choices to make; his decisions are all made for him and thereby his actions are somehow ratified. All Edmond's experiences are contained in this speech and, as such, it is a kind of brief chronicle of his postdomestic life.

Edmond goes off, on the Man's advice, to "The Allegro," in order to find a woman and have sexual relations with her. He quickly finds that commerical sex is both expensive and unsatisfactory; in fact, in his attempts to indulge in it, he is repeatedly thwarted because he has brought with him too much of his middle-class, business mentality as well as a need to be fair in all negotiations. Because he feels he is being exploited, he argues about the price he must pay for the B-girl's drinks and her company:

> *Edmond:* I'll give you five. I'll give you the five you'd get for the drink if I gave them ten. But I'm not going to give them ten.
> *B-girl:* But you have to buy me a drink.
> *Edmond:* I'm sorry. No.
> *B-girl:* Alright. *(Pause.)* Give me ten.
> *Edmond:* On top of the ten?
> *B-girl:* Yeah. You give me twenty.
> *Edmond:* I should give you twenty.
> *B-girl:* Yes.
> *Edmond:* To *you.*
> *B-girl.* Yes.
> *Edmond:* And then you give him the five?
> *B-girl:* Yes. I got to give him the five.
> *Edmond:* No. (scene 4, pp. 28–29)

This sounds more like the business negotiations of two executives than a dialogue between a prostitute and her client. Edmond is determined not to be exploited, but there is here also a hint of his concern for the girl; he does not wish to be part of any scheme in which she may be abused at the hands of pimps or barroom "managers." Throughout the play, he emphasizes his respect for those who work and takes the trouble to find the best "deal" for the worker in question. Edmond has an unswerving sense of fariness, which may be due to an intense regard for the work ethic. In his eyes, to work is to be a good, respectable citizen who is prepared to pull his own weight. Quite where this leaves him once he has severed all ties is unclear, but his concern persists. Perhaps the most striking example of Edmond's belief in the sanctity of work occurs when the woman in the subway has run away from him, screaming for help. He is incensed and distraught that she should have mistaken his innocent approach as a sinister prelude to a violent attack. He cries in desperation: "*You* don't know who I am. . . . Is everybody in this town *insane*? . . . Fuck you . . . fuck you . . . fuck you . . . fuck the *lot* of you . . . fuck you *all* . . . I don't *need* you . . . I worked all of my life!" (scene 13, p. 59). The repeated obscenities only serve to emphasize the helplessness Edmond feels. His reaction is to shout abuse at no one in particular, rather like a deranged drunk in the middle of the road. His assertion that he doesn't "need" anyone is plainly untrue; more than anything else, Edmond needs support and solace.

Edmond's respect for the work ethic surfaces again just before he fatally wounds Glenna. He sings the praises of working women:

> *Edmond:* . . . A working woman. Who brought life to what she did. Who took a moment to *joke* with me. That's . . . that's . . . that's . . . god *bless* you what you are. (scene 16, p. 75)

Edmond is profoundly grateful that at least one person has treated him courteously and without contempt. He is so ecstatic he can barely articulate his words and he stammers "that's" three times without concluding the sentence. At this moment Glenna is the ideal being to Edmond. She is an open, kind-hearted woman with no malice or cruelty in mind. The terrible irony is that, like Büchner's *Woyzeck*, Edmond later kills the one person with whom he may have found lasting happiness and contentment.

Mamet's play has frequently been compared to *Woyzeck*, a fragmentary, unfinished play about a simple—even imbecilic—army private who murders his unfaithful wife. Michael Billington finds *Edmond* "fascinating [in] its echoes of Büchner's *Woyzeck*, in its fragmentation and stark emphasis on human destruction."[71] Douglas Watt believes that *Edmond* has an "obvious kinship with Büchner's early 19th century dramatic shocker [and this fact] emphasizes the somewhat Germanic tone (even the dialogue sounds like a translation at times) and that it could effectively be fleshed out by a Berg-like score."[72] *Woyzeck* powerfully depicts the social and economic iniquities that lead both to the wife's faithlessness and her murder by her husband. Like *Edmond*, it is extraordinarily compact and economic in style, comprised of a quick succession of short scenes that are executed in pared down, yet brilliantly realistic language. There are striking similarities on a purely verbal level, as well as in the atmosphere of fatalism that runs through both plays. In the shop of an old Jew, Woyzeck purchases the knife he will use to murder his wife:

> *Woyzeck:* The gun's too dear.
> *Jew:* You buy or you don't buy, which is it?
> *Woyzeck:* How much is the knife?
> *Jew:* Lovely and straight it is. You want to cut your throat with it?—So what's the matter? I give it to you as cheap as anybody else. Cheap you can have your death, but not for nothing. What's the matter? You'll have your death all right, very economical.
> *Woyzeck:* It'll cut more than bread.
> *Jew:* Tuppence.
> *Woyzeck:* There.[73]

When Edmond pawns his ring, he overhears another customer enquiring about a knife; he becomes interested and enquires himself:

> *Edmond:* Why is it so expensive?
> *Owner:* Why is it so expensive? . . . This is a *survival* knife. G.I. Issue. World War Two. And that is why.
> *Edmond:* Survival knife.
> *Owner:* That is correct.
> *Edmond:* Is it a good knife?
> *Owner:* It is the best knife that money can buy. *(He starts to put knife away. As an afterthought.)* You want it?
> *Edmond:* Let me think about it for a moment. (scene 12, p. 57)

There are obvious similarities here; the brief, clipped sentences, the inference in both cases that the knife might be used for more than cutting bread, the impatience on the part of the knife-seller, and the Jewish-sounding rhythms that both dramatists incorporate into this character's speech. What is perhaps most striking about these excerpts is the extraordinary sense of menace each writer manages to incorporate into a seemingly simple exchange. A powerful subtext of violence is present in both works. In *Woyzeck*, the Captain exhorts the protagonist to take more care:

> *Captain:* What's the hurry, Woyzeck? Stop a bit. You rush through the
> world like an open razor. You'll give somebody a nasty cut.[74]

As Edmond similarly rushes towards his doom, Mamet depicts an
image of one who has been literally 'sharpened' by life's cruelties
and whose final act of murder is via a "nasty cut." Indeed, Douglas Watt has observed that the whole play is rather like "a raw
wound."[75]

Another source of inspiration is undoubtedly Theodore Dreiser's *An American Tragedy.* Mamet has cited Dreiser's work as an
early influence; it, too, charts the downfall of an innocent. Dreiser's first and last emphasis in this novel is on enclosure, on the
stifling claustrophobia of city life. The ominous beginning describes "the tall walls of the commercial heart of an American
city"[76] and the dark epilogue again details "the tall walls of the
commercial heart of the City of San Francisco—tall and grey in the
evening shade."[77] As Alfred Kazin observes, "enclosure is fundamental to the social logic behind *An American Tragedy.* It is a logic
that Dreiser's method forces us to accept. . . . Dreiser does not
leave anything out of his almost one thousand pages. . . . The
compulsion behind Clyde's life has transferred itself to the narrative. The inevitability that Dreiser brings to every detail is like
Clyde's progress to the chair. The reader feels as trapped as
Clyde."[78]

Mamet's script for *Edmond* contains a similar compulsion; it
begins and ends with a discussion about destiny and all that
comes between seems to follow an already established pattern.
Like Clyde, Edmond remains to the last an unconscious prisoner
of fate. Raskolnikov, the intellectual murderer in Dostoyevsky's
Crime and Punishment, was Dreiser's favorite character in fiction.
Although he based his character upon Dostoyevsky's creation to
some extent, the two men could hardly be more different—one is
an intellectual and the other an easily confused, far from intelligent shopworker. Although the reasons that Raskolnikov, Clyde,
and Edmond commit murder seem dissimilar at first, they are in
fact closely linked. Raskolnikov strikes at the mediocrity and
cheapness he sees as characteristic of his society, and thus decides
to murder to show the world—and himself—the triumph of his
will. Clyde rids himself of the girl who stands between him and
his ambitions, his self-realization; to him, Roberta represents all
that is pallid and half-hearted about the world he wishes to leave
behind. Edmond kills Glenna because of his unshakable egotism;

she clutches at the threads of comfort her banal life has offered and thereby denies Edmond the means of vindicating his new, truly liberated way of life. The common denominators in each case are the need to break free from a restrictive and suffocating society, and the selfishness of each man.

An American Tragedy was dramatized by Erwin Piscator and entitled *The Case of Clyde Griffiths*. Since this play was eventually staged by The Group Theatre with Lee Strasberg directing, it is possible that Mamet became aware of the novel through his involvement with founding member Sanford Meisner and his association with Harold Clurman. As Clurman recalls, the play was poorly received. "The reason for the reviewers' dislike of the play . . . was not that it was a poor piece of writing, but that it interpreted the plot of *An American Tragedy* . . . in terms of the class struggle. The Piscator dramatization employed a Speaker who dunned the audience with a single refrain: "We have given a name to Fate. It is the Economic System."[79] It is not difficult to understand how Mamet, with his concern over the capitalist system in his country and his interest in fate, should have been drawn to such sources.

Despite the almost universal acclaim Mamet has received for *Edmond*, there remain a few critics for whom it is a grave disappointment. Frank Rich feels that Mamet was out of form when he wrote the play, suggesting that he was "spinning hooey and neglecting his valuable gifts."[80] He goes on to compare *Edmond* with plays such as *American Buffalo, Sexual Perversity in Chicago,* and *The Water Engine:* "[In these plays] . . . Mamet has demonstrated an uncommon ability to hear the voices of inarticulate Americans and to limn the society that oppresses them. Though the thematic concerns are similar in *Edmond,* the author's ear has gone tone deaf, and his social observations have devolved into clichés."[81] Rich seems to have completely missed the point of what Mamet is trying to achieve in the play. If the characters speak in what he describes as "tone deaf" dialogue, it is because they are incapable of speaking in any other way. They are part of the society that has created them and that has taken away the beauty of language in its never-ending pursuit of the prosaic and functional. Communication is reduced to the bare essentials in which not a word is wasted to get from point A to point B. Where there *is* a suggestion of lyricism, it quickly becomes apparent that this is part of a verbal strategy, designed to entrap a listener in its intrigues. For example, the Three Card Monte speaks in a beguiling and mesmeric rhythm, but this has been carefully cultivated to persuade and coerce naïve would-be gamblers to participate in his dubious game. He sounds seductive—like the Whore before she gets down to basics—and mesmerizing as he sets about spinning his linguistic web. The sheer hypnotic pull of his words draws Edmond closer to the game. He has been advised to "figure out which card has *got* to win . . . and bet the *other* one" (scene 6, pp. 35–36). As Colin Stinton has observed, this becomes Edmond's life-strategy as well as his gambling technique—he takes action that is unexpected and sometimes perverse in an effort to "beat life's game."[82] The Sharper notices Edmond loitering on the sidelines and senses a possible quarry:

> *Sharper:* You going to try me again? . . .
> *Edmond:* Again? . . .
> *Sharper:* I remember you beat me out of that *fifty* that time with your
>   girlfriend . . .
> *Edmond:* . . . When was this?
> *Sharper:* On four*teen*ff street. . . . You going to try me one more
>   time? . . . (scene 10, p. 46)

The Sharper draws Edmond toward him by utilizing in one short sentence two forms of flattery that will almost certainly bring about the desired effect. He gives a puff to Edmond's supposed gambling expertise and to his sexual vanity; he takes a chance by referring to a fictional past game in which Edmond "beat" him out of "fifty." There is here a sense that both men are fully aware that this is a lie but are each willing to participate in it. Mamet places the Sharper socially by his pronunciation of "four*teen*ff" street and by the "African-American" inflections in his voice, as well as by stressing his streetwise manner. As soon as he has Edmond's attention, he moves into the linguistic routine specifically designed to catch his prey:

> *Sharper:* . . . Play you for that fifty . . . Fifty get you one hundred, we
>   see you as fast as you was . . . Pay on the red, pass on the black . . .
>   Where is the queen? . . . You pick the queen you win . . . *Where* is
>   the queen? . . . Who saw the queen? . . . You put up fifty, win a
>   hundred . . . Now: who saw the queen? . . . (ibid., p. 47)

The Shill loses his money, and Edmond decides to try his luck. Again, the Sharper uses flattery: "Ah, *shit*, man, you too fass for me" (ibid.). However, Edmond's choice is the wrong one and he loses his money. The Sharper's sequence of words beginning with, "Where is the queen?" and ending with, "Who saw the queen?" works as a kind of mesmeric chant. It is reminiscent of the rhythms used by black Baptist preachers at prayer meetings, where the flow and harmonic elements of their speech are crucial to engage the sympathies and responses of the congregation. Indeed, the speech of the Preacher in *Edmond* follows very similar lines: the following extract from his exhortations for a sinner to come up to the dais to testify indicates how close the two methods of linguistic coercion truly are:

> *Preacher:* "Oh no, not me!," You say, "Oh no, not me. Not *me*, Lord, to whom you hold out your hand. Not *me* to whom you offer your eternal grace. Not *me* who can be saved. . . ." But *who* but you, I ask you? *Who* but you. (scene 17, p. 79)

In both extracts, there are many strong vowel sounds, and the rhyming quality of the words lulls the listener and engages him in a rhythmic confection intended to elicit a response.

Mamet also uses a kind of Orwellian inversion in *Edmond*. Not only have words changed their meaning or, at least, taken on new implications, they also serve to demonstrate how little ordinary discourse can be taken at face value. In an essay in which he discusses the misappropriation of much contemporary language, Mamet observes,

> My generation grew up in a time where constant aggression publicly avowed came to be the norm of our foreign policy. We had changed the name of the Department of War to the Department of Defense, and went about making war continually and calling it defense until today we doubt if there *is* such a thing as defense; or if, in fact, the real meaning of defense is not "aggression." We have come to accept all sorts of semantic inversions, as George Orwell told us we had.[83]

When Edmond buys the knife he will use to murder Glenna, the weapon is referred to as a "survival knife;" thus, the boundaries between life and death become semantically blurred. He declares the necessity to "live" seconds before he stabs her to death and his new-found sense of life affirmation is tragically transposed to self-destruction. The word "pledge" no longer refers to human commitment but to an object pawned for money. When the item is once again required, it can then be "redeemed." Thus, two words that originally indicated a serious undertaking and a kind of salvation have been reduced to mere fiscal terms. The Manager at the "health club" is really the Madame of a brothel—Edmond's activities there will be billed to him only as having occurred in

"Atlantic Ski and Tennis." When he is accosted outside the Peep Show by the Pimp, he asks if the whore in question will be "clean." Even a word like this has taken on a new and sinister meaning. What once referred only to hygiene or fastidiousness now relates to someone who is free from venereal disease and who is honest and up to no tricks. Actions, as well as words, have been similarly inverted or altered. All attempts to make contact with another individual are seen as incipient threats, games have been devalued into fraudulent cons, and affection, in the form of prostitution, must be bought.

It is difficult not to feel that reviewers who have given poor notices to *Edmond* because of its 'failure' to utilize language effectively have been extremely unfair. Even if one quibbles about the work's bluntness and its harshly prosaic verbal style, there is still much to admire. Of the language used in *Edmond* Connie Booth comments: "The dialogue reminds me of the sort of difference which exists, say, between Rodgers and Hart and Stephen Sondheim. You might not come out of a Sondheim musical humming some of the tunes because they are often too dense and complex. The Rodgers and Hart music might be more accessible . . . but it won't make the impact of Sondheim's best work."[84] In the same way that *American Buffalo* was misunderstood as nothing more than a slice of realism, it would appear from some critical opinion that something similar has occurred with *Edmond*. The play cannot be viewed as simple realism, a slice of "low life," if only because of the exceptionally compact and economic structure of its text and scenes. There is surely a sense of the abstract about the play. One cannot possibly view Edmond's downfall in purely naturalistic terms, since he moves so rapidly from one crisis to another. His destruction is almost surrealistic in its intensity and nightmarish imagery. The play is intended as an allegory—as Mamet himself has pointed out, "an American Rake's Progress."[85] As Edmond wanders frightened and alone through the Nighttown-like darkness of New York's red-light districts, he becomes rather like Bunyan's Pilgrim whose progress, it will be recalled, led him to Vanity Fair, where all the empty things of the world are sold. Edmond, too, encounters emptiness and desolation but, unlike Bunyan's adventurer, his wanderings do not end in heaven but in prison. He does, however, find a kind of peace at the play's conclusion and this is another aspect of the work that has much troubled its adverse critics.

The end of Mamet's play *is* rather far-fetched, but only if viewed as the culmination of a series of real-life escapades. If it is meant as a haunting picture of a man who has, because of the intolerable pressures upon him, brought about his own ruin but inadvertantly found tranquility, then it is completely believable. Edmond finds a spurious kind of happiness in prison, even though he has been made to confront each of his prejudices and to accept what before he had found repugnant. His sexism, racism, and contemptuous attitude toward homosexuals are all inverted when he is forced to become the "wife" of a black, homosexual prisoner. At first, he is devastated by his experiences and seems to have become a mere shadow of his former self. He tells the Prison Chaplain that he is "so *empty* . . ." (scene 21, p. 95) and that he is "sorry about everything" (ibid., p. 96). All anger and frustration has disintegrated; it is as if Edmond has died inside. When the Chaplain asks him why he murdered Glenna, Edmond does not know. He can only respond with inarticulate stuttering—the collapse of his sensibility is reflected in the breakdown of his language:

> *Edmond:* I . . . *(Pause.)* I . . . *(Pause.)* I *don't* . . . I . . . I *don't* . . . *(Pause.)*
> I . . . *(Pause.)* I don't . . . *(Pause.)* I don't . . . *(Pause.)* I don't think . . .
> *(Pause.)* I . . . *(Pause.)* (ibid., p. 97)

The repetition of the personal pronoun, which had so recently been used to boldly proclaim Edmond's new-found confidence, is now an indication of his struggle to make sense of what has happened to him. His idea of himself as a vital person has dissolved, leaving behind only an impotent stuttering, heartbreaking in its desperation.

Once Edmond has recovered from these dreadful early days in prison, which ironically follow his admission that he believes he will enjoy being there, there seems to be a real change in him. It is as if he has been somehow cleansed. His optimistic ideas about freedom of choice and the need for self-expression are negated as he is confined in a prison even more inhibiting than the one he chose to leave, yet he insists that he is at last content. He has undergone what appears to be a kind of catharsis, an extreme kind of behavior modification in which he has been exposed to his fears and prejudices until they have been either decimated or reversed. Edmond is at peace because there are no longer any pressures on him other than those he has apparently come to accept as part of his new life. All choices are now made for him, all decisions are taken from his hands. In a perverse way, Edmond is happy for the first time; he is free as he has never been since prison has allowed him a liberation of spirit that had hitherto been markedly absent. Edmond had agreed with the man in the bar that "the pressure is too much" in modern society (scene 3, p. 23) and, when he tells his wife the reasons for his murder of Glenna, he says "I think I'd just had too much coffee" (scene 19, p. 87). Edmond has had too much of a contemporary rat race and, since coffee symbolizes at least part of the exhausting ritual that urban toil necessitates, these strange words are in fact quite accurate. Prison allows Edmond release from reality, an escape from everything that had oppressed him. As Miranda Richardson points out "Edmond's world has been so busy, so fraught. There has been so little time for him to be himself. In the prison, he weeps when he wants to, gets angry when he wants to. It is an ordered, structured society; he need take no responsibility for his actions, and he can at last *relax*."[86] The sense of release and relaxation is powerfully apparent in the play's final scene when Edmond and his cellmate (his prison "husband") lie on their bunks and philosophize about life and death. For the first time, Edmond can talk about spiritual issues and there is in this scene a harmony and peace that exists at no other time in the work. The two men cue each other's responses in the way that true friends do, and listen to one another's remarks with interest and respect. At one point, they consider the possibility that animals are the creatures on earth who have within them the ultimate knowledge:

> Prisoner: We say they're only *dogs*, or *animals*, and *scorn* them . . .
> Edmond: . . . Yes.
> Prisoner: We scorn them in our fear. But . . . don't you think? . . .
> Edmond: . . . It could very well be . . .
> Prisoner: But on their native *world* . . .
> Edmond: . . . Uh-huh . . .
> Prisoner: . . . they are *supreme* . . .
> Edmond: I think that's very . . .
> Prisoner: And what *we* have done is to disgrace ourselves.
> Edmond: We have. (scene 23, pp. 104–5)

It may be that in this scene, Mamet is satirizing the rather eccentric philosophical conversations that can take place on park benches as well as in prisons, but this in no way reduces its impact as a touching demonstration of solidarity. Edmond's humility here is a far cry from the arrogance he had displayed to Glenna. For the first time, he actually listens to what another person is saying rather than perfunctorily acknowledging their contributions. When the Prisoner observes that the human race has "disgraced" itself, Edmond is quick to agree; he knows only too well what ignorance and selfishness can produce and his admission of his own culpability in the general malaise is effectively delineated.

The play ends with the stage picture of Edmond crossing his cell to kiss goodnight the man who has made him both a sexual slave and a confidante. The peace that Edmond has at last found has been bought at the expense of his former life. Although an audience must feel some consolation that contentment of a sort has finally been gained, there is at the play's conclusion an overwhelming sense of sadness and waste. It is with some frustration, therefore, that one notes the gross reductivism of sentiments such as "considering what has gone before . . . the notion that Edmond finds redemption and release in a homosexual relationship with his violator seems, at the least, simplistically contrived and incredible."[87] Once again, a realistic interpretation has been forced upon an expressionistic image. It appears Mamet's fate to be misunderstood as a realist because of his brilliantly concise and ostensibly realistic dialogue, but it is a great pity that important allegorical issues are missed along the way.

Edmond is all too recognizably human. In him is embodied all of Mamet's fears about humanity's dilemma in the modern world. He is a mass of contradictions: kind-hearted, selfish, immoral, fair, courageous, and afraid. Although Edmond's actions are extreme, he is a universal spokesman. He makes serious mistakes, but at least he does try to improve his lot, which, in the New York dramatized here, takes considerable courage.

When Mamet asked an interviewer who was deeply unimpressed with the play, "Didn't you feel any compassion for him?"[88] he spelt out his aim in writing the piece. Edmond is the embodiment of all the terrors of our age, an ordinary man with an unrealistic and tainted dream of happiness. In him is incorporated a warning. If this is missed, and the play is dismissed as an impossible fantasy or a work that fails to demonstrate the dramatist's true abilities, then very important issues have been raised in vain.

5

Glengarry Glen Ross

At the end of Arthur Miller's *Death of a Salesman*, Charley offers a valediction on Willy Loman:

> for a salesman, there is no rock bottom to the life. . . . He's a man way out there in the blue, riding on a smile and a shoe shine. . . . A salesman is got to dream, boy. It comes with the territory.[1]

Like Willy, the salesmen in Mamet's *Glengarry Glen Ross* all have their dreams. They dream of the rich customer who will enable them to stop working for those who exploit them and they dream, continually, of success. For several generations of writers who have criticized the American Dream, the salesman has symbolized its shortcomings. It is true that such a profession can be the route to great wealth, the means for an ordinary man to make good by sheer hard work, but this is not the aspect that such writers choose to emphasize. To them, a society that advocates this kind of "self-improvement" is a consumer society based on materialism and has, at its heart, an emptiness that cannot be assuaged by yet more money in the bank. Just as the salesmen's lives are fueled by the promise of happiness and contentment in return for material success, so too are the lives of their clients; the clients are as much a part of the capitalist hegemony as the men from whom they purchase their symbols of material success. Their purchases are invested by the salesmen with amazing, life-enhancing properties that somehow hold the promise of a better future. The truth is, however, usually rather different. In the same way as the salesmen's endless quest for spurious success is essentially a chimera, so the goods they sell are probably quite worthless. The salesmen are, therefore, exploiting those who, like them, need to dream and to believe in a brighter future. It is a vicious circle.

Probably the most famous literary salesman is Miller's Willy Loman, whose frustrated dreams eventually split his family and destroy him. His relentless quest for success, together with an unrealistic view of the world, results, as Eleanor Clark puts it, in his being "done . . . in" largely due to "the capitalist system."[2] Similarly, G. F. Babbitt in Sinclair Lewis's satirical novel, *Babbitt*, neglects his emotional life in the belief that "the one purpose of the real-estate business was to make money for George F. Babbitt,"[3] although he finds that success does not bring him the happiness he seeks. Hickey, that hypocritical shatterer of illusions in Eugene O'Neill's *The Iceman Cometh*, is undone not directly through capitalism—although there is certainly a suggestion that the need for professional kudos is at least partly to blame for his tragedy—but through his need to hang onto the "pipe dreams" he exhorts his friends to eschew. Hickey is the archetypal salesman in literature, a peculiar mixture of both victim and oppressor whose downfall is brought about by self-delusion and societal pressure.

Mamet has commented on the theme of capitalism that runs through both *Glengarry Glen Ross* and *American Buffalo* (which was written about nine years earlier). Both plays are, he says, "set deeply in the milieu of capitalism [which is] obviously an idea whose time has come and gone."[4]

He goes on to explain how

> in America we're still suffering from loving a frontier ethic—that is to say, take the land from the Indians and give it to the railroad. Take the money from the blacks and give it to the rich. The ethic was always something for nothing. It never really existed when the American frontier was open . . . it never was anything more transcendent than something for nothing . . . The idea of go West and make your fortune, there's gold lying in the ground, was an idea promulgated by the storekeepers in the gold rush and the railroads in the westward expansion as a way of enslaving the common man and woman . . . playing on their greed. As W. C. Fields said, you can't cheat an honest man. So, because we've been rather dishonest about our basic desire to get something for nothing in this country we've always been enslaved by the myth of the happy capitalist. Familiar American pieties are always linked to criminality. That's why they're familiar American pieties.[5]

Elsewhere he notes that "American capitalism comes down to one thing. . . . The operative axiom is 'Hurrah for me and fuck you.' Anything else is a lie."[6] Thus, Mamet lays the blame for modern-day greed and corruption on the ethics that have existed since the early days of the American Republic. From the outset, people have been urged to live falsely, to seek financial success by any means open to them, including cheating and stealing. Mamet believes that this has led to the diminishment of important emotional bonds whose value is then viewed only as a means of achieving pecuniary gain. His plays are frequently concerned with the fact that ordinary human relationships have been corrupted and subverted by social fiats, and *Glengarry Glen Ross* is perhaps the most frightening example of this tendency. The archaic—although still powerful—New World ethos of seizing rapaciously what is denied by right is exposed as both immoral and callous and, in these plays, Mamet draws attention to the deforming effect upon individual morality. His characters are, therefore, essentially very unhappy; on the surface they may be tough and smiling, but underneath this brittle veneer, they are aware of a terrible void in their lives. Mamet has noted how

> the American ethic of business, of boosterism, never made anybody happy. It has made a lot of people rich, but it never made anybody happy. So we live in a very, very unhappy country here. I have always considered it to be part of my job to talk about the things that I see, and certainly the most pervasive aspect of America is that we are so damned unhappy over here, but we are smiling all the time.[7]

Glengarry Glen Ross is, he says, an attempt to write about "those guys you see on planes. They all sit together, and you can never understand what they're talking about, and they all have these papers filled with columns and figures. They're all named Bob. And when they laugh, it's 'Ha-*ha!*'—this imitation laugh."[8] During an interview with Mel Gussow, Mamet recalled a conversation he had had with his wife's stepfather about the cruelty and ruthlessness of the world of salesmanship. He had been told how "as an effect of the recession, how 'vicious the competition was for jobs and sales, especially among older men.' He described one incident in which an older salesman was so terrified about making a presentation that he had a heart attack on the spot, 'and the new president of the company stepped over his body to leave the room.'"[9]

Mamet's characters must convince themselves that material gain is the ultimate achievement—there is simply nothing else. In this world, business has become an end in itself; people frantically pursue their individual goals for success and happiness and find it to be an endless pursuit. Once they reach one pinnacle, they must move on to another. Mamet demonstrates how inextricably people can become enmeshed in their jobs, almost losing their identity behind a job title. Certainly his salesmen seem to have little life outside the office. One of them actually says, "A man's his job" (act 2, p. 44), which suggests that he has become a mere extension of his livelihood. There are very few moments in the play when the characters use any language that is not expressly concerned with business and even when they do it quickly becomes apparent that it is a ploy designed to coerce a colleague or cheat a client. When Roma talks to a customer about his wife, he uses the vocabulary of the boardroom to make his point:

> *Roma:* . . . You have a contract with your wife. You have certain things you do *jointly,* you have a *bond* there . . . (act 2, p. 55)

It is as if the world has ceased to exist outside of the office; Roma and his cronies have distorted speech so much through cunning and artifice—and downright professional obsession—that it seems they no longer have a need for language that does not immediately relate to their business interests. Mamet is not, however, out to condemn such characters, but merely to expose a system that has created them. He insists that it was not his intention to offer an indictment or a commentary: "My job is to create a closed moral universe,"[10] he says, and to leave evaluation to the audience. To Mamet, the "play is about a society based on business . . . a society with only one bottom line: How much money you make."[11]

The premise upon which *Glengarry Glen Ross* is based is, in a way, a paradigm of capitalism. The company's bosses have organized a sales competition in which the salesman with the highest "grosses"—financial profit—wins a Cadillac and is automatically guaranteed the best "leads" (addresses of prospective land buyers), the runners-up win a set of steak knives, and the losers are sacked. That the successful salesman is given the best leads while the runners-up are forced to accept inferior leads from the "B" list or are even dismissed, underlines the unfairness of a system that penalizes those who are weak and needy but rewards those who least need such support. With no other choice but to capitulate to the demands of their employers, it is not surprising that the salesmen should rail against the iniquities of an unfair system. Their jobs may be their lives, but they should be *better* jobs; despite their refusal to look beneath the shallowness of their lives, there remains a level at which they are conscious of a serious deficiency.

Corrupted by the constant need to beat their colleagues at any cost, these men have become expert manipulators. Their ability to cajole and confuse with superbly calculated verbal onslaughts is quite mesmerizing. Jack Shepherd, who played Richard Roma in the National Theatre production remarks that they are "vicious existentialists, experts in deception, superb liars. . . . persuasive, ruthless, competitive, disloyal."[12] These men think nothing of trampling over anyone who stands in their way. Theirs is a world in which loyalty and trust have almost no place and where language can no longer be trusted as a means of straightforward communication. Merely listening to the wrong words can mean dire consequences, as Aaronow finds to his cost. A major theme in this play is the corruption of the function of language, and Robert Cushman has observed how Mamet drives home his point about the unreliability of language through his characters' "intoxicating mixture of evasions, pleadings, browbeatings, stonewalling and spiel."[13] The language in *Glengarry Glen Ross* is quite stunning in its versatility, and Mamet's command over dialogue reaches its most dazzling pitch. What is perhaps most striking is the almost operatic quality of some of the verbal set pieces. The terse, sometimes stychomythic quality of his earlier dialogue still exists here, but Mamet now seems to be experimenting with new and more lengthy forms of linguistic control. There are in this work a number of bravura monologues and brilliantly sustained "duets" that the salesmen utilize to bewilder and impress their audience. In *Sexual Perversity in Chicago,* some of Bernie Litko's absurdly inflated fantasies take a similar form, but even they are a pale prelude to the heights achieved here. Mamet demonstrates with consummate skill his ability to condense and expand salient aspects of the American language into what truly become the "tainted arias"[14] of which Christopher Bigsby has spoken. Roma's mesmerizing monologue in the company of the inarticulate Lingk, Levene's poetic and almost orgasmic evocation of a great sale, and the brilliant entrapment of Aaronow into criminal culpability by his colleague, Moss, surpass even Mamet's own dizzying standards of linguistic invention.

The world of sales and salesmanship offers myriad opportunities for those who enjoy spinning a yarn and acting a part. In the brutally competitive world in which he moves, the salesman must become expert in linguistic technique; so long as he can keep his narrative flowing and uninterrupted he is able to feel, at least momentarily, safe. Through the pattern of his words, he can manipulate and persuade and thus his fantasies of success and those of his client can become a temporary reality. As Barbara

Hardy observes, storytellers of any kind must be "fluent and vivid . . . artists who keep an eye on the subject, on the listeners, and on the occasion. They are sincerely involved and engrossed in their stories but are self-consciously practised in that manipulation of effect which belongs to all oratory and is essential to the art of narrative improvisation."[15] In *Glengarry Glen Ross*, Mamet's salesmen spill out their endless, brilliant chatter to anyone who is prepared to listen but at the heart of their manipulation lies aridity and emptiness. Behind the foul-mouthed, incessantly "macho" bravado lies a desperate bluster, a braggadocio show of power by men who are only too aware of their own powerlessness. They may live by victimizing their colleagues and clients, but the most abject victims of their trade are themselves.

This play is Mamet's most successful to date. It was premiered at the National Theatre in London in 1983, winning two British drama awards before opening on Broadway where it won the Pultizer Prize in 1984. Despite the fact that it is by far the most abrasive and scatalogical that Mamet has yet written, it has been much praised for its poetic qualities. Benedict Nightingale comments upon the "gaudy, swaggering poetry [Mamet] has fashioned out of the street-wise idiom of Chicago [which] sucks us in, carries us along, bouncing us over minor implausibilities like a stream over rusty cans."[16] Connie Booth describes the work as one of "poetic brilliance . . . It is caustic, sharp, and tragic. The language isn't easy or melodic but it is certainly true poetry in every sense of the word."[17] Mamet was worried about the play when he read it through for the first time. The mixture of an episodic first act with a conventionally structured second act prompted him to send a copy to Harold Pinter for his comments. Pinter told him that, in his opinion, the only thing wrong with the play was that it was not currently in production. Mamet now believes that its structure gives the work an extra dimension, and adds to its appeal. He has noted, "people love my new play . . . Because I finally had the will to write a second act. I wrote a million episodic plays. I can write them with my left hand. So what? Who cares? Fortunately, I got sick of it before [the audience] did."[18]

Because *Glengarry Glen Ross* details the experiences of those whose lives lack any sense of morality, it ironically becomes a kind of morality play. Benedict Nightingale believes that it "certainly. . . . is a moral play [but] not a moralizing one. It seeks to "tell the truth" about the usually invisible violence men inflict on themselves and each other as they grab for gold; not to preach redundant sermons about it."[19] Mamet believes that the play not only tells the truth but is also "a good play"[20] in its own right, in that it accurately reflects the realities of the real-estate world in which he was once involved. He based the work on his experiences of working as an assistant office manager in a "fly-by-night"[21] concern in downtown Chicago. After graduating from college in Vermont, he came to Chicago to find work as an actor but quickly discovered that "theatrical work was scarce" and that he was "virtually unemployable in any case, being without either skills or experience."[22] He decided to register with a temporary employment agency, and recalls, "the agency sent me out for a two day job as a typist in a real-estate office. I stayed a year. . . . The office. . . sold tracts of undeveloped land in Arizona and Florida to gullible Chicagoans."[23] He describes the firm as being "one of those offices . . . on the way to the airport [and one of those companies for which] you hear an ad on television that says 'Interested in the Arizona way of life? No salesman will call,' and the next thing that happens is that a salesman calls."[24] Mamet recalls the kind of work he undertook while employed there:

> The firm advertised on radio and television. . . . Interested viewers would telephone in for the brochure and their names and numbers were given to me. My job was to call them back, assess their income and sales susceptibility, and arrange an appointment with them for one of the office salesmen. . . . This appointment was called a lead— in the same way that a clue in a criminal case is called a lead i.e., it may lead to the suspect, the suspect in this case being a prospect. It was then my job to assess the relative worth of these leads and assign them to the salesforce. The salesmen would then take their assigned leads and go out on the appointments, which were called *sits* i.e. a meeting where one actually sits down with the prospects.[25]

Mamet thoroughly enjoyed his year in the real-estate office, and expresses a deep and unqualified admiration for the men with whom he worked: "I loved those guys," he says, "They made my life interesting for a year."[26] He got so involved in the work that he even considered making real estate his career! He says that had he stayed on after the year, he "would have done it forever. . . . be very, very wealthy. . . . divorced and . . . living in Chicago and the Bahamas."[27] As an afterthought, he adds that he might also "have spent time in prison."[28] The world he depicts in *Glengarry Glen Ross* teeters on a knife-edge of immense financial reward and its concomitant professional kudos, and base criminality. In *American Buffalo*, Mamet portrays a group of small-time crooks who thought themselves legitimate businessmen; in *Glengarry Glen Ross,* his subjects *are* businessmen but they all behave like crooks. The very terminology used by the salesmen and already described by Mamet points to a close link with the criminal world. The ambiguity between realms is entirely deliberate: the actual break-in perpetrated by the desperate salesmen is merely a concrete realization of crimes brazenly carried out during working hours in the course of "business." Robbery is only one of the crimes delineated here: Levene resorts to bribery not once, but twice in a desperate effort to keep his head above water; Moss blackmails Aaronow by calmly threatening to denounce him to the police should he decline to rob the office, and Roma explodes with a violence more suited to a gangster than a businessman when his successful deal has been ruined by an unthinking colleague.

In spite of their callousness and selfishness, Mamet's characters engage and retain our sympathies. It is possible to despise what they represent and to bemoan what a materialistic, grasping society has made them, but it is difficult to despise them as individuals. Mamet based the characters to some extent on the men with whom he had worked at the real-estate office; he was fascinated by their dedication to their craft and their single-minded pursuit of the big sale. He recalls, "the men I was working with could sell cancer. . . . They were amazing. They were a force of nature. These men. . . . were people who had spent their whole life in sales, always working for a commission, never working for a salary, dependent for their living on their wits, on their ability to charm. They sold themselves."[29] This is reminiscent of Arthur Miller's response when asked what Willy Loman actually sold; his answer: "Himself".[30]

During rehearsals, Mamet tried to convey some of the power of his ex-colleagues to the actors involved, and Jack Shepherd recalls Mamet's excitement when talking about these men:

[Mamet] remembers them as being intensely dynamic. They took cocaine to keep high, and there was an almost sexual quality to the quest for selling. The sense of release when a sale was made was quite extraordinary, almost orgasmic. During the process of selling, they became very neurotic, unattached, and distanced from their families. The sale became *the* all-important experience. It was utterly addictive. They drank heavily and, when in the throes of a big sale, indulged in lots of casual sexual relationships.[31]

The analogy between selling and drug taking is a telling one, and is borne out in Levene's desperate cry: "I NEED A SHOT. I got to get on the fucking board. . . . I need your help" (1.1, p. 7).

Shepherd also recalls the rehearsal period as a particularly harrowing time. Tensions often rose too high and fights broke out:

> We all went mad. The amount of information you had to take in was staggering. Things got very, very heated and tempers were lost. A chair got thrown at one point. There is just so much to remember at any one time in Mamet's work; you begin to feel like a computer that is overloading. Mamet knows exactly what he wants . . . he is very fast, very dynamic. His speech is also very quick. The rhythms in him and in his plays are similar. In trying to pick up something of the Chicago accent from him, you cannot help but pick up his quick-fire streetwise personality as well. We tried to give the impression, during rehearsals, of rapid interaction, of sharing something over a very short period. You have to struggle to remember so much about your part, the lines, the sensation, the character, and so on. You feel rather like a thoroughbred horse; you tend to overstrain to compensate for feelings of bewilderment and confusion. It's all very, very speedy.[32]

In order to add to the authenticity of the piece, Mamet gave his actors copies of Dale Carnegie's *How to Make Friends and Influence People* and, during rehearsals for the American production, brought in real-life sales personnel to give short lectures to the cast. In an article about the play, Samuel G. Freedman recalls how "Herb Cohen, the author of *You Can Negotiate Anything*, spoke to the actors. Salesmen from International Business Machines and Xerox and even a Fuller brush saleswoman lectured them on sales technique and taught them sales jargon."[33] Mamet remembers that "the Fuller Brush lady was great . . . The whole pitch was reduced to a science. They're very fond of slogans: 'Plan your work and work your plan.' Everything moves toward the close."[34]

In *Glengarry Glen Ross*, relationships appear to exist only to facilitate commercial success and to establish which party is in control. Duplicity among friends is commonplace, and language and philosophy are casually prostituted. The first act is a superb demonstration of how a complex network of domination and submission underlies any encounter. It consists of three short, almost Pinteresque scenes set in a Chinese restaurant, each of which is structured around an encounter between two characters. In any conversation, it is often not the actual content that offers the most insight into its speakers, but its emphatic and persuasive rhythms. The first of these encounters provides an excellent example of this. Shelly Levene, a once-great salesman now down on his luck and faced with the prospect of dismissal, appeals for help from Williamson, his cold-hearted and apathetic office manager:

> *Levene:* John . . . John . . . John. Okay. John. John. Look: *(Pause.)* The Glengarry Highland's leads, you're sending Roma out. Fine. He's a good man. We know that he is. He's fine. All I'm saying, you look at the *board*, he's throwing . . . wait, wait, wait, he's throwing them *away*, he's throwing the leads away. All that I'm saying, that you're wasting leads. I don't want to tell you your *job*. All that I'm saying, things get *set*, I know they do, you get a certain *mindset* . . . A guy gets a reputation. We know how this . . . all I'm saying, put a *closer* on the job. There's more than one man for the . . . Put a . . . wait a second, put a *proven man out* . . . and you watch, now *wait* a second—and you watch your *dollar* volumes . . . You start closing them for *fifty* 'stead of *twenty-five* . . . you put a *closer* on the . . .
> *Williamson:* Shelly, you blew the last . . .
> *Levene:* No. John. No. Let's wait, let's back up here, I did . . . will you please? Wait a second. Please. I didn't "blow" them. No. I didn't "blow" them. No. One kicked *out*, one I *closed*. (1.1, p. 3)

To analyze this one speech of Levene's (which is also the opening speech of the play) is to learn almost everything there is to know about him and the life he leads. The naturalistic, repetitive opening line reveals his tentative, although persistent, manner—the crafty, insidious approach of the professional salesman never leaves him. As he repeats the name "John" with varying degrees of pause and emphasis, patience and exasperation, he builds up a kind of rhythmic litany with which he hopes to nudge Williamson into sympathetic understanding. Since Williamson has the power to "make" or "break" him, Levene musters every scrap of his psychological know-how to achieve his effect. He tries to sound friendly, but firm; he strives to appear confident and in control. He uses subtle flattery, and is very careful not to criticize his colleagues in any meaningful way, but prefers instead to turn around his doubts about their performance by referring always to the fact that *he* could make the company more money. Similarly, he is at pains not to infer that Williamson does not know his job, merely that a man in his position can occasionally become a little confused, and think of only one solution to a problem. He struggles to strengthen his hold on a rapidly disintegrating career with nothing stronger than carefully chosen words. The repetition of "All I'm saying"—although he is plainly going to say a great deal more—points not only his calculated ingenuousness but also to his growing nervousness.

The rhythms of desperation are incorporated into Levene's speech. His phrasing is in marked contrast to the complacent tones of Williamson whose speech throughout the scene reflects security and superiority. The fact that Levene does most of the talking is no accident; his refusal to let Williamson speak is further evidence of his terror. Levene prefers his audience's silence to the risk of allowing another—possibly condemning—voice to join in. Mamet builds into Levene's speech the frantic delaying tactics of a man who is afraid to stop talking: "Wait, wait, wait . . . wait a second . . . now wait a second." There is no indication in the script that Williamson is trying to interrupt, which makes Levene's exhortations to "wait" simultaneously pitiful and funny. At the same time, Mamet can also suggest that the silent actor may be trying to say something but is constantly beaten down by the garrulousness of the speaker. Therefore, Mamet's interruptive device can be utilized in production in two, equally amusing and telling ways.

Levene and Williamson converse in what sounds like a kind of code. It is the almost incomprehensible jargon of the real-estate world in which "leads," "the board," "Glengarry," and "closers" are the main components of linguistic exchange. Baffled by the arcane jargonistic language used by the characters, the audience is forced to respond at a completely different level; even if the audience is unsure as to what is taking place, it is quite clear that one of the men is in trouble and will go to any length to extricate himself from it. The "salespeak" is, in fact, so confusing that Mamet felt the need to add a brief glossary in the program notes for the National Theatre production. Many critics have commented upon its "specialist" quality. Milton Shulman calls it "coded insider jargon,"[35] Jack Tinker refers to the salesmen's "impenetrable machine-gun conversation"[36] and Jack Kroll comments upon how "Mamet's salesmen have created a lingo of their own, a semantic skullduggery that can fake out a prospective buyer with non-sequiturs, triple talk and a parody of philosophical wisdom that is breathtaking in its jackhammer effrontery."[37]

As well as being thoroughly bewildering to the uninitiated, this jargonized language also begs a purely American interpretation. Jack Shepherd's initial reaction to Mamet's script was confusion. The elliptical sentences, stammering, and jargon seemed to him to be an indecipherable puzzle: "I remember when I first saw the script for *Glengarry*, my reaction was that it looked like code. It

made no sense if you merely read it with an English accent with
the sense of an English idiom in your head but, once you began to
pick up the rhythm, you could begin to enjoy yourself."[38]
Elsewhere, he elaborates: "*Glengarry Glen Ross* is not an easy play
to read: the language is English but the style is American. Many
of the lines are incomplete. The grammar is often weird. The
idiom is unfamiliar. Arcane. . . . The rhythms are slick, fast,
syncopated."[39] Mamet's salesmen have, in fact, evolved their own
brand of esoteric, almost impenetrable jargon. They are seduced
by the sheer exhilaration they can conjure up with language and
John Barber notes that part of the fascination the audience feels
lies in the fact that the salesmen are "totally in love with the
clackety-clack of their yackety-yak."[40] Levene's verbal helter-skel-
ter establishes at a very early stage that he and his colleagues have
only one subject of conversation—selling—whether the sale is a
piece of land, or, tragically, themselves. The opening scene between Levene and Williamson recalls a similar situation in Miller's
Death of a Salesman when Willy Loman faces dismissal because of
his poor performance record. There are differences, however.
Willy is reluctantly fired by what Dennis Welland has described as
a " 'nice guy,' forced into a situation that he doesn't know how to
handle 'nicely' "[41] whereas Levene comes up against the frigidity
of modern-day business in the shape of the reptilian Williamson.
Although Levene finally manages to retain his job through bribery, Mamet is still able to suggest that the business world that his
salesmen face is a far bleaker prospect than the one that Willy
Loman endures.

The second scene also dramatizes the plight of a salesman
down on his luck. Aaronow is worried that his sales figures are so
low that he will not be able to get "on the board" and will probably
lose his job. Moss plans to break into the office or, rather, coerce
someone else to break in for him, and steal the all-important
leads. As he sits in the restaurant with Aaronow, he begins to
insidiously work on his colleague's sensibilities; he gradually
moves the conversation around to hypothesizing about a possible
robbery, sometimes drowning out Aaronow's rather weak and
monosyllabic responses altogether and sometimes turning his
words around to flatter Aaronow into thinking that the thoughts
expressed in them were *his* ideas, rather than those of Moss:

Moss: The whole fuckin' thing . . . The pressure's just too great. You're
ab . . . you're absolu . . . (1.2, p. 12)

As he plants the seeds of the idea into his colleague's mind, Moss tells him that the leads could be easily sold to their boss's rival, Jerry Graff. There then follows a hilarious exchange during which Aaronow questions Moss as to whether he is actually "talking" about the possibility of a robbery, or merely "speaking" about it:

> *Aaronow.* . . . I mean are you actually *talking* about this, or are we just . . .
> *Moss.* No, we're just . . .
> *Aaronow:* We're just *"talking"* about it.
> *Moss:* We're just *speaking* about it. *(Pause.)* As an *idea.* (Ibid. p. 18)

Of this scene, Colin Stinton remarks:

> Through his superlative command over language, Mamet can identify the mental processes through which characters move. They some-times "hit" a word which they feel will give their conversation the emphasis and meaning they desire, but that word can be quite arbi-trary. There are wonderful examples of this in *Glengarry Glen Ross* and, in particular, when the two salesmen make a false distinction between talking about a crime and merely speaking about it. In their minds there is some differentiation between the two . . . To "talk" implies that they are actually planning to do it but to "speak" means only that they are entertaining the possibility of it being done![42]

Eventually, Aaronow is caught. Because Aaronow has listened, Moss informs him that he is as guilty as he would be had he actually committed the crime:

> *Moss:* . . . My end is *my* business. Your end's twenty-five. In or out. You tell me, you're out you take the consequences.
> *Aaronow:* I do?
> *Moss:* Yes. *(Pause.)*
> *Aaronow:* And why is that?
> *Moss:* Because you listened. (Ibid., p. 23)

This is surely the ultimate betrayal of the trust implied in ordinary conversation; Aaronow is designated as a criminal simply because he "listened."

Mamet's characters have so thoroughly molded and deformed language to suit their own ends that it is quite impossible to be sure of the truth of anything they say or, indeed, where it might lead. In *The Caretaker*, Mick accuses Davies of duplicity and, as he coolly regards the trembling vagrant, observes: "I can take nothing you say at face value. Every word you speak is open to any number of different interpretations. Most of what you say is lies."[43] He could be speaking to one of the salesmen in Mamet's play. In their efforts to manipulate and persuade, they have ceased to use language as a means of communication. Therefore, in order to find out something about their genuine emotions, it is necessary to look elsewhere. As with many of Pinter's characters, it is in what they leave unsaid that they reveal most about themselves. Thus, there is an honesty in silence that is certainly absent in their endless, forced garrulousness.

Aaronow's subsequent refusal to name Moss as the probable culprit of the office break-in tells us more about his character than any of the stammerings, evasions, and inarticulacies we have thus far heard. We know already that he is a weak and gullible man but we are quite unaware of any of his strengths. There is a sense of loyalty inherent in Aaronow, which he demonstrates simply by keeping quiet. The notion of honesty through silence is something that Strindberg touches on in his *Ghost Sonata* when his Old Man observes "I prefer silence. Then one can hear thoughts, and see the past. Silence hides nothing. Words conceal."[44]

There is no moral law at work in this real-estate office, merely a system of reward and punishment. The world portrayed here is truly a Darwinian jungle in which survival of the fittest is the prevailing maxim. Because they are all in the same position, Mamet's salesmen can legitimize the most horrendous acts of betrayal without flinching. Mamet has observed that, when connected in some way to a large organization or state ideology, people can behave in ways quite unacceptable to them in any other context: "The code of an institution ratifies us in acting amorally, as any guilt which might arise out of our acts would be borne not by ourselves but shared out through the institution. . . . [If these acts] are done in the name of some larger group, a *state*, a *company*, a team [then] those vile acts are somehow magically transformed and become praiseworthy."[45] This kind of mentality pervades *Glengarry Glen Ross*. When Levene has cheated two elderly people out of $82,000, Roma congratulates him warmly: "That was a great sale, Shelly" (act 2, p. 43) and Levene has nothing but contempt for the couple:

> Levene: . . . convert the mother fucker . . . *sell* him . . . *sell* him . . . *make him sign the check. (Pause.)* The . . . Bruce, Harriett . . . the kitchen, blah: They got their money in *government* bonds . . . I say

fuck it, we're going to go the whole route. I plat it out eight units. Eighty-two grand. (act 2, p. 42)

Levene speaks of actually "selling" the customer, as if he is no longer a human being but merely a commodity to be exploited. There is a kind of frenzy in Levene's words; the underlinings and obscenities emphasize his excitement and ruthlessness. In his mind, he is back in the house with his victims; he *sees* in his mind the scene he had savored—so much so that he refers to "the kitchen" for no apparent reason other than the fact that he is visualizing it. It is all or nothing for Levene. He persuades his clients to sign a contract for "the whole route" although it must be patently obvious to him that they can ill afford it, whether they have "*government* bonds" or not. The emphasis in this speech is upon force; the client *must* be converted, to be *made* to sign "the check." It is an aspect of selling that is repeated throughout the play—one character is always trying to force another to do something.

In the third of these opening scenes, we have our first glimpse of the salesman incarnate, the almost maniacal Richard Roma. Roma is a superbly crafted character, and one that many critics have designated as the most powerful in a very powerful work. He has been variously described as "slicker than oil,"[46] "the whizz-kid spieler with the almost manic drive,"[47] "superbly slick,"[48] and "a sharp hustler."[49] Roma is the youngest of the sales force, in his "forties" as opposed to the "fifties" of his colleagues, and utilizes whatever youthful thrust he can muster to gain the advantage over them.

When the scene begins, two men are sitting at different booths in a restaurant, although there is a kind of conversation already in progress. It is immediately apparent that this conversation is a very one-sided affair, Roma completely dominating the proceedings with what is virtually a monologue, Lingk responding infrequently and hesitantly, if at all. The over-familiar manner adopted by Roma leads the audience to believe that these two are well-acquainted and it is only in the last moments of the scene that Roma introduces himself as a total stranger and reveals his true motive—he is trying to sell land. The audience is, therefore, as completely deceived as Lingk; we, too, have only Roma's puzzling words as clues and it is extremely difficult to fathom what he has in mind since his speech is an amalgam of simplified existentialism, intrusive sentimentality, and preacher-like exhortations for the necessity to stand up and be counted.

Rather perplexingly, Mamet has described this speech as "inspirational . . . classic Stoic philosophy"[50] but most critics have
taken it to be little more than cleverly worded nonsense. If the
piece is analyzed, it is difficult to disagree with them. Far from
being "inspirational," it is vacuous and pretentious. The only type
of listener who would be impressed by such verbiage would be
someone like Lingk, a gullible, easily swayed individual, apparently with few opinions of his own. Roma exhorts Lingk to live
each day to the fullest, accept life for what it is, and to face the
consequences of any mistakes:

> *Roma:* . . . I say *this* is how we must act. I do those things which seem
> correct to me *today.* . . . And if security concerns me, I do that
> which *today* I think will make me secure. And every day I *do* that,
> when that day *arrives* that I need a reserve, a) odds are that I have it
> and, b) the *true* reserve that I have is the strength that I have of *acting
> each day* without fear. . . . Stocks, bonds, objects of art, real estate.
> Now: what are they? *(Pause.)* An opportunity. (1.3, p. 25)

There is a neurotic rhythm in Roma's words that propels his train
of thought from one sentence to the next. He is utterly caught up
in his performance. He continually asks rhetorical questions, answering them before Lingk can think what to say. Roma's quick-
fire phrasing and pretentious tone no doubt deeply impress his
innocent victim, who probably believes he is hearing the important inner thoughts of an intellectual. Roma is careful not to
mention anything that may give his game away too soon. When
the subject of "real estate" is 'innocently' dropped into the conversation, it is only alongside "stocks, bonds [and] objects of art,"
items of worth that can offer "opportunity." However, there remains a sense in which this *is* more than a prelude to a sales
pitch—it is Roma's way of justifying his actions. Perhaps he is
talking as much to himself as to Lingk:

> *Roma:* . . . When you *die* you're going to regret the things you don't
> do. You think you're *queer.* . . ? I'm going to tell you something:
> we're *all* queer. You think that you're a *thief*? So *what*? You get
> befuddled by a middle-class morality? . . . You fuck little girls, so *be*
> it. There's an absolute morality? May *be.* . . . Bad people go to hell?
> I don't *think* so. A hell exists on earth? Yes. I won't live in it. That's
> *me.* You ever take a dump made you feel you'd just slept for twelve
> hours?
> *Lingk:* Did I. . . ?
> *Roma:* Yes.
> *Lingk:* I don't know.

Roma: Or a *piss*. . . ? A great meal fades in reflection. . . . The great
  fucks that you may have had. What do you remember about them?
Lingk: What do I. . . ?
Roma: Yes.
Lingk: Mmmmm. . . ?
Roma: . . . For *me,* I'm saying, what it is, it's probably not the orgasm.
  Some broads, forearms on your neck, something her *eyes* did. There
  was a *sound* she made . . . or, me, lying, in the, I'll tell you: me lying
  in bed: the next day she brought me *café au lait*. . . . What I'm
  saying, What is our life: *(Pause.)* it's looking forward or it's looking
  back. And that's our life. That's *it*. (1.3, pp. 23–24)

Roma casually infers that Lingk may be "queer," "a thief," or be
inclined to "fuck little girls," without pausing to consider that
these could be taken as grossly offensive remarks. He phrases his
words so that Lingk does not have the opportunity to object; he
seems to implicate himself in these offensive acts as much as he
does Lingk. By framing his remarks as pseudohypothetical questions and by speaking quickly and without many pauses, Roma
confounds and hypnotizes his prey. As he notices Lingk's growing confusion at all the talk of "middle-class morality" and "hell on
earth," Roma suddenly moves the monologue onto another tack:
he begins to talk about bodily functions and sex, two subjects
with which even the most inarticulate of men can identify. However, Lingk is totally bewildered and is unsure how he should
respond to his new "friend's" verbal display. Tony Haygarth, the
actor who played Lingk in both the original National Theatre
production and in the Mermaid's revival, made much of the
character's insecurity and nervousness and, at the same time,
conveyed his pathetic attempts at bonhomie and "macho" understanding. Taking Roma's lead, Haygarth's Lingk responded to his
words with a kind of desperate mime, opening and closing his
arms, grimacing, smiling, or frowning when he believed it was
appropriate to do so. Unfortunately for him, he often chose the
incorrect reaction, leading to a querulous raised eyebrow from
Roma. Roma's cruel manipulation of a man who is so clearly
confused and who clearly wishes to make a true friend, is thus
truly horrifying, but this fact does not detract from the grim
humor that pervades the scene.

Mamet is able to show how Roma's mind works as he casts
about in his subconscious for the next piece in his linguistic
jigsaw. The most common punctuation mark in the text of *Glengarry Glen Ross* is the comma, and Roma uses it relentlessly. As
Christopher Bigsby notes, the comma allows "mismatched

phrases and random ideas [to be] strung together in a protective flow of sound."[51] As Roma details his experiences with women, he begins one sentence only to leave it after a word or two and then move onto another, and yet another. The pauses afforded by the use of the comma allow him to further build his story, to embroider it, and to render it effective for the attentive—although hopelessly bewildered—ears of his quarry.

The call to action, to face facts and proceed with life, fills Mamet's plays. Roma's speech is, as Jennifer Allen points out "similar to one of Teach's in *American Buffalo* ('We must face the facts and act on them') and to a declaration by the eponymous hero of *Edmond,* who invites a woman to 'change [her] life' with him (and, unstrung before this incident, stabs her when she refuses)."[52] Roma moves rapidly toward the moment when *he* will metaphorically impale Lingk with a verbal coup de grace so efficient it could hardly be bettered. Watching this scene is akin to watching a spider edge ever closer to the fly caught in its net:

> Roma: . . . I want to show you something. *(Pause.)* It might mean *nothing* to you . . . and it might not. I don't know. I don't know anymore. *(Pause. He takes out a small map and spreads it on a table.)* What is that? Florida? Glengarry Highlands. Florida. "Florida. *Bullshit.*" And maybe that's true; and that's what *I* said: but look *here*: What is this? This is a piece of land. Listen to what I'm going to tell you now: (ibid., p. 26)

It is no accident that Mamet ends this speech with a colon rather than a period; Roma's patter is relentless and without mercy. He will go on and on until Lingk finally capitulates and offers to buy some land. The unfortunate man is trapped; he has no choice but to "listen" to whatever Roma hurls at him. He may even be confused enough to believe that buying the land was his own idea in the first place, so deft and swift is the salesman's technique. The linguistic slip in Roma's, "It might mean *nothing* to you . . . and it might not," suggests a stressful excitement. The double negative makes no sense but Roma is beyond worrying at this point. He knows that it is only a matter of moments before he can play his trump card, and that Lingk is quite incapable of fighting back. The tone is one of camaraderie and sincerity. Roma implies that he had once been skeptical about the value of such land but that was before he had learned the truth—possibly the same "truth" he has been telling Lingk during his bravura performance. To "Florida," he links the term "Bullshit." He casually lets slip the mellifluous words "Glengarry Highlands," and allows Lingk the briefest of moments to savor the sound of "Glengarry." Both "Glengarry" and "Glen Ross" sound, and are intended to sound, reliable and romantic; they are probably the softest, most serene words uttered in the entire play. In the same way that Charles Dickens created a symbol of American greed in *The Life and Adventures of Martin Chuzzlewit* by calling the phony real-estate venture "Eden,"[53] so too Mamet chooses his title with care. Those who might be tempted to invest in land would, in all likelihood, be most attracted to areas with pleasing and substantial names as if, by their very sound, they guaranteed satisfaction. It is probably no coincidence that there is an acreage development in Sinclair Lewis's *Babbitt* that is similarly designated as "Glen Oriole."[54]

Roma's betrayal of Lingk's trust has thus been extended to the audience; what was taken to be genuine, if bewildering, conversation must now be reevaluated as lies and fatuous platitudes. Once again, the function of language as a means of communication has been subverted and forced to serve corrupt ends.

Another excellent example of Mamet's linguistic control occurs in Levene's ecstatic evocation of his successful sale. He generates an almost sexual excitement as he details the moment when the clients signed the all-important contract:

Levene: . . . Now I handed them the pen. I held it in my hand. I turned the contract eight units eighty-two grand. "Now I want you to sign." *(Pause.)* I sat there. Five minutes. Then, I sat there, Ricky, *twenty-two minutes* by the kitchen *clock. (Pause.)* Twenty-two minutes by the kitchen clock. Not a *word*, not a *motion*. What am I thinking? "My arm's getting tired?" *No*. I *did* it. I *did* it. Like in the *old* days, Ricky. Like I was taught . . . Like, like, like I used to do. . . I did it.
Roma: Like you taught me.
Levene: Bullshit, you're . . . No. That's raw. . . well, if I *did*, then I'm *glad* I did. I, *well*. I locked on them. All on them, nothing on me. All my thoughts are on them. I'm holding the last thought that I spoke: "Now is the time." *(Pause.)* They signed, Ricky. It was *great*. It was fucking great. It was like they wilted all at once. No *gesture* . . . nothing. Like together. They, I swear to God, they both kind of *imperceptibly slumped*. And he reaches and takes the pen and signs, he passes it to her, she signs. It was so fucking solemn. I just let it sit. I nod like this. I nod again. I grasp his hands. I shake his hands. I grasp *her* hands. I nod at her like this. "Bruce . . . Harriett . . ." I'm beaming at them. I'm nodding like this. I point back in the living-room, back to the sideboard. *(Pause.) I didn't fucking know there was a sideboard there!!* He goes back, he brings us a drink. Little shot-glasses. A pattern in 'em. And we toast. In silence. *(Pause.)*

Roma: That was a great sale, Shelly.
Levene: . . . Ah fuck. (act 2, pp. 42–43)

Levene's pride in his achievement is almost tangible, his enthusiasm irresistibly infectious. We may shudder at his sheer immorality, but it is difficult not to enjoy a frisson of excitement on his
behalf as he lovingly recreates the "moment of truth." Mamet
cleverly manipulates his audience's feelings; he knows exactly
how to retain sympathy for his characters even as they are shown
to be ruthless and hopelessly corrupt. Having observed Levene as
a pathetic underdog at the beginning of the play, we then witness
his joy as he recaptures some of his past glory. He is like a man
rejuvenated; the underdog has triumphed—at least temporarily.
     Levene's tale is almost like a thriller; there is power and sus-
pense written into every line. He becomes an author at such
times, as fluent and confident as a Dashiell Hammett or a Raymond Chandler. There is a sense, of course, in which the entire
play is a thriller. There is a robbery, police intervention, and a
surprising twist to the denouement. That it should be Levene
who tells the most "thrilling" story is deeply ironic given that he is
the culprit of the robbery and the ultimate victim of the piece.
     Roma is impressed enough with his elder colleague's sales-
manship to offer a word or two of flattery, implying that he owes
his own success to Levene's example. This naturally reinforces
Levene's sense of achievement, despite his modest dismissal, and
Mamet captures most humorously his protestations and counter-
compliments. It is difficult, in fact impossible, to tell whether
Levene and Roma are expressing genuine approbation for each
other's work or their words are as fatuous and manipulative as the
words they reserve for their clients. Certainly Roma's instructions
to Williamson at the end of act 2 sound quite unlike the sentiments of a man who places great emphasis on friendship and
loyalty:

> *Roma:* Williamson: listen to me: when the *leads* come in. . . . I want my
> top two off the list. For *me.* My usual two. Anything you give
> Levene. . . . I GET HIS ACTION. My stuff is *mine,* whatever *he* gets.
> I'm taking half. . . . My stuff is mine, his stuff is *ours.* (act 2, p. 64)

Moments earlier, he had broached with Levene the advantages of
being "partners," of splitting "everything right down the middle"
(ibid., p. 63). It will also be recalled that in the opening moments
of the play, Levene criticizes Roma's ability, observing that "he's
throwing the leads away" (1.1, p. 3).

As Levene recounts his tale, his phrasing becomes more fluid and hypnotic; his timing is as exact as that of the kitchen clock whose movements he so accurately remembers. He elongates some moments and telescopes others. He chooses not to spell out, word for word, how he thrusts the contract at the couple, but hurries the sentence in a brief, abbreviated rush: "I turned the contract eight units eighty-two grand." It contains all the information he wishes to convey. Grammatical accuracy is dismissed in favor of highlighting the essential components of the phrase—the number of units sold and the amount of money involved. The actual moment of signing, on the other hand, is detailed in the most minute terms. Levene takes immense pleasure in recalling how he felt Bruce and Harriett had *"kind of imperceptibly slumped"* and how they "wilted." The breakdown of the couple's resolve is therefore celebrated like a battle victory; the defeated have, through constant battering, lost their will to fight and they lie down in an attitude of abject surrender. As the contract is finally signed, Levene's speech becomes almost religious, with ceremonial and liturgical overtones: "And he reaches and takes the pen and signs, he passes it to her, she signs. It was so fucking solemn." The religiosity of his words sits very uncomfortably with the emphatic obscenity! As he moves toward the climax of his tale, a climax that seems almost orgasmic particularly when one notes his final "Ah fuck," it is as if he has lost himself in a sexual dream. In the Mermaid Theatre's production, Levene's final exclamation was accompanied by his slumping sideways across his chair as if he had, indeed, reached a kind of climax. The actor (Derek Newark) remained in this pose for several seconds, his eyes glazed and fixed straight ahead, completely overtaken by the power of his own storytelling.

Before he reaches this moment of what is, to him, akin to sexual gratification, Levene moves through a period of spiritual transcendence. He recalls how, in his growing ecstasy, he pointed "back in the living room" to the sideboard, which he had not hitherto realized had even existed. The irony of Levene experiencing a spiritually mesmeric moment as he fleeces a browbeaten couple out of a great deal of money is captured perfectly; there is a sublime nastiness in hearing this man relate his success story in these quasi-religious terms. The final irony occurs when he recalls the "little shotglasses" with which the sale is celebrated, glasses he remembers as having "a pattern in 'em." The noxious sentimentality of his words can be interpreted either as a nod toward the brilliance of his own achievement, his awareness of the "pattern" in the glasses taking place at a moment of heightened "aesthetic" understanding, or a genuine instant of compassion for his victims, whose failure to fight him is poignantly realized in the image of their offering of libations—even if the offer does emanate from Levene's suggestion. The final words celebrating his achievement, and broken in the middle by a rather theatrical period, consolidate the mood of sentimental (and spiritual) exultation: "And we toast. In silence."

As Levene's story progresses, he changes tense. What was at first related in the past tense suddenly becomes an evocation of events as they are actually taking place. Thus, he verbally enacts the scene for Roma just as he had performed his play about selling with consummate success at the Nyborg household. By dint of words alone, both men enjoy reliving the event, participating in the triumphant sale as its recollection stimulates their imagination.

Mamet has always been interested in the process of storytelling, and two plays that are particularly concerned with telling a story—as well as, of course *Glengarry Glen Ross*—are *Lakeboat* and *Dark Pony*. Christopher Bigsby notes how, in the face of a missing intimacy in their lives, Mamet's characters "compulsively elaborate fantasies, create plots, devise scenarios or simply exchange rumour and speculation."[55] In *Lakeboat*, the men who work on the merchant marine ship pass their time by turning mundane events into exciting adventures. Their lives are empty, passionless, and comprised mainly of drinking, gambling, and chattering aimlessly about sex. They spend hours doing nothing more than gazing at sets of gauges or making sandwiches. It is not then surprising that fiction should play such a large part in their daily existence, even if that fiction does not evolve from their own imaginations. Nearly all their stories bear the hallmarks of routine film plots, full of hackneyed clichés and simplistic morality. Virtually every piece of dialogue in the play involves storytelling. It begins with the Pierman asking, "Did you hear about Skippy and the new kid?" (scene 1, p. 17) and the variations on this theme that reverberate throughout the work form the backbone of the plot. Nothing is certain; everything is hearsay or frankly made up.

These men are reminiscent of James Joyce's *Dubliners* who, as Barbara Hardy observes,

> move through their nights and days, telling stories to themselves and to each other. However mean their existence, however thin their feelings, however numb their reflections, they are never so paralysed

as to be incapable of narrative. Their language and symbolism may be feeble, second-hand or banal, but the form, function and individuality of their stories prove that they are imagined as imaginative. They tell over the past and sketch out the future. They exchange overt or covert confessions, pleas and defences. . . . many of them are capable of fervent and energetic lies, dreams, projects, boasts, anecdotes, reminiscences, aspirations, fantasies, confidences and disclosures.[56]

Joyce, like Mamet, allows us to "encounter the poor in spirit by letting them speak and think for themselves. In scrupulously avoiding a contrast between his style and theirs. . . he teaches us not to condescend."[57]

The sheer survival value of storytelling is powerfully depicted in *Lakeboat*; just as the salesmen in *Glengarry Glen Ross* need the seductive potency of a well-rehearsed narrative with which to entrap their clients, the men who work on the lakeboat need fiction to make life tolerable. In the half-real world they inhabit, the dislocation of both time and identity necessitates an outlet, and that outlet is realized through an ongoing fictional representation about past events that may or may not have actually occurred.

Dark Pony is a short work totally concerned with the telling of one story. A man drives home late at night with his young daughter and, as he drives, he tells her a well-loved and familiar story about an American Indian boy called Rain Boy and his adventures with a magical pony. Part of the pleasure the child feels lies in the tale's predictability and the security of knowing how it will end; the story is lyrical and set out in a kind of verse and, although brief, conjures up a reassuring picture of a world in which all is well in the end. It is easy to see why Mamet should have written such a work, with its insistent rhythms and vividly imaginative plot; he enjoys working with fairy tales, and feels they offer a good guide to playwriting: "Bruno Bettleheim in *The Uses of Enchantment* writes that the fairy tale (i.e. the drama) has the capacity to calm, to incite, to assuage, finally, to *affect*, because we listen to it non-judgementally—we identify *sub*consciously (i.e., non-critically) with the protagonist."[58]

The salesmen in *Glengarry Glen Ross* must rely on their ability to tell a good story; if they are to be successful, their gambits must, like the fairy tale, be able to "incite, to assuage . . . to *affect*." Mamet has remarked that nearly all his characters use affective language in some way. He notes, "their language has been forced to serve their terms, which is why the dialogue in most of my plays is affective; the dialogue absolutely serves the turn of the speaker—In the drama, the character—if well-written—is going to use all of the tools at his disposal to get his ends."[59] Elsewhere, he has said that the characters in *Glengarry Glen Ross* "all use words to influence actions. They build what's called a line of affirmatives. A customer is never allowed to say no: 'You'd like to make money, wouldn't you?' they say. Another great trick is not answering objections: 'That's an excellent point. Let's talk about that later.' "[60]

Mamet's salesmen are not only superlative storytellers but also great actors. Their whole life is an act designed to impress, deceive, or coerce and they take great pride in acting out their "war stories" (act 2, p. 38) for each other and performing their carefully manipulative sales spiels for their clients. Mamet recalls that his colleagues in the real-estate office "were primarily performers. They went into people's living rooms and performed their play about the investment properties."[61] When the break-in necessitates the renegotiation of existing contracts, the salesmen effortlessly invent a masquerade, which they will act out for the benefit of clients. Williamson explains the plan to them:

> *Williamson:* The word from Murray is: leave them [the leads] alone. If we have to get a new sig he'll go out himself, he'll be the *President*, just come *in*, from out of *town* . . . (act 2, p. 36)

Mamet based this idea partly on the real-life ploys used daily in the real-estate office where he worked: "As [the client] had been told that no salesman would call, my basic telephone pitch went something like this: 'Mr. . . . This is Stewart Hodgkins from the . . . agency. . . . I'm sorry to bother you at home, but our company's International President, Mr. Williams . . . is, coincidentally, going to be in the Chicago area for two days this week on his way to New York . . .' "[62]

The salesmen have another opportunity to fall into their improvizational acting routine when Lingk unexpectedly turns up at the office to renege on his contract. Roma, with incredible timing and alacrity of mind, tells Levene that they must act out a make-or-break charade:

> *Roma:* You're a client. I just sold you five waterfront Glengarry Farms. I rub my head, throw me the cue "Kenilworth." (act 2, p. 45)

Having "suddenly" noticed Lingk, Roma then moves into the next stage of the routine:

Roma: (Looking up). Jim! What are you doing here? Jim Lingk, D. Ray
   Morton.
Levene: Glad to meet you.
Roma: I just put Jim into Black Creek . . . are you acquainted with . . .
Levene: No . . . Black *Creek.* Yes. In *Florida?* . . . My *wife* told me to look
   into . . .
Roma: Beautiful. Beautiful rolling land. I was telling Jim and Jinny, Ray,
   I want to tell you something. *(To Levene:)* You, Ray, you eat in a lot of
   restaurants. I know you do . . . *(To Lingk:)* Mr. Morton's with Amer-
   ican Express . . . he's *(To Levene:)* I can tell Jim what you do . . .
Levene: Sure.
Roma: Ray is Director of all European Sales and Services for American
   Ex . . . *(To Levene:)* But I'm saying you haven't had a *meal* until
   you've tasted . . . I was at the Lingk's last . . . as a matter of fact,
   what was that Service Feature you were talking about. . .
Levene: Which . . .
Roma: "Home Cooking" . . . what did you call it, you said it . . . it was
   a tag phrase that you had . . .
Levene: Uh . . .
Roma: Home . . .
Levene: Home cooking . . .
Roma: The monthly interview. . . ?
Levene: Oh! For the *magazine* . . .
Roma: Yes. Is this something that I can talk ab . . .
Levene: Well, it isn't coming *out* until the February iss . . . *sure.* Sure,
   go ahead, Rick.
Roma: You're sure?
Levene: (nods) Go ahead. (ibid., pp. 46–47)

This is all not only brilliantly funny but it also demonstrates the
risks that professionals like Roma are willing to take. Levene
"thinks on his feet," but even he struggles a little when confronted with such linguistic wizardry. Roma mentions an obscure
piece of land, "Black Creek" and Levene must think for a moment
how to respond. Once he realizes what is expected of him, however, he begins to invent and to embroider his own fictions,
emphasizing the word "creek" as a way of demonstrating to Lingk
that the name had only momentarily slipped his mind. Supposing
Lingk to be a married man and, by his shy and uncertain presence
possibly a hen-pecked one at that, Levene carefully but expertly
adds that his wife "told" him to look into the possibilities of such
an acquisition. Roma latches onto the personalized touch, and
begins to flatter Lingk with compliments about his wife's cooking.
Roma guesses correctly that the man's presence in the office can
mean only one thing: that he wishes to cancel his contract. In a

desperate attempt to flatter, confuse, disorient the hapless Lingk, Roma changes the subject every few seconds, seldom finishing a sentence before leading into another. He infers that he is going to relate something that he told "Jim and Jinny" but then he veers off, still in the same sentence, into an implication that the cooking he found at their house was rather exceptional. However, he does not actually get around to saying this for some time, so involved is he in trying to impress Lingk with his friendship with a high-flying business executive, and his offering of what almost amounts to classified information about the "executive's" precise job title. Hilariously, later in the same scene, D. Ray Morton's professional status changes once again: he is suddenly promoted ·to "*the* Senior Vice-President American Express" (ibid., p. 47).

In the full knowledge that he is playing with fire, Roma decides to throw in another invention, this time involving a "service feature." Again, Levene is momentarily nonplussed but soon catches on and begins to enjoy himself. He triumphs with a superbly slick show of bogus friendship: "Well, it isn't coming *out* until the February iss . . . *sure*. Sure, go ahead, Rick." His tone suggests intimacy, good and sound friendship, and trust. If Roma wishes to tell his "friend" Lingk about the finer details of American Express publishing, then so be it; there is more than a hint of "any friend of yours is a friend of mine" in Levene's manner. Confronted with such a display of bonhomie and trust, poor Lingk must wonder how he can even begin to say what he has promised his wife—that he must cancel the contract and nullify the check. However, in a moment of extreme courage, he manages to stammer out that his wife has called the Attorney General; he has informed her that the contract is not binding if cancelled within three days. Roma is genuinely appalled:

Roma: *Who* did she call?
Lingk: I don't know, the Attorney Gen . . . the . . . some Consumer office, umm . . .
Roma: Why did she do *that*, Jim?
Lingk: I don't know. *(Pause.)* They said we have three days. *(Pause.)* They said we have three days.
Roma: Three days.
Lingk: To . . . you know. *(Pause.)*
Roma: No I don't know. *Tell* me.
Lingk: To change our minds.
Roma: Of *course* you have three days. *(Pause.)* (ibid., p. 49)

In order to make the trembling Lingk suffer, Roma implies that his personal feelings have been hurt. He calls Lingk by name to emphasize and consolidate the "friendship" that exists between them. When Lingk prevaricates, Roma senses his fear and tries to undermine his confidence still further with aggressive tactics: "No I don't know. *Tell* me." His mind works frantically to find ways in which he can either further confuse Lingk or buy more time to think up other strategies. He tries to evade the issue by pretending that he is too busy to talk about the contract until the following week, by which time Lingk's legal rights will be cancelled:

> *Roma:* Jim, Jim, you saw my book . . . I *can't, you* saw my book . . .
> *Lingk:* But we have to *before* Monday. To get our money ba . . .
> *Roma:* Three *business* days. They mean three *business* days.
> *Lingk:* Wednesday, Thursday, Friday.
> *Roma:* I don't understand.
> *Lingk:* That's what they are. Three business . . . if I wait till Monday, my time limit runs out.
> *Roma:* You don't count Saturday. (ibid., p. 49)

Lingk persists despite being browbeaten by Roma. Eventually, as a final attempt, Roma tries the following:

> *Roma:* When did you write the check?
> *Lingk:* Yest. . .
> *Roma:* What was yesterday?
> *Lingk:* Tuesday.
> *Roma:* And when was that check cashed?
> *Lingk:* I don't know.
> *Roma:* What was the *earliest* it could have been cashed? *(Pause.)*
> *Lingk:* I don't know.
> *Roma:* Today. *(Pause.)* Today. Which, in any case, it was not, as there were a couple of points on the agreement I wanted to go over with you in any case. (ibid., p. 50)

Once he has seized upon the idea of the uncashed check, Roma is unstoppable. Lingk cannot even finish a word—"Yest . . ."—before Roma plunges ahead in breathless abandon. As he realizes that he is safe, Roma can relax a little and Mamet suggests this lull—even exhaustion—by the breakdown of grammar and the repetition of "in any case." This is like the relief felt after the exhalation of a deep sigh, and Roma can begin to pick up the fragments of his frayed nerves. For good measure and as an added puff to his confidence he implies that, as an honest and decent businessman he would not have cashed the check in any case since there were a "couple of points" he wished to discuss. Not only has Lingk misread the entire situation and distrusted Roma's intentions, but he has also maligned and hurt the feelings of a "buddy" with the ethics of a saint.

The extent of the guilt Lingk feels is evident later in the scene when he actually apologizes for being cheated. In spite of Roma's denials to the contrary, Lingk learns that the check has, after all, been cashed. Roma has been revealed as a liar, yet Lingk is incapable of rational thought at such a moment:

> *Lingk:* Oh, Christ. . . . I know I've let you down. I'm sorry. For . . . Forgive . . . for. . . I don't know anymore. *(Pause.)* Forgive me. (ibid., p. 56)

Lingk seems to believe that he has broken a bond of friendship, even though he must be aware that he has been callously used. Such a need to believe in the power of friendship and the unimpeachability of loyalty is Mamet's way of suggesting that there *is* more than the cynical, cruel relationships enjoyed by the salesmen. Of their number, it is only Aaronow who gives any indication of a sense of loyalty. Such moments of genuine affection may be fragile and few, given the amount of corruption that rages throughout the play, but they nevertheless persist. Such behavior would be absolutely unthinkable for a man like Roma, whose desire to succeed overrides all emotional considerations. His feigned friendship with Lingk is perfidious in the extreme, and his only reaction to the man's distress is to turn his back on him and launch into a terrifying verbal assault on Williamson, the much-despised office manager who has been responsible for Roma's loss of "six thousand dollars. And one Cadillac" (act 2, p. 56).

After a vicious stream of profanities, Roma's blistering contempt is summed up as he gropes for words and finds what is, to him, the ultimate insult: "You fuckin' *child* . . ." (act 2, p. 57). Throughout the play, there is much emphasis upon selling being a "man's job," a sense of being out there on the streets, on the "front line." A little after this outburst, Roma bitterly remarks to Levene: "I swear . . . it's not a world of men . . . it's not a world of men, Machine . . . it's a world of clock watchers, bureaucrats, office holders . . . What it is, it's a fucked-up world . . . there's no adventure *to* it. . . . We are the members of a dying breed." (act 2,

p. 62). This brings to mind Willy Loman's nostalgia for the "good old days" of selling. He, too, remembers how "in those days there was personality in it. . . . There was respect and comradeship, and gratitude in it. Today it's all cut and dried, and there's no chance for bringing friendship to bear—or personality."[63] It has already been observed that a heady sense of tough masculinity pervades the play and it is significant that Shelly Levene's nickname should be "The Machine" with all the hard-working macho imagery that implies. The challenge of the sale is repeatedly articulated in mock-heroic language, which would not be amiss in cowboy or gangster films; the salesmen elevate themselves above the rest of the world and, particularly, above those who merely sit at a desk. Earlier in the play, Levene also insults Williamson's abilities when the latter has called into question the validity of his sale:

> *Levene:* Why should the sale not stick? Hey, fuck *you*. That's what I'm saying. You have no idea of your job. A man's his job and you're *fucked* at yours. . . . You can't run an office. I don't care. You don't know what it *is*, you don't have the *sense*, you don't have the *balls*. You ever been on a sit? *Ever?* (act 2, p. 44)

Williamson is thus denounced as little more than a secretary—and an inefficient one at that—who isn't fit to mix with real men who must work for a living. This feeling of hardened professionals striving to survive in a hostile wilderness gives rise to a certain degree of fellowship among the men although, as mentioned elsewhere, it is difficult to know how genuine such sentiments are. In this brutally competitive world, perhaps the expression of friendship is one means of ensuring that a "pal" will stand up for one's rights when times are hard. Even the cynical Roma occasionally indulges in this kind of supportive strategy. When Aaronow tells him of his fear of losing his job, and of his incompetence, Roma praises him:

> *Roma:* . . . Fuck that shit, George. You're a *hey*, you had a bad month. You're a good man, George. . . . You hit a bad streak. (act 2, p. 32)

When Levene is exalted at his good fortune with the Nyborg sale, Moss all but ignores him, resenting his success. As a result of this display of coldness towards a colleague, Roma confronts him:

> *Roma:* . . .Fuck *you*, Dave, you know you got a big *mouth*, and *you* make a close the whole *place* stinks with your *farts* for a week. . . .

> what a big *man* you are. . . . Your *pal* closes, all that comes out of
> your mouth is *bile,* how fucked *up* you are . . . (act 2, p. 41)

In spite of these rare displays of a kind of friendship, any relationship that exists between the men can be only skin-deep. They
can identify only with each other's problems and crises through
work—there is nothing outside of the office they can share. They
are salesmen, first and foremost, and any attempt to view themselves as anything else is doomed to failure. Thus, when Levene
begs Williamson to give him some of the precious leads and to
judge him independently of his current achievements, he is
bound to fail:

> *Levene:* I'm asking you. As a favor to me? *(Pause.)* John. *(Long pause.)*
>   John: my *daughter* . . .
> *Williamson:* I can't do it, Shelly. (1. 2, p. 10)

and later, once Williamson has realized that it is indeed Levene
who has broken into the office and stolen the leads, Levene again
begs for mercy:

> *Levene:* John: . . . my *daughter* . . .
> *Williamson:* Fuck you. (act 2, p. 62)

Levene brings up his daughter to try and sway Williamson's
decision, but to no avail. The only time we hear of anything other
than salesmanship is when one of the workers is either in trouble
or working towards a sales coup. Williamson knows this as well as
Levene, and refuses to let personal considerations intrude. Besides, in the existential world of the salesman, each man is *only* a
salesman; he is not what he has done, or what his personal life has
made him, but what he is at the present time. He can be judged
only in terms of his current capabilities and, in Levene's case, this
is not very much.

Perhaps the most resonant emotion that one feels upon seeing
the play performed is the terrible sense of waste. It is at once a
comical and terrible sight to see intelligent men groveling toward
success at any cost. They muster every scrap of their ingenuity to
survive, but that survival is empty at its core. Christopher Bigsby
makes an analogy between Mamet's salesmen and the aging cow-
boys in Arthur Miller's film, *The Misfits.* In that work, the protagonists capture wild horses to be used as meat in dog food.

They use all their worthy talents toward that squalid end, wasting both their energy and their expertise. In *Glengarry Glen Ross,* the salesmen "stake their fortunes and possibly their lives . . . on nothing more adventurous than selling land (valuable or worthless) to people who are themselves seduced by an old dream, an avaricious myth of sudden profit."[64] It is very sad that these men, with their brilliant skills in the manipulation of language and their apparently fathomless depths of imagination cannot put their skills to more worthwhile use.

Glengarry Glen Ross was almost universally applauded by the critics and is generally considered to be Mamet's best play. A few examples of the kind of critical response it received will illustrate the depth of feeling it inspired. Robert Cushman felt that it was "the best play in London. . . . Here at last, carving characters and conflicts out of language, is a play with real muscle. Hereafter, all the pieces we have half-heartedly approved because they mentioned 'important' issues as if mentioning were the same as *dealing* with will seem second-rate. *Glengarry Glen Ross* mentions nothing, but in its depiction of a driven, conscienceless world it implies a great deal."[65] Dennis Cunningham observed that "David Mamet's *Glengarry Glen Ross* is a theatrical event, altogether extraordinary, an astonishing, exhilarating experience. . . . a ferocious comedy, a riveting drama, even a shocking mystery."[66] Christopher Edwards declared the play to be "by far the best thing showing in London."[67] Kevin Kelly called it "a short but masterful play,"[68] and John Barber nominated it as "a small masterpiece."[69]

There remain, however, those who refuse to acknowledge the merits of the piece. Kenneth Hurren avers that "Mamet has big ideas but writes very small plays. . . . the foul-mouthed dialogue is about as authentic as a three-dollar bill. . . as an indictment of American capitalism it is superficial tosh"[70] and Douglas Watt is very scathing indeed: "Down the drain once more with David Mamet. . . . [This] lacks the genuine humor and pathos and, especially, the delicate balance of *American Buffalo.* To elevate it to the status of a bitter comment on the American dream would amount to cosmic foolishness. It is what it is, a slice of life that sends you out of the theatre neither transported nor even informed, just cheerless."[71]

Each of these reviewers seems to have missed by quite a wide margin Mamet's intentions in the play. It seems to me extraordinary how Kenneth Hurren can claim that the dialogue "is about as authentic as a three-dollar bill"; it is generally accepted among

Mamet's critics that his ability to form the American vernacular
into realistic-sounding dialogue is his greatest gift as a playwright. Mamet does not set out to present himself as a naturalistic
dramatist; what he *tries* to do is write dramatic poetry that incorporates the idiom of the American streets. Douglas Watt's criticism of the play as being "a slice of life" is equally misguided for
reasons already stated. Although he praises *American Buffalo*, it
would appear that he viewed that work too as totally naturalistic.
It is also extremely difficult to understand how he could fail to
notice the genuine humor in *Glengarry Glen Ross* and why he
should comment upon its lack of balance. It is perhaps the most
perfectly balanced of all Mamet's plays, the characterization and
mood which are set up in the opening three scenes are then
opened out and explored in the concluding act. Watt's assertion
that it would be "cosmic foolishness" to elevate the work to a
comment on the American Dream is also rather puzzling, as is
Kenneth Hurren's view that, as "an indictment of American capitalism it is superficial tosh." The play is neither of these in
isolation, but it surely implies quite serious criticism of both the
debased American Dream and the corrupting nature of capitalism.

Like Mamet's other plays, *Glengarry Glen Ross* can be viewed on
several different, even contrasting levels: it can be seen as a black
comedy, a thriller, a morality play with serious political overtones,
a straightforward account of the world of real estate sales, and a
study of male companionship and competition. Its chief value,
however, lies in Mamet's superb use of language; the play is an
unsurpassed demonstration of linguistic skill by a playwright
already lauded for his dialogue. His interest in storytelling
reaches its zenith in this work—his salesmen are both fabulators
and consummate actors who are able to set up a fictional "reality"
with ease. But it is not merely their ability to construct stories that
make Mamet's salesmen interesting; it is why they choose to do
so. They sell not only real estate but also hope and consolation, as
much to themselves as to their hapless clients. So alone in the
world are they that they need words to construct alternative
worlds. It is their tragedy that they have subverted language to
such a degree that they can barely articulate genuine needs and
emotions. Selling is their whole lives, and they do not really exist
outside of the workplace. Despite their corruption, they are
worthy of our sympathy; a ruthless, capitalist society has set them
on the wheel, and for them there is no turning back. However, the

will to believe in a brighter future—both for the salesmen and for their customers—is seen by Mamet as being very powerful. Their joint ability to create and believe in fictions that contain hope is the tenacity of optimism.

Conclusion

The purpose of this book has been to demonstrate how, via his very original use of free verse, David Mamet uses language as dramatic action. From the outset, however, Mamet is faced with a dichotomy: he wants to dramatize the apathy and corruption of modern America and to identify its debilitating effects upon his characters, but he is also drawn to their debased language as a positive vehicle for his poetry. What is remarkable is the successful resolution he finds to this problem.

The speech of Mamet's characters may have become deformed as a result of taking for its model that which is already corrupt— the ever present mythmaking lie that assails them from all corners of the media-machine—but there remains a level at which it can still be viewed as a celebration of tenacity, a means of a communication that is vibrant and alive. For these individuals, language has become a weapon with which to attack a threatening world, a way of sustaining confidence and building security. Their speech may be blunted and basic, but it is seldom without interest—in fact, it is usually downright fascinating. It is clear that Mamet is thrilled by the theatrical possibilities this kind of language affords a playwright who is first and last a verse dramatist.

No matter how unethical or amoral Mamet's characters may be, we empathize with and even like them. They are so real, so magnificently crafted that it is quite possible to identify with their plight and at the same time deplore what a grasping, nihilistic society has made them. Furthermore, Mamet's plays are extremely funny; even in their darkest moments, there is injected a flash of humor that tempers the tragedy.

Although, finally, Mamet's view of the world is optimistic, and much comedy is included to convey his dramatic point, his poetry is replete with negative imagery and sadness. The emotions of his characters have become blunted by relentless media battering and their reliance upon popular stereotypes that, they believe, will confirm their place in the world and provide them with energy and status. With their true feelings hidden from the public gaze, they struggle to give credence to the lies they have adopted as truths. Mamet is a moralist who bemoans, through his drama, the fecund venality he believes exists at all levels of American society, whether in the form of media propaganda, spurious "business" negotiations at either end of the social spectrum, devalued emotional and sexual relationships, or simply an arrogant capacity for selfishness and greed. His drama is not an easy experience, either for his actors or the audience; it is exceptionally fast-moving and direct—its dazzling dialogue ricochets around the auditorium like so many blue-tinged bullets, the obscenities nearly colliding as they spill from their speakers' mouths.

Above all, the body of work produced by David Mamet is a superb demonstration of the talents of a man primarily concerned with language and what can be achieved by its careful manipulation. Through his imaginative and original use of idiomatic speech, Mamet utilizes every word to forward the action, depict character, establish mood, and add to the overall shape of his work. As a "language playwright," he is unsurpassed in contemporary American theatre.

Notes

Introduction

1. Samuel Beckett, "Dante . . . Bruno. Vico . . . Joyce," in *Our Exagmination Round his Factification for Incamination of Work in Progress* (New York: Grove Press, 1962), p. 14.

2. Robert Storey, "The Making of David Mamet," *Hollins Critic* 16, no. 4 (October 1979): p. 1.

3. Jack Kroll, "The Muzak Man," *Newsweek*, 28 February 1977, p. 79.

4. Richard Eder, "David Mamet's New Realism," *New York Times*, 12 March 1978, p. 40.

5. John Lahr, in Program notes for *Glengarry Glen Ross* (London: National Theatre, 1983).

6. C. W. E. Bigsby, *Contemporary Writers—David Mamet* (London: Methuen, 1985), p. 14.

7. Ross Wetzsteon, "New York Letter," *Plays & Players* 23, no. 12 (September 1976): p. 39.

8. Storey, "Making of David Mamet," p. 1.

9. *Dictionary of Literary Biography: 20th Century American Dramatists* vol. 7, ed. John MacNicholas (Detroit: Gale Research Co., 1981), p. 66.

10. Christopher Edwards, "Perfect Pitch," *The Spectator*, 15 March 1986, p. 36.

11. Bigsby, *Contemporary Writers*, p. 14.

12. *Kaleidoscope*, Radio 4, (B.B.C. Radio) 19 April 1985.

13. David Mamet, *Writing in Restaurants* (New York: Viking Penguin Inc., 1986), p. 130.

14. Ibid.

15. Bigsby, *Contemporary Writers*, p. 135.

16. Constantin Stanislavski, in *Stanislavski's Legacy*, ed. and trans. by Elizabeth Reynolds Hapgood (London: Eyre Methuen, 1981), p. 20.

17. Mamet, *Writing in Restaurants*, p. 12.

18. Ibid.

19. Bigsby, *Contemporary Writers*, p. 124.

20. Jack Kroll, "Mamet's Jackals in Jackets," *Newsweek*, 9 April 1984, p. 109.

21. Mel Gussow, "The Daring Visions of Four New, Young Playwrights," *New York Times*, 13 February 1977, p. D13.

22. Jack Shepherd, interview with author, 13 March 1986, National Theatre, London.

23. Gussow, "Daring Visions." p. D13.

24. John Ditsky, "He Lets You See the Thought There," *Kansas Quarterly* 12, no. 4 (1980): pp. 25, and 33.

25. Bigsby, *Contemporary Writers*, p. 28.

26. Stanislavski, *Stanislavski's Legacy*, p. 81.

27. Ibid., p. 83.

28. Miranda Richardson, interview with author, 8 December 1986, National Theatre, London.

29. August Strindberg, Preface to *Miss Julie* in *Strindberg: Plays: One*, trans. Michael Meyer (London: Methuen, 1982), p. 98.

30. Ibid., p. 99.

31. Ibid.

32. Gareth Lloyd Evans, *The Language of Modern Drama* (Totowa, N.J.: Rowman & Littlefield, 1977), p. 181.

33. Wetzsteon, "New York Letter," (September 1976): p. 38.

34. Harold Clurman in Introduction to *Odets: Six Plays* (London: Methuen, 1982), p. xi.

35. C. Gerald Fraser, "Mamet's Plays Shed Masculinity Myth," *New York Times*, 5 July 1976, p. L7.

36. Ditsky, "He Lets You See," p. 26.

37. Wetzsteon, "New York Letter," (September 1976): p. 37.

38. Jack V. Barbera, "Ethical Perversity in America: Some Observations on David Mamet's *American Buffalo*," *Modern Drama* 24, no. 1 (September 1981): 272.

39. Jack Shepherd, interview with author, 13 March 1986, National Theatre, London.

40. Jack Shepherd, "An Actor's Diary," *Drama* 4, no. 154 (1984): 54.

41. *Dictionary of Literary Biography*, p. 66.

42. Ibid., p. 69.

43. Arthur Miller, *The American Clock* (London: Methuen, 1983), act 2, p. 42.

44. Wetzsteon, "New York Letter," *Plays & Players* 24, no. 9 (June 1977): p. 37.

45. Program notes for *Glengarry Glen Ross*.

46. Colin Stinton, interview with author, 22 March 1986, National Theatre, London.

47. Ibid.

48. Ibid.

49. Leo Sauvage, "Corrupted Salesmen," *New Leader* 67, no. 7 (16 April 1984): pp. 20–21.

50. Edward Bond, Preface to *Lear* in *Plays: Two* (London: Methuen, 1972) p. 3.

51. Linda Winer, "David Mamet: A Serious Win," *USA Today* Life section, 17 April 1984, p. 30.

52. Mamet, *Writing in Restaurants*, p. 26.

53. Martin Esslin, *Pinter the Playwright*, (London: Methuen, 1970), p. 49.

54. Colin Stinton, interview with author, 22 March 1986, National Theatre, London.

55. Mamet, *Writing in Restaurants*, p. 14.

56. Colin Stinton, interview with author, 22 March 1986, National Theatre, London.

57. Ibid.

58. Ibid.

59. Bigsby, *Contemporary Writers*, p. 124.

60. Mamet, *Writing in Restaurants*, p. 68.

61. Colin Stinton, interview with author, 22 March 1986, National Theatre, London.

62. Freddie Jones, interview with author, 17 November 1986, B.B.C. Television Studios, Acton, London.

63. Richard Gottlieb, "The 'Engine' that Drives Playwright David Mamet," *New York Times*, 15 January 1978, p. D4.

64. Shepherd, "An Actor's Diary," p. 54.

65. Shepherd, interview with author, 13 March 1986, National Theatre, London.

66. Stinton, interview with author, 22 March 1986, National Theatre, London.

67. Jack Shepherd, National Theatre Study Notes for *Glengarry Glen Ross* (London: National Theatre, 1983), p. 8.

68. Stinton, interview with author, 22 March 1986, National Theatre, London.

69. Shepherd, interview with author, 13 March 1986, National Theatre, London.

70. David Mamet, *American Buffalo* (London: Methuen, 1978), p. 4.

71. Stinton, interview with author, 22 March 1986, National Theatre, London.

72. Jean Vallely, "David Mamet Makes a Play for Hollywood," *Rolling Stone,* 3 April 1980, p. 44.

73. David Mamet, National Theatre Study Notes for *Glengarry Glen Ross,* p. 5.

74. Vallely, "David Mamet," p. 46.

75. Mamet, National Theatre Study Notes for *Glengarry Glen Ross,* p. 5.

76. Vallely, "David Mamet," p. 46.

77. Ibid.

78. David Mamet, "Mamet in Hollywood," *Horizon,* February 1981, p. 54.

79. Vallely, "David Mamet," p. 46.

80. David Mamet, *The Postman Always Rings Twice* (screenplay), unpublished manuscript (London: Lorimar Distribution Ltd., 1979), p. 6.

81. Ibid., pp. 6–7.

82. James M. Cain, *The Postman Always Rings Twice* in *The Five Great Novels of James M. Cain* (London: Picador, 1985), p. 6.

83. Mamet, *Postman* screenplay, p. 39.

84. David Mamet, *The Verdict* (screenplay), unpublished manuscript (London: Twentieth Century Fox Film Co. Ltd., 1981), p. 1.

85. Ibid.

86. Mamet, *Writing in Restaurants,* p. 71.

87. Bigsby, *Contemporary Writers,* pp. 19–20.

88. Mamet, *Writing in Restaurants,* p. 71.

89. Samuel Beckett, *The Unnameable* (London: Calder & Boyars, 1958), p. 132.

90. Fraser, "Mamet's Plays," p. L7.

91. Mamet, "Epitaph for Tennessee Williams," *Rolling Stone,* 14 April 1983, p. 124.

Chapter 1: *Sexual Perversity in Chicago*

1. Mamet, *Writing in Restaurants,* p. 30.

2. Karl Marx cited in Erich Fromm, *Beyond the Chains of Illusion: My Encounter with Marx & Freud* (London: Abacus, Sphere Books, 1980), pp. 46–47.

3. Bigsby, *Contemporary Writers,* p. 50.

4. Eder, "David Mamet's New Realism," p. 40.

5. Fraser, "Mamet's Plays," p. L7.

6. Ibid.

7. Tom Wolfe, *The Kandy-Kolored Tangerine-Flake Streamline Baby* (London: Jonathan Cape, 1981), p. 46.

8. Fraser, "Mamet's Plays," p. L7.

9. Ibid.

10. Peter Stothard, *Plays & Players* 25, no. 5 (February 1978): pp. 30–31.

11. Marshall Walker, *The Literature of the U.S.A.* (London: Macmillan, 1983), p. 194.

12. John Elsom, *The Listener,* 8 December 1977, p. 774.

13. Jules Feiffer, *Carnal Knowledge* (London: Penguin, 1972), pp. 10–12.

14. Ibid., pp. 18–19.

15. Stinton, interview with author, 22 March 1986, National Theatre, London.

16. Ibid.

17. Connie Booth, interview with author, 2 December 1986, Hampstead, London.

18. Stinton, interview with author, 22 March 1986, National Theatre, London.

19. Richardson, interview with author, 8 December 1986, National Theatre, London.

20. Fraser, "Mamet's Plays," p. L7.

21. Ibid.

22. Ibid.

23. Ibid.

24. Bigsby, *Contemporary Writers,* p. 48.

25. Wetzsteon, "New York Letter," (September 1976): pp. 37–39.

26. *The South Bank Show,* London Weekend Television, 20 March 1985.

27. Shepherd, interview with author, 13 March 1986, National Theatre, London.

28. Stephen Brook, *New York Days, New York Nights* (London: Picador, 1985), p. 47.

29. Stinton, interview with author, 22 March 1986, National Theatre, London.

30. Friedrich Hebbel cited in *Playwrights on Playwriting,* ed. Toby Cole (New York: Hill & Wang, 1982), p. 286.

31. Nicholas de Jongh, *The Guardian* 19 March 1984 p. 11.

Chapter 2: *American Buffalo*

1. Folk tune quoted in Mamet, *American Buffalo,* title page.

2. *The South Bank Show,* 20 March 1985.

3. Ibid.

4. Ibid.

5. June Schlueter and Elizabeth Forsyth, "America as Junkshop: The Business Ethic in David Mamet's *American Buffalo,*" *Modern Drama* 26, no. 4 (December 1983): p. 497.

6. Bigsby, *Contemporary Writers,* pp. 133–34.

7. Ibid., p. 134.

8. David Mamet, *Ozark Magazine,* May 1984, p. 38.

9. Bigsby, *Contemporary Writers,* p. 84.

10. *South Bank Show,* 20 March 1985.

11. Ibid.

12. Mamet, *Writing in Restaurants,* p. 66.

13. Ibid., p. 67.

14. Ibid., p. 65.

15. Jennifer Allen, "David Mamet's Hard Sell," *New York,* 9 April 1984, p. 40.

16. Richard Christiansen, "The Young Lion of Chicago Theatre," *Chicago Tribune Magazine,* 11 July 1982, p. 11.

17. Gussow, Daring Visions, p. D13.

18. *South Bank Show,* 20 March 1985.

19. Ibid.

20. David Mamet, "The Things Poker Teaches," *New York Times Magazine,* 20 April 1986, p. 52.

21. Bigsby, *Contemporary Writers,* p. 75.

22. Saul Bellow, *Herzog* (London: Weidenfeld & Nicholson, 1965), p. 11.

23. Gottlieb, " 'Engine' that Drives Mamet," p. D4.

24. *South Bank Show,* 20 March 1985.

25. Gottlieb, " 'Engine' that Drives Mamet." p. D4.

26. Mamet, National Theatre Study Notes for *Glengarry Glen Ross,* p. 4.

27. Mamet to Jack V. Barbera, 6 June 1980, cited in Barbera, "Ethical Perversity," p. 274.

28. Thorstein Veblen, *The Theory of the Leisure Class: An Economic Study of the Evolution of Institutions* (London: Macmillan, 1925), p. 17.

29. Joseph Conrad in Preface to *The Nigger of the Narcissus* (Middlesex, England: Penguin Modern Classics, 1985), p. 13.

30. Mamet, *Writing in Restaurants,* p. 65.

31. Caryl Churchill, *Softcops* (London and New York: Methuen's New Theatrescripts, 1984), p. 6.

32. Shepherd, interview with author, 13 March 1986, National Theatre, London.

33. Ibid.

34. Thornton Wilder, "Some Thoughts on Playwriting" in Cole, ed., *Playwrights on Playwriting,* p. 112.

35. Wetzsteon, "New York Letter," (September 1976): p. 38.

36. *Dictionary of Literary Biography,* p. 66.

37. Eugene O'Neill to Barrett H. Clarke, 1946, cited in Clifford Leech, *Eugene O'Neill* (Edinburgh and London: Oliver & Boyd, 1966), p. 100.

38. John Simon, National Theatre Study Notes for *Glengarry Glen Ross,* p. 4.

39. Bigsby, *Contemporary Writers,* p. 80.

40. G. L. Brook, *Varieties of English* (London: The Macmillan Press, 1973), p. 83.

41. Carl Sandburg quoted on *The Story of English,* B.B.C.2 Television, 22 September 1986.

42. Brook, *Varieties of English,* p. 126.

43. Milton Shulman, "Strong Words, Electric Shocks," *London Evening Standard,* 3 August 1984, p. 26.

44. Raymond Chandler, *The Notebooks of Raymond Chandler* (London: Weidenfeld & Nicholson, 1977). p. 20.

45. John Osborne, *The Entertainer,* scene 8, p. 62.

46. Stinton, interview with author, 22 March 1986, National Theatre, London.

47. Ibid.

48. Eder, "David Mamet's New Realism," p. 42.

49. John Beaufort, *Christian Science Monitor,* 23 February 1977. Review cited in *New York Theatre Critics Reviews,* vol. 38 (1977): p. 368.

50. Edwin Wilson, "A Phlegmatic *American Buffalo,*" *Wall Street Journal,* 23 February 1977, p. 24.

51. Brendan Gill, "No News from Lake Michigan," *The New Yorker,* 28 February 1977, p. 54.

52. Christopher Porterfield, "David Mamet's Bond of Futility," *Time,* 28 February 1977, p. 55.

53. Ibid.

54. Gottlieb, " 'Engine' that Drives Mamet." p. D4.

55. Bigsby, *Contemporary Writers*, p. 85.

56. Schlueter and Forsyth, "America as Junkshop," 492.

57. Porterfield, "Mamet's Bond of Futility," p. 55.

58. Harold Clurman, "Theatre," *The Nation*, 12 March 1977, p. 313.

59. Schlueter and Forsyth, "America as Junkshop," p. 493.

60. Storey, "The Making of David Mamet," pp. 1–11.

61. Frank Rich, "Al Pacino in *American Buffalo*," *New York Times*, 28 October 1983, p. C3.

62. Clive Barnes, "Pacino's Back for a Knockout in *Buffalo*," *New York Post*, 27 October 1983. Review cited in *New York Theatre Critics Reviews*, vol. 44 (1983): pp. 143–44.

63. Clive Barnes, *New York Post*, 5 June 1981. Review cited in *New York Theatre Critics Reviews*, vol. 42 (1981): p. 187.

64. Clive Barnes, "Mamet's *Glengarry*: A Play to See and Cherish," *New York Post*, 26 March 1984. Review cited in *New York Theatre Critics Reviews*, vol. 45 (1984): p. 335.

65. Robert Cushman, *Plays & Players*, no. 372 (September 1984): p. 25.

66. Howard Kissel, *Women's Wear Daily*, 28 October 1983. Review cited in *New York Theatre Critics Reviews*, vol. 44 (1983): p. 142.

67. Dennis Cunningham, WCBS (radio station), 28 October 1983.

68. David Skerritt, cited in John Beaufort, "*Buffalo* is Back—A Tragicomedy Starring Al Pacino," *Christian Science Monitor*, 8 November 1983. Review cited in *New York Theatre Critics Reviews*, vol. 44, (1983): p. 144.

69. Stothard, *Plays & Players*, (February 1978): pp. 30–31.

70. Shepherd, National Theatre Study Notes for *Glengarry Glen Ross*, p. 8.

71. Booth, interview with author, 9 December 1986, Hampstead, London.

72. Booth, letter to author, 14 November 1986.

73. Wetzsteon, "New York Letter," (September 1976): p. 39.

74. Kroll, "The Muzak Man," p. 79.

75. Barbera, "Ethical Perversity in America," p. 270.

76. Carl Sandburg, *Chicago* in *Complete Poems* (New York: Harcourt, Brace & World Inc., 1950), p. 3.

77. Allen, "Mamet's Hard Sell," p. 41.

78. Ibid.

79. Ditsky, "He Lets You See," pp. 27–29.

80. Robert Brustein in Introduction to *Chekhov: The Major Plays*, translated by Ann Dunnigan (New York: Signet Classic, New American Library, 1964), p. xi.

81. Wetzsteon, "New York Letter" (September 1976): p. 38.

82. Bigsby, *Contemporary Writers*, p. 133.

83. Ibid., p. 69.

Chapter 3: *A Life in the Theatre*

1. Mel Gussow, "Mamet Wins with *A Life in the Theatre*," *New York Times*, 5 February 1977, p. 10.

2. Mel Gussow, "Illusion Within an Illusion," *New York Times*, 20 October 1977, p. 12.

3. David Mamet, "A Sad Comedy about Actors," *New York Times*, 16 October 1977, p. D7.

4. Ibid.

5. Mamet, *Writing in Restaurants*, p. 106.
6. Ibid.
7. Ibid., p. 105.
8. Jones, interview with author, 17 November 1986, B.B.C. Television Studios, Acton, London.
9. Mamet, *Writing in Restaurants*, p. 104.
10. Ibid., pp. 104–5.
11. Tom Stoppard, *Rosencrantz and Guildenstern are Dead* (London: Faber & Faber, 1980), act 2, p. 46.
12. Ditsky, "He Lets You See," p. 31.
13. Patrick Ryecart, interview with author, 9 March 1987, National Theatre, London.
14. Mamet, *Writing in Restaurants*, p. 106.
15. Michael Coveney, *Financial Times*, 19 July 1979, p. 21.
16. Luigi Pirandello cited in Raymond Williams, *Drama from Ibsen to Brecht* (Middlesex, England: Penguin, 1981), p. 179.
17. Williams, *Drama from Ibsen to Brecht*, p. 174.
18. Michael Billington, *The Guardian*, 19 July 1979, p. 12.
19. Stoppard, *Rosencrantz and Guildenstern*, act 1, p. 30.
20. Gussow, "Illusion Within an Illusion," p. 12.
21. David Mamet, *A Life in the Theatre* (New York: Samuel French, Inc., 1975), p. 6.
22. Ibid.
23. Ryecart, interview with author, 9 March 1987, National Theatre, London.
24. Milton Shulman, "Disasters on Cue," *London Evening Standard*, 19 July 1979, p. 27.
25. Sheridan Morley, *Punch*, 1 August 1979, p. 42.
26. Colin Ludlow, *Plays & Players*, 26, no. 11 (August 1979): pp. 25 and 28.
27. Ryecart, interview with author, 9 March 1987, National Theatre, London.
28. Tennessee Williams cited in C. W. E. Bigsby, *A Critical Introduction to Twentieth-Century American Drama—Williams, Miller, Albee*, vol. 2 (Cambridge: Cambridge University Press, 1984), p. 47.
29. Ryecart, inteview with author, 9 March 1987, National Theatre, London.
30. Mamet, *Writing in Restaurants*, p. 105.
31. Ryecart, interview with author, 9 March 1987, National Theatre, London.
32. Jones, interview with author, 17 November 1986, B.B.C. Television Studios, Acton, London.
33. Ryecart, interview with author, 9 March 1987, National Theatre, London.
34. Shulman, "Disasters on Cue," p. 27.
35. Stinton, interview with author, 22 March 1986, National Theatre, London.
36. Ryecart, interview with author, 9 March 1987, National Theatre, London.
37. Ibid.
38. Ibid.
39. Shulman, "Disasters on Cue," p. 27.
40. Gussow, "Illusion Within an Illusion," p. 12.
41. Jones, interview with author, 17 November 1986, B.B.C. Television Studios, Acton, London.
42. Ryecart, interview with author, 9 March 1987, National Theatre, London.
43. Ibid.
44. Jones, interview with author, 17 November 1986, B.B.C. Television Studios, Acton, London.

45. Ryecart, interview with author, 9 March 1987, National Theatre, London.
46. Ibid.
47. Jones, interview with author, 17 November 1986, B.B.C. Television Studios, Acton, London.
48. Ryecart, interview with author, 9 March 1987, National Theatre, London.
49. Rudyard Kipling, *Actors*, cited in Mamet, *A Life in the Theatre*, p. 7.
50. Billington, *The Guardian*, p. 12.
51. Gussow, "Mamet Wins," p. 12.

Chapter 4: *Edmond*

1. Program notes for *Glengarry Glen Ross*.
2. Booth, interview with author, 2 December 1986, Hampstead, London.
3. Program notes for *Glengarry Glen Ross*.
4. Bigsby, *Contemporary Writers*, p. 133.
5. Carl Jung in *Jung—Selected Writings*, ed. Anthony Storr (London: Fontana, 1983), p. 349.
6. Jack Kroll, "Hearts of Darkness," *Newsweek*, 8 November 1982, p. 82.
7. Jung, *Selected Writings*, p. 355.
8. Bellow, *Herzog*, pp. 106–7.
9. Fromm, *Beyond the Chains of Illusion*, pp. xi–xii.
10. Norman Mailer cited in Charles Ruas, *Conversations with American Writers*, (London: Quartet Books, 1986), p. 28.
11. *South Bank Show*, 20 March 1985.
12. Susie Mackenzie, "Base Instincts," *Time Out*, 28 November 1985 p. 18.
13. Benedict Nightingale, "Is Mamet the Bard of Modern Immorality?" *New York Times*, 1 April 1984, p. 5.
14. *South Bank Show*, 20 March 1985.
15. Ibid.
16. Ibid.
17. Jung, *Selected Writings*, p. 402.
18. *South Bank Show*, 20 March 1985.
19. Ibid.
20. Frank Rich, "Mamet's *Edmond* at the Provincetown," *New York Times*, 28 October 1982, p. C20.
21. Matt Wolf, *City Limits*, 29 November 1985, p. 63.
22. Mackenzie, "Base Instincts," p. 19.
23. Ibid.
24. Stinton, interview with author, 22 March 1986, National Theatre, London.
25. Bellow, *Herzog*, p. 151.
26. Joseph Conrad, *Heart of Darkness* (London: Pan Books Ltd., 1976), p. 13.
27. T. E. Kalem, "I Hate New York," *Time*, 8 November 1982, p. 82.
28. Francis King, *Sunday Telegraph*, 8 December 1985, p. 14.
29. Richardson, interview with author, 8 December 1986, National Theatre, London.
30. Milton Shulman, *London Evening Standard*, 4 December 1985, p. 28.
31. Michael Conveney, *Financial Times*, 4 December 1985, p. 13.
32. Steve Grant, *Time Out*, 12 December 1985. Review cited in *London Theatre Record*, vol. 5 (20 November–3 December 1985): p. 1195.
33. Kroll, "Hearts of Darkness." p. 82.

34. Stinton, interview with author, 22 March 1986, National Theatre, London.

35. Sheridan Morley, *Punch*, 8 January 1986, p. 28.

36. Rich, "*Edmond* at the Provincetown," p. C20.

37. Mamet, "Mamet in Hollywood," p. 54.

38. Christiansen, "The Young Lion of Chicago Theatre," p. 9.

39. *South Bank Show*, 20 March 1985.

40. Jim Hiley, *The Listener*, 12 December 1985. Review cited in *London Theatre Record*, vol. 5, p. 1197.

41. Christopher Lasch, *The Culture of Narcissism: American Life in an Age of Diminshing Expectations* (New York: Norton, 1978), p. xv.

42. Tom Wolfe, *The Purple Decades* (London: Jonathan Cape, 1983), p. 265.

43. Woody Allen, *Manhattan* (screenplay) in *Four Films of Woody Allen* (London: Faber & Faber, 1983), p. 267.

44. Mamet, *Writing in Restaurants*, p. 66.

45. Lasch, *The Culture of Narcissism*, title page.

46. Ibid., p. 11.

47. Bigsby, *Contemporary Writers*, p. 103.

48. Richardson, interview with author, 8 Decmeber 1986, National Theatre, London.

49. Stinton, interview with author, 22 March 1986, National Theatre, London.

50. Richardson, interview with author, 8 December 1986, National Theatre, London.

51. Clive Barnes, "Stark Telling of Mamet's *Edmond*," *New York Post*, 28 October 1982. Review cited in *New York Theatre Critics Reviews*, vol. 43 (1982): pp. 162–3.

52. Richardson, interview with author, 8 December 1986, National Theatre, London.

53. Michael Billington, *The Guardian*, 4 December 1985, p. 11.

54. Richardson, interview with author, 8 December 1986, National Theatre, London.

55. Ibid.

56. Wallace Shawn, *Aunt Dan & Lemon* (London: Methuen [Royal Court Writers Series], 1985), p. 36.

57. *South Bank Show*, 20 March 1985.

58. Edmund Burke, "Letter to the Sherriff of Bristol," cited in Howard Kissel, *Women's Wear Daily*, 28 October 1982. Review cited in *New York Theatre Critics Reviews*, vol. 43 (1982): pp. 159–60.

59. Burke cited in *Penguin Dictionary of Quotations*, ed. J. M. and M. J. Cohen (Middlesex, England: Penguin, 1960) p. 81.

60. Kissel, *Women's Wear Daily*, pp. 159–60 as per note 58.

61. Coveney, *Financial Times*, 4 December 1985, p. 13.

62. Kissel, *Women's Wear Daily*, 28 October 1982 pp. 159–60 as per note 58.

63. Barnes, "Stark Telling of Mamet's *Edmond*", pp. 162–163.

64. Coveney, *Financial Times*. 4 December 1985, p. 13.

65. Booth, interview with author, 2 December 1986, Hampstead, London.

66. Stinton, interview with author, 22 March 1986, National Theatre, London.

67. Booth, interview with author, 2 December 1986, Hampstead, London.

68. Lasch, *The Culture of Narcissism*, p. xiv.

69. *South Bank Show*, 20 March 1985.

70. Stinton, interview with author, 22 March 1986, National Theatre, London.

71. Billington, *Guardian*, 4 December 1985, p. 11.

72. Douglas Watt, "*Edmond* Goes Round the Bend," *Daily News*, 28 October 1982. Review cited in *New York Theatre Critics Reviews*, vol. 43 (1982): p. 160.

73. Georg Büchner, *Woyzeck* in *The Plays of George Büchner*, trans. Victor Price (Oxford: Oxford University Press, 1971), scene 18, p. 126.

74. Ibid., scene 9, p. 118.

75. Watt, "*Edmond* Goes Round the Bend." p. 160 as per note 72.

76. Theodore Dreiser, *An American Tragedy*, (London: Constable & Co., 1926), p. 3.

77. Ibid., p. 406.

78. Alfred Kazin, *An American Procession: The Major American Writers from 1830–1930—The Crucial Century* (New York: Secker & Warburg, 1985), p. 341.

79. Harold Clurman, *The Fervent Years: The Group Theatre and the 30s* (New York: Da Capo Press, Inc., 1975), p. 175.

80. Rich, "*Edmond* at the Provincetown." p. C20.

81. Ibid.

82. Stinton, interview with author, 22 March 1986, National Theatre, London.

83. Mamet, *Writing in Restaurants*, pp. 66–67.

84. Booth, interview with author, 2 December 1986, Hampstead, London.

85. *South Bank Show*, 20 March 1985.

86. Richardson, interview with author, 8 December 1986, National Theatre, London.

87. John Beaufort, *Christian Science Monitor*, 8 November 1982. Review cited in *New York Theatre Critics Reviews*, vol. 43 (1982): p. 163.

88. Mackenzie, "Base Instincts," p. 19.

Chapter 5: *Glengarry Glen Ross*

1. Arthur Miller, *Death of a Salesman*, (London: Penguin, 1980), Requiem, p. 111.

2. Eleanor Clark cited in Dennis Welland, *Miller the Playwright* (London and New York: Eyre Methuen, 1983), p. 39.

3. Sinclair Lewis, *Babbitt* (New York: Harcourt, Brace & Co., 1922), p. 49.

4. Bigsby, *Contemporary Writers*, p. 111.

5. Ibid.

6. Program notes for *Glengarry Glen Ross*.

7. *Kaleidoscope*, Radio 4, (B.B.C. Radio) 19 April 1985.

8. Allen, "Mamet's Hard Sell," p. 41.

9. Mel Gussow, "Real Estate World a Model for Mamet," *New York Times*, 28 March 1984, p. C19.

10. Ibid.

11. Ibid.

12. Shepherd, National Theatre Study Notes for *Glengarry Glen Ross*, p. 7.

13. Robert Cushman, *The Observer*, 11 September 1983, p. 31.

14. Bigsby, *Contemporary Writers*, p. 126.

15. Barbara Hardy, *Tellers and Listeners: The Narrative Imagination* (London: The Athlone Press, 1975), p. 135.

16. Nightingale, "Bard of Modern Immorality," p. 5.

17. Booth, interview with author, 2 December 1986, Hampstead, London.

18. Allen, "Mamet's Hard Sell," p. 41.

19. Nightingale, "Bard of Modern Immorality," p. 5.

20. *Kaleidoscope*, Radio 4, (B.B.C. Radio) 19 April 1985.

21. Mamet, National Theatre Study Notes for *Glengarry Glen Ross*, p. 6.

22. Ibid.

23. Ibid.

24. Allen, "Mamet's Hard Sell," p. 40.

25. Mamet, National Theatre Study Notes for *Glengarry Glen Ross*, p. 6.

26. Allen, "Mamet's Hard Sell," p. 40.

27. Gussow, "Real Estate World," p. C19.

28. Ibid.

29. Mamet, National Theatre Study Notes for *Glengarry Glen Ross*, p. 6.

30. Welland, *Miller the Playwright*, p. 46.

31. Shepherd, interview with author, 13 March 1986, National Theatre, London.

32. Ibid.

33. Samuel G. Freedman, "Pulitzer-Winning Mamet Praises *Glengarry* Cast," *New York Times*, 18 April 1984, p. C21.

34. Allen, "Mamet's Hard Sell," p. 40.

35. Milton Shulman, *London Evening Standard*, 25 February 1986, p. 26.

36. Jack Tinker, *Daily Mail*, 25 February 1986, p. 24.

37. Kroll, "Mamet's Jackals in Jackets," p. 109.

38. Shepherd, interview with author, 13 March 1986, National Theatre, London.

39. Shepherd, National Theatre Study Notes for *Glengarry Glen Ross*, pp. 7–8.

40. John Barber, "The Hard Sell," *Daily Telegraph*, 26 February 1986, p. 11.

41. Welland, *Miller the Playwright*, p. 40.

42. Stinton, interview with author, 22 March 1986, National Theatre, London.

43. Harold Pinter, *The Caretaker* in *Plays: Two* (London: Eyre Methuen, 1981), act 3, p. 82.

44. August Strindberg, *The Ghost Sonata* in *Strindberg: Plays One*, trans. Michael Meyer (London: Methuen, 1982), p. 179.

45. Bigsby, *Contemporary Writers*, p. 123.

46. Kenneth Hurren, *Mail on Sunday*, 2 March 1986, p. 37.

47. Martin Hoyle, *Financial Times*, 25 February 1986, p. 25.

48. Glenna Syse, "*Glengarry Glen Ross* Rings up Another for Mamet," *Chicago Sun Times*, 7 February 1984, p. 44.

49. Michael Billington, *The Guardian*, 11 September 1983, p. 27.

50. Allen, "Mamet's Hard Sell," p. 41.

51. Bigsby, *Contemporary Writers*, p. 124.

52. Allen, "Mamet's Hard Sell," p. 41.

53. Charles Dickens, *The Life and Adventures of Martin Chuzzlewit*, chapter 21 (Oxford: Oxford University Press, 1971), p. 341.

54. Lewis, *Babbitt*, p. 14.

55. Bigsby, *Contemporary Writers*, p. 22.

56. Hardy, *Tellers and Listeners*, p. 206.

57. Ibid., p. 209.

58. Mamet, *Writing in Restaurants*, p. 13.

59. *Kaleidoscope*, Radio 4, (B.B.C. Radio) 19 April 1985.

60. Allen, "Mamet's Hard Sell," p. 40.

61. Mamet, National Theatre Study Notes for *Glengarry Glen Ross*, p. 7.

62. Ibid., p. 6.

63. Miller, *Death of a Salesman*, act 2, pp. 63–64.

64. Bigsby, *Contemporary Writers*, p. 120.

65. Cushman, *The Observer*, 11 September 1983, p. 31.

66. Dennis Cunningham, WCBS (radio station), 25 March 1984.

67. Christopher Edwards, "Perfect Pitch," *The Spectator*, 15 March 1986, p. 36.

68. Kevin Kelly, *The Boston Globe*, 10 February 1984, p. 49.
69. Barber, "The Hard Sell," p. 11.
70. Hurren, *Mail on Sunday*, 2 March 1986, p. 37.
71. Douglas Watt, "A 'Dearth' of Honest Salesmen," *Daily News*, 26 March 1984. Review cited in *New York Theatre Critics Reviews*, vol. 45 (1984): p. 335.

Select Bibliography

Allen, Woody. *Manhattan*. In *Four Films of Woody Allen*. London: Faber & Faber, 1983.

Beckett, Samuel. *Our Exagmination Round his Factification for Incamination of Work in Progress*. New York: Grove Press, 1962.

————. *The Unnameable*. London: Calder & Boyars, 1958.

Bellow, Saul. *Herzog*. London: Weidenfeld & Nicholson, 1965.

Bigsby, C. W. E. *Contemporary Writers—David Mamet*. London: Methuen, 1985.

————. *A Critical Introduction to Twentieth-Century American Drama—Williams, Miller, Albee*. Vol. 2. Cambridge: Cambridge University Press, 1984.

Bond, Edward. *Lear*. In *Plays: Two*. London: Methuen, 1972.

Brook, G. L. *Varieties of English*. London: The Macmillan Press, 1973.

Brook, Stephen. *New York Days, New York Nights*. London: Picador, 1985.

Büchner, Georg. *Woyzeck*. In *The Plays of Georg Büchner*. Translated by Victor Price. Oxford: Oxford University Press, 1971.

Cain, James, M. *The Postman Always Rings Twice*. In *The Five Great Novels of James M. Cain*. London: Picador, 1985.

Chandler, Raymond. *The Notebooks of Raymond Chandler*. London: Weidenfeld & Nicholson, 1977.

Chekhov, Anton. *Chekhov: The Major Plays*. Translated by Ann Dunnigan. New York: Signet Classic, New American Library, 1964.

Churchill, Caryl. *Softcops*. London and New York: Methuen's New Theatrescripts, 1984.

Clurman, Harold. *The Fervent Years: The Group Theatre and the 30s*. New York: Da Capo Press, Inc., 1975.

Cole, Toby, ed. *Playwrights on Playwriting*. New York: Hill & Wang, 1982.

Dreiser, Theodore. *An American Tragedy*. London: Constable & Co., 1926.

Esslin, Martin. *Pinter the Playwright*. London: Methuen, 1970.

Feiffer, Jules. *Carnal Knowledge*. London: Penguin, 1972.

Fromm, Erich. *Beyond the Chains of Illusion: My Encounter with Marx & Freud*. London: Abacus, Sphere Books, 1980.

Hardy, Barbara. *Tellers and Listeners: The Narrative Imagination*. London: The Athlone Press, 1975.

Jung, Carl. *Jung—Selected Writings*. Edited by Anthony Storr. London: Fontana, 1983.

Kazin, Alfred. *An American Procession: The Major American Writers from 1830–1930—The Crucial Century*. New York: Secker & Warburg, 1985.

Lasch, Christopher. *The Culture of Narcissism: American Life in an Age of Diminishing Expectations*. New York: Norton, 1978.

Leech, Clifford. *Eugene O'Neill.* Edinburgh and London: Oliver & Boyd, 1966.

Lewis, Sinclair. *Babbitt.* New York: Harcourt, Brace & Co., 1922.

Lloyd Evans, Gareth, *The Language of Modern Drama.* Totowa, N.J.: Rowman & Littlefield, 1977.

MacNicholas, John, ed. *Dictionary of Literary Biography: 20th-Century American Dramatists.* Vol. 7. Detroit: Gale Research Co., 1981.

Mamet, David. *A Life in the Theatre.* New York: Samuel French, Inc., 1975.

————. *All Men Are Whores: An Inquiry.* In Mamet, *Goldberg Street: Short Plays & Monologues.* New York: Grove Press, Inc., 1985.

————. *American Buffalo.* London: Methuen, 1978.

————. *A Sermon.* In *Goldberg Street: Short Plays & Monologues.*

————. *Cold.* In *Goldberg Street: Short Plays & Monologues.*

————. *Dark Pony.* In *Reunion* and *Dark Pony.* New York: Grove Press, Inc., 1979.

————. *Duck Variations.* New York: Samuel French, 1977.

————. *Edmond.* New York: Grove Press, Inc., 1983.

————. *Glengarry Glen Ross.* London: Methuen, 1983.

————. *House of Games.* London: Methuen London Ltd., 1988.

————. *In the Mall.* In *Goldberg Street: Short Plays & Monologues.*

————. *Lakeboat.* New York: Grove Press, Inc., 1981.

————. *Mr. Happiness.* In *The Water Engine* and *Mr. Happiness.* New York: Grove Press, Inc., 1977.

————. *Pint's a Pound the World Around.* In *Goldberg Street: Short Plays & Monologues.*

————. *The Postman Always Rings Twice* (screenplay). Unpublished manuscript. London: Lorimar Distribution, 1979.

————. *Prairie du Chien.* In *The Shawl* and *Prairie du Chien.* New York: Grove Press, Inc., 1985.

————. *Reunion.* In *Reunion* and *Dark Pony.* New York: Grove Press, Inc., 1979.

————. *Sexual Perversity in Chicago.* New York: Samuel French, Inc., 1977.

————. *The Shawl.* In *The Shawl* and *Prairie du Chien.* New York: Grove Press, Inc., 1985.

————. *Squirrels.* New York: Samuel French, Inc., 1974.

————. *Speed the Plow* (unpublished manuscript). New York: deposited with Rosentone/Wender (Literary Agents), 1986.

————. *The Verdict* (screenplay). Unpublished manuscript. London: Twentieth Century Fox Film Co. Ltd., 1981.

————. *The Water Engine.* In *The Water Engine* and *Mr. Happiness.* New York: Grove Press, Inc., 1977.

————. *The Woods.* New York: Grove Press, Inc., 1979.

————. *Writing in Restaurants.* New York: Viking Penguin Inc., 1986.

Miller, Arthur. *The American Clock.* London; Methuen, 1983.

————. *Death of a Salesman.* London: Penguin, 1980.

Odets, Clifford. *Odets: Six Plays.* London: Methuen, 1982.

Osborne, John. *The Entertainer.* London: Faber & Faber, 1957.

Pinter, Harold. *The Caretaker.* In *Plays: Two.* London: Eyre Methuen, 1981.

Ruas, Charles. *Conversations with American Writers*. London: Quartet Books, 1986.

Sandburg, Carl. *Complete Poems*. New York: Harcourt, Brace & World Inc., 1950.

Shawn, Wallace. *Aunt Dan & Lemon*. London: Methuen (Royal Court Writers Series), 1985.

Stanislavski, Constantin. *Stanislavski's Legacy*. Edited and translated by Elizabeth Reynolds Hapgood. London: Eyre Methuen, 1981.

Stoppard, Tom. *Rosencrantz and Guildenstern are Dead*. London: Faber & Faber, 1980.

Strindberg, August. *The Ghost Sonata* and *Miss Julie*. In *Strindberg: Plays: One*. Translated by Michael Meyer. London: Methuen, 1982.

Veblen, Thorstein. *The Theory of the Leisure Class: An Economic Study in the Evolution of Institutions*. London: Macmillan, 1925.

Walker, Marshall. *The Literature of the U.S.A.* London: Macmillan, 1983.

Welland, Dennis. *Miller the Playwright*. London and New York: Eyre Methuen, 1983.

Williams, Raymond. *Drama from Ibsen to Brecht*. Middlesex, England: Penguin, 1981.

Wolfe, Tom. *The Kandy-Kolored Tangerine-Flake Streamline Baby*. London: Jonathan Cape, 1981.

———. *The Purple Decades*. London: Jonathan Cape, 1983.

Index

time change. There is evidence that traffic accidents increase during the week after the twice-yearly time shifts, suggesting that even small circadian changes can affect alertness and muscle reaction.[21]

The greatest stress on the body occurs when we repeatedly ignore the 24-hour light-dark cycle by working in shifts around the clock. Some are able to adjust well to shift work, but many do not. Nonetheless, an estimated 15 to 25 percent of those living in industrialized countries work in shifts, a total of approximately 60 million people.[22] Working in a rotating shift of 8:00 A.M. to 4:00 P.M.; 4:00 P.M. to midnight; and midnight to 8:00 A.M. is similar to spending one's life alternately working in New York, Paris, and Tokyo.[23] Shift workers have an increased incidence of coronary artery disease, sleep disorders, respiratory problems, lower back pain, and intestinal disorders, including ulcers. They also have higher rates of job stress and emotional problems, with men frequently resorting to heavy drinking, and women turning to sleeping pills and tranquilizers as well as alcohol. Shift workers experience a significant loss of alertness and ability to make decisions, resulting in increased numbers of errors and accidents. Yet many people in positions of great responsibility have shift schedules. These include physicians, nurses, airline personnel, police forces, the crews of submarines that carry nuclear weapons, and workers at chemical and nuclear plants. Some scientists believe that the 1979 accident at the Three Mile Island nuclear power plant could have been partly due to the shift schedule of the crew on duty.

Those who do not rotate shifts but regularly work nights have similar problems. In this case the problems are not because of abrupt time changes, but because the night worker must ignore the internal rhythms set by the light-dark cycle. The night worker must try to be alert when the body wishes to rest, and must try to sleep when the body is ready for activity. Although the body can adjust to night work, full adjustment takes at least one week. However, it is difficult to stay on this schedule. When a shift worker has free days, she or he naturally returns to normal daytime activity in order to be in time with family, friends, and normal business hours. The result is a state of constant circadian disharmony.

As information on the importance of the circadian timing system becomes more widely known, individuals, groups, and companies have begun seeking professional help to minimize the negative effects of shift work (see the listing for Light Therapy Information Service in the Resources section at the back of this book). Among other techniques, researchers are using carefully timed bright artificial light or the administration of melatonin to help shift workers adjust to their schedules.

LIFE IN NORTHERN LATITUDES

We evolved as a species in temperate or subtropical latitudes that had a 24-hour day-night cycle. As the human race grew and spread, some groups settled near or above the Arctic Circle. There the inhabitants experience continuous darkness during the winter and continuous daylight during the summer. Only during spring and autumn are they exposed to a 24-hour day-night cycle.

In the absence of daily sunrise and sunset, time loses its usual meaning. In either perpetual daylight or perpetual darkness, there is no particular reason to be active or to rest at any certain time. During the perpetual daylight of summer, Arctic Eskimos* are just as likely to go hunting and trapping at "night" as during the "day." During the winter, when the sun never rises, their outdoor activities were once governed largely by the two or three hours of dusk in the middle of the day, until electricity spread to their communities.

---

*Some natives of the North American Arctic prefer to be called Inuit rather than Eskimo, since the latter is sometimes perceived to be pejorative. The author uses the latter term throughout the book because it is more widely known, and means no offense in its use.

In the absence of 24-hour time cues such as sunlight, electric lights, or regular school or work schedules, the circadian system evidently weakens. In the past, researchers noted significant differences between the circadian rhythms of native Eskimos and those of visitors who had previously lived in a regular daylight cycle. During midwinter and midsummer the circadian rhythms of the visitors desynchronized or split apart, while the Eskimos had very weak and sometimes undetectable circadian rhythms. When visitors to the Arctic Circle had lived there a year, their desynchronized rhythms also weakened. Evidently with the spread of electricity and regular school and work schedules, Eskimos now show stronger circadian rhythms.

A number of important health consequences are associated with living in high latitudes, especially during midwinter's continuous darkness. These include major changes in mood, insomnia, and, in some women, disruption of the menstrual cycle. Mental illness, suicide, and violence are more frequent in populations living at high latitudes than at low latitudes.[24] However, other factors, such as the harsh environment and the disruption of native societies, also contribute to these statistics. Researchers on polar expeditions have reported their own experiences of extreme mood changes, inability to concentrate, and complete disruption of the sleep-wake cycle. (See chapters 3, "Sleeping and Waking," and 5, "Mood and Behavior.")

Scientists have not yet defined all the health consequences of living without a 24-hour light-dark cycle. However, the known health effects correlate with research on the broader relation of light to mood, eating and sleeping patterns, and fertility. All of these are discussed in subsequent chapters.

CHAPTER 2

Fertility and Childbirth

*Nothing could easily be found that is more remarkable
than the monthly flux of women. Contact with it turns
new wine sour, crops touched by it become barren,
grafts die, seeds in gardens are dried up, the fruit of
trees falls off, the bright surface of mirrors in which it
is merely reflected is dimmed, the edge of steel and the
gleam of ivory are dulled, hives of bees die, even bronze
and iron are at once seized by rust . . . sexual
intercourse brings disease and death upon the
man. . . . So much greater then is the power of a
menstruous woman.*

PLINY, ca. 70 A.D.[1]

ANCIENT BELIEFS LINK light to fertility and to birth
itself. A woman's reproductive cycle was associated with
the cycles of the moon; in some cultures it was believed that the
moon caused menstruation. The word *menses* originally meant a
lunar month. Although some scientists have thought there could
be some truth to this belief, until recently the idea that light of
any kind could influence human reproduction was generally considered unscientific and often ignored. However, research sug-

gests that in the course of evolution, sunlight and possibly moonlight did regulate our ancestors' cycles of sexual activity and birth, and that light still influences our fertility and reproductive health.

MATING DANCES

In many mammals, light has clear and striking effects on fertility that may help clarify the more subdued influence of light on our own reproduction. Timing is essential to an animal's fertility and to the survival of its young. Birth must occur during a favorable season and at a time of day during which the animal is relatively safe from predators. Terrestrial animals use the time cue of sunlight to register the length of daylight and therefore the season.

Most mammals mate only when the female is in estrus, the state of sexual excitement during which she will accept the male and is capable of conceiving. Estrus is timed by the circadian system, the biological rhythm discussed in the previous chapter. Each day the retina sends routine "time of day" signals to the animal's hypothalamus, where the pacemaker, or rhythm coordinator, is located. On one day of each fertility cycle, when estrogen levels are high, this routine signal initiates the process of releasing eggs for fertilization. The female animal's male partner may be ready to breed at any time, or may breed only in certain seasons. In seasonally breeding males, light triggers a similar cascade of events to prepare the testicles for sperm production in time for the female's estrus. Thus, the sun sets the clock that times the male animal to the female and both to their environment in a fascinating and complex plan of nature.

An animal's circadian system "plans ahead" for the season of birth, which is usually spring or summer, when conditions are optimal for survival of the young. In most animals there is a fixed time between conception and birth, called the gestation period, varying in length from one species to another. Estrus is therefore usually timed according to an animal's gestation period, occurring either as day length increases (for short gestations) or as it decreases (for longer gestations).

Once the eggs have been fertilized, birth is also timed. The fetus can send signals to the mother concerning its own stage of development, including its readiness to be born. In many animals the birth process may be initiated by the fetus's biological clocks, set to the mother's clocks, so that birth occurs in the proper season, on the proper day, at the proper time of day.

MOONLIGHT AND FERTILITY

To regulate this intricate birth planning according to day length, it is logical for terrestrial life to use the sun as its time cue. However, sea life also needs to time conception and birth for optimal survival of its offspring. The sea's rhythms are the tides, and aquatic and amphibious animals therefore require a different time cue, the moon. The high and low tides in the oceans, as well as the less turbulent reactions of some lakes and rivers, correspond to the rotations of the earth and the moon in relation to each other (see Introduction, Figure 2). Much of sea-borne life times its mating and reproduction according to moon-light. The cycles of light intensity tell waterborne creatures when the tides will be most suitable for survival of their young, just as solar day length conveys similar messages to land animals.

Since ancient times, people dwelling near the oceans have noticed that the size of edible shellfish varies with the phases of the moon. Today, in Mediterranean countries and around the Red Sea, crabs, mussels, oysters, and sea urchins are said to be "full" at full moon and "empty" at new moon. Some gourmets claim that the flavor also varies.

Such differences in size and flavor, long thought of as supernatural affinities to the moon, can be explained by the in-fluence of moonlight as a time cue. For example, the oyster queen develops her reproductive organs to coincide with the full moon of each lunar month during her breeding season. In some sea urchins, just before full moon, the ovaries and testes are filled with eggs or spermatozoa, which are spawned into the sea at the full moon. Such timing is essential to ensure that all members of a species will become sexually active at the same time and that the offspring will not be immediately washed out to sea at high tide.

Laboratory studies show that several species have biological clocks that keep an approximate lunar rhythm even when deprived of exposure to moonlight and the tides.[2] These rhythms are called circalundian, an approximate lunar day, or circalunar, an approximate lunar month. Some researchers believe that a biological clock system for timing lunar-tidal periods may be as widespread among living creatures as the solar-day or circadian timing system. Like circadian rhythms, circalundian and circa-lunar rhythms give advance warning of important cyclic changes in the environment. They also enable the creature to know the appropriate time for breeding even when the moon is hidden by clouds for many weeks. Just as land animals in laboratories can be tricked into breeding out of season by the use of artificial light, so seaborne creatures will breed in laboratories according to simulated moonlight.[3] Some animals even show lunar rhythms in their sensitivity to light, being least light-sensitive around the time of the new moon and most light-sensitive around the time of the full moon. The latter is called the animal's "critical time," when its rhythms can be most easily reset using artificial moon-light.

Some animals use both moonlight and tidal water dis-turbances as time cues, while others use both the moon and the sun. Amphibious animals, such as crabs, often need both circadian and circalunar rhythms. Their breeding cycles are timed to the phases of the moon, the seasons of the year, and the time of day.

A few terrestrial animals also breed according to lunar rhythms, especially nocturnal animals living in equatorial rain forests. Apparently, some respond directly to moonlight without having internal lunar rhythms. Among lunar breeders are certain primates, those animals considered closest to humans in evolutionary development. Some primates ovulate and are sexually active only during the full moon.

As humans we now live largely in an environment of our own making, and we have devised our own methods of birth control. It is therefore difficult to study and assess the effects of light on our fertility and birth. However, scientists working on this subject note that every stage of our fertile years, from sexual development through mating, conception, and birth, shows rhythms or patterns related to circadian or circalunar timing. Current studies indicate that the influence of sunlight and circadian and seasonal rhythms on our fertility is far greater than that of moonlight and circalunar rhythms. Nonetheless, the sparse research on moonlight and the menstrual cycle is intriguing and worth our attention.

The assumption of a link between the menstrual cycle and the 29.5-day rotation of the moon is not strengthened by studies of women's monthly periods, which vary widely both in the same woman and between women. Women's cycles usually range from 20 to 36 days in length, with much shorter or longer cycles still considered normal. However, several studies have shown that menstrual cycles close to the lunar cycle of 29.5 days are more likely to be fertile than longer or shorter cycles.[4] Data also suggest that those women whose menstrual cycles are close to the length of the lunar cycle tend to menstruate during the full moon.[5] Even those with irregular cycles may tend to have their flow during the light half-cycle of the moon. In addition, the mathematical average of all menstrual cycle lengths is not 28 days, as is commonly believed, but 29.5 days, exactly the length of the lunar month.[6] The average duration of pregnancy is 266 days, almost exactly nine lunar months.[7]

Some researchers think that the menstrual cycle may have once been an exact lunar rhythm, but that indoor life with artificial lighting prevents most women from having their cycles properly timed by moonlight. According to oral and written accounts from the 1930s, women's menstrual cycles are manifestly "dependent on the moon" in some tropical regions.[8] A medical

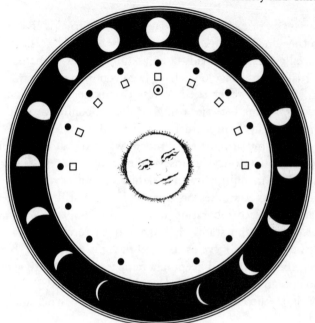

9 LUNAR CYCLES: AVERAGE LENGTH OF PREGNANCY

● 29.5 DAYS: LUNAR CYCLE AND
    MATHEMATICAL AVERAGE OF MENSTRUAL CYCLE

□ MENSTRUAL FLOW: PEAK TIMES

⊙ MENSTRUAL FLOW IN WOMEN WHO HAVE
    CLOSE TO 29.5-DAY CYCLES: PEAK TIME

Figure 7. *Clock of fertility.*

text written in 1821 states that many women in warmer climates
menstruate in accordance with lunar phases. The author says that
"only women who live a rather unchanged, simple way of life
and those belonging to so-called primitive tribes will menstruate
largely under the influence of the moon, beginning the cycle
around the time of the new moon."[9]

Menstrual rhythms may also be influenced by a woman's
sense of smell, and possibly by an exchange of skin chemicals
with her partner while making love. Studies suggest that the
scent and perhaps touch of other women and men can encourage

regular cycles of close to 29.5 days.[10] Female friends living near each other and in frequent, regular contact tend to have synchronized cycles.[11] In small, closely knit societies, a shared lunar menstrual rhythm may once have been common among women.

One researcher tried to test the influence of moonlight by doing two small studies using artificial moonlight to stabilize the menstrual cycle in women with irregular periods. Dim (100 watt) light, simulating the full moon, was shone at night during an approximated midcycle for several months. The results suggest that artificial moonlight can regulate a woman's cycle to exactly 29 days.[12] Larger studies on this method are still lacking. The only attempt at corroboration was done by Louise Lacey, author of *Lunaception*, who states that she and 27 (out of 29) women successfully set their cycles using dim light at night.[13] By stabilizing their cycles and keeping a temperature chart, they either avoided pregnancy or conceived, as they had planned. Those who used this method the longest reported eventual synchrony with the moon.

SUNLIGHT, PUBERTY, AND MENSTRUATION

Some scientists think that the menstrual cycle has gone through an evolutionary change from lunar to solar rhythms, both of which have weakened. Others suggest that women have simultaneous solar-day and lunar-day clocks. Whatever the case may be, solar-day clocks are now easier to define because of the abundant evidence linking solar or circadian rhythms to the menstrual cycle and to puberty itself.

Since 1909 some researchers have suspected that the pineal gland is involved in the timing of puberty in both women and men. The pineal secretes the hormone melatonin, which is regulated by light and darkness. The ovary contains a melatonin receptor, indicating that the ovary's function may be directly influenced by this hormone. Studies of children, adolescents, and young adults suggest that melatonin may control sexual maturation in both sexes by suppressing certain reproductive hormones until the appropriate time.[14] The suppressed hormones, called gonadotrophins, stimulate the ovaries or testes. This would indicate that the circadian system times our own puberty, just as it does in many animals.

In women, part of puberty is the beginning of the menstrual cycle, called menarche. A girl's first period usually begins when she is about 12½, though any time from 9 to 18 years is normal. Menarche may have seasonal rhythms; some data indicate that it occurs predominantly during the winter in the Northern Hemisphere.[15] Perhaps seasonal variations in light influence its timing. However, studies are conflicting, and light is only part of a more complex picture, since a girl must also attain a certain minimum of body fat before her first period will begin. Nonetheless, it is striking that altitudes also affect menarche. The higher the altitude at which a girl lives, the later her first period is likely to be, no matter what the climate.[16] The median age of girls at menarche increases by about three months for every 100 meters of altitude.[17] High altitudes may affect menarche through the intensity of light as well as the higher amount of short-wavelength radiation.

Once menstruation begins, girls have a daily rhythm in the first flow of blood in each cycle, which occurs most often between 4:00 A.M. and noon.[18] Menstrual periods that begin in the morning between eight and twelve tend to be shorter than those beginning in the afternoon.[19] The menstrual cycle is itself an intricately rhythmic cycle of hormonal secretions that are linked to circadian rhythms of body temperature and sleep. The circadian average of core body temperature fluctuates with the menstrual cycle, rising slightly after ovulation and falling again when the next menstruation begins. Women who have attempted the rhythm method of birth control are familiar with these fluctuations. Sleep evidently changes during menstruation; women often have difficulty falling asleep, and sleep longer, during this time. Studies suggest that a woman's reproductive hormones alter the timing of her dreams during menstruation, although possibly only fertile cycles (when ovulation occurs) have this effect. Some women report that their dreams are more vivid and associated with strong colors during menstruation.

Melatonin levels in women fluctuate with the menstrual cycle and may influence the surge in hormones that precedes ovulation. One of the gonadotrophins is secreted in nightly patterns that recur in cycles according to the phase of the sleep and menstrual cycles. The timing of the sleep-wake cycle and the ovulatory cycle are apparently locked together. This may explain why altered sleep patterns are so often a part of premenstrual syndrome (PMS), the cluster of physical and emotional changes that some women experience just before menstruation.

The depression some women experience as part of PMS may also be related to a disturbance in circadian timing. One study suggests that premenstrual depression can be helped by treatment with bright light in the evening to shift the circadian phase.[20]

In both women and men the gonadotrophic hormones, called luteinizing hormone and follicle-stimulating hormone, are released in approximate hourly pulses that accelerate during the day and slow down at night. This pulse, generated in the hypothalamus, is all that the pituitary gland needs to direct the complex monthly ovarian cycle in women. If this pulse is destroyed, or if its beat varies too widely from one pulse per hour, gonadotrophic hormones cannot function normally. Researchers say that this pulse, on which our fertility depends, is clearly connected with circadian rhythms, although the nature and significance of the connection are not yet known.[21]

In some women, alterations in the 24-hour light-dark cycle can alter menstrual rhythms. For example, traveling through large changes in time zones can evidently induce menstrual irregularity. Airline stewardesses frequently have menstrual problems, including irregular cycles, increased or decreased flow, and pain or pelvic congestion after long flights. In addition, women who work at night or in rotating shifts experience more irregular or painful menstrual periods, fewer pregnancies, more problems during pregnancy, and higher rates of stillbirths than do women working during the day.

All menstruating women may be affected by gradual seasonal variations in day length. One large study shows a menstrual curve roughly parallel to the sun's movements, with shorter cycles during longer days, and longer cycles during shorter days.[22] This finding is controversial, however; some researchers report seasonal variations and others do not. Reactions to sunlight may also vary, with some women having less light-sensitive menstrual rhythms that do not alter with the seasons.

Many Alaskan women who live in villages above the Arctic Circle tell of menstrual variability, especially longer cycles during the winter. These women apparently expect fewer menstrual periods in winter as a normal variation. Some go to clinics thinking they are pregnant because their periods have ceased. In one village such false alarms were related to the long hours of winter darkness. Such current reports are similar to observations made more than 90 years ago by a polar explorer who claimed that during the long polar night, women in the world's northernmost Eskimo tribe ceased menstruating almost entirely.[23]

As we age, levels of melatonin decline in men and women. Just as light-regulated melatonin may influence the timing of puberty, it may also time the end of women's reproductive years. Scientists are currently debating this question. While many men produce viable sperm into their eighties, the average age of women's menopause is 52. The final years of a woman's fertility bring changes in the monthly rhythms of hormonal secretions. During these menopausal years some women experience waves of sudden body temperature changes called hot flashes. These are associated with the lowered estrogen production of the ovaries during menopause. Some women also experience insomnia during menopause, especially frequent night awakenings, generally considered to be caused by hot flashes. However, recent research shows that these awakenings actually precede hot flashes and may occur with the preliminary downward setting of the body's temperature system.[24] These are further signs that circadian rhythms, such as those of sleep and body temperature, are intertwined with the menstrual cycle. Animal studies suggest that estrogen helps to balance circadian timing. Menopausal changes in estrogen levels appear to throw circadian rhythms temporarily off balance in some women, causing disrupted sleep and abrupt temperature rises. When women with these difficulties take synthetic estrogens, hot flashes and night awakenings are diminished or cease altogether, and REM sleep (the stage of sleep characterized by rapid eye movements and vivid dreams) increases.[25]

CYCLES OF AROUSAL AND FERTILITY

We can, and do, make love at any time of the month or year. Although many obstacles can stand in the way of sexual intimacy and fulfillment, we are able to experience desire and become aroused regardless of the day, month, or season if circumstances permit. However, some of us notice distinct patterns in our sexual arousal. This is especially true for women in their menstrual years, many of whom experience a rhythmic flux in sexual desire related to the ovarian/menstrual cycle. Although studies vary as to the precise time of a woman's greatest sexual receptivity, most find that it occurs around the time of or during the menstrual flow.[26] Such monthly rhythms may be due to the cyclic fluctuations in certain hormones, especially androgen, which affects sexual desire in both men and women.

> I often notice that I feel much more sensual during my period and a few days afterward than I do during the rest of the month. I tend to daydream about making love then, and when I don't have a partner I'm more likely to masturbate. During those days I feel as though all my nerves are open and that my breasts are swollen and unusually sensitive. I've always considered this my own personal birth control. But of course the

presence and touch of a man I'm attracted to can
arouse me any time of the month.

49-YEAR-OLD WOMAN

During their fertile years, therefore, many women tend to be
most easily aroused during the time of month when they are least
likely to conceive. Since this predilection is neither overwhelming
nor universal, it does not appear to affect fertility.

However, when traditional Eskimo culture was still intact, both men and women living in far-northern regions evidently experienced marked seasonal variations in sexual desire.
In 1897 one researcher noted:

> The genital sense of these people [Eskimos in
> northwest Greenland] is decidedly periodical. They
> seek gratification to some extent throughout the
> year, but during the [long winter] night the sexes
> are more or less indifferent to each other. There
> is a grand outburst of sexual rage soon after the
> return of the sun. It comes with such force and
> overtakes them with such suddenness that they
> frequently quiver for days with passions. This
> culminates during the first summer days with
> what might be called an epidemic of venery,
> when wives and husbands are frequently ex-
> changed with becoming grace and good inten-
> tions. For the rest of the year life resolves itself
> into a hard matter-of-fact existence . . . during
> which they have little time or ambition to nurse
> or gratify amorous instincts.[27]

Evidently most observers of life in the Arctic regions have noticed
a change in attitude toward the opposite sex in the spring and
summer. Earlier statistics on sexually transmitted diseases in the
Canadian Arctic indicated a major increase in sexual activity
during the spring and summer, with a peak in the month of

May.[28] However, such seasonal patterns of sexual interest have evidently weakened in the last few years, perhaps discouraged by the spread of daily wage employment in place of the traditional seasonal camp-life of hunting and trapping.

Some of those living in more temperate zones say they also feel seasonal differences in arousal, noticing an increase in the spring and summer months.

> I think I'm more easily sexually aroused in the spring, definitely the spring. It's warmer, and everyone takes off their winter clothes, they look better. Walking around without a coat on makes you feel sort of exposed and more sexual. Also, when you're in a sexually stimulated environment—and nature is sexually very stimulated in spring—I think we do feel that.
>
> 46-YEAR-OLD WOMAN

> I remember when I was with Fred, he just couldn't get it up at all in the winter. He just wasn't interested. Sex was totally nonexistent for him in the winter. He would change in the spring.
>
> 34-YEAR-OLD WOMAN

There is no information on the extent of this tendency, nor whether it is related to light or warmth or a greater sense of physical well-being generated by both. According to one theory, the decrease in melatonin during the long daylight encourages arousal. However, as many of us have experienced when long, warm days become hot, humid ones, the extreme temperatures and high humidity can dampen our interest in sex, especially when we are new to the climate.

Several reproductive hormones seem to shift twice a year, becoming either more or less active around the time of the two major changes in climate and day length: spring/summer and fall/winter. In menstruating women, the levels of estrogen target cells peak in the spring, and other hormones shift seasonally as well, both before and after menopause. Data from several countries show seasonal testosterone rhythms in men, with a peak in the average daily level in autumn and a trough in the spring.[29] Rhythms of sex hormones may influence rhythms in sexual desire. Several studies suggest that we are generally more sexually active in the months of late spring through fall.[30] However, rhythms in reproductive hormones do not always correspond with the peak season of conception.

Nonetheless, some scientists interpret the evidence of seasonal hormonal shifts in women as remnants of fertile and infertile seasons. According to this theory, our evolutionary ancestors had seasons of menstrual cycles in which ovulation occurred and seasons of cycles in which ovulation did not occur. Seasonal fertility in women may have been part of an evolutionary transition from lunar to solar time. As humankind moved away from the equator, survival of the young through seasonal births may have become crucial, so that the sun's seasonal changes took precedence over lunar rhythms of ovulation.

Traces of this rhythm may still affect our fertility and the health of children today. According to one researcher, some women ovulate regularly only in the spring and late autumn, and seldom or not at all in winter and summer.[31] If these are seasons of fertility, then some women may have phases similar to seasonally breeding animals in which their ovaries do not properly prepare an egg for ovulation, so that the egg is released either immature or overripe. Some data suggest that if such an egg is fertilized, a difficult pregnancy or spontaneous abortion is more likely.[32]

Births of infants with congenital handicaps tend to peak in certain seasons, although the season varies with the handicap. For example, congenital hip dislocation occurs most frequently in autumn births in the Northern Hemisphere and, judging by Australian statistics, in the Southern Hemisphere as well.[33] Births of infants with Down's syndrome peak in the winter. Some researchers attribute these rhythms to the seasonal status of the

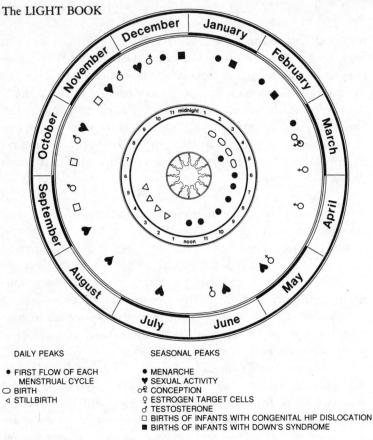

DAILY PEAKS

- • FIRST FLOW OF EACH
     MENSTRUAL CYCLE
- ○ BIRTH
- ◁ STILLBIRTH

SEASONAL PEAKS

- • MENARCHE
- ♥ SEXUAL ACTIVITY
- ♂♀ CONCEPTION
- ♀ ESTROGEN TARGET CELLS
- ♂ TESTOSTERONE
- □ BIRTHS OF INFANTS WITH CONGENITAL HIP DISLOCATION
- ■ BIRTHS OF INFANTS WITH DOWN'S SYNDROME

Figure 8. *Daily and seasonal rhythms in reproduction.*

mother's hormones. Although light-modulated biological rhythms appear to underlie these peaks, in some birth defects seasonal differences in climate and nutrition could affect egg and sperm.

Evidently biological rhythms are crucial to several aspects of timing in a woman's ovulatory cycle. This is illustrated in a technique called *in vitro fertilization,* in which a ripe egg is removed from the ovary, fertilized with sperm in a laboratory dish, then released within the uterus in the hope that it will attach to the uterine wall and develop. The first pregnancies achieved through in vitro fertilization occurred in 4 attempts out of 79.[34] Of those four successful conceptions, all occurred after release of the fertilized ovum between the hours of 10:00 P.M. and midnight. The physicians who carried out these procedures acknowledged that circadian rhythms must have played an important part in this phenomenon. The timing may be related to rhythms in a woman's reproductive hormones—for example, the luteinizing hormone. Research on the role of biological rhythms in achieving pregnancy is still lacking and might be especially welcomed by infertile couples.

RHYTHMS OF LABOR AND BIRTH

Conception and birth do not occur at random times of the year dispersed equally over all twelve months. Instead, births rise and fall in frequency the world over, building patterns that scientists have studied for more than 160 years. The patterns are not uniform and unchanging but vary historically and according to latitude. For these reasons, scientists disagree about the causes of the patterns. Some maintain that only social factors such as religious observances, work load, and prevalence of birth control are responsible, while others consider that temperature and/or seasonal variations in light share the responsibility.

In an attempt to reexamine these questions, a recent study analyzed birth rates in more than 200 regions covering more than 3300 years. This study shows that annual rhythms in conception and birth vary with latitude according to the seasons in both the Northern and Southern Hemispheres.[35] North and south of 30-degree latitude, average conception rates peak around the spring equinox. These data strongly suggest that day length, supplemented by temperature, is the major control of our rhythms of conception and birth. Other research supports this conclusion. Historically it appears that fertility control by light has weakened due to increasing indoor life, leading first to a transient period of control solely by temperature, then to a general weakening of both sunlight and temperature and to a rise in the power of social factors such as holiday seasons. Some researchers call this trend *denaturalization,* a separation from nature brought about by the radical changes in our lives due to industrialization and city life.

Just as there are seasonal rhythms in conception and birth, so are there rhythms in the timing of birth within each day and possibly within each lunar cycle. Labor normally begins with spontaneous, rhythmic contractions of the uterus and/or the rupture of the membrane that carries the fetus within protective water called amniotic fluid. Studies show that spontaneous rupture of the membrane occurs most frequently during the full and/ or new moon.[36] According to a belief widespread among hospital personnel, labor units are very busy around the time of the full moon. Some researchers postulate that the moon's effect comes at the time of conception, due to its influence on behavior and on the menstrual cycle. If conception is influenced by the full moon, then birth would occur around the time of the full moon nine months later. However, studies are conflicting, and the moon's influence, if any, on the beginning of labor may not be through its light. According to the theory of biologic tides, the gravitation of the moon can influence body fluids such as menstrual fluid and amniotic fluid. The moon's influence may also be through the association of the full moon with a drop in barometric pressure, with the pressure change itself inducing labor.

Research over the past 160 years also shows that spontaneous births do not occur equally at all times of day. Most labors begin in the dark hours, and most births occur in darkness or early dawn.[37] In 1935 such birth rhythms led some prescient European physicians to state that unidentified "cosmic influences" evidently govern the timing of labor.[38] Since then, increased knowledge of the influence of the 24-hour light-dark cycle on our biological rhythms has led to several studies on birth timing, with striking results. Spontaneous labor is most likely to begin around or after midnight, and birth is most likely to occur between 2:00 and 5:00 A.M.[39] This timing is apparently consistent in North America and western Europe regardless of the season.

Labor that begins during the night tends to be shorter

and associated with fewer cesarean deliveries than labor that begins in the morning.[40] Some researchers postulate that labor can occur under two different circumstances: one of complete preparation and proper circadian timing, in which labor is shorter and begins at night; and one in which hormonal preparation is inadequate, labor is longer, and circadian timing no longer functions. This is related to the theory that birth defects are more likely to occur when a woman conceives "out of season." Some researchers hope that further knowledge of the hormones involved in circadian rhythms of childbirth might help prevent premature births, a major national health problem.

Some studies suggest that stillbirths, and births of infants with low vitality or serious medical problems, also tend to occur at a particular time: from 2:00 to 5:00 P.M.[41] These rhythms can be partly the result of inadequate hospital care or of circadian rhythms in the fetus's or mother's response to drugs used during delivery. Nonetheless, they also suggest that the circadian timing of birth can indicate an infant's state of health and its readiness to be born. However, when physicians induce birth by using drugs, forceps, or surgery, they naturally prefer the daytime. Induced births occur most often between 12:30 and 4:30 P.M.,[42] a time possibly more conducive to the health of the attending physician than to that of the mother and child.

Since circadian physiology is not part of a birth attendant's usual medical training, the idea that biological rhythms can play a role in birth is not widely recognized among obstetricians, midwives, and nurse-midwives. Even those who might be aware of such rhythms have little chance of acting accordingly within a regimented hospital setting.

> Many of the things we do to a woman when she enters the hospital prevent her from honoring any rhythm that might be there. From putting her in a hospital gown in a room without windows, strapping her to a fetal monitor—how is she supposed to let a natural event unfold? Once a

woman walks through a hospital door, it's very
difficult to know if her own rhythms have a chance.

30-YEAR-OLD NURSE-MIDWIFE

However, midwives may be somewhat less likely than obstetricians to disrupt birth rhythms. Midwives do not perform cesareans, and they are more likely to learn about and respect birthing rhythms through their hours of attending women in labor. Possibly these are among the reasons why Holland, which has the highest rate of home births attended by midwives, also has one of the lowest infant mortality rates in the world.[43]

Researchers still speculate on the original and underlying causes of circadian rhythms in the timing of labor. Perhaps the timing of labor is simply the result of circadian timing in conception, with labor beginning 266 days later, to the hour. It could also be related to the 24-hour timing in women's reproductive hormones on the day of birth. On the other hand, survival of mother and child may have once dictated that birth occur during a relatively safe time of day. During the hours of labor and birth a mother, animal or human, is helpless to defend herself against attack. The birth-giver needs to feel as secure as possible and, in some cases, must be ready to keep up with her migrating or nomadic clan during the daytime. Even the signal that sets off the birth process is not fully understood. Possibly the circadian system within the fetus initiates labor through a crescendo of hormonal messages, and the cycle of birth and life begins again.

CHAPTER 3

Sleeping and Waking

When I lived in Fairbanks, Alaska, I used to stay up until about 3 or 4 A.M. in the summertime, which I had never done before. I didn't know why I was doing it. It was just something that happened. I had a lot of energy because of the light, so that the sleeping mechanism didn't kick in. I noticed it would get a little dusky sometime around 3 A.M. and that a large part of why I was staying up was a craving for that little bit of darkness. I wondered if it was physical. I could feel a craving for that duskiness and felt relaxed when it came.

47-YEAR-OLD WOMAN

LIGHT AFFECTS THE timing and duration of our sleep, and to some extent our need for sleep. Usually we take this for granted, hardly questioning why we are active during the daylight hours and rest during darkness. Although this is the most obvious rhythm of our lives, insights into the link between sleep and the light-dark cycle are new. In fact, sleep is still a relatively mysterious state, its causes and functions largely unknown. However, in order to understand the roles of light and

43

darkness in our sleeping and waking, we must examine what is known about the cause, stages, and purpose of sleep.

THE PROCESS OF SLEEP

A sleeper cannot convey the experience of sleeping. For this reason, until the twentieth century sleep research often involved periodically awakening the sleeper, a procedure that largely defeated its purpose. Sleep became more accessible in the 1920s with the discovery that electrical waves arise in the brain and can be recorded. Brain-wave recordings, the discovery in 1951 of rapid eye movement (REM) sleep, and studies on light and body temperature begun in the early 1980s together provide the basis of current knowledge.

Often we think of sleep as a simple and uniform state of rest into which the brain passively sinks. This image is misleading. Sleep is a varied, complex, and active process during which most nerve cells in the brain send rapid electrical impulses to one another, much as they do during waking.

Generally, each night our sleep passes through a repeated sequence of stages. Researchers have identified and labeled these stages by recording the electrical waves that the brain emits; the slower and longer the wave patterns, the deeper the sleep. We begin by "falling asleep," which is the transition from waking to sleeping, called stage one sleep. We then progress into sleep itself (stage two); deep sleep, also called delta sleep (stages three and four); and, after a brief return to stage two, move on to rapid eye movement or REM sleep (stage five). Stages two through five then repeat themselves with variations in length from four to five times in one night's sleep. The sequence runs 1-2-3-4-2-5-2-3-4-2-5 and so on. Deep sleep becomes briefer in the course of a night or may even disappear, while REM sleep becomes progressively longer.

During REM sleep, the last stage of each cycle, we have our most vivid dreams, and our eyes show bursts of rapid movement beneath the closed lids. During this stage our faces and limbs twitch; heartbeat, respiration, and blood pressure become irregular; the penis or clitoris becomes engorged with blood and erect; and the uterus may increase its contractions. The entire central nervous system becomes so intensely active that some researchers call REM a third state of existence, distinct from other sleep stages and from wakefulness. During this stage the nerves connecting the brain to the limbs are deadened and we are paralyzed, perhaps to protect us from acting out our dreams.

Theoretically, we could go through our sleep cycles randomly, sleeping an hour or two here and there or sleeping 20 hours at a time. This would cause many of us to lose our jobs. However, we do not sleep in consolidated blocks of a certain timing and length in order to accommodate our work schedules. We sleep during the night because our bodies have a unique relationship with the cycle of sunrise and sunset, causing us to feel lazy and sleepy during the dark hours, and wakeful and alert during daylight. The circadian system's biological clock(s) are synchronized to the light-dark cycle and time our sleep and wakefulness accordingly.

Our sleep-wake rhythms appear to be determined by hormones secreted in 24-hour cycles as part of the circadian system. These hormones regulate body temperature rhythms and determine our states of sleepiness or alertness. Normally, we become sleepy between 6:00 P.M. and midnight, when body temperature is rapidly falling, and we are most alert about six hours after waking, when body temperature is near its highest. When we go to bed during the downward curve of the body temperature cycle, as most people do, we sleep until the next upward temperature curve, an average of 7.8 hours.[1]

The timing and duration of sleep are never free from the influence of the group of hormonal rhythms marked by body temperature. This is true even when we are up and active for long periods of time and sleep little. In such cases if we were to go to bed near the trough of body temperature, about 6:30 A.M., we would generally awaken in a short period of time in spite of our fatigue, because body temperature would be slowly rising. If, however, we went to bed during the midafternoon, when body temperature is at its highest, we would generally sleep through until the next upward slope of the temperature curve, namely the next morning. In other words, no matter when we go to bed, we tend to awaken at the body's upward temperature curve. A mere difference of one-half degree of body temperature measured on the thermometer (36.5 versus 37 Celsius) can mean the difference between fragmented or extended sleep.

Anyone who has stayed up all night will recognize the alertness that comes with morning. This is due to our continuous circadian rhythms in the desire for sleep, which fluctuate with body temperature whether we sleep or not. Studies show that when we are sleep-deprived, our fatigue will increase during the time we would normally have been in bed, and each morning we will become relatively more alert.[2] We would have the greatest difficulty staying awake from around 1:00 to 5:00 A.M., when the urge to sleep is all but irresistible. We would be least fatigued in the afternoon, at the peak of body temperature. However, we might experience a brief afternoon dip in alertness, which frequently occurs no matter how much we slept the night before and regardless of the size of the noontime meal.

Not only the length but also the structure of sleep is determined by circadian rhythms. REM sleep is closely related to body temperature. The first episode of REM sleep can begin two hours earlier or later, depending on whether a person goes to bed during the temperature maximum or minimum. Even if, for several days, you were kept awake for a variable number of hours so that your bedtime occurred during different hours of the day and night, the length of your sleep, the type of sleep (REM or non-REM), and your sleepiness or alertness would all be related to your body temperature at that time. This is why "catching up" on sleep during the daytime never fully compensates for sleep lost at night. It also explains why shift workers who have to sleep by day suffer from both insufficient and inefficient sleep.

Because our sleep-wake cycles are so closely linked to a biological clock timed by sunlight, it becomes clear why length of and need for sleep fluctuate with the seasons. As the days lengthen, so does the body's alertness phase. The early sun awakens us, and long, light evenings encourage activity, decreasing our need and desire for sleep. A New York population survey shows that seasonal fluctuations in sleep length are in strict agreement with the seasonal change in sunrise.[3] People sleep the least from June through August and the most from December through February. Sleep length averages out around the equinoxes of March and September. Some Scandinavians, who experience unusually long seasonal daylight and darkness, report a difference of two hours or more in average sleep length between summer and winter.

> When I take my family back to Sweden in the summer we all sleep so much less, but we feel just as refreshed, more refreshed! Even when I go to bed late, I get up early the next morning and it's like I had been asleep ten hours, so refreshed. My children just can't go to bed, they don't want to go to bed, and they don't need it either. Here in Boston if they go to bed late, the next day it's awful, they are tired and irritated. But in Sweden in the summer it doesn't bother them, they don't need that much sleep.
>
> 40-YEAR-OLD WOMAN FROM MALMÖ, SWEDEN

The structure of sleep also changes with the seasons. Some studies show that we are likely to spend more time in deep sleep during the winter, increasing the efficiency of our sleep, while other studies show no seasonal change in deep sleep.[4] The lengthening days of spring and summer progressively change the timing of REM sleep, indicating a seasonal shift in body temperature rhythms.

Sleep length, depth, and structure also vary with age.

47

We are not born with a functioning sleep-wake cycle. As so many sleep-deprived parents know, newborns appear to enter life ignoring night and day, sleeping approximately two-thirds of the time but in short bouts. Actually, studies show that when infants are fed on demand rather than at times set by their parents, they sleep more during the night than during the day, even though they have not yet developed a regular light-regulated, sleep-wake cycle.[5] Over the first months of life the infant's periods of wakefulness gradually lengthen at certain times of day, and sleep becomes concentrated at others. Slowly a sleep-wake cycle emerges, as the infant's biological rhythms become coordinated and eventually adjust to the 24-hour rhythm of night and day. Newborns and infants also spend as much as 40 to 50 percent of their sleep in REM, whereas in adulthood REM takes up about 20 percent of sleep.[6]

When we reach old age we sometimes notice that the length and quality of our sleep change once again. In our older years sleep often becomes fragmented, and we may find ourselves nodding off during the day and repeatedly awakening at night. Many of the elderly report that they only sleep three, four, or five hours a night and are up by 2:30 A.M.[7] Deep sleep becomes both shorter and shallower, and is entirely absent in some elderly people. REM sleep often begins earlier and may also become shorter. In a way, sleep in old age resembles sleep in infancy. These changes may be caused by a circadian system that again makes itself independent of the light-dark cycle.

The Why and How of Sleep

The light-dark cycle may also play a direct but minor role in the functions of sleep. Some researchers theorize that by imposing a period of rest, sleep helps an organism obtain food and avoid dangers in the environment. Animals that can see in the dark, such as the bat, either have no 24-hour sleep-wake cycle or are active at night and sleep during the day. Animals that eat grass and run in herds, such as cows and sheep, sleep in short periods over the whole light-dark cycle. In this way there are always a few animals awake and alert for predators. According to this theory, because humans cannot see well in the dark, we sleep at night to stay out of trouble. Other theories suggest that sleep reduces the need for food and therefore conserves energy; that sleep allows intensive use of the nervous system during activity; and that REM sleep facilitates learning and/or brain development, or reinforces personal behavior patterns.

All these theories may be correct, yet together they cover only part of sleep's functions. Our experience of sleep tells us that it replenishes the body and restores energy. Normally, we go to bed tired and awaken invigorated. No matter how commonplace and obvious this function seems, science cannot analyze or explain it. Some studies suggest that chemical changes occur in the cells, perhaps involving the shift in hormones secreted during sleep.[8] However, the actual process has not been discovered, although it appears to be necessary to life.

As we all know, the need to sleep grows progressively stronger the longer we stay awake. Although circadian rhythms continuously regulate our state of alertness, still the longer we are deprived of sleep, the harder it is to stay awake. A person who has not slept for a long time needs only to sit down and he or she will nod off immediately, no matter what time of day. Research suggests that the increasing pressure to sleep is caused by peptides, chemicals made up of amino acids, which accumulate in the brain during wakefulness and are broken down or destroyed during sleep. The longer these peptides accumulate, the greater the need for sleep and the longer and deeper the subsequent sleep will be. Scientists have discovered such substances in animals, but their chemical structure and how they act on the central nervous system are not yet understood.

LIGHT-RELATED SLEEP PROBLEMS

According to surveys, most adults sleep six to nine hours a night, with eight to nine hours reported most often.[9] Only very small percentages report five hours or less or ten hours or more.

49

Usually we sleep in one nightly phase, although in some cultures and during some times of life, a siesta or afternoon nap is also common. Studies show that women sleep an average of about one hour longer than men when they are isolated from time cues such as sunlight.[10]

Some of us tend to be "morning people," or "larks," while others are "evening people," or "owls." The difference is often slight. "Larks" generally have a sleep schedule one hour in advance of "owls," even though sleep length is often the same.[11] This one-hour discrepancy accords with a small difference in the circadian rhythms of body temperature. In some people these differences can be seasonal rather than constant, with the same person rating herself or himself a "morning type" in the spring and an "evening type" in the winter.

You can assess yourself as a "morning," "evening," or "intermediate" person by answering the accompanying questionnaire (from J. A. Horne and O. Östberg, "A Self-Assessment Questionnaire to Determine Morningness-Eveningness in Human Circadian Rhythms").[12] The appropriate score for most questions is the number beside your answer box, except for numbers 1, 2, 10, and 18, when you put an x in the appropriate place along the scale. Your score is the number (between the arrows) below your x. For number 17, put x's in the appropriate boxes. Your score is the number (between the arrows) below your outer right-hand x. Add all score numbers to assess your type:

Definitely Morning Type:	70–86
Moderately Morning Type:	59–69
Neither Type:	42–58
Moderately Evening Type:	31–41
Definitely Evening Type:	16–30

Some of us have more pronounced preferences for going to bed either early or late, and also feel notably more alert and energetic in the morning or evening. Some people awaken easily in the early morning, feeling rested and refreshed and working

LARK OR OWL QUESTIONNAIRE

1. Considering only your own "feeling best" rhythm, at what time would you get up if you were entirely free to plan your day?

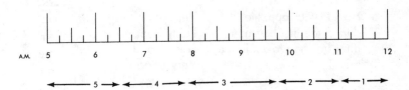

2. Considering only your own "feeling best" rhythm, at what time would you go to bed if you were entirely free to plan your evening?

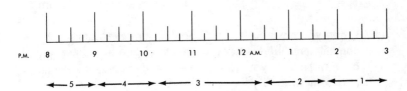

3. If there is a specific time at which you have to get up in the morning, to what extent are you dependent on being woken up by an alarm clock?

Not at all dependent ☐ 4
Slightly dependent ☐ 3
Fairly dependent ☐ 2
Very dependent ☐ 1

4. Assuming adequate environmental conditions, how easy do you find getting up in the morning?

Not at all easy ☐ 1
Not very easy ☐ 2
Fairly easy ☐ 3
Very easy ☐ 4

51

5. How alert do you feel during the first half-hour after having woken in the morning?

Not at all alert ☐ 1
Slightly alert ☐ 2
Fairly alert ☐ 3
Very alert ☐ 4

6. How is your appetite during the first half-hour after having woken in the morning?

Very poor ☐ 1
Fairly poor ☐ 2
Fairly good ☐ 3
Very good ☐ 4

7. During the first half-hour after having woken in the morning, how tired do you feel?

Very tired ☐ 1
Fairly tired ☐ 2
Fairly refreshed ☐ 3
Very refreshed ☐ 4

8. When you have no commitments the next day, at what time do you go to bed compared to your usual bedtime?

Seldom or never later ☐ 4
Less than one hour later ☐ 3
1–2 hours later ☐ 2
More than two hours later ☐ 1

9. You have decided to engage in some physical exercise. A friend suggests that you do this one hour twice a week, and the best time for him is between 7:00–8:00 A.M. Bearing in mind nothing else but your own "feeling best" rhythm, how do you think you would perform?

Would be in good form ☐ 4
Would be in reasonable form ☐ 3
Would find it difficult ☐ 2
Would find it very difficult ☐ 1

10. At what time in the evening do you feel tired and as a result in need of sleep?

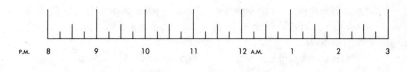

P.M.   8   9   10   11   12 A.M.   1   2   3

←—5—→ ←—4—→ ←————3————→ ←—2—→ ←—1—→

11. You wish to be at your peak performance for a test that you know is going to be mentally exhausting and will last for two hours. You are entirely free to plan your day. Considering only your own "feeling best" rhythm, which ONE of the four testing times would you choose?

8:00–10:00 A.M.	☐ 6
11:00 A.M.–1:00 P.M.	☐ 4
3:00–5:00 P.M.	☐ 2
7:00–9:00 P.M.	☐ 0

12. If you went to bed at 11:00 P.M., at what level of tiredness would you be?

Not at all tired	☐ 0
A little tired	☐ 2
Fairly tired	☐ 3
Very tired	☐ 5

13. For some reason you have gone to bed several hours later than usual, but there is no need to get up at any particular time the next morning. Which ONE of the following events are you most likely to experience?

Will wake up at usual time and will NOT fall asleep	☐ 4
Will wake up at usual time and will doze thereafter	☐ 3
Will wake up at usual time but will fall asleep again	☐ 2
Will NOT wake up until later than usual	☐ 1

14. One night you have to remain awake between 4:00–6:00 A.M. in order to carry out a night watch. You have no commitments the next day. Which ONE of the following alternatives will suit you best?

Would NOT go to bed until watch was over ☐ 1

Would take a nap before and sleep after ☐ 2

Would take a good sleep before and nap after ☐ 3

Would take ALL sleep before watch ☐ 4

15. You have to do two hours of hard physical work. You are entirely free to plan your day. Considering only your own "feeling best" rhythm, which ONE of the following times would you choose?

8:00–10:00 A.M. ☐ 4
11:00 A.M.–1:00 P.M. ☐ 3
3:00–5:00 P.M. ☐ 2
7:00–9:00 P.M. ☐ 1

16. You have decided to engage in hard physical exercise. A friend suggests that you do this for one hour twice a week, and the best time for him is between 10:00–11:00 P.M. Bearing in mind nothing else but your own "feeling best" rhythm, how well do you think you would perform?

Would be in good form ☐ 1

Would be in reasonable form ☐ 2

Would find it difficult ☐ 3

Would find it very difficult ☐ 4

17. Suppose that you can choose your own work hours. Assume that you worked a FIVE-hour day (including breaks) and that your job was interesting and paid by results. Which FIVE CONSECUTIVE HOURS would you select?

```
┌┬┬┬┬┬┬┬┬┬┬┬┬┬┬┬┬┬┬┬┬┬┬┬┐
└┴┴┴┴┴┴┴┴┴┴┴┴┴┴┴┴┴┴┴┴┴┴┴┘
12 1 2 3 4 5 6 7 8 9 10 11 12 1 2 3 4 5 6 7 8 9 10 11 12
MIDNIGHT                  NOON                  MIDNIGHT
←—1—→ ←—5—→ ←4→ ←3—→ ←—2→ ←——1——→
```

18. At what time of the day do you think that you reach your "feeling best" peak?

```
┌┬┬┬┬┬┬┬┬┬┬┬┬┬┬┬┬┬┬┬┬┬┬┬┐
└┴┴┴┴┴┴┴┴┴┴┴┴┴┴┴┴┴┴┴┴┴┴┴┘
12 1 2 3 4 5 6 7 8 9 10 11 12 1 2 3 4 5 6 7 8 9 10 11 12
MIDNIGHT                  NOON                  MIDNIGHT
←——1——→ ←5→ ←4→ ←—3——→ ←—2—→ ←1→
```

19. One hears about "morning" and "evening" types of people. Which ONE of these types do you consider yourself to be?

Definitely a "morning" type	☐ 6
Rather more a "morning" than an "evening" type	☐ 4
Rather more an "evening" than a "morning" type	☐ 2
Definitely an "evening" type	☐ 0

most efficiently during the morning hours. Their energy declines by late afternoon and if possible they go to bed early. Others arise reluctantly and continue to feel half-asleep during the first part of the day, often being accused of "getting up on the wrong side of the bed." They have little appetite at the start of the day and often eat little or no breakfast. Not until afternoon do their alertness and mood begin to improve, and they gradually feel more dynamic. These people do their best work in the evening and are often active until the small hours of the morning.

Those of us who have these marked preferences do not necessarily experience them as problems, especially when our preferred hours do not vary too widely from our work schedules. In such cases we may call ourselves "larks" or "owls" and let the matter lie. However, noticeable morning fogginess is not easily excused in some professions and can be severely detrimental. Ironically, when evening people try going to bed earlier in the hope of feeling more alert in the morning, usually they either cannot fall asleep or their sleep is disturbed and unrefreshing. Some evening people can only sleep well if they sleep at times that differ widely from the light-dark cycle, such as 4:00 A.M. to noon. Since such a sleep-wake schedule is inappropriate for most families and workplaces, the affected person goes to bed earlier only to find that he or she cannot sleep. Thus the evening person develops a case of severe insomnia with all its accompanying physical and emotional trials. This type of insomnia is one of several caused by a problem in the circadian timing of sleep.

Sleep Scheduling Disorders

People whose circadian rhythms are not properly timed have great difficulty in getting their sleep-wake cycles to coincide with day and night. Such difficulties can be exacerbated by dark bedroom shades that shut out the morning light. While some cannot fall asleep until the early morning hours, others are troubled by sleep that is fragmented and shallow, with frequent awakenings. Still others can fall asleep easily but may be irre-

sistibly sleepy by 8:00 P.M. and awaken promptly at 2:00, 3:00, or 4:00 A.M. as if by an internal alarm. Some people experience repeated periods of going to sleep and awakening progressively later each day, alternating with periods of a normal and stable sleep-wake cycle. Sleep researchers now recognize many of these forms of insomnia as problems in sleep timing. Only recently were such disorders officially classified as part of a distinct type of insomnia called sleep scheduling disorders.

Statistics on insomnia do not reveal how many people suffer from sleep scheduling disorders. However, small surveys have shown that among those who have difficulty falling asleep, 7 to 10 percent have a type of sleep scheduling disorder called delayed sleep phase syndrome, or DSPS.[13] Some researchers think that DSPS is actually much more common than these statistics indicate. Many with DSPS never seek professional help. Some even alter their work schedules to accommodate their sleep times—taking, for example, a 3:00 P.M. to 11:00 P.M. job. Yet, since they do not seek help, they are not counted statistically.

When people with any type of sleep scheduling disorder do seek medical help, they usually receive prescriptions for sedatives, hypnotics (sleep-promoting drugs), or anti-anxiety drugs to induce sleep. Statistics show that for all types of insomnia, more than 22 million prescriptions for sleep-inducing drugs were written in 1985.[14] This figure does not include drugs issued in hospitals or nursing homes, or nonprescription sleep medications.

When we take prescribed sleep medication, usually the pills are of a type called benzodiazepines, such as diazepam (Valium), flurazepam (Dalmane), and triazolam (Halcion). Recent studies show that benzodiazepines can reset the brain's pacemaker, or biological clock.[15] Some researchers think that benzodiazepines induce sleep by retiming the sleep-wake cycle to the light-dark cycle. Benzodiazepines may directly reset the pacemaker or alter the light-dark information from the retina to the brain. Further study is needed to determine the exact effects of benzodiazepines and other sleep-inducing drugs on the timing of sleep. (See p. 63 for information on light therapy for sleep scheduling disorders.)

Seasonal Sleeplessness

Just as insomnia can occur as a result of a sleep-wake cycle out of time with the light-dark cycle, so it can also occur when there is no light-dark cycle to time it. Those living in regions near or within the Arctic and Antarctic Circles experience one to four months of either constant daylight or constant darkness each year, depending on latitude. When the body's circadian rhythms cannot be coordinated by the sun's rhythms, the sleep-wake cycle becomes desynchronized from the body temperature cycle and acquires other rhythms, from 25 to 30 hours or even 50 rather than the normal 24.[16] Circadian rhythms in general become less pronounced in response to the unchanging light or darkness. As a result, sleep patterns can alter drastically and appear to be regulated primarily by accumulated exhaustion rather than by circadian rhythms. Such sleep changes vary and are perceived differently, depending on the person and on whether they are caused by constant light or constant darkness.

Midsummer insomnia, for example, is associated with a lack of desire and need for sleep. It is difficult to go to bed at night when the sun is still bright. Therefore, people are more likely to be up and active as long as possible, rather than tossing and turning in bed, unhappy that they cannot sleep. For this reason, lack of sleep in midsummer is not necessarily felt as deprivation but rather as a change in lifestyle.

In Sweden in the summer you get kind of confused. A friend of mine told me she was once cleaning her house and suddenly noticed it was one A.M.! Even the birds are up singing in the middle of the night. They don't sleep either. In the spring you hear them all day and all night.
35-YEAR-OLD WOMAN FROM GÖTEBORG, SWEDEN

I'm from Massachusetts, and when I first started spending my summers in Stockholm I never used to be able to go to sleep. I would walk home with my husband from a party about midnight, and when we reached home at one A.M. I felt like it was time for breakfast because the sun was rising. One night after I had gone to sleep about two A.M. I awakened because my baby was crying. The sun was pouring in the window and I thought it must be time to get up, but I looked at the clock and it was only four-thirty A.M.! But the sun was so bright—I was just totally off, I didn't know what time of day it was.

32-YEAR-OLD WOMAN

Some people attempt to keep a regular sleep rhythm by using blackout systems. In Alaska, Norway, and Sweden, for example, heavy curtains and window shades for spring and summer nights are common.

These lifestyle changes and their consequences can be extreme. Among the north Canadian Eskimos, for example, sleep-wake rhythms during the spring and summer become almost completely random and are regulated primarily by weather and hunting conditions. Families follow no predictable, 24-hour routine. In periods of poor weather they may sleep. If the weather is good they hunt, trap, and fish, staying up 24 hours or longer until they collapse from exhaustion.[17] After such extended periods of activity, they may sleep 16 or 22 hours at a time. This becomes their summer rhythm. Those who are wage earners go out to hunt seals or set fishing nets after work. Often they lose their sense of time and find they have stayed up all night. Social visits take place at all hours, with visitors dropping in at three or four in the morning. School attendance among Eskimo children drops to its lowest. Children begin taking long hikes, day or night. Many stay up all night and then go fishing, hiking, or hunting rather than to school.

Polar researchers describe similar midsummer experiences

in their written accounts of Arctic and Antarctic expeditions. They recall doing routine tasks at 4:00 A.M. and then sleeping 22 hours at a time.[18] Some evidently suffered from their insomnia and tried to gain some semblance of a light-dark cycle by hanging black cloths over their windows at night. Other explorers appeared to take their sleeplessness in stride:

> We went unwillingly to bed, preferring to sleep just as the occasion offered; the sleep was short yet refreshing. One had the feeling of never resting and never tiring, which contrasted strongly with the physical helplessness of the dark period. We were disposed to be friendly toward one another, very willing to listen and likewise to talk.[19]

Conversely, insomnia resulting from 24-hour darkness often has all the usual connotations of deprivation and fatigue. In northern Norway an estimated one-third of schoolchildren and adolescents and one-quarter of adults suffer from sleeplessness, which Norwegians call midwinter insomnia.[20] Their experiences range from moderate difficulties falling asleep to an almost total lack of sleep during the night. Those with midwinter insomnia seem to lack the normal feeling of drowsiness during the evening but feel very tired in the morning and, more or less, during much of the day. This type of insomnia usually lasts from the end of November to the middle or latter part of January.

Among Eskimos living in a settlement in Holman Island, northern Canada, the problem is evidently kept at bay as long as there is work to be done. Active trappers and wage earners report little difficulty maintaining regular work schedules, now aided by electricity and regular television programming.[21] However, when winter holidays arrive, sleep rhythms become noticeably altered, and people in the settlement stay up later and later, then sleep through half or all of the day. So many residents reverse their patterns at such times that those who have to stay on a regular schedule, such as health-care personnel, find themselves out of time with the rest of the population. Nonetheless, adult Eskimos in this area evidently do not perceive their winter changes in sleep patterns as insomnia. Instead, they let their bodies glide into unusual rhythms during the holiday period and ignore the time of day, just as they do during midsummer.

Schoolchildren in the settlement have a more difficult time. Children generally tend to respond more sensitively to changes in the light-dark cycle than do adults, and their sleep-wake rhythms are more likely to go awry in the constant darkness. The pressure on the children to attend school is not as great as their parents' pressures to go to work, and Eskimo children quickly acquire rhythms that are out of time with the adult population. With sleep-wake rhythms askew, school becomes a place where exhausted children arrive at irregular hours and fall asleep at their desks. An anthropologist in Holman noted in his journal:

> December 10 [1979]—This is the last week of school before Christmas break, and almost all of the children in the upper grade levels are staying up all night. Despite their fatigue, they are still coming to school and falling asleep in front of the teacher.

> December 11—While children in the older grades are staying up all night and coming to school in the morning, a substantial number of younger children are staying up late, sleeping through the morning, and coming to school in the afternoon only. The teachers also note that the degree of mental and physical exhaustion is so pronounced among most children that academic progress has slowed to a standstill. [22]

Researchers stationed at the two poles have recounted their altered sleep-wake patterns during the months of constant darkness. Some fell into a pattern of short naps at various times of day and night. Others describe alternating periods of a constant inclination to sleep and complete insomnia. At one research station in New Zealand during the winter darkness, everyone in the camp was a member of the "Big Eye Club," of which the only qualification for membership was insomnia. Some club members recount that although they felt tired—even exhausted—at the same time they felt restless when they tried to sleep.

> It is now difficult to get out of our warm beds in the morning. There is no dawn—nothing to mark the usual division of night and morning until nearly noon. During the early part of the night it is next to impossible to go to sleep, and if we drink coffee we do not sleep at all. When we do sink into a slumber, it is so deep that we are not easily awakened.[23]

> For many sleep was difficult, broken, and accompanied by dreams; one often lay for hours without being able to fall asleep. Heaviness followed in the morning, as if after a night on the watch; endeavors during the day to make up for the sleep lost resulted simply in a worse night afterwards.[24]

Polar researchers have noted that when they did sleep, body temperature and the need to urinate rose rather than fell, indicating desynchronized circadian rhythms.

Sleep and Mood

Unusual sleep patterns are common among those who experience major shifts in mood and behavior such as depression, mania, and schizophrenia. The depressed either sleep unusually long hours and have difficulty awakening, or awaken in the early morning hours and are unable to sleep longer. Depression is often most severe just after waking and improves over the course of the day. Sleep tends to be agitated and inefficient, with less deep sleep. Conversely, studies show that REM sleep is excessive in the depressed and in people with other psychiatric disorders, and dreams may be unusually intense.[25] Some depressed people recover when they are deprived of REM sleep by repeated awakenings, and many antidepressant drugs reduce REM sleep. In some cases complete sleep deprivation for a night can relieve depression, but also worsen mania. In some forms of depression the major problem appears to be delayed sleep and the inability to awaken. Shifting the sleep-wake cycle is a successful antidepressive treatment in such cases, suggesting that the feelings of depression were an extension of sleep.

Some treatments for sleep disorders and for depression consist in changing the person's bedtime and the period of time spent asleep. Some researchers believe that mood disorders and sleep disorders are both related to circadian rhythms, with sleep disorders caused either by a shift in sleep in relation to other rhythms, or by a forward or backward shift of all 24-hour rhythms together. Others postulate that deep sleep and mood are related through a part of the sleep-regulation process independent of circadian rhythms. In either case, sleep evidently has much to tell us about mood and behavior if science can unravel its meaning.

Moonlight and Artificial Light

Knowing that sunlight sets the sleep-wake cycle, researchers have begun to study other forms of light that might have the same effect. Studies have shown that ordinary room lighting can influence and synchronize circadian rhythms. Therefore, depending on timing and intensity, room lighting may affect sleep patterns. It is also possible that in the absence of electric light, moonlight can alter the sleep-wake cycle.[26] This may explain a folk belief, still prevalent in the Shetland Islands, that moonlight should never fall on the face of a sleeping person. Such beliefs indicate that humankind has long intuited the power of light over sleep.

Some researchers now use unusually bright lamps (10,000 lux) to reset the sleep cycle, relieve some forms of insomnia, and increase daytime alertness and energy. They find that bright artificial light, of appropriate intensity and duration, can alter the body's temperature rhythm and change the timing, length, and quality of sleep. Such lamps can be used to help those whose sleep-wake cycles are markedly out of time with the light-dark cycle. For example, people with delayed or advanced sleep phase syndromes have sleep and wake times that are intractably later (delayed) or earlier (advanced) than desired, although they sleep normally during those hours.

Because it is easier to shift the sleep-wake cycle forward (clockwise) than back (counterclockwise), some researchers prefer using light to schedule bedtimes progressively later until a person has "lost" a day. Others use light to shift the cycle back by scheduling bedtimes progressively earlier. Both methods have been successful for the small numbers of people treated thus far. However, light therapy does not permanently alter circadian rhythms. The person must continue to receive plenty of properly timed outdoor or bright indoor light in order to maintain the new sleep pattern.

In Norway, midwinter insomnia has been treated by exposure to a half-hour of intense light (2000–2500 lux) in the morning over a five-day period.[27] Although those treated have not increased their sleep time, they can fall asleep earlier and are drowsy at the appropriate time, namely in the evening rather than in the morning. Schoolchildren in the far north who have uncontrollable waves of fatigue at random times of the day during the dark period are helped by a daily dose of bright light before going to school.

Researchers are now using light in an attempt to coalesce the fragmented sleep of the elderly. Supplementary light, properly timed, might improve the quality of our sleep as we age and increase our energy. To have this effect, bright artificial light must be able to strengthen circadian rhythms weakened by age as well as to reset the sleep-wake cycle. Studies to help the elderly in this manner are under way.

If you think you may be suffering from delayed or advanced sleep phase insomnias, midwinter insomnia, or age-related sleep problems, and they are disrupting your life, call the Light Therapy Information Service, listed in the Resources section, for the names of physicians using light therapy to treat these conditions.

CHAPTER 4

Eating and Drinking

My weight goes down in the summer without any effort at all. And I immediately feel myself putting on fat in October without eating any more or doing anything differently—especially as I've gotten older. It's really incredible! I think it's probably good for the body to put on a little fat for the winter.

34-YEAR-OLD WOMAN

LIKE OUR HABITS of sleeping and waking, we tend to take our eating rhythms for granted. In the industrialized world, this rhythm is usually three meals a day, with perhaps one to three snacks in between, unless we are deprived by poverty or illness. Yet are all our meals equally important to health? Does body weight fluctuate with the seasons? Do we digest food equally well any time of the day or night? Why do some of us eat or drink in uncontrollable binges or stop eating altogether? Research on biological rhythms is addressing these questions, since our eating and drinking patterns are related to the light-dark cycle.

HUNGER AND DIGESTION

The Flexible Control of Digestion

We use the familiar term "mouth-watering" to describe a meal or dish that looks irresistibly tasty. "Mouth-watering" refers to the saliva produced for digestion by the salivary glands when it is secreted in anticipation of food. This anticipation is an example of the way in which the circadian system learns from experience. Since the body uses the light-dark cycle through the circadian system to measure intervals of time, it can use its previous eating experience to foretell when that same meal will arrive again. For example, if you regularly have lunch at 12:30 P.M. your metabolic system will set itself accordingly, thus assuring that the necessary digestive enzymes, as well as insulin and glucagon, are ready to process each subsequent lunch. The body's circadian system controls the digestive system, with its innate rhythms synchronized by the cycles of light and darkness.

This control is lenient enough to leave the digestive system somewhat flexible, since food is not always available at the same time each day. However, digestive enzymes take several days to adjust to a new eating routine, and they only adjust within limits. They have preferred times for absorbing food into the bloodstream or lymphatic system and using it for energy and other needs. Some enzymes in the small intestine do not adjust at all to altered mealtimes, keeping instead a steady circadian rhythm. Such enzymes only adjust when the entire circadian system shifts, as it would after a lengthy stay in a different time zone. For these reasons, sensitive stomachs and intestinal disorders are common among those who constantly fly across time zones or work in rotating shifts.

Food is essential to life. Therefore, rhythms of food availability partly determine whether animals and humans are active during the day (diurnal), at dusk (crepuscular), or at night (nocturnal). Those who depend on catching fish to eat or sell often fish at night, knowing that many fish swim to the surface only during the dark. In this case the importance of securing food overrides the normal circadian rhythms of sleep.

Animals use light and circadian rhythms for their eating and drinking in ways unique to each species. The honeybee, for example, can learn and remember the time of day when any given type of flower opens and closes its petals. It wastes no energy flying to a flower only to find its petals closed and its pollen inaccessible. For this reason, if you regularly breakfast outdoors you may find bees waiting for your breakfast honey before you even bring it out onto the terrace.[1] In families of hares, the doe and her young separate during the day and reunite shortly after sunset for suckling. They return for this meal precisely on time, gradually altering that time with the sun as the weeks and months go by.

Of course, not every meal is so reliable. For predators, food is not always available at exactly the same time from day to day. A falcon, for example, may find no prospective meal roaming about at 12 noon. It will try again at a different time, and when successful will return every day at that new time until prey availability changes again.

Hunger and Circadian Rhythms

We like to think that we eat because we are hungry. However, an empty stomach does not inevitably lead to eating. When we are anxious, afraid, exhausted, or sick we may have no desire to eat even though our bodies need food. When involved in intense work on an exciting project, we may forget to eat and not notice that we have missed a meal. On the other hand, we may eat constantly when we feel lonely or depressed. German speakers acknowledge this fact with the word *Kummerspeck*, meaning weight that is added through worry and care. We may also continue eating when already full: who accepts dessert out of hunger? Even a person whose stomach has been surgically removed can still experience feelings of hunger and satiety.

Hunger is obviously an insufficient explanation of why

we eat when we do. In fact, hunger and the regulation of eating are phenomena still not entirely understood, and theories have abounded concerning the importance of stomach or intestinal secretions and contractions. More recent research reveals that hunger, satiety, and digestion begin in the brain, and that the regulation of our eating habits involves a wide variety of factors, including circadian rhythms in brain signals, the pleasurable qualities and chemical properties of food, and the body's response to eating.

Hunger is not solely dependent on the time elapsed since the last meal, but instead is part of the body's complex of circadian rhythms. This is dramatically illustrated in the daily eating habits of people who have experimentally spent days alone and enclosed in windowless rooms, isolated from sunlight or other clues as to the time of day. In such cases the body's circadian timing system gradually changes. The sleep-wake cycle can become shorter than 24 hours, but usually lengthens and can become up to 50 hours long. Studies show that in such cases, people who are used to eating three meals a day and perhaps a snack continue to do so, even when their "day," meaning hours of activity, is twice as long as normal. The three meals are stretched out over the "day" accordingly. The time between waking up and eating breakfast might be 6 or 8 hours; the time between breakfast and lunch might be 8 to 10 hours; with dinner perhaps 11 hours later.[2] Those in the outside world who arose at the same time would have had two meals and a snack by the time the isolated person ate breakfast. Of course, those in isolation are not aware of this difference. They have lost a sense of earthly time and think they are living on the usual 24-hour schedule. Although some people in isolation increase the size of their meals, they lose weight since they consume little more than half of their usual calories per 24-hour period.

Why does a person whose internal clock no longer runs on solar time stretch mealtimes to such lengths? It appears that when the circadian rhythm of wakefulness is shortened or lengthened, a person's metabolism and psychological processes are compressed or stretched as well. Since mealtimes in isolation are always at well-regulated intervals in relation to the length of the "day" involved, researchers speculate that the body already "knows" at the time of awakening how long its "day" will be and sends internal signals to eat accordingly. Such experiments in isolation units help clarify how the circadian rhythms of sleep/wakefulness and eating/drinking are intertwined, with the latter dependent on the former.

From "Start Eating" to "Stop Eating"

Hunger is regulated by functions in the brain not directly under our control. If these functions ceased, we could starve without ever feeling hungry, or eat ceaselessly without ever feeling full. Instead, the body has pathways through which it tells the brain whether it is sated or empty. It is vital for the brain to know the body's current energy level so that it can regulate eating behavior accordingly. The brain has several sensors or "windows" through which it views the body's nutritional state. Information from these sensors is then processed within the brain, mainly the hypothalamus, through a system of chemical messengers. The hypothalamus then modulates appetite and eating behavior accordingly. This system has been studied in animals, and it appears to be largely applicable to our own eating habits as well.

Studies suggest that the hypothalamus has a "start-eating" center and a "stop-eating" center: first "start" inhibits "stop," then vice versa.[3] Special chemical messengers stimulate one or the other in turn. For example, a brain chemical called norepinephrine stimulates appetite, while serotonin specializes in satiety. When people take the serotonin-related drug fenfluramine, they respond by eating smaller meals even when the food is particularly desirable. They also eat more slowly and remain sated longer.[4] Amphetamines (prescribed for head colds and hay fever and used as diet pills) block appetite, while antipsychotic drugs (prescribed for hallucinations and delusions) stimulate appetite by blocking the signals for satiety. When volunteers receive experimental injections of substances that reduce serotonin, they become hungrier and eat larger meals.[5] Both serotonin and norepinephrine are under the influence of the circadian system.

The alimentary tract, the long canal that extends from the mouth to the anus, also affects satiety. Receptors in the mouth monitor the amount of food we eat. So powerful are these receptors that they can leave an animal temporarily satisfied after a meal even if all the food passes out through an opening in the esophagus, leaving the stomach empty. Partly because of these receptors, it is healthy for us to eat slowly, chew well, and pause before second helpings, giving the monitors time to register satiety in the brain.

Substances in the blood, such as glucose and the hormones insulin, cortisol (derived from cortisone), and epidermal growth factor (EGF) also influence our eating patterns. These substances fluctuate with circadian rhythms of activity. In animals, cortisone, glucagon, insulin, EGF, and other peptides encourage the eating of energy-rich nutrients and influence the chemical messengers involved in hunger and fullness. Daily cortisone levels are highest just before an animal's eating cycle. There is evidence that cortisol influences our own food intake, and that abnormal increases in appetite and weight are related to cortisone levels.[6] Glucose, which reaches its highest level during the day, also appears to influence the chemical messengers that regulate eating.

The food we eat also helps regulate eating patterns. As certain nutrients enter the bloodstream, they make their presence known to the brain and affect the chemical messengers that regulate eating. A large carbohydrate meal causes a chain of events resulting in an increase in the chemical messengers that form serotonin. Consequently, the person is likely to prefer protein at the next meal, which then decreases these same chemicals. Sometimes diets high in protein or fat and low in carbohydrates can trigger carbohydrate binges, the body's reaction to deprivation. Drugs that alter the chemical messengers for eating not only change body weight, but in some cases cause a person to crave or reject carbohydrates, and possibly protein as well. In these ways our brains register and modulate essential nutrients, letting us know what foods we need.

Rhythms of Digestion and Metabolism

Our bodies' needs for essential nutrients may have another link to light and darkness. The eating control system appears to prefer certain nutrients at certain times of day. For example, the body evidently puts carbohydrates to maximal use around noon.[7] Such studies indicate that the ideal breakfast would be mainly carbohydrate, while the ideal supper would be largely protein, preferably from vegetables, whole grains, legumes, and fish. The two meals have different purposes: breakfast provides energy for the activity of the day, and supper anticipates the body's needs for the hours of darkness, sleep, and fasting.

Once food is digested and absorbed through the intestines into the bloodstream or lymphatic system, the body can use it. The body's process for using food is called metabolism, and the speed at which it uses food is the rate of metabolism. Most of us know that metabolism changes when the body needs energy at a more rapid rate than usual—for example, during exercise. We have also heard of a so-called basal or basic metabolism, as measured at some point on an ordinary day. This is a misconception, still widespread even among physicians. A basal rate of metabolism does not exist. Instead, metabolism has a prominent circadian rhythm, with a peak in the early afternoon.[8] Metabolism varies independently with the time of day, whether or not a person has recently eaten or exercised.

Metabolism is evidently linked to other circadian rhythms since it is modified by sleep and waking. Metabolism may also vary with the seasons, reaching its peak during winter.[9] This finding is controversial and may be due to dietary factors rather than biological rhythms. However, global statistics reveal that people living near or within the Arctic Circle have an average metabolism 10 percent higher than those living in the tropics.[10] This same study showed worldwide seasonal changes in metab-

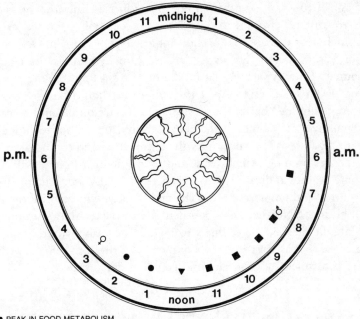

● PEAK IN FOOD METABOLISM
■ GREATEST USE OF CALORIES
▼ MAXIMAL USE OF CARBOHYDRATES
♀ PEAK IN ALCOHOL METABOLISM (WOMEN)
♂ PEAK IN ALCOHOL METABOLISM (MEN)

Figure 9. *Daily rhythms for food and drink.*

olism with a winter peak in the temperate zones. Temperature
cannot fully account for these seasonal rhythms, leaving the possibility that changes in light affect metabolism. If this is true,
our bodies' use of food would be affected by both the daily and
the seasonal timing of light, and perhaps by its intensity as well.
This theory is supported by evidence that the body has seasonal
variations in glucose and glycogen, with a peak in December and
a trough in July.[11]

   Hibernating mammals have marked seasonal variations
in metabolism that accord with their different needs for the in-
active period of winter. Some researchers think that seasonal
variations in human metabolism are the remains of the protective

seasonal function of hibernation. According to this theory, we have seasonal changes in our ability to metabolize fat and carbohydrates. During the warmer, longer days of April to October our tissues and organs expect to use carbohydrate as the chief source of energy, storing fat for use during the approaching winter. From October to April the stored fat should be used and completely metabolized. The seasonal expectations should reveal themselves as changes in the body's ability to metabolize fat and carbohydrates. This theory is still controversial and conflicts with other research on carbohydrate and fat metabolism. Nonetheless, some studies indicate that our bodies gradually store fat in the summer and fall and use it as the main fuel in winter.[12] Research in both the Northern and Southern Hemispheres shows seasonal peaks in the body's readiness to metabolize carbohydrates, suggesting that at least remnants of metabolic rhythms remain with us, controlled by the changing length in daylight.

SEASONAL PATTERNS IN EATING AND WEIGHT

Many animals that do not hibernate also undergo seasonal changes in metabolism and weight. In this way their bodies adjust to extremes of temperature and scarcity of food. However, since the body cannot adjust overnight, it is too late to make the necessary adjustments once the temperature change and food scarcity have occurred. Instead, the animal uses the gradually changing day length of late summer and fall as a cue to begin its internal preparations for winter.

Hamsters, for example, prepare for winter by adding body fat in order to store energy and provide insulation. Small rodents called voles, on the other hand, conserve energy by losing weight, thus decreasing energy requirements. In experimental laboratories, hamsters and voles grow fat or thin respectively when artificial light is used to gradually shorten their day, signaling an approaching winter. In conjunction with these preparations for winter, some animals change their eating habits, increasing their consumption of carbohydrates in the autumn, with protein consumption remaining unchanged throughout the year.

Researchers are studying whether traces of seasonal eating adjustments exist in the human body. Of course, for most people in the world the seasonal difference in food availability is the most important source of both dietary and weight changes. These seasonal variations have little impact on industrialized countries, however, because of the importing of food from other climates, growth of food in greenhouses, and food preservation techniques.

The question remains whether we have inherited a light-regulated control for changes in our food choice and body weight. It would seem logical that some dietary changes should occur, because the body requires more energy during the cold winter months to maintain its core temperature. However, studies on seasonal variation in the total calories consumed in industrialized countries are conflicting, with the majority showing no such variation.[13] Nonetheless, several studies show seasonal variation in the consumption of specific nutrients—for example, a tendency in the autumn and winter to eat more starches and fiber such as wheat products, potatoes, and rice.[14] Many of us notice similar personal seasonal changes in appetite and food preference.

> I like heavier foods in the winter: good, thick soups, and more bread and pasta. I'm hungrier when it's cold, and I want hot, filling meals to keep me warm. In warm weather I definitely have an urge for lighter things like salads, and lots of corn, and fruits. I think we all eat differently in the summer. That's probably normal.
>
> 50-YEAR-OLD WOMAN

> I have noticed in the last few years that around Christmastime I get really heavily into Christmas pastries. I mean good, homemade pastries, with lots of nuts in them and sugar and flour. Also some fruit, tangerines—typical Christmas kind

> of food. And I live for several weeks over Christmas almost off that, not feeling as though I am eating candy, not feeling as though I'm eating badly and feeling guilty or anything like that. I feel that I am eating exactly right.
>
> 46-YEAR-OLD WOMAN

Some researchers think that seasonal food preferences may be part of a circadian-regulated system of seasonal variation in the body's energy balance, just as daily preferences help keep a 24-hour chemical balance.

Some people, like some animals, have a tendency to gain weight in the winter and lose it again in the spring. The former is certainly true of children and adolescents, who have marked seasonal growth spurts, with growth in height greatest in the spring and growth in weight greatest in the autumn. In children and adolescents, weight can increase five times as much in the fall as it does in spring, with some children actually losing weight in spring.[15] Well-nourished children appear to show seasonal differences in weight less than do poorly nourished children.

Researchers do not yet understand the causes of this seasonality in weight gain during our growing years. However, it is evidently not dependent upon temperature and is likely to be regulated by light-induced seasonal variations in hormonal secretions.

As we grow, the weight we gain is not only fat but muscle and other tissues as well. In some people, however, the seasons continue to affect weight in adulthood after growth is complete. According to a survey in New York City, nearly half the population (47 percent) reported gaining weight in late fall and winter.[16] Other studies also indicate a tendency toward winter increase in weight, with a decrease before the summer.[17]

> I'm always heavier in winter than in summer by five pounds or maybe ten. I automatically gain weight from about November or December and

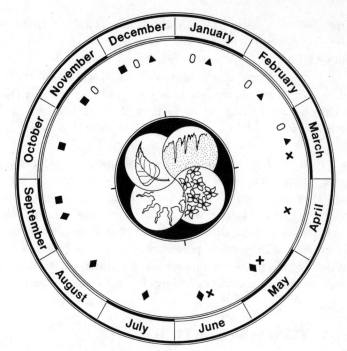

▲ PEAK IN METABOLISM (IN TEMPERATE ZONES)
○ TENDENCY TO GAIN WEIGHT
♦ TENDENCY TO LOSE WEIGHT
■ GREATEST GROWTH IN WEIGHT IN ADOLESCENTS
✕ PEAK IN ALCOHOL ABUSE

Figure 10. *Seasonal rhythms in drinking, metabolism, and weight.*

begin losing it again in March or April. It has nothing to do with conscious dieting or exercise —it just happens. My body just fluctuates this way.

42-YEAR-OLD WOMAN (EXTREMELY LIGHT-SENSITIVE)

Temperature, food choice, and seasonal variations in light may all contribute to this tendency.

In each of us, the body's basic shape and size are largely inherited. You are likely to take after your genetic mother or father in your tendency to be heavy or slim. This has little to do with family eating habits, since it is true of those who were adopted in infancy as well. Nonetheless, it appears that even those who have been on the heavy side since early childhood have seasonal fluctuations, tending to add weight in winter. Therefore, those who are cutting down on fatty foods to lose weight for health reasons may lose more weight in spring than in winter.

Our seasonal changes in weight may well be related to the protective layer of fat in hibernating animals. Added winter tissue stores energy and insulates against cold. Several studies show that our overall body insulation increases from summer to winter.[18] Perhaps this is why unseasonable heat or cold often seems harder to bear than the same temperature during the expected season. A person's perception of cold out of doors is 14 Celsius degrees higher in summer than in winter—a reaction that some researchers think is caused by changes in body insulation.[19]

MEAL TIMING AND WEIGHT

An old saying goes: "Breakfast like a king, lunch like a prince, and dine like a pauper." In contrast to this saying, many of us begin the day with a hasty breakfast or none at all, consuming 50 to 75 percent of our daily food at the evening meal.[20] What difference does it make if we prefer to dine like kings and breakfast like paupers?

As we have seen, the body's digestive fluids are not equally ready at all times to receive whatever we choose to eat. Therefore, optimal nutrition may depend not only on what and how much we eat, but also on when we eat during the day. Research suggests that a fixed number of calories is used in different ways when consumed in one meal as breakfast, in one meal as dinner, or as multiple meals throughout the day.

Most of us would lose weight if we ate only one meal a day, no matter when we took that meal. However, two studies showed that people lost a weekly average of 1.4 pounds more when they ate breakfast as their only meal of the day than they did when they ate dinner as their only meal.[21] This held true even when the choice and amount of food for that meal were unlimited. Some who ate their single meal at dinner even gained weight. When calories were restricted to 2000 per meal, the weight loss for the breakfast-only schedule was 2.5 pounds more than for dinner-only.

It seems that the digestive organs do not handle a calorie the same way in the morning as they do in the evening. For this reason, the timing of our meals may be as important as their size and food type in determining weight loss or gain. Of course, part of this difference has to do with activity: we are more likely to use calories for energy during the day's activities rather than during a quiet evening. However, the difference also lies in the circadian timing of the circulating hormones such as cortisol, plasma growth hormone, and insulin, which affect digestion and assimilation. The circadian rhythms of these three hormones can adjust to changes in the timing of a meal, but not equally well at all times of day. As far as metabolism is concerned, they are at their best during the earlier part of the day.

For these reasons we may be what we eat, as the saying goes, but we are also when we eat.[22] Some researchers think that concern for the timing as well as the content of meals should be part of our daily program for health.

EATING DISORDERS AND ALCOHOLISM

Binge-eating, refusing to eat, and drinking alcohol in excess can become chronic patterns and are signals of physical or emotional distress. Unusual eating and drinking habits may be related to the light-dark cycle. Most brain chemicals involved in such behaviors, and sometimes the behaviors themselves, have circadian and seasonal rhythms. Eating and drinking problems are often associated with disturbances in other circadian rhythms as well, such as sleep. Researchers are now studying aspects of problematic eating and drinking in relation to daily or seasonal rhythms.

Anorexia, Bulimia, and Food Cravings

Anorexia (also known as anorexia nervosa) refers to chronic, compulsive dieting. Bulimia (also called bulimia nervosa) is characterized by recurrent binge-eating, usually followed by purging through vomiting or the use of laxatives. Although these two eating disorders are often thought of as opposites, they actually have much in common. Both are most prevalent among women, and both can be caused by, for example, a fashion for extreme thinness. The pressure to be thin often leads to anorexia or to severely restrictive low-calorie diets. These periods of complete or semi-starvation can evidently unbalance the brain's chemicals that signal satiety. After a period of semi-starvation, the deprived will gorge themselves and sometimes vomit. This behavior is now known as bulimia. The chemical imbalance is transient but can recur with each low-calorie diet, possibly leading to permanent overeating. In this way the absence of food can upset the circadian rhythms of chemicals involved in hunger and satiety, causing lifelong eating problems.

It appears that in both anorexia and bulimia, the imbalances in brain chemicals can also be the cause rather than the effect of voluntary starvation or binge-eating. For example, many of those who are anorexic or bulimic have unusual hormonal patterns in the hypothalamus, pituitary, thyroid, and adrenal. These patterns are also found in some cases of depression. Many depressed people are also anorexic, and many who are anorexic or bulimic also have periods of severe depression, a family history of depression, or both. This suggests that the same brain chemicals are causing all three problems.

Some people experience a form of seasonal binge-eating during the fall and winter months. They usually crave carbohydrates and do not purge. Like other bulimics, people with the seasonal variety experience their binging as eating out of control.

When I was extremely anxious I could easily go
through a dozen doughnuts—and still feel the
need for more, and add half a gallon of ice cream
to it. Chocolate especially I could eat, candy bar
after candy bar, and never feel satiated. Frequently when I binged I would be aware even
when I was eating that it did not taste good to
me. But a certain calmness would come with it.
And when I was done, when I could no longer
stomach any more, there was also a tremendous
feeling of self-disgust, the feeling that you're not
in control. And this from a person who was always extremely self-disciplined. But the need for
the food was so great that I didn't care.

41-YEAR-OLD WOMAN

While high-carbohydrate meals generally tend to make
people sleepy, bulimics who crave carbohydrates say they feel
more alert after such a meal. This suggests a specific disturbance
in the brain's chemistry. Seasonal bulimia is accompanied by the
fall/winter depression called seasonal affective disorder (see chapter 5), and some researchers think that the same brain chemicals
cause both problems. Three of the brain chemicals under suspicion
are dopamine, melatonin, and serotonin, the latter two having
seasonal rhythms. All forms of bulimia may have seasonal exacerbations or seasonal rhythms of occurrence, a possibility requiring further study.

Some researchers think of both mood disorders and eating
disorders as results of a similar underlying chemical imbalance
within the brain. In some people the imbalance could provoke a
pronounced change in mood, in others an unusual eating pattern,
and in many both symptoms simultaneously. For those bulimics
who crave a specific type of food such as carbohydrates, the food
may then act as a drug to correct the chemical imbalance.

The underlying flaw may lie in the circadian system itself,
in which the rhythmic daily or seasonal secretions of crucial

hormones are overabundant, inadequate, or desynchronized. This theory is supported by the striking association between patterns in eating, weight, sleeping, and mood, all of which are linked to circadian physiology. One study of those with severe mood changes showed that reduced, broken sleep and early waking were associated with weight loss, while longer, unbroken sleep and later waking were associated with weight gain.[23] Anorexia and weight loss are generally found together with what is called endogenous depression or melancholia. This type of depression is generally accompanied by insomnia, particularly in the early morning hours, and the depressive feelings are usually at their worst in the morning. This form of anorexia and depression peaks in the spring.

Added to these connections are the rhythmic premenstrual changes in some women, called premenstrual syndrome or PMS. A study of 300 nurses showed an association between the occurrence of cravings for food and/or sweets on the one hand, and depression and premenstrual fluid retention on the other.[24] Women who experience PMS also frequently eat more, sleep longer, and crave carbohydrates. In addition, studies indicate that among women who are bulimic, binge-eating is most frequent in the five days preceding the menstrual period.[25]

Seasonal carbohydrate craving responds rapidly and dramatically to therapy using bright artificial light. Light treatment may correct a deficiency in the hormone serotonin, thereby eliminating the need to binge on carbohydrates. One study suggests that light therapy has a specific effect on the regulation of appetite for carbohydrates, greater than its effect on appetite in general.[26] Some researchers think that light therapy could be effective for other forms of bulimia as well, perhaps those with signs of seasonal exacerbations. This possibility remains to be tested.

> I could have been miserable because none of my clothes fit. I could have decided, "I'm going to stop this." But when the need would arise, then nothing mattered except having whatever I had

chosen to eat. It would get to the point where I would go to the store and buy a big bag of M&M's and a dozen Reese's peanut-butter cups, and I would sit and go through the whole thing. Then the self-disgust would be tremendous and I would be all right for a little while and say: "I will never do this again"—until next time. . . . I was amazed to find that light could be substituted for all this.

41-YEAR-OLD WOMAN

Many of those who suffer from bulimia have had successful treatments with several different classes of antidepressant drugs. Presumably these drugs correct the underlying biochemical disturbance causing both depression and binge-eating. However, researchers do not yet know which chemicals in the drugs are effective, or why.

Alcoholism

Drinking an alcoholic beverage with lunch or at the end of the day is a common routine in the Western world. Although such customs need not pose a problem, wine, beer, and spirits all contain ethanol, a drug that affects the brain even in small amounts and is potentially addictive. In fact, ethanol is one of the two most commonly used drugs in the United States, the other being caffeine.[27]

Like other drugs, alcohol can affect the circadian rhythms that are normally set by the light-dark cycle. The stimulating or depressing effects we notice when we drink alcohol are evidently linked to alcohol's ability to alter the timing of hormones. For example, one incident of intoxication alters the circadian organization of the adrenal system for three days, raising adrenaline to more than 10 times its normal level.[28] Men who become addicted to alcohol lose the circadian rhythms of the hormone testosterone, probably one of the factors responsible for the deterioration in sexual function among male alcoholics. Alcohol in excess disrupts the circadian rhythm of sleep, and a sleep disorder is one of the first symptoms of alcoholism. However, in the case of sleep it is not clear whether alcohol works through the circadian system, through other mechanisms, or both.

Some people may also use alcohol in an attempt to correct deficiencies of certain brain chemicals normally secreted in circadian rhythms, making alcohol craving similar to food craving. According to one study, 54 percent of alcoholics report craving sweets at all times and especially when coming off alcohol.[29] Some alcoholics who succeed in breaking their drinking habits become compulsive binge-eaters, and many bulimics have a history of previous alcohol dependence. Depression and anxiety also often accompany alcoholism. Some investigators now think that vitamin and mineral supplements and nutritious foods might help reduce alcohol craving by supplying the brain with necessary nutrients. Further research is needed on similarities among compulsive eating, compulsive drinking, and severe mood changes, and the relationship of all three to circadian rhythms.

I have read that a very large percentage of those who have both an eating disorder and winter depression are children of alcoholics—and I am one. And I can make no distinction between an alcoholic's need for alcohol and mine for food. All I would have to do is have one candy bar, then I'd need more. Going completely without them would have been much better. So I equated *that* with the fact that an alcoholic cannot have any more drink. I kind of assumed that in some way I inherited this, but that I sought relief in ways other than alcohol. You know, there was a time in my life when I would look down on an alcoholic and be rather disgusted. I don't feel that I could possibly do that now.

41-YEAR-OLD WOMAN

Circadian rhythms reveal themselves in several aspects of alcoholism. First of all, a person's risk of becoming alcoholic may be partly determined by the concentration in the blood of certain hormones such as estradiol and cortisol.[30] These hormones have circadian, circaseptan (approximately seven-day), and seasonal rhythms, suggesting that a susceptible person may have rhythms of particular sensitivity to alcohol addiction or to relapse while recovering from alcoholism. These hormonal rhythms could underlie the regular drinking sprees of some alcohol-dependent people, with a timing that tends to remain the same in many successive attacks.

Secondly, alcohol varies in its effects according to time of day in all who drink it. A Bloody Mary before breakfast is likely to make you tipsy faster, but also more briefly, than a martini before dinner. Alcohol has circadian rhythms of metabolism regulated by the light-dark cycle and independent of the timing of meals. During the daytime alcohol disappears more speedily from the body than in the evening and at night. This variation can amount to as much as 25 percent of the hourly rate of alcohol metabolism.[31] One study shows that peak time of alcohol metabolism differs between women and men, around 3:00 P.M. for women and around 8:00 A.M. for men.[32] However, in general it appears that for both sexes alcohol drunk in the evening or at night produces a more lasting effect than a drink of the same size earlier in the day. This rhythm is probably related to the circadian rhythms of enzymes in the liver that process ethanol.

Animal studies suggest that we may also react to alcohol differently—for example, feel either stimulated or depressed—depending on the time of day we drink.[33] Even the more dangerous effects of alcohol, such as subnormal body temperature (hypothermia), could vary with the time of day, with early morning possibly the riskiest time. These differences may be due to circadian fluctuations in hormones of the central nervous system that are sensitive to ethanol. For example, the abnormal drop in body temperature may depend on the hormone serotonin's circadian phase of sensitivity to alcohol.

For unexplained reasons, animal research implicates lunar as well as circadian rhythms in the effects of alcohol, showing that deaths resulting from alcohol consumption are greater during the full moon than at new moon, with the peak time for both in the middle of the night.[34]

Our reactions to alcohol could also vary with the seasons. Cyclic seasonal changes affect the sensitivity of the central nervous system, and this could influence physical dependence on alcohol, just as it influences dependence on other drugs such as morphine. One study suggests a seasonal trend in alcohol abuse, with a peak in the spring.[35] Some evidence also shows increased outpatient treatment for alcoholism during winter and increased hospitalizations for alcoholism during spring.[36] Preliminary data indicate that some of those suffering from alcoholism have seasonal drinking patterns similar to seasonal affective disorder, with repeated exacerbations in fall and winter.[37]

Therefore, if you drink alcohol, the number of drinks you have had is not an accurate indication of your ability to function or the harm done to your body. Further research on daily, weekly, monthly, and seasonal fluctuations in alcohol sensitivity would be welcomed by all who drink socially, by recovering alcoholics, and by professionals dedicated to preventing and treating alcohol addiction. Meanwhile, those of us who are addicted may help ourselves by keeping a calendar of the hours, days, weeks, and seasons of drinking binges or compulsions to drink. We could use such a calendar to alert ourselves and our therapists to especially vulnerable times.

CHAPTER 5

Mood and Behavior

OFTEN WE NOTICE that light affects our moods. While candlelight suggests coziness and intimacy, a poorly lit room can make us gloomy and uneasy, especially at night. Weather can have similar effects, with persistently gray skies giving us a sense of discontent or cheerlessness.

> I start a bright sunny day with a little bit more
> on my side. I have all my life noticed that when
> I first open my eyes in the morning I feel dif-
> ferently about different kinds of weather, and
> most particularly about light and dark. It has to
> do with optimism and pessimism—it feels like
> an upper or a downer.
>
> **55-YEAR-OLD WOMAN**

Dark clouds overhead are familiar symbols of sadness and foreboding, while the sun stands for joy and rebirth. So deeply engrained are these symbols in our thinking that some of us associate character traits with warmth and sunshine.

> Generally I think that people are happier in places where the sun shines. When I go to Arizona, for example, it's very un-Boston. I mean people talk to you and they smile more. People on the highways don't seem so angry. Who knows what it's really related to, but people there are more expansive and more open and happier. It's hard to just chalk it all up to sunshine, but I'm sure it has something to do with it.
>
> 42-YEAR-OLD WOMAN

Our reactions to sunlight often become evident as winter approaches and the days grow shorter. Even those who are usually unperturbed by the gradually lengthening darkness receive a jolt in October when the clocks are turned back an hour. The change to standard time is widely disliked. Some call it an "annual masochistic ritual too few people have had the courage to oppose."[1] An adjective frequently used to describe the time change is "depressing."

> That Sunday in October when we set the clock back an hour is always the saddest day of the year for me. Suddenly it's dark by 5:00 P.M. It's as though the night were closing in, threatening to take over. I try to make especially nice plans for that day to help myself get through it.
>
> 50-YEAR-OLD WOMAN

As the days become shorter and winter finally sets in, many people find it more difficult to get up in the morning because it is still dark. If left to ourselves, without alarm clocks, most of us would awaken later in the winter and earlier in the spring and summer, according to the morning light. In general we tend to sleep more from November through February than during the rest of the year.[2] In winter we may also eat more to keep our bodies warm, and prefer heavier foods rather than the lighter salads and fruits of summer. Weight gain during the winter months is common, especially since we also tend to be less physically active. Curling up with a good book often seems more appealing than getting out into the cold and exercising.

In other words, our daily habits change as our bodies adapt to the longer nights and colder days. In its extreme form, this adaptation is called hibernation. The word *hibernate* stems from the Latin *hibernare*, "to pass the winter." It refers to the dormant or resting state in which some animals spend the winter months. As humans, the pressures of our lives rarely allow us to adapt or "hibernate" as much as we might wish.

The relative lethargy and heaviness of winter can translate into feeling sluggish and run-down. People generally feel worst during January, February, and March, and best during April, May, and June.[3] A New York City population survey suggests that in some areas of the United States, seasonal swings in mood and behavior are the norm. The survey's 200 respondents reported changes in the late fall and winter as follows: lower energy, 50 percent; increased weight, 47 percent; increased sleep, 42 percent; decreased social activity, 31 percent; feeling generally worse from late fall throughout the winter, 31 percent.[4]

In some people, these reactions to winter are exaggerated and at times difficult to live with. Winter then becomes a bleak season in which mild sadness is coupled with lowered motivation. An estimated 25 percent of those who experience seasonal mood swings have variations in behavior severe enough to pose a personal problem.[5]

I have to push myself harder in the winter, over-come a resistance in myself. I used to wonder what was the matter with me, why I was drag-

ging around and couldn't concentrate when
everyone else seemed so perky.

55-YEAR-OLD WOMAN

SHORT DAYS, DAYLESS NIGHTS

It is dark! dark! Dark at noon, dark at midnight,
dark every hour of the day.

FREDERICK A. COOK IN THE ANTARCTIC, JUNE 1898

The further we live from the equator, the shorter are the winter
days and the more likely we are to notice the effects of darkness.
Some regions have three to six hours of feeble light during midwinter, while others have only two hours of light per day.

> In Stockholm in midwinter we have light from
> about nine a.m. to three P.M., but the sun is
> always very low, so it's not as though the sun
> were shining. It's more like evening all the time.
> In the city further north where I used to live, it
> was only light from about eleven A.M. to one
> P.M. When I walked home from work to have
> lunch, the sun was just going down. But then
> it never really comes up.
>
> 40-YEAR-OLD WOMAN FROM UMEA, SWEDEN

Changes in mood and energy have long been accepted as
part of life in many northern areas. Mental illness, suicide, and
violence occur more frequently among Arctic residents than among
those at lower latitudes, although the long darkness is only one
of the possible causes. Suicidal behavior increases in December
and January even outside the Arctic, and the high suicide rates
in areas such as Seattle, Washington, and Sweden may be associated with the lack of winter sunshine.

Nonetheless, responses to light and darkness are quite

complex and individual. Many take the months of long darkness in stride, especially those who grew up in or near the Arctic and are therefore acclimatized. Some enjoy the long nights, saying that the snow reflects whatever light there is and makes the day seem brighter. Others grit their teeth every winter or suffer so noticeably from the darkness that they eventually move to a more southern latitude.

> My husband grew up in Stockholm. But as soon as he finished school, he left. He couldn't stand it, he got so depressed being there where it's dark so early in the afternoon. And many times we have talked about moving from the U.S. back to Sweden. But he says, "I can never move back to Stockholm. It's too dark for me."
>
> 39-YEAR-OLD WOMAN

In most areas close to the Arctic or Antarctic, the sun does make a daily appearance during the winter, if only briefly and feebly. In polar regions, however, those who see the sun set at the end of November (Arctic) or mid-May (Antarctic) know it will not rise again for more than two months—not an easy thought to bear. In northwest Canada, for example, once the winter sun disappears below the horizon, only darkness and twilight alternate, with midwinter bringing only a one- to two-hour period of very dim twilight at midday.

Natives of polar regions and non-native researchers have told of their mood and personality changes during the dark period. These conditions range from lethargy and depression to outbursts of hysteria and hallucinations. Eskimos have their own terms for these states of mind, such as *pibloctoq*, in which a person runs out over the ice, screams, gesticulates, and tears off clothing despite temperatures of minus 40 degrees Fahrenheit. The attack usually ends in sobbing or falling asleep.

Polar explorers describe a creeping mental lethargy during the dark period that makes any mental endeavor extremely difficult. They report being incapable of concentration and finding the desire and capacity to work greatly reduced:

> We had placed before us the outline for indus-
> trious occupation; but we did little of it. As the
> darkness increased our energy waned. We became
> indifferent and found it difficult to concentrate
> our minds or fix our efforts to any one plan of
> action.[6]

> One wakened up heavy and indisposed, with the
> feeling [called] "wooden." . . . The wish was
> present to begin work seriously; the pipe was lit
> and the pen filled, but one got no further. The
> pen became dry and was again dipped in the ink;
> the pipe was smoked out, refilled and started
> again, always in the belief that something really
> was to be done or being done. It was only when
> the bell rang for dinner some hours later, with
> nothing done, that the inevitable conclusion was
> accepted that one was unable to work.[7]

Accompanying the lethargy is progressive depression which, according to the explorer Dr. Frederick Cook, afflicts every polar expedition through the long night. His journals kept during the Belgian Antarctic expedition repeatedly mention the disheart-ening and destructive effects of the "soul despairing darkness" and "unbroken blackness":

> We strain the truth to introduce stories of home
> and of flowery future prospects, hoping to infuse
> a new cheer; but it all fails miserably. We are
> under the spell of the black antarctic night and,
> like the world which it darkens, we are cold,
> cheerless, and inactive. We have aged ten years
> in thirty days.[8]

The moonlight comes and goes alike during the hours of midday as at midnight. . . . Oh, for that heavenly ball of fire! Not for the heat—the human economy can regulate that—but for the light—the hope of life.[9]

SEASONAL AFFECTIVE DISORDER (SAD)

Most of us do not live in such extreme light-dark conditions. Nonetheless, many people outside the polar regions react to the shortened days of winter as intensely as polar explorers react to 24-hour darkness. These light-sensitive people develop an almost constant feeling of fatigue and drowsiness and tend to sleep much more than usual during the winter months, as long as 10 to 12 hours, or even 13 to 14 hours on weekends. Feelings of sadness, irritability, and anxiety set in, and lack of concentration and social withdrawal often occur, including a decrease in sexual desire. Many develop a craving for carbohydrates such as potatoes, bread, rice, and pasta, and eat them in large amounts.

Some of these reactions to winter have their logic and were possibly adaptive or useful at an earlier stage in human development. However, in our urban, nine-to-five lives that pay no heed to the seasons, these reactions are disruptive and detrimental. Consequently they have been observed by mental-health professionals and termed winter depression, seasonal depression, or, more recently, seasonal affective disorder (SAD).

Although the label SAD is relatively new, the suspicion that some mood disturbances are related to the seasons dates back to antiquity. For more than two thousand years physicians believed that mania was caused by heat and was most prevalent in the summer, and that depression was caused by cold and was most prevalent in the autumn.[10] In the last 150 years researchers have observed seasonal variations in episodes of mental disorders and in suicide, an indirect reflection of depression. Finally, in 1967 the chronobiologist Franz Halberg published a paper relating depression to biological rhythms.[11] Halberg postulated that the seasonally depressed have internal rhythms not properly timed to the 24-hour cycles of sunlight and darkness. Other researchers soon began testing Halberg's hypothesis, leading eventually to renewed interest in recurrent winter depressions, which were given the name SAD.

SAD is now a subject of continuous study. It is related to day length, overcast skies, and lowered temperature, and appears to be most prevalent in northern latitudes, although it occurs to a lesser extent further south and in parts of the Southern Hemisphere. SAD can begin in childhood, adolescence, or adulthood, and women make up 74 to 94 percent of all those treated for the condition.[12] However, these figures are made up of people who volunteered for research studies to treat winter depression and may not reflect the actual extent of the condition among men. Men may simply be more reluctant to openly acknowledge their problems and to seek help by volunteering. A survey in New York City shows no significant differences in the numbers of men and women who reported winter problems, no matter how mild or severe.[13]

For some people with SAD, feelings of anxiety can begin as early as August or September. This late-summer anxiety, which some describe as a feeling of panic, may be due to the approaching winter announced by the shortening days, or it may have a biological basis of its own.

> I moved to New England twenty years ago in December and the first thing I noticed was that it was dark all the time! Every year it gets harder to take and every year I start thinking about it earlier. I sit on the beach in August and think about how horrible the winter is going to be.
>
> **40-YEAR-OLD WOMAN**

Usually, changes in mood and behavior begin in October or November, often beginning with an increased need for sleep and a change in food preference. People with SAD find it difficult to wake up in the morning and set about their daily tasks, and they develop a distinct craving for carbohydrates. Both of these needs become stronger as winter advances.

> In general, when winter comes what my body wants to do is hibernate. When it's dark I want to go to bed and pull the covers over my head and sleep. I have to force myself out of the house. I find myself going to bed earlier and earlier and daydreaming about going to warm places, feeling more negative about life in general. Mostly it's a sense that I can't stand it one minute more. Get me out of here!
>
> 40-YEAR-OLD WOMAN

To a casual acquaintance a person with SAD may not appear to have obvious difficulties, but those who have the condition can suffer severely. They are likely to have no energy and great difficulty listening attentively, thinking, and concentrating, as if they had the flu. They become so withdrawn that the thought of going to a party is agony. Although some experience no change in their eating patterns or eat less than usual, eating most often becomes compulsive.

> I got to the point that I was into binge-eating so much that I joined an eating-disorder group. When I was extremely anxious my automatic response was to look for those high-calorie foods, and I would eat them and eat them and eat them. I feel very successful this year because for the first time I have not gotten into the Halloween candy. There was one year—and of course it would be the end of October—where I went through a hundred little bars of candy before Halloween ever came, and I had to go out and buy a whole new bag of it.
>
> 41-YEAR-OLD WOMAN

In severe cases of SAD, weight gain in winter can reach 30 pounds, and the pressure to sleep extra hours—sometimes until afternoon—is so great that a normal workday schedule is impossible. Some of those with SAD go through only one or two of these behavioral changes, but always on a regular, seasonal basis. Added to these behaviors is often self-blame for not being able to meet the everyday demands that come from others or from within.

> I have very high expectations of myself and I used to blame myself for not living up to them. I would berate myself for my bad, undesirable qualities: laziness, lack of patience, wanting somebody to take care of me, wishing I didn't have to work so hard. Thinking that these were all personal bad qualities made it all the harder.
>
> 55-YEAR-OLD WOMAN

In the spring, the feelings and behaviors of those with SAD reverse, and they become highly mentally alert and creative, energetic, sociable, and optimistic. They usually eat less and may lose most of the weight gained during the winter. Some people experience even more markedly opposite behavior in the spring or summer—becoming hyperactive, with greatly decreased need for sleep and food, and signs of talkativeness, grandiosity, and exaggerated sexual drive. Although the majority appear to experience this mood swing as positive and exhilarating, in some cases it is extreme enough to become a behavior problem called hypomania, a mild form of mania.

SAD in children and adolescents is generally milder and less clear-cut than in adults. Nonetheless, the condition impairs a child's functioning and can lead to difficulties in school. The children and adolescents treated for SAD tell of fatigue, sleep changes, increased or decreased appetite, carbohydrate craving, and headaches. They experience problems in school and/or withdrawal from activities with their peers. All of these reactions leave with the coming of spring.

In taking a closer look at SAD, physicians have discovered other characteristics that link it to the seasons and to light. Many people with seasonal mood swings seem especially drawn toward sunlight. They prefer houses with many windows, and keep the hedges trimmed low and the windows unshaded. They shop in brightly lit supermarkets at night, and may walk around their own houses or apartments turning on lights.

> I notice every moment of sunshine during the day. Any variation in light I notice. And I get this tremendously strong feeling when I'm lying on the beach in the sunshine: I always feel as though this weight is being lifted off me. It's really physical, it seems to be. I can lie there and feel something lifting.
>
> 40-YEAR-OLD WOMAN

For the susceptible, a move to a poorly lit office or home can bring on despondency.

> I used to work in an office up on a high floor with windows overlooking space and I had sky out the window. Then I changed jobs and had an inside office with no windows, and even the rooms with windows looked into an inside air shaft. You couldn't see the sky—and I need the sky.
>
> 55-YEAR-OLD WOMAN

Many people with SAD say they have good and bad days, both during and after periods of depression, and that these mood swings are related to weather conditions. A spell of cloudy weather can cause depression, even during summer. Some improve when they take winter holidays in the mountains, and even feel better after visits to a solarium. Traveling south often has a positive effect. Conversely, moving from a southern to a northern climate can initiate depression.[14] Even moving from a sunny to a cloudy part of the same country can cause the first of a series of seasonal depressions.

> My problem in winter clearly started when I moved from Kansas to Boston. The feelings I had that first winter were noticeably different, particularly getting on the streetcar in the morning in the darkness to go to work, and coming out of work in the darkness to come home. I remember being acutely aware of feeling like a mole and hating it. I felt like I was living underground and desperately yearning for the light. I didn't know how I was going to survive the winter again.
>
> 55-YEAR-OLD WOMAN

People who are seasonally depressed show other differences in their bodies' rhythms. For example, those with SAD appear to conceive their children more often during late summer than at any other time of the year, as opposed to the general U.S. population, which shows a peak in conception in winter. In fact, some researchers have observed that women who have SAD do not conceive in winter. This may be due to the lack of sexual interest associated with depression, or to changes in a depressed woman's ovulatory cycle.

The quality of sleep also appears to alter during the winter months in the seasonally depressed. The phase of deep sleep called delta decreases, whereas the phase of dreaming and rapid eye movement (REM) increases. Some researchers speculate that these differences may be related to earlier rhythms in humans or to the seasonal rhythms of hibernation, reproduction, and feeding in some animals.

Researchers note that many of the symptoms of SAD, such as increased consumption of high-carbohydrate foods, increased appetite and weight, decreased activity and sexual drive, and social withdrawal, are energy conserving behaviors. Conversely, the spring/summer behaviors dissipate energy. The changing seasons are associated with changes in energy requirements and food availability, natural stimuli for these behaviors. Animals can go through dramatic preparations for seasonal survival: from thin to fat (or vice versa), from dark coat to white, from sexually active to disinterested, from active to lethargic. Some investigators are drawn to the idea that SAD could be related to seasonal rhythms similar to those in certain animals, although this theory is controversial.

Sunlight or extremely bright lamps have the power to regulate secretions of the hormone melatonin. Melatonin has been especially interesting to some SAD researchers because in animals it signals how long the days and nights are and consequently what season it is, when to mate, and when to hibernate. These observations inspired investigators to try treating SAD by artificially producing "spring" with light powerful enough to imitate the sun and alter melatonin secretions.

Bright-Light Therapy

> I finally decided that I would have to make a personal adjustment to my problem with winter. It does make me feel somewhat unique, and everyone wants fellow sufferers, or at least acknowledgment, and I wasn't getting it. When I read about this light study in the newspaper I was thrilled. I mean, I'm always thrilled when someone comes up with scientific evidence to prove what I already knew. I cut the article out, duplicated it, sent it to a couple of people I used to live with and said: Look! What I have is real.
>
> 40-YEAR-OLD WOMAN

The idea of treating depression with artificial light is not new. As early as 1924 a British researcher observed: "It is obvious what a stimulating and beneficial influence artificial sunlight can exert on those whose fund of energy is seriously depleted by nervous or mental disorder, especially during the dull, sunless, and depressing months of our British winter."[15] Since the 1980 discovery that high-intensity artificial light can suppress melatonin secretions, studies using light to treat SAD have been continuously under way.

Researchers frequently use lamps of approximately 2500 lux, the amount of light to which one would be exposed by looking out a window on a sunny spring day. This is five to ten times brighter than ordinary room lighting. The light is placed at eye level, and study participants are usually instructed to sit about three feet from the light and to engage in their usual activities such as reading, writing, or eating. They then report their responses on a daily basis and are interviewed by a trained clinician according to a standard depression rating scale for SAD. The timing and dosage of the light vary widely. Some researchers expose participants daily to two hours of bright light in the early morning; others use light in the evening instead of (or as well as) the morning light (two to six hours total); a third group experiments with two to four hours of bright light at midday. A few studies have used a mere half-hour of bright light in the morning or evening, or have had the participants scatter the timing within certain limits.

> I borrowed the lights from the psychiatrist who was doing this study and took them home for two weeks. I was supposed to sit under them an hour a day, letting them shine on both sides of my face. She gave me a list of times to choose from so that I could fit it into my work schedule: early morning, noontime, or early evening. She told me that any time was fine but not to use the same time twice in a row. This worked for me. In general the lights gave me a tremendous sense of well-being no matter when I used them. It was something I looked forward to—the actual experience of sitting there under the lights.
>
> 40-YEAR-OLD WOMAN

People with SAD report a sense of calmness and alertness under the lights, and frequently an energy surge after approximately 20 minutes. They feel more cheerful and energetic, sleep and eat less, concentrate well, become sociable, and stop craving carbohydrates. In many cases they feel and behave as they would in spring or summer. These changes frequently take place within two to three days of beginning therapy. Once light therapy ceases, those with SAD often relapse into depression within a few days or weeks, although for some who have a milder form of SAD the beneficial effects can last longer.

A review of 29 studies conducted in the United States, England, and Switzerland shows that the early morning appears to be the most clearly beneficial time to use the lights. [16] However, some find that another time of day is best, or that improvement is equal using light in the morning, midday, or evening. For some people, a higher intensity of light, around 10,000 lux, makes them feel better in a shorter period of time. This intensity is the level of light outdoors within half an hour of sunrise.

Research also suggests that exposure to properly timed light of normal room intensity (less than 500 lux) can alleviate SAD. [17] For example, a bedside light apparatus that simulates the gradual dawn light of a spring day is effective in some people with SAD, even though most of the light exposure occurs during sleep. Some researchers suspect that the pattern of the dynamic twilight signal is especially effective on the body's biological rhythms, and that the eye is acutely sensitive to light during the twilight hours. These factors may explain the surprising effect of relatively weak light even through closed eyelids.

How Does Light Work?

Research shows that it is mainly the visible light waves entering the eyes that produce antidepressant effects, with the waves in the green region of the sun's spectrum being perhaps the most beneficial. [18] Most studies indicate that the invisible light of the ultraviolet range is not necessary in treating SAD, although some people may respond to ultraviolet or infrared light on the skin rather than through the eyes. It is not clear, however, in what way visible light through the eyes exerts its beneficial effects. Researchers have proposed various theories, some concerning light's reinforcement of the body's oscillating rhythms, others having to do with advances or delays in the timing of rhythms.

However, studies are conflicting, and explanations of how light works are still controversial. Light therapy may work differently in different people, and in a more complex manner than originally thought, involving numerous hormonal interactions. Besides melatonin, other hormones under study include serotonin, norepinephrine, prolactin, and thyroxine, as well as other hormonal secretions of the adrenal glands and thyroid. Some researchers speculate that light may also influence mood and behavior independently as well as through its effects on the circadian system.

Experiments suggest that the positive response to light may involve the way the eyes send information to the brain.[19] After light therapy, those with SAD experience an improvement in their attention and reaction to visual information. This could explain why some of those with SAD say that their faces, especially their eyes, change after light therapy.

> The anxiety when I need the light and can't get it is tremendous. I can do without it for three days, but I know that by the fourth day I'm going to be in trouble. I can always tell by my face when I need the light. My face goes through a transformation—my appearance actually changes. I don't know if I can define it but it is through my eyes. On the third or fourth day without light, my eyelids swell and there is a strain in my eyes. I always felt that I looked so much better with a tan in the summer, and I always assumed it was the tan. I now realize it is not the tan, it is the light.
>
> 41-YEAR-OLD WOMAN

Apparently reactions to light therapy are individual, with different people responding to different lengths of light exposure as well as to various strengths of light. These variations may be related to the person's unique sensitivity to light, geographical origin, and depth of depression.

> I had a friend, an older woman about thirty years older than me who had never even heard of SAD. But yet, on the suggestion of her doctor, she sat in front of a makeup light for an hour every day. Now she had absolutely no knowledge of SAD! She had a home in New Hampshire and one in Florida. And she said to me, "You know, it's the funniest thing, when I go to Florida I don't need to do this."
>
> 41-YEAR-OLD WOMAN

The suspicion remains that bright light may simply act as a placebo, or sugar pill. That is, since the depressed expect to be helped by light therapy, their strong belief itself may actually bring about the improvement. Some depressed people evidently improve with the dim yellow light often used by researchers as a control, or means of comparison. This supports the idea that light therapy simply acts as a placebo. However, the suspicion that bright light acts only through the power of the imagination is contradicted by investigations in which dim light had no effect, and by the powerful statements made by those who undergo successful treatment.

> When someone first suggested that I stare at light bulbs four hours a day, my initial reaction was: "You've got to be kidding." I was totally turned off to this idea. I was totally resistant except for the fact that I was desperate. The first couple of days it was agony. On the third day it wasn't so bad. By the fourth day I had such remarkable improvement—not only improvement but I found

> a certain comfort in the light. And once I get
> into it, that's how I feel. And when I'm having
> a hard time, then it's my light I want.
>
> 41-YEAR-OLD WOMAN

Also, the percentage of those responding to bright-light therapy is unusually high, and this response has been shown separately in many different treatment centers. In all, 75 to 85 percent of seasonally depressed people treated so far have improved as a result.[20]

Light therapy has important positive aspects. Improvement is rapid and can be repeated, because the body evidently does not become less sensitive to light as it does to some drugs. Therapy does not disrupt one's daily routine. It can be started or continued at home or even at some workplaces. Perhaps most crucial, a person who uses light therapy actively participates in the therapy and can often dictate its timing. This gives the depressed person a greater sense of control, so necessary to mental and physical health.

> I hate these feelings in winter. They disrupt the
> flow of my life and I resent them. Talk about
> powerlessness! In November it's this tremendous
> feeling that I'm sliding down a dark tunnel. I
> know I'm going to get depressed and sad and
> unhappy, and there's nothing I can do about it.
> Now I have access to these special lights, and
> this is the first time I have ever felt that there
> was something I could do about it.
>
> 40-YEAR-OLD WOMAN

Bright artificial light can also have negative effects. Under the influence of light therapy some depressed people become unusually and nervously active and irritable and experience eyestrain, headaches, nausea, or insomnia. A few discontinue light treatment for these reasons, although a reduction in the dosage of light or a change in the timing can sometimes eliminate any uncomfortable effects. In general, light strength and duration must be individually adjusted to avoid either a lack of response as a result of underdose, or undesirable effects resulting from overdose. Light acts on those with SAD as a drug and should be carefully monitored.

Research indicates that artificial light of the strength used to treat depression can harm the skin and eyes if it contains the ultraviolet A and B spectrum.[21] The lamp's rays may be powerful enough to cause cataracts to form in the eye or to damage essential molecules in the skin such as deoxyribonucleic acid (DNA), increasing the risk of skin cancer. The fact that some people develop a tan from ultraviolet rays during light therapy indicates its potency. However, this potential for harm depends somewhat on the type of lamps used. Lamps containing ultraviolet A and B are less safe yet no more effective for most people than lamps emitting a minimum of ultraviolet radiation. For these reasons some researchers now strongly recommend lamps that exclude the ultraviolet range as far as possible for safety's sake.

Pregnant women have participated in light therapy, although questions of any risks concerning its use during pregnancy are not yet answered. Some researchers think that until data on light therapy during pregnancy are available, the therapy is preferable to depression for both mother and fetus. The mother's body chemicals are probably enhanced by the therapy, possibly improving the fetus's rhythmic environment. However, each woman needs to weigh the possibility of risks against light therapy's benefits.

Other Mental Afflictions and SAD

> One should be especially on one's guard against the most violent changes of the seasons . . . and the most dangerous: both solstices, especially the summer solstice, both the equinoxes, especially the autumnal.
>
> HIPPOCRATES, ca. 400 B.C.[22]

Research on SAD has prompted some investigators to try to place it within the context of other mental problems. Many aspects of SAD are found in other forms of depression, suggesting that the underlying causes could be the same. The majority of those who have been treated for SAD report a family history of depression or mania, and familial alcohol-related problems are common.

The 24-hour rhythms of eating and sleeping are important components of many mood disorders. For example, most forms of depression include some form of sleep disturbance, with the depressed sleeping for either unusually long or short periods. Quite by chance, researchers discovered that some forms of depression evidently feed on sleep. After an all-night discussion with a therapist, severely depressed people were suddenly free from all symptoms of depression. Sleep deprivation had a repeatedly cheering effect, and when allowed to sleep again, the depressed relapsed into gloom. Some researchers suspect that sleeplessness works as an antidepressant because it alters sleep cycles that are out of time with other internal rhythms. The depressed also frequently experience either a loss of appetite or, in the case of SAD, a ravenous appetite with cravings for certain foods.

Depression in general is associated with disturbances in the 24-hour rhythms of hormonal messages sent from the hypothalamus to the pituitary and adrenal glands and back again. These messages involve hormones that are known to affect mood. One of the most important of these hormones is cortisol, which is normally produced on a 24-hour cycle. In a depressed person that cycle is often disrupted so that the level of cortisol in the blood remains high when it should be low. Similarly, the hypothalamus sends signals to the thyroid gland, which secretes its hormones accordingly. Disturbances in this circadian cycle can affect a person's moods and activities. People with very low levels of thyroid hormones are often listless and apathetic, while those with high levels may be anxious and tense.

In general, there are remarkable rhythmic trends in mental afflictions other than those classified as SAD. One seasonal rhythm is the reverse of SAD: a few people become regularly depressed in summer and hyperactive and energetic in winter. Many of those who suffer from depression have seasonal rhythms, with peaks in the spring and fall.

Mania is a disorder characterized by extreme nervousness, activity, and sleeplessness, which contrasts with the sadness, lethargy, and drowsiness of depression. Some people experience alternating periods of extreme ups and downs called manic depression. Some of those who are manic-depressive have seasonal rhythms in their moods, becoming either manic or depressive in spring and/or fall. Some researchers now think that the rapid increase or decrease in light during these seasons causes hormonal turbulence, stimulating extremes in mood in the susceptible. This might help explain the fact that suicides peak in the spring, with a second peak in the fall. [23]

> I've had six hospitalizations for manic-depressive illness. All of them have been in the fall or in the spring. I have had both manic and depressive episodes in the spring and fall, so I associate the spring and fall with my mood disorder. My doctor feels that in the spring I'm getting manic or depressed because the amount of sunlight is increasing rapidly, and my body has a hard time adapting to that. In the fall the opposite thing is going on, and again I'm having a very difficult time adjusting to that from day to day. He explained that there are certain receptors in the brain that are affected by the amount of sunlight, and the receptors take in the sunlight and create different chemical reactions within the brain based on the amount of sunlight that they get.
>
> 36-YEAR-OLD MAN

Mental afflictions can also have monthly rhythms in intensity. Many nurses working in psychiatric wards notice increased agitation when the moon is full. Some people with manic depression say that they are more emotional during the full moon.

> There are seven of us in my therapy group, and we all seem to feel that during a full moon our emotions are likely to be more feverish. We're likely to get into arguments, to be depressed, to be crying. There's a great deal of turmoil around a full moon. In my own case I don't necessarily feel that it's the amount of moonlight. But *that* particular phase of the moon seems to coincide with some real emotional intensity.
>
> 36-YEAR-OLD MAN

Evidently these observations are not new. The word *lunacy* stems from the Latin word for moon, because intermittent "insanity" was thought to be caused by changes in the moon.

Mental illnesses can also have cycles longer than a year, or shorter cycles of 48 hours or less. One study shows that among the manic-depressive, the manic phase is associated with three- to four-hour advances in body temperature rhythms, and with an earlier bedtime compared to the depressive phase.[24] Those who have a disorder called schizophrenia often have extremely early bedtimes, around 7 P.M., in spite of encouragement from others to stay up later. Studies show that the 24-hour body temperature rhythms of those with schizophrenia are advanced in timing compared with similar rhythms in other people.[25] Epileptic fits can be rhythmic, with some afflicted people having a daily fit at almost the same time every 24 hours. Some extreme personality changes show 48-hour rhythms, with a person undergoing a complete personality change from one 24-hour phase to the next, living in effect two separate lives on alternate days.

These rhythmic associations among many forms of mental affliction appear to point to the body's circadian system as an underlying link. Abnormal biological rhythms are perhaps triggered by stress-related changes in the brain in those susceptible, or by a flaw in the way the brain interprets light.

Further evidence supports the theory that circadian disorders may contribute to psychiatric disturbances. For example, people whose sleep-wake cycles are experimentally shifted suffer severe emotional reactions, including depression and hostility. Conversely, some of those suffering from depression cease to feel depressed when they try unusual bedtimes—for example, going to bed at 5:00 P.M. and arising at 2:00 A.M. Researchers presume that this "treatment" is effective because it coordinates the sleep-wake cycle with the body's other circadian rhythms, which are set abnormally forward in time, causing depression.

Further clues lie in the success of drug treatment for depression or mania. Psychiatrists have long used drugs such as lithium and sodium valproate to treat certain mood disorders without knowing why the drugs are effective. Animal studies show that both of these drugs alter circadian rhythms.[26] Some researchers think that the drugs act on a specific chemical within the brain called gamma-aminobutyric acid, which resets one of the brain's pacemakers according to the light-dark information from the eye. Other research suggests that such drugs act by altering the way the brain interprets light.

Some investigators who are studying the pieces of this puzzle have begun experiments with light treatment for depressions other than SAD. The results of these studies so far have been conflicting. However, work in progress indicates that certain types of depression may be alleviated by light therapy.[27]

There are many open questions concerning SAD and other disturbing mood changes. Whatever the answers may prove to be, it seems that we and the health professionals who care for us can benefit from a greater awareness of the possible effects of light and biological rhythms on our mental health. Therapists may otherwise mistakenly attribute mood problems solely to past childhood experiences or to current problems in relationships or at work. Those of us who are parents, teachers, or counselors may wish to keep the possibility of SAD in mind when a child's school difficulties appear to be seasonal.

New discoveries on depression and mania have broad implications in the field of mental health and in future psychiatric training and research. The idea of studying the eye and understanding wavelengths of light is new to psychiatry. In training future mental-health professionals, it could be useful to strengthen the combination of psychiatry, the study of mental disorder; neurology, the study of the brain and nervous system; and endocrinology, the study of hormones. These three fields may be inextricably intertwined when it comes to the practical matter of helping those in need.

> I had been hospitalized during a manic episode in April. About the middle of the following August I got very depressed. I would feel very low upon waking up in the morning and feel very good about going to bed at night. And I'd go to bed early—about nine o'clock at night. I would wake up in the morning on weekends and have crying fits—I didn't know what to do, where to turn, or how to make myself better. I just didn't know what to do besides dying. . . . I was hospitalized after trying to kill myself on September 20th, right on the fall equinox. As a matter of fact, it was a rainy day.
>
> 36-YEAR-OLD MAN

Understanding the effects of light on our moods can also help those of us who are mildly but noticeably affected by light deprivation. Sadness at Christmas may not always be due to the loneliness of those who do not or cannot celebrate this holiday. For those who do celebrate, Christmas and Hanukkah can be ideal rituals to help carry us through the shortest days of the year.

Those of us suffering from more severe mental disturbances often see ourselves as odd or weak-willed. Our moods tend to be surrounded by a mystique, making it more difficult for us to bear them. Comprehending our problems can help remove the stigma and make it easier for us to accept our behavior, help ourselves, and seek appropriate treatment.

Labeling SAD was very helpful for me. It allowed me not to forget the connection between my behavior and winter and got me over the self-blame. So that if I start having a sinking feeling I say to myself: "It's all right, Joanna, you know what this is, you'll be all right, you can ride with it, it will pass." So I am able to reassure myself rather than blame myself.

60-YEAR-OLD WOMAN

The idea is to ride it out. For example, I was recently very worried about my coming job evaluation that I have every October. I was afraid the evaluation would be bad, and I was anticipating that things in my job would soon be in very serious turmoil. But now that I think about it I realize this is not really so much what's going on in my job as what's happening to me because of the fact that it's now getting dark at seven o'clock and two months ago it was getting dark at 8:45. It's a big difference, an hour and a half of light.

36-YEAR-OLD MAN

Helping Ourselves through the Dark Times

As information on SAD increases, those with the condition are getting together for mutual help. Support groups have sprung up in several parts of the country. You can contact NOSAD, the Washington, D.C.–based organization for seasonal affective disorder, listed in the Resources section, to ask if a group exists in your area. Consider starting a support group yourself by putting a notice in your local newspaper and in the NOSAD newsletter. The newsletters of both NOSAD and the Society for Light Treatment and Biological Rhythms provide current information on SAD and on light therapy.

111

For day-to-day living with SAD, the following suggestions may be useful:

1. Try to spend at least one hour a day outdoors during daylight hours. During the winter this may mean taking a walk during your lunch hour, or taking short midmorning or early-afternoon breaks. You will benefit not only from the light but also from the air and exercise.
2. If possible, work and live in rooms with windows that let in plenty of light. Avoid offices with no windows.
3. During the day, go to the window and look at the sky at frequent intervals.
4. If you have the time and money, take a winter trip to a place in a southern latitude. Not only will the trip be helpful, looking forward to it will be therapeutic as well.

> For me depression was cumulative. Even though in February it begins to get lighter, I felt it most severely then. It's as if by sheer willpower I held myself together through the worst of it and then couldn't stand it any longer. So when my kids had February vacation I made sure we went south for a week.
>
> **55-YEAR-OLD WOMAN**

5. Allow yourself to eat the food you crave.

> I used to overeat because I would snack on all the healthy food in the refrigerator—all the leftover protein, all the leftover veggies—and still not feel satisfied. Then I would give in and eat five cookies at the end. Now I just let myself have the five cookies. They are what I really want anyway.
>
> **55-YEAR-OLD WOMAN**

6. Remind yourself that your moods have a cause and that they are not "your fault."

7. If your depression is lasting and interferes with your happiness and daily activities, seek help from a trained professional experienced in diagnosing and treating SAD. Call the Light Therapy Information Service listed under Resources to locate one in your area.

CHAPTER 6

Skin and Bones

J UST AS LIGHT entering the eyes coordinates chemical changes within us, so rays of solar energy cause chemical reactions within the skin, the body's largest organ, as well as in the eyes themselves. Visible rays in the blue spectrum act on the eyes alone. Those acting through the skin as well as on the eyes are invisible ultraviolet rays, subdivided according to wavelength as ultraviolet A, B, and C, shortened to UVA, UVB, and UVC (see Figure 3 in the Introduction).

The amount of ultraviolet radiation that reaches us and affects our health is determined by a series of filters through which the rays must pass. About one-third of ultraviolet radiation is absorbed by water and by ozone, a form of oxygen in the earth's atmosphere. Ozone absorbs UVC so strongly that these wavelengths generally do not reach the earth's surface. It also filters UVB, which varies in intensity according to the ozone concentration.

Once the rays reach our skin, their penetration is filtered once again by a pigment in the skin called melanin. The amount of melanin we are born with determines our skin color. Varying amounts of melanin bring a palette of interesting tones to the skin's outer layer, from shades of pale beige through hues of yellow, olive, sienna, and chocolate brown. The more melanin in the skin, the darker it is and the less ultraviolet can pass through.

When we expose our bodies to ultraviolet rays, the radiation can strike the surface of the skin and penetrate to deeper skin layers. The effects of ultraviolet radiation depend on the seasonal angle of the earth to the sun, altitude, latitude, time of day, length of sun exposure, and age and skin tone of the person involved. Given the right circumstances, some of the skin's cells will use ultraviolet radiation to benefit the body's skeleton.

BUILDING BONES

The "Sunshine" Vitamin

When the sun reaches the skin, units of radiant energy in the UVB range, called photons, which can pass through the ozone and melanin barriers, penetrate into the skin. A chemical called provitamin D_3 within the skin's outer layer (the epidermis) and second layer (the dermis) absorbs these photons and is transformed into previtamin D_3, the precursor of a hormone. Within three days this prehormone turns itself into a complete hormone called vitamin D, also known as the "sunshine" vitamin.[1] Once this chemical process in the skin is complete, vitamin D enters the bloodstream, attaches itself to a special protein, and travels to the liver and kidney, where it is modified into its final form for active use in the body's bone-building process. Vitamin D is essential for the balance of calcium and phosphorus necessary for a healthy skeleton.

If you are light-skinned, young or middle-aged, live close to the equator, and step out into the noontime sun in June, your exposed skin will begin producing previtamin D_3 within 5 to 10 minutes.[2] Actually, at any age, anywhere, and any time between

115

9:00 A.M. and 5:00 P.M., a light-skinned person's skin makes all the vitamin D it is going to make in a relatively short time. The timing can vary, but researchers estimate that within about 15 to 30 minutes of exposure to spring or summer sun, previtamin D_3 reaches a plateau.[3] Once this plateau is reached, sunlight destroys further previtamin D_3 no matter how much longer you remain in the sun. This control prevents the skin from producing a vitamin D overdose. The body can build up stores of vitamin D in fat cells for later use, but too much stored vitamin D can be poisonous to the body. In some people, vitamin D stores acquired in the spring and summer sun can last throughout the winter.

If you are of African or Jamaican ancestry, your skin's melanin provides a stronger filter of UVB rays than in a person of, for example, northern European ancestry. For this reason, although your skin has the same capacity to produce vitamin D as that of a lighter-skinned person, you may need as much as six times more sunlight for the necessary chemical reaction to take place.[4] Presumably, those with shades of deep olive or brown skin indigenous to areas around the Mediterranean Sea require sun exposure somewhere between the timing of the very light- and the very dark-skinned.

Time of day, season, altitude, and latitude greatly influence the capacity of the skin to produce previtamin D_3. Time of day determines the intensity of UVB rays, which are 10 times more powerful around midday than after 3:00 P.M.[5] The latitude and season also determine the angle and, therefore, the intensity of the sun's rays. For example, at the latitude of New York City, the total amount of UVB reaching the earth is seven times higher in summer than in winter.[6] The altitude determines how focused or scattered the UVB rays are when they reach you. These influences are so strong that the level of vitamin D in your blood corresponds to the latitude and altitude of your place of residence. Vitamin D levels can fluctuate with the seasons; they are likely to be highest at the close of summer and lowest at the end of winter. If you live in Boston, vitamin D conversion from sunlight will be highest in June and July, but the sun on your skin from November through February will not boost your vitamin D at all. [7] People living only 10 degrees north of Boston will not convert vitamin D from October through March, whereas residents of Los Angeles can synthesize at least some vitamin D even in January, but less than those living in Puerto Rico. [8]

Bone Growth and Resorption

Vitamin D synthesis takes place even in the simplest life forms. Scientists do not yet know what function vitamin D has in single-celled organisms, but they are certain that no vertebrates, including humans, could exist without it because of its importance in building bones.

Like all other parts of our bodies, bones are continuously in the process of cyclic change. New bone builds on the outside, while inner layers of old bone are reabsorbed into the body. We essentially have a new skeleton every 10 years. Nonetheless, bones remain the same size during early to middle adulthood, since bone-building and resorption occur at equal rates. This is not true in childhood and adolescence, when bone-building outstrips resorption, causing bones to grow in size. Nor is it true from midlife (between 35 and 40) into old age, when bone resorption gradually exceeds bone gain and bones become somewhat hollow and less resistant to pressure, jarring, and bending.

At all ages, the body forms new bone by laying down a mixture of bone-forming cells (osteoblasts), a protein (collagen), and a cementlike substance. Together these make up the bone matrix, or reinforced concrete of the body. At the same time, minerals such as calcium and phosphorus begin depositing in the matrix, making bones our hardest tissue.

Throughout life, our bodies require exercise to encourage the bone-building process, as well as an adequate dietary supply of bone-building minerals and substances to help the body absorb and use minerals. For example, an adequate supply of vitamin D is essential because it enables the intestines to absorb calcium and phosphate so that bones can use them.

Since two sources of bone strength, vitamin D and exercise, are often associated with outdoor activities, it is not surprising that our bones can have seasonal rhythms of strength. Studies of postmenopausal women in Scotland show that bone mineral content rises from winter to summer and falls from summer to winter.[9] Vitamin D activities are higher in summer than winter, and phosphorus and calcium levels rise from winter to summer, with the intestines absorbing calcium best in summer and worst in winter. The underlying cause of these seasonal changes is likely to be the increased exercise during sunny seasons and vitamin D synthesized by the spring and summer sun, although biological rhythms regulated by seasonal light changes may also play a role.

For children, one of the results of inadequate vitamin D is a bone disease called rickets. When a child's body does not have sufficient vitamin D, the bones cannot mineralize properly. Consequently they soften and become deformed by the weight of the body. During the eighteenth and nineteenth centuries, European and some American cities grew denser, and young children played mainly in narrow, sunless alleys. New industries added air pollution, which screens out ultraviolet light. This combination brought years of semidarkness to inner cities, and rickets affected up to 90 percent of children in some of the largest cities.[10]

As awareness of the problem grew and vitamin D began to be added to milk and other foods, rickets was almost completely eliminated. However, in the United States and some other countries rickets appears to be reemerging in small numbers as a disease of inner-city children. Children with darker skin who live in northerly latitudes are more prone to develop rickets than their light-skinned neighbors, especially during the winter months. This is evidently true of black children in the United States and of Asian children in Scotland. Added dangers for children of all skin tones are inadequate amounts of vitamin D from fortified milk, fish, or from a daily supplement such as cod-liver oil.

Adults can also suffer health consequences from vitamin D deficiency. If the body has too little vitamin D the bone matrix, a rubbery substance that has been laid down by osteoblasts, cannot be mineralized. This condition, called osteomalacia, softens the bone. It is essentially the same condition as rickets in children but can occur at any age in adulthood.

A more familiar form of bone weakening is called osteoporosis, a potential problem of our older years. Osteoporosis is the result of a combined loss of bone matrix and bone mineral, leaving bones porous, brittle, and unusually susceptible to fractures. Basically, osteoporosis is a worsening or acceleration of the normal aging process. Both osteomalacia and osteoporosis can lead to bone fractures in our older years, making sufficient vitamin D a cause for concern.

Many of us drink little or no milk as adults, possibly thinking that vitamin D is essential only for the growing bones of children. Perhaps for this reason, in spite of the availability of vitamin D–fortified foods in the United States, vitamin D deficiency may be a problem among some elderly people. Preliminary studies suggest that in many cases, low vitamin D is associated with hip fractures, a cause of disability and even death among the aged.[11] Since the sunlight of northerly latitudes is too weak to produce vitamin D during the winter, those living in Canada and the northern parts of the United States, Europe, and the Soviet Union may risk developing rickets or osteomalacia by the end of winter unless they eat plenty of vitamin D–rich foods or take vitamin D supplements. One study of young men on a normal (but not vitamin D–fortified) diet showed that when deprived of sunlight for five or six weeks, their bodies' stores of vitamin D were depleted, and calcium absorption began falling after only three weeks.[12] For these reasons adults and children alike take cod-liver oil during the winter in northern Norway, where the sun does not rise above the horizon for two months. They call the substance "bottled sunshine."[13]

The elderly have the additional problem of skin changes with age. For unknown reasons the skin's content of provitamin

D_3 decreases with increasing age, and its ability to produce pre-vitamin D_3 can fall by more than half, making a vitamin D–rich diet essential in our older years.

THE DARK SIDES OF SUNLIGHT

If the production of vitamin D were the only effect of UVB on the skin, we could simply try to stay outdoors as long as possible during the warmer months. Unfortunately, vitamin D production is the only indisputably positive effect of ultraviolet light on the skin.[14]

At the same time that UVB rays are encouraging the skin to produce vitamin D, those same rays and others can cause a host of different chemical events, some of them in the eye. Just as the skin acts as a barrier to protect the internal cells and organs from ultraviolet damage, so our eyes have protective shields, the lens and the cornea. The lens, a tiny oval capsule, lies immediately behind the iris, the colored part of the eye, and the pupil, the opening in the iris. The lens absorbs ultraviolet waves and protects the eyeball, especially the retina, from harm. Normally the lens is transparent and focuses light on the light-sensitive cells of the retina, which transmit visual information to the brain.

Chemical changes in the transparent proteins of the lens can cause it to become cloudy or even opaque, forming what is called a cataract. In some people, cataracts seem to occur as a result of cell changes in the normal aging process. However, evidence is strong that ultraviolet light stimulates cataract formation.[15] Studies indicate that the UVB wavelengths are those causing the damage, although UVA may promote the effects of UVB or cause harm on its own.[16] Some researchers suspect that the chemical tryptophan within the lens proteins is susceptible to changes resulting from ultraviolet light. With time the proteins become pigmented and may lose their transparency.

In the United States cataract surgery is the most common surgical procedure for those over 65. In India and Africa, where

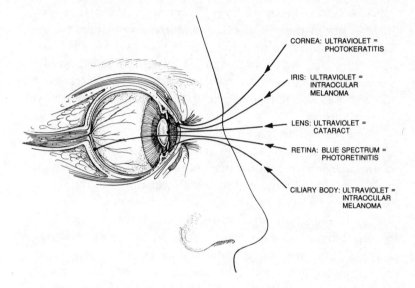

CORNEA: ULTRAVIOLET =
PHOTOKERATITIS

IRIS: ULTRAVIOLET =
INTRAOCULAR
MELANOMA

LENS: ULTRAVIOLET =
CATARACT

RETINA: BLUE SPECTRUM =
PHOTORETINITIS

CILIARY BODY: ULTRAVIOLET =
INTRAOCULAR
MELANOMA

Figure 11. *The sun's harm to the eyes.*

the skin's melanin protects against the near-equatorial sun, the eyes have no similar extra protection. Cataracts and resulting blindness are a major social and economic burden in these countries. Physicians and paramedics from England and the United States fly in and establish "eye camps," performing hundreds of cataract operations each day. [17]

UVB can also cause temporary but painful damage to the cornea, called photokeratitis. This damage is generally caused by sunbathing on a sandy beach or skiing without wearing sunglasses or goggles. These outdoor activities can lead to a powerful dose of ultraviolet light because snow and sand reflect UVB, causing it to radiate from below as well as from above.

Studies suggest that the ultraviolet spectrum of sunlight is an important factor in developing cancer of the eye called intraocular malignant melanoma. [18] Possibly this eye cancer is related to the skin cancer called melanoma since the same cells, called melanocytes, are involved. Those with darker skin have the least risk of this eye cancer; among those with lighter skin, brown eyes bring the least risk, while blue eyes are the most vulnerable. Unprotected sun exposure during childhood may be especially hazardous for those most vulnerable to eye cancer, since the lens does not fully function as an ultraviolet screen until young adulthood.

Even visible light in the blue spectrum is potentially harmful to the eye, damaging the retina in high doses. Such damage is not a concern for most of us, however, because high doses from sunlight are only acquired by staring into the sun, a pastime to which our eyes have a natural aversion.

Theoretically, artificial light could harm our eyes with the same blue and ultraviolet wavelengths. Actually, we are largely protected from such harm by our natural aversion to staring at any uncomfortably bright light, making acute eye injury due to artificial light rare. Nonetheless, the possibility of slow, cumulative eye damage, such as cataract formation, is a concern for those using bright lamps as therapy for problems related to biological rhythms. Many researchers now strongly suggest that people undergoing such therapies should use lamps emitting a minimum of ultraviolet radiation, because the ultraviolet range is evidently unnecessary in treating most people.

Simultaneously, ultraviolet waves cause harmful chemical events in the skin, changing the way skin looks and feels, and affecting our health. Part of the purpose of some of the skin's molecules is to absorb ultraviolet radiation so that it will not penetrate deeper into the body. However, these same molecules, such as DNA (deoxyribonucleic acid), RNA (ribonucleic acid), and the proteins keratin, collagen, and elastin, are also essential to cell function and reproduction. For a fraction of a second after absorbing ultraviolet radiation, the molecules are in an excited state and undergo changes that harm the skin's cells. Some rays penetrate to deeper layers, causing blood vessels to swell and giving light skin the reddish hue of sunburn. Even exposure too brief to redden the skin can harm the cells' DNA. To make matters worse, biological rhythms in epidermal cells may cause DNA content to reach a peak around noon, exactly the time when the sun is most potent.[19] However, studies on epidermal rhythms are conflicting.

Once molecules have been damaged, the skin takes action to defend itself and the tissues beneath it from further harm. Melanocytes swell and branch out in their efforts to produce more melanin. Melanin rises like a cloak to shield the vital molecules below. What we know as heightened color or a tan is melanin's defensive reaction to radiation. Simultaneously, cells in the epidermis divide rapidly for several days, causing the outer skin layers to thicken to about twice their normal depth. These changes help the skin adapt to the seasons and add further layers of protection for the body's inner tissues. Nonetheless, they are a sign that skin damage has already occurred. Damage accumulates with each exposure to the spring or summer sun, even if each exposure is brief. In a sense, the skin must sacrifice itself as protector of the body's inner organs.

The darker the skin, the more sun is required for this chain of harmful events to unfold. A person who tans easily, for example, is less susceptible to further damage than one who only burns and freckles in response to sun, since in the tanned person melanin has risen strongly as a shield. However, a tan is not a badge of security. First of all, a tan induced mainly by UVA rays, such as those used in many tanning booths or home tanning devices, is less protective against further damage than a tan caused by UVB rays. This is because UVA rays penetrate more deeply and induce color in the basal layer of skin, whereas after UVB exposure melanin rises upward through the epidermis and stratum corneum, the outer layers of skin. Secondly, a tan acquired over the summer offers only limited protection against further burning. Such a tan can take only two to three times more sun than untanned areas before it flares up again. Nature offers far better protection. Those who have moderately pigmented skin, such as shades of olive or pale brown, can take three to five times more sun before burning than those of paler hues. The very dark-skinned of a deep chocolate brown can take up to 30 times more sun without burning.[20]

Assessing Your Risk of Sun Damage

Dermatologists currently divide skin types into six categories of sun sensitivity, from the most to the least vulnerable to ultraviolet radiation.[21]

1. Always burn, never tan
2. Always burn, then slight tan
3. Sometimes burn, always tan
4. Never burn, always tan
5. Heavily pigmented (for example, darker Mediterraneans, Native Americans)
6. Most heavily pigmented (usually of African or Jamaican origin)

Those with skin types 1 and 2 often have light skin and blue eyes, may be redheads, and may or may not freckle. However, some people with dark brown hair and blue or green eyes have type 1 or 2 skin.

Chemically Induced Sensitivity

Some of us become unusually sensitive to sunlight through eating or touching chemicals that increase the skin's reaction to the long waves of ultraviolet radiation called UVA. Some perfumes and colognes contain oil of bergamot, an extract of the peel of an orange grown in southern Europe. This oil contains 5-methoxypsoralen, which responds dramatically to UVA, causing bizarre configurations on the neck where the scent has been applied and trickles down. These and other responses are usually transitory but can persist for weeks or months. In some cases, harmful cosmetic articles already removed from the market are still causing severe reactions in those who used them because the ingredients induced a permanent hypersensitivity to sunlight.

Drug and Cosmetic Ingredients That Can Cause Hypersensitivity to UVA

Uses	Generic or Chemical Name
Acne treatment	Retinoic acid (tretinoin), Retin-A
Antiseptics, deodorants, antifungal agents	sulfonamides (sulfamethoxazole, sulfisoxazole, trisulfapyrimidines), nalidixic acid, trimethoprim and sulfamethoxazole, halogenated salicylanilides, halogenated carbanilides, halogenated phenols
Antibiotics	tetracycline and tetracycline derivatives: chlortetracycline, demeclocycline, doxycycline, methacycline, minocycline, oxytetracycline
Anticonvulsants	carbamazepine, trimethadione
Antidepressants	amitriptyline, desipramine, doxepin, imipramine, nortriptyline, protriptyline
Antidiabetics (glucose-lowering agents)	sulfonylureas (acetohexamide, chlorpropamide, tolazamide, tolbutamide)
Antihistamines	diphenhydramine, promethazine, triprolidine, chlorpheniramine
Antimicrobials/anti-infective agents	griseofulvin
Antipsoriatics (also used in cosmetics)	coal tars and coal-tar derivatives, wood tars, and petroleum products
Diuretics (and antihypertensives)	chlorthalidone, furosemide, thiazides, and combinations
Dyes	acridine, anthracene, eosin (in lipstick), erythrosin, fluorescin, methyl violet, methylene

Uses	Generic or Chemical Name
	blue, orange red, rose bengal, toluidine blue, trypaflavin, trypan blue
Estrogens and proges-terones	mestranol and norethynodrel, diethylstilbestrol
Melanogenics (also used in cosmetics)	furocoumarins (5-methoxypsoralen, 8-methoxypsoralen, 4,5,8-trimethyl-psoralen)
Nonsteroidal anti-inflammatory drugs	benoxaprofen, ibuprofen, naproxen, piroxicam
Perfumes and toilet articles (essential oils in cosmetics)	containing: ethereal oils, oil of bergamot, oil of cedar, citron, lavender, lemon, lime, rosemary, sandalwood, musk ambrette
Sunscreens	containing: benzophenone, PABA, PABA esters, porsol 1789
Tranquilizers	chlorprothixene, doxepin, haloperidol, loxapine, thiothixene; phenothiazines: acetophenazine, chlorpromazine, fluphenazine, perphenazine, prochlorperazine, thioridazine, trifluoperazine, triflupromazine

Adapted from FDA Consumer, *Department of Health and Human Service, HHS Publication No. (FDA) 81-8149, reprinted from October 1980.*

Those whose skin is sensitized in this way can develop a rash even from fluorescent lamps or from sun exposure through a window glass. Transparent glass can block some or all UVB depending on its manufacture, but not UVA.

    Carrot processors, celery pickers, and others who are in continuous contact with certain vegetables can react severely to UVA. Carrots, celery, and other plants contain a substance called psoralen, which becomes active when exposed to UVA, causing the skin to flare up in sunlight. Simply handling a plant while gardening does not seem to cause psoralen to irritate the skin, but getting the plant's pulp or juice on the skin might.

Some people have an inherited tendency toward extreme sun sensitivity. This condition, called porphyria, causes the skin to sting, burn, and swell when exposed to sunlight, leaving scars from broken blood vessels in the skin, and in some cases damaging cartilage. The porphyrias are a group of genetic disorders that occur when the body produces large amounts of porphyrins, pigments highly sensitive to the visible range of the sun's rays. This problem can be latent in the body and not show itself until middle age. Years of taking estrogens, such as those found in birth control pills, or of drinking alcohol can eventually bring on some types of porphyria in those predisposed. This is a particularly disabling condition since the skin cannot be exposed to visible light without harm, even indoors through closed windows or under fluorescent lights.

For those without a special light sensitivity, the possible effects of fluorescent light on the skin are a matter of debate among researchers. Rays from light bulbs are only a fraction of the strength of the sun, and they have much less potential for harm. Nonetheless, fluorescent lamps, the most widely used lighting in workplaces, emit measurable quantities of ultraviolet waves. This is especially true of the high-intensity brands. Researchers disagree on how much UVA, UVB, and UVC such lamps produce, and the amount can vary from one lamp to another. Some researchers state that most diffusers in lamp fixtures absorb all UVB, while others say fluorescent lamps do send out UVB radiation and some emit UVC as well. Fluorescent lamps are undoubtedly a source of small amounts of UVA. Some calculations suggest that exposure to fluorescent lamps could result in cumulative skin damage, including increases in skin cancer.[22] Nonetheless, whatever skin damage is caused by artificial light, it is only a small part of the total harm done to the skin through sun exposure.

The lamps used in light therapy for mood or sleep problems may also harm the skin if they emit light in the ultraviolet range. However, this potential hazard can be avoided. As mentioned earlier, lamps with only barely measurable amounts of ultraviolet light are apparently just as effective in treating most people.

Skin Aging and Skin Cancer

Over the years we walk countless times out into the spring and summer sun, or play and lie on beaches. Countless times the skin reacts to sunlight, and damage accumulates. UVA penetrates into the deeper skin layers, altering the balance of connective tissues and causing sagging and fine wrinkling. UVB permanently changes the skin's surface, which becomes coarse and acquires a mottled coloring of brown spots and dilated capillaries in those with paler skin. Even infrared light, which we feel as heat, may contribute to the process. Although we may think of these changes as inevitable signs of aging, they are solely due to sun damage and do not occur in sun-protected areas of the body at any age.[23] In other ways, however, sun damage can be seen as an acceleration of the normal aging process, especially the damage in deeper skin layers, and other skin changes on the surface such as dryness, cracks, and bruises.

Simultaneously, other sun-induced alterations take place. With age the skin loses some of its ability to perform its vital functions, such as sensing danger or pleasure, healing wounds, and producing oil and sweat. Research suggests that ultraviolet radiation accelerates these losses.[24] In addition, ultraviolet rays appear to encourage the very essence of the skin's aging process by shortening the life span of cell strains in both the dermis and epidermis. The more rapidly cell strains die, the weaker and "older" the skin becomes.

With time, if too much damage has occurred, skin cells can become disordered in size and build small, sometimes colored scabs of horny skin here and there on sun-exposed parts of the body. This condition, called actinic keratosis or solar keratosis,

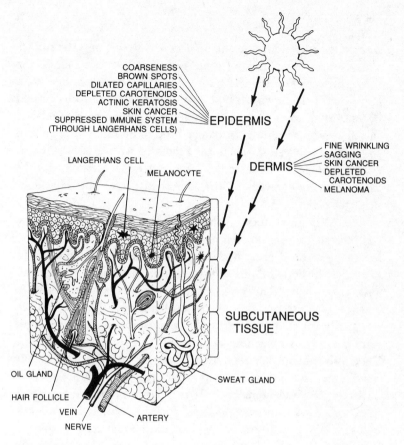

Figure 12. *The sun's harm to the skin.*

is more frequent among the light-skinned and is a warning that cells may eventually lose control of their growth and become cancerous. Actinic keratosis develops predominantly in midlife and old age. Unfortunately, during these same years the normal aging process reduces the skin's ability to produce melanin, the body's major barrier against ultraviolet light. In our older years the skin also cannot respond to injury or repair damage to a cell's DNA as well as it once could.

These events help to pave the way for irretrievable damage to the DNA of skin cells, leading to cancer of several types of skin cells. Basal cells and squamous cells grow along the surface of the skin, and cancers of these cells usually spread along the skin's surface as well. The term "skin cancer" commonly refers to cancers of these two cell types, which can be successfully treated by surgery in most cases. Ultraviolet rays appear both to initiate these cancers through DNA damage and to promote their growth by stimulating certain chemical processes within each cell and cell membrane. Animal studies suggest that UVA encourages the cancer-causing damage of UVB and can also act alone to produce skin cancer. [25]

When melanocytes, the cells that produce melanin, grow out of control, the possible consequences are more dangerous. Melanocytes lie deeper in the skin, and cancerous melanocytes can enter the body's fluids and spread to distant parts of the body with fatal results. This type of skin cancer, called melanoma, is apparently caused or promoted by ultraviolet light. When we repeatedly expose ourselves to ultraviolet radiation, melanocytes react not only by branching and swelling but also by multiplying. They also multiply in response to a single powerful dose of ultraviolet radiation, familiar to us as a blistering sunburn. Research indicates that melanoma can be triggered or promoted by one or more painful blistering sunburns during childhood or adolescence, and, in some cases, by cumulative sun damage over a lifetime. [26] Evidence suggests that UVB contributes to both the initiation and growth of melanoma. [27] The numbers of people afflicted with melanoma vary with geographical location, with the greatest prevalence among those living near the equator. Melanoma incidence also appears to fluctuate in cycles. These cycles may be caused by cyclic changes in the sun that increase the ultraviolet rays reaching us, although this theory is controversial.

A Link to the Immune System

Ultraviolet rays also endanger our health in ways only recently discovered. The skin contains cells that belong to the body's immune system. One type is called the Langerhans cell, which resides in the skin's outer layer and spots potentially harmful substances, passing them on to be destroyed by other immune cells. Langerhans cells normally decrease with age and can further decrease by as much as 50 percent in habitually sun-exposed skin, compared with the sun-protected skin of the same person.[28] Relatively low levels of ultraviolet radiation can also incapacitate Langerhans cells, which then cease to pass on harmful substances to be destroyed. Instead, harmful substances slip by the Langerhans cells and stimulate suppressor lymphocytes, cells that suppress immune reaction. Since suppressor lymphocytes circulate throughout the body, what begins as a local effect of ultraviolet light becomes a suppression of the entire immune response.

Ultraviolet radiation also alters the numbers and proportions of various immune cells in the blood and decreases the activity of so-called natural killer cells that destroy virus-infected and cancer cells.[29] Even brief sunbaths in the midday summer sun can deplete carotenoids, the body's active form of vitamin A, which resides in the skin.[30] Evidently women lose more vitamin A than men after the same dose of ultraviolet light. Most of these alterations appear to return to normal within two weeks of sun exposure, but some persist for longer.

The discovery that the skin mediates between sunlight and the immune system is relatively new, and all that this may imply for our health is not yet known. However, research already indicates that the ability of ultraviolet light to suppress immunity can depress the skin's allergic response to poisons and may play a fundamental role in the development of skin cancer.[31] Normally the immune system protects against skin cancer as it does against all other diseases. Ultraviolet light, however, not only induces skin cancer but prevents the normal immune response against it. This link may also explain how ultraviolet light contributes to the growth of melanomas on parts of the body not exposed to the sun.

Researchers do not yet know if ultraviolet light interferes with the body's resistance to other types of cancer or to infectious diseases. Some organisms that produce disease gain entry into the body through the skin, and some viruses, bacteria, and fungi produce disease within the skin. Animal studies on the effects of ultraviolet radiation on infectious diseases are in progress.

A Glance into the Future

The protective layer of ozone that filters the ultraviolet light reaching us has already decreased an average of around 2 percent over the past 20 years.[32] Ozone-depleting chemicals, called chlorofluorocarbons, are likely to continue damaging ozone in the stratosphere for many years, in spite of the agreement of several countries to achieve an 85 percent reduction in such chemicals as soon as possible and a complete halt by the year 2000. Chlorofluorocarbons are used in foam insulation, fire extinguishers, refrigerants, and air conditioners, and in manufacturing cars, electronic parts, and computer chips. They are released into the air and eventually rise to the stratosphere. A chlorofluorocarbon molecule takes at least 40 years to reach the ozone layers, so that the effects of full production still lie ahead, as well as the unknown potential of continuing chlorofluorocarbon production at a slower rate for several years.

When left unharmed, the naturally thin layer of ozone is very efficient in absorbing ultraviolet rays from the sun. Although the sun sends out large amounts of UVC, UVB, and UVA radiation, only the UVA and a very small amount of UVB actually penetrate through ozone and reach the surface of the earth. The amount of ultraviolet radiation in sunlight that reaches the earth is dependent on the concentration of ozone molecules in the atmosphere.

One of the major consequences of ozone damage will be an increase in the amount of ultraviolet radiation reaching us. This is especially true of UVB waves, but ozone damage could also increase the already large amounts of UVA. The possible consequences to our health are difficult to predict, but apparently every percentage point of lost ozone will count. According to predictions, for every 1 percent reduction in ozone, basal and squamous cell carcinomas will increase by 3 to 6 percent and melanoma will increase between 1 and 1.5 percent.[33] The incidence of eye cataracts is likely to rise, and the effects on the immune system could be a cause for alarm. If the need to avoid sunlight becomes extreme, health problems related to desynchronized biological rhythms may increase. Although the light-skinned will suffer most, people of all skin hues will have an increased risk of ultraviolet-related assaults on health.

LIVING WITH ULTRAVIOLET LIGHT

Studies on ultraviolet light have raised many health-related questions. We want to know the best ways to protect ourselves from ultraviolet rays, and how much direct sunlight is both healthy and safe. We wonder if we should always wear sunscreens, or if this would block too much of the skin's ability to produce vitamin D. This is an especially vital question for light-skinned women around the years of menopause or older, who may be concerned about osteoporosis. There are no answers to such questions suitable for all of us, because so much depends on skin shade, age, and special vulnerabilities such as unusual sun sensitivity. However, some information is available that is useful in deciding the best course for each of us.

Sunscreens and ultraviolet light. Many sunscreens absorb radiation in the UVB range but offer no protection from UVA. The higher the sunscreen's SPF (sun protection factor) number, the greater the UVB protection, with those rated SPF 15 or higher giving good UVB protection. Only sunscreens containing benzopherone or porsol 1789 give some UVA protection as well.

However, even when sunscreens prevent sunburn and skin damage, they may not protect against suppression of the immune system.[34] Perhaps ultraviolet light affects the immune system independent of visible skin damage, a point of controversy among researchers. The dark-skinned could be equally vulnerable to immune suppression, but this is not yet known. For these reasons, sunscreens should only be considered a supplement to protective clothing and broad-brimmed hats.

Sunscreens and vitamin D.   Unfortunately, exactly those rays that sunscreens absorb best, namely the UVB range, are those that synthesize previtamin D_3 in the skin. Experiments show that even a sunscreen of SPF 8 can interfere with the skin's synthesis of vitamin D.[35] This poses a dilemma for those who want to protect the skin yet get a sufficient amount of vitamin D. However, you need not be concerned about getting too little vitamin D from sunlight unless you are deficient in this vitamin. You can request a blood test to ascertain your vitamin D level, called 25-OH-D, keeping in mind that it is likely to vary with the seasons. A level at or above 10 ng/ml (nanograms per milliliter) is usually considered sufficient.

Vitamin D from food and supplements.   A few foods and food supplements are also good sources of vitamin D and do not depend on sunlight to make them biologically active in the body. Depending on the latitude of your home during the winter months, you may need about 400 IUs (international units) of vitamin D a day exclusively from foods such as fortified milk (one quart provides 400 IUs), a spoonful or tablet of cod-liver oil, or multi-vitamin pills containing vitamin D. Eggs, liver, and some fish also contain vitamin D but in smaller, fluctuating amounts, some of which can be lost in the cooking process.

Exposure to the sun.   Some researchers suggest using sunscreens constantly and making sure your diet is sufficient in vitamin D. Or, you might compromise with sporadic (once or twice weekly) exposures to the sun using no sunscreen. Between the hours of 10:00 A.M. and 2:00 P.M. Eastern Standard Time, or 11:00 A.M. and 3:00 P.M. Daylight Savings Time, only 10 to 15 minutes of sun on hands, arms, and face without sunscreen two or three times a week should suffice for vitamin D synthesis, depending on your age and skin shade.[36] During earlier or later hours between 9:00 A.M. and 5:00 P.M., 15 to 30 minutes should suffice.

Artificial light. If you are unable to go out of doors due to long illness or disability and are low in vitamin D in spite of a vitamin D–rich diet, you could consider using an especially bright artificial light, one that includes the ultraviolet spectrum, for a few minutes each day. Two studies on middle-aged and elderly men exposed to a lamp that simulated weak summer sunlight showed that the men had better calcium absorption after one month.[37] Use the light only under your doctor's supervision and have your vitamin D levels checked to see if the light works for you. Remember that sitting by a sunny but closed window is not likely to improve your vitamin D, because window glass absorbs some or all UVB radiation. If you are mobile, walk rather than sit in the sun. The exercise will also help strengthen your bones.

Sunglasses. Your eyes also need protection. The Food and Drug Administration now requires that sunglasses be labeled as "cosmetic," "general purpose," or "special purpose," according to the protection they provide from ultraviolet light. Read the brochure, available at stores, describing the appropriate uses for each type of lens. If you have had cataract surgery, your surgeon may have implanted the newer artificial lenses with UV-absorbing pigments. If this is not the case, your eyes now lack the protection of a lens and you will need to wear sunglasses consistently, at least in spring and summer, and perhaps tinted glasses year-round. Even with the new lenses you may need extra protection. Discuss your need for sunglasses with your ophthalmologist.

Drugs and UVA sensitivity. Be aware that certain drugs may make the lenses of your eyes more sensitive to UVA. These include sulfonamides (prescribed for certain urinary tract infections, bronchitis, and other bacterial infections); phenothiazines (prescribed for severe psychiatric problems such as depression and schizophrenia); and psoralens (prescribed for the skin condition psoriasis).

Vitamins and cataract prevention. Some research indicates that vitamins C and E may help prevent cataract formation.[38] In one study the cataract-free people averaged 300 to 600 IUs of vitamin E and 300 milligrams of vitamin C daily.

Diet and skin cancer.   Animal studies suggest that a diet high in unsaturated fat encourages the development of skin cancer, perhaps by promoting a process called peroxidation, a chemical step toward cancer.[39] Unsaturated fats are liquid at room temperature and include vegetable or nut oils such as safflower, soy, and linseed. Conversely, vitamin A (beta-carotene), vitamin C, and a food additive called BHT (butylated hydroxytoluene) are being tested for their possible protection against skin cancer.

CHAPTER 7

Wellness and Disease

W HEN YOU WALK into your doctor's office for a routine checkup, keep in mind that you are not the same person in the morning as you are in the afternoon, nor are you the same person in summer as you are in winter. Because of your body's rhythms, coordinated by the cycle of sunlight and darkness, your fluids and tissues are in a state of constant cyclic flux, changing with the time of day and the season. If you are a woman, you also have monthly rhythms throughout your menstruating years and, on a more subdued level, even after menopause. Therefore, when your doctor listens to your heart and lungs, tests your blood pressure, checks your weight, and takes blood and urine samples, the exam is capturing only one moment in the body's fluctuating time. This is like "taking a snapshot of a roller coaster," and results in a static and therefore inadequate picture of the internal motions that define your health.[1]

137

THE ROUTINE PHYSICAL

Every cell in the body has numerous parts, and each part has daily tasks. Most cells also reproduce themselves, not by mating but by dividing. As a cell divides, the mother cell passes on the vital information of what the daughter cells will be and do. Eventually the mother cell dies, the daughter cells divide, and thus the generations of cells continue. Cell division ensures that each cell knows its own place and function within the body; it knows when to divide, and when to die. Each cell's functions have circadian rhythms, and every cell is part of a network of cells that helps determine the particular circadian rhythms of each organ or fluid. At any given time of day, cells in different parts of your body are at different stages in their daily functions, depending on the organs to which they belong.

Since cells have a circadian time structure, your body's fluids and organs will be at different stages depending on when the physician examines them. For example, the doctor or nurse will check your blood pressure by wrapping a cuff around your upper arm, inflating it, and listening to the pulses that occur as the arteries contract and expand with the pressure of blood pumped by the heart. Blood pressure refers to the amount of pressure on an artery as blood is pushed through it. Your physician will note your blood pressure as two numbers: the systole number, referring to the greater pressure as the heart contracts, and the diastole number, the lower pressure as the heart relaxes.

However, blood pressure is notoriously difficult to pin down. It fluctuates with emotions and activities, and even differs according to body posture (sitting, lying down) at the time of measurement. It also fluctuates independently with the time of day. Generally, all of us have higher blood pressure in the afternoon and evening than in the morning, and some have dangerously high blood pressure only at night. Rhythms in blood pressure are influenced by the size of the arteries, the force of the heart's contraction, the amount of blood being pushed through, and by adrenal hormones, all of which have circadian rhythms.

(However, rhythms in blood pressure, as well as other rhythms in health and disease discussed below, pertain to people on the usual cycle of sleeping and waking, and do not necessarily hold true for night workers.)

Next, the physician will ask you to take a few deep breaths so that she or he can listen to your lungs. The lungs also vary in capacity throughout the day. At night the airways to the lungs are less ample, the lungs are less powerful, and the hormones that expand the bronchial tubes are at a low level. These changes leave you more susceptible to respiratory problems at night, a time when your doctor is unlikely to examine you.

If your health-care practitioner takes your temperature as well, she or he will consider anything below 98 or above 99 degrees Fahrenheit as a sign of trouble. However, these interpretations are too narrow, since they do not take into account the normal circadian flux of body temperature that drops in the evening and rises in the morning.

The contents of your blood and urine samples also will vary widely in the course of the day, depending partly on the phase of the hormones circulating through and out of the body, as well as on rhythms in white blood cells.

Your physician will listen to your heart. The rate at which your heart beats varies over the course of the day and night, normally increasing during the day, with a peak in the afternoon. Sometimes this peak coincides with the peak in body temperature. The heart's circadian rhythm is built into each heart cell. Even when the heart is destroyed, individual heart cells that are kept alive in laboratories continue to beat with a circadian rhythm.

Heart rate may be synchronized to the body's other rhythmic functions by the light-dark cycle. Apparently, most people who live near or within the Arctic Circle and have adapted over generations to the extreme seasonal differences in light do not suffer changes in heart rhythm when the sun becomes scarce or disappears during the winter. However, some Antarctic explorers unused to living without sunlight experienced alarming differences in their heart functions. During the long polar darkness their hearts became unsteady, irregular, spasmodic, easily disturbed, and extremely changeable from day to day. The explorer Dr. Frederick Cook perceived that "the sun seems to supply an indescribable something which controls and steadies the heart. In its absence it goes like an engine without a governor."[2]

WHEN YOU ARE ILL

> That period of twenty-four hours formed by the regular revolution of our earth, in which all its inhabitants partake . . . is apparent in all diseases.
> **CHRISTOPHER WILLIAM HUFELAND, M.D., 1797**[3]

Just as we are not equally alert and responsive at all times of day, so are our bodies not equally capable at all times of resisting assaults such as infections, diseases, or poisons. The body has daily, monthly, and seasonal rhythms in its level of tolerance and susceptibility. These are our "times of least resistance."[4]

For example, generally we are most sensitive to pain at night and least sensitive during the afternoon. Of course, specific health conditions have their own rhythms of pain: rheumatoid arthritis is often more painful in the early morning, while low-back pain increases with the pressure of sitting during the day. Rhythm in pain sensitivity simply means that our experience of a continuous pain varies, perhaps due to the rhythms of a natural painkiller within our bodies, or to rhythms in brain function.

Some health conditions are also rhythmic in their effects. These rhythms are related to the normal ones in the organs involved. For example, breathing difficulties in asthma are much more common during the night and upon awakening in the early morning than during the rest of the day. This is logical since the lungs and air pathways are rhythmically predisposed toward breathing difficulties during the dark hours. This circadian susceptibility is worsened by the fact that the lungs are adversely affected by lying prone. At night the airways are also more sus-

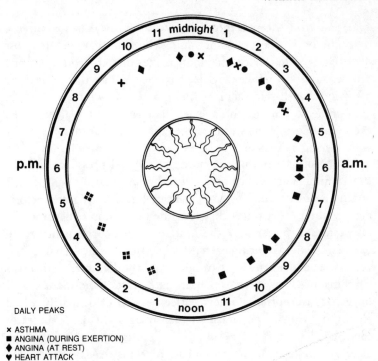

DAILY PEAKS

x ASTHMA
■ ANGINA (DURING EXERTION)
♦ ANGINA (AT REST)
♥ HEART ATTACK
● STROKE (BLOOD CLOT)
❖ STROKE (BURST ARTERY)

Figure 13. *Hours of least resistance.*

ceptible to the chemicals involved in the body's allergic response. For this reason, if you have asthma, one brief daytime
exposure to a substance to which you are allergic can cause repeated nightly asthmatic attacks. In addition to this circadian
rhythm, many women who have asthma experience more frequent and/or more severe attacks immediately before or during
their menstrual periods, presumably because of changes in ovarian and adrenal hormones.

Because of the normal rhythms of the gastrointestinal
tract, those suffering from ulcers are likely to notice both daily
and seasonal rhythms in their discomfort. Gastric acid secretions
are lowest during the late morning and highest at night. There-

141

fore, pain from ulcers is most likely to occur or to be most intense at night or in the early morning. The fact that we are most sensitive to pain during the night makes matters worse. Animal studies suggest that we may also have seasonal rhythms in gastric secretions, with some acids reaching a peak in winter and others in summer.[5] This might help explain why peptic ulcers often recur only during one season of the year, with that season varying from person to person.

Normal rhythms in heart rate, blood pressure, and the functioning of arteries coincide with rhythms in heart pain, called angina pectoris, and rhythms in heart attacks. Angina pectoris occurs when the arteries that feed the heart muscle become obstructed and cannot give the heart enough nourishment. Some experience angina during exercise or exertion, most often between 6:00 A.M. and noon. This timing is partly due to the circadian rhythms in blood pressure, heart rate, certain hormones, and oxygen consumption. Others notice heart pain primarily while sitting or lying down, most frequently at night or in the early morning. This latter type of angina results from spasms in the arteries that feed the heart, and its rhythms may be partly due to the circadian difference in the flexibility of these arteries. Arteries are less flexible in the early waking hours than in the afternoon.

Heart attacks occur three times more often at 9:00 A.M. than at 11:00 P.M.[6] Perhaps the abrupt and often rushed morning shift from sleep to activity acts together with circadian rhythms in the heart, arteries, and blood, building too great a load in those predisposed to heart problems. Heart disease occurs most often in the winter in both the Northern and Southern Hemispheres,[7] bringing under suspicion seasonal rhythms in blood cholesterol levels and in certain adrenal hormones. However, in some countries with hot climates and no air conditioning, heart disease peaks in the summer as well as the winter, leading some researchers to suspect a combination of the body's innate rhythms and climatic harshness as the cause.

When the brain rather than the heart is deprived of

nourishment, the resulting damage is called a stroke. Strokes caused by a blood clot blocking an artery occur most often late at night when blood pressure is lowest, suggesting that a clot is most dangerous when the force of blood being pumped to the brain is weakest. Strokes caused by a burst artery occur most often in the afternoon, when blood pressure is highest. This type of stroke also peaks in the winter.

Those who have diabetes often notice periodic ups and downs in their condition. Diabetes occurs when the digested form of carbohydrates and starches, called glucose, cannot enter the body's cells to nourish them. Glucose needs the assistance of a hormone called insulin in order to enter the cells. A group of diseases called diabetes mellitus can occur if the body does not produce enough insulin, or if the cells become insensitive to it. Insulin has both daily and seasonal rhythms, and diabetes similarly has daily and seasonal rhythms of severity. The seasonal rhythms are most striking, with diabetics needing less insulin from late spring to early fall, and in summer experiencing a minimum of problems associated with the disease.

Even more common illnesses, such as colds and flu, are influenced by biological rhythms. The runny or congested nose we experience with a cold or flu is likely to be most troublesome in the early morning. Many of us have noticed that we are more likely to come down with the flu during the winter months. In fact, in both the Northern and Southern Hemispheres, infectious diseases of the respiratory system such as colds, flu, and pneumonia peak in the winter.[8] Menstruating women may also have monthly rhythms of infection, with bacterial infections more likely around the time of ovulation, and viral infections more common just before or during menstruation. Preliminary reports also suggest that we have daily rhythms in our susceptibility to infections, with bacterial infections more likely to begin during the morning, and viral infections during late afternoon or evening.

One explanation for these rhythms is the cyclic fluctuation in the immune system itself. The immune system attempts to

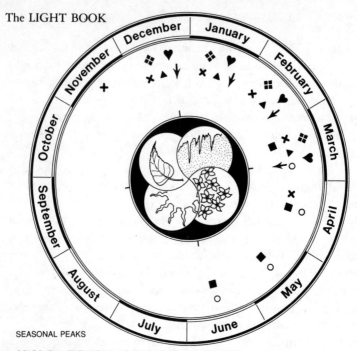

SEASONAL PEAKS

▲ COLDS, FLU, PNEUMONIA (AS IN NORTHERN HEMISPHERE)
× DIABETES (SEVERITY)
↓ SEMINOMA (DIAGNOSIS)
■ PROSTATE CANCER (DIAGNOSIS IN MEN UNDER 60)
○ BREAST CANCER (DIAGNOSIS)
♥ HEART DISEASE (AS IN NORTHERN HEMISPHERE)
❖ STROKE (BURST ARTERY)

Figure 14. *Seasons of susceptibility.*

protect us against all degrees of harm, from the common cold to
cancer. Our bodies produce highly specialized cells in the bone
marrow, some of which travel in the circulating fluids. Depending
on their specific function, immune cells recognize dangerous germs
or cancer cells and bind to them, engulf and digest them, inject
them with lethal proteins, send out warning signals, activate
other cells in the immune system, and signal the system to stop
when its task is complete.

So-called natural killer cells make up the first line of
immune defense against viruses, bacteria, and malignant cells.
This front line does not remain equally aggressive throughout

144

the day; it has a circadian rhythm of activity, with a peak in the morning. Some of the cells of the two essential arms of the immune system, called T and B cells, peak at night and have weekly rhythms as well. Animal studies show that the levels of T, B, and other immune cells are synchronized by the light-dark cycle.[9] The proper functioning of both T and B cells is vital for resistance to infections and to cancer.

In premenopausal women, certain immune cells are weakest around the time of ovulation. Some researchers think that the immune system suppresses itself at this time for fertility's sake, probably to restrain the immune cells from attacking and rejecting a fertilized egg. Natural killer cells apparently have a different rhythm, and are most active during the second half of the menstrual cycle.

Research on weekly, monthly, and seasonal rhythms in immunity is just beginning. However, reports from the Canadian Arctic already suggest that the two-and-a-half-month period of constant darkness in winter increases the resident Eskimos' susceptibility to disease.[10] The absence of direct sunlight may weaken immunity, partly by desynchronizing the immune system. However, this theory is controversial, and factors other than lack of sunlight could be responsible.

Diagnosis and Treatment

Drugs vary in their power to relax, cure, heal, or alleviate pain, depending on when they are taken. Your body can be completely unresponsive to a medicine taken at one time of the day or night, yet be highly affected by the same dose at another time. However, your physician is likely to tell you to take your medication on a fixed schedule, such as "three times a day, with meals." The purpose of this routine is to help you remember to take your medicine, and also to alleviate harm to the lining of the stomach by having it coated with food when the drug is taken. The false assumption behind this routine is that your body's functions are constant during the day and night, when in fact each cell, tissue, organ, and system of organs changes in time in its susceptibility to medicines. This holds true for a drug's potential to harm as well as its potential to heal.

In Western medicine, a few European scientists were the first to recognize the body's timed receptivity to drugs. In 1814 these scientists noted that opium and other drugs taken to relax the body should not be given in the morning but in late evening, because at this time "the forces of nature turn toward sleep and repose."[11] This observation itself slept for over 150 years until scientists in the 1970s began testing certain drugs according to the time of day they were taken. This testing continues, with optimal timing, called *chronotherapy*, partly established for certain drugs. The following list describes uses and effects:[12]

- *Aspirin:* to avoid harm to the stomach, take around 8:00 P.M.
- *Sleeping pills:* for greatest soporific effect, take close to the time that normal sleep would occur.
- *Antihistamines* (for colds and allergies): most will make you sleepy no matter when you take them; the exception is ter-fenadine, which will make you vigilant regardless of timing.
- *Bronchodilator* (for asthma): take one-third of the daily dose in the morning and two-thirds in the evening for best relief of asthma at night, when symptoms are most severe.
- *Steroids* (for asthma, rheumatoid arthritis, and other health conditions): reduce undesired side effects by taking in the morning and/or early afternoon.
- *Indomethacin:* take at noon for most effective relief of rheumatic pain and stiffness.

Special areas of study in chronotherapy are under way: the monthly response to drugs in menstruating women; drug timing for children, pregnant women, and the elderly; seasonal changes in a drug's effects; the power of some drugs to alter circadian rhythms; and the consequences of taking more than one drug at a time.

The Body's Rhythms and Cancer

Normal cells, as we have seen, have strict instructions about where they belong and when to divide. Cancer cells, however, may divide so rapidly that they take over an organ and prevent it from functioning normally. They can also travel to other organs and continue dividing there, having lost their sense of place and purpose. In many cases, if these cells cannot be controlled by the immune system, removed by surgery, or destroyed by drugs, they will eventually overwhelm vital organs.

Cancer cells have various rhythms. For example, some have a timing 12 hours out of phase with the organ's normal cells.[13] Evidently a cancer cell is either more or less harmful depending on the degree of its loss of normal circadian rhythms. Some researchers think that slow-growing tumors are partly made up of cells that divide in a rhythm similar to the organ's normal cells. For example, some breast cancer cells evidently divide according to the rhythms of sex hormones, just as normal breast cells do. Conversely, aggressive, fast-growing tumors mainly contain cells that have lost all normal rhythmicity.

A cell can lose its circadian rhythm for several reasons, perhaps the most common being damage to the cell's information code by poisons in food, water, or air; X rays; ultraviolet rays; and other sources. Our cells are not equally vulnerable to damage at all times of day. Animal studies show that potentially hazardous chemicals or X rays can be harmless or can induce cancer, depending on the time of day we are exposed to them.[14] While chemicals differ in their times of greatest hazard, X rays appear to be potentially more harmful during the day than in the late night hours.

In some cases, once cancer has developed, biological rhythms may play a role in its detection and spread. Cancer of the testicles, called seminoma, is most frequently diagnosed in the winter, presumably due to the seasonal changes in testicle cell division. Conversely, statistics from Israel and the United States show that women most often notice a malignant breast lump in the spring.[15] In one study, this seasonal rhythm of detection mainly occurred when breast cancer was at an advanced stage and already detectable in another organ as well. Researchers suspect that this seasonal rhythm reflects tumors that are growing rapidly due to a seasonal change in hormones such as estrogen, which can encourage the growth of breast cancer cells. Estrogen receptor levels are highest from April through June in postmenopausal women, and possibly in premenopausal women as well. Prostate tumors are also sensitive to estrogen. One study shows that in men under 60, the diagnosis of prostate cancer is seasonal and virtually identical to the pattern of breast cancer diagnosis.[16] Research also suggests that cells in the uterus and fallopian tubes have a seasonal sensitivity to the hormones estrogen and progesterone, but it is not yet known if this affects the spread of a growing cancer in those organs.

Treating Cancer Rhythmically

Knowledge of the rhythms in our bodies' cells can change the way physicians treat cancer. Currently, if you undergo surgery, radiation therapy, or chemotherapy, your treatment is scheduled for whatever time of day is convenient for health-care personnel and for you. In other words, each therapy is a shot in the dark, perhaps occasionally hitting cancer cells at the optimal time, but often not. Studies show that properly timed treatment of cancer can be beneficial. This is mainly true for radiation and chemotherapy, but may also influence the surgical removal of a tumor, called a biopsy.

Preliminary studies suggest that in premenopausal women who have breast cancer, the timing of a biopsy may affect the spread of the disease, with midcycle (ovulation) being the most favorable time.[17] Researchers do not know why this may be, but suspect that sex hormones interact with stress hormones secreted during surgery. The balance of these hormones then affects any circulating cancer cells, the immune system, or both. If this suspicion is confirmed by further data, then proper surgical timing could be invaluable to premenopausal women with breast cancer.

Tumor cells are most sensitive to radiation therapy at one particular time of day. A cancerous tumor has its own temperature, which can be measured; the time of peak temperature is when the tumor cells are most susceptible to radiation. A study on people with cancer of the mouth showed that their tumors shrank most rapidly when irradiated at the tumors' peak temperatures.[18] After two years, more than 60 percent of those treated according to the daily peak of tumor temperature were alive, while only 35 percent of those treated at lower tumor temperatures had survived.

Rhythms in cell activity are equally important in chemotherapy. Chemotherapy drugs attack all cells, normal and cancerous ones alike. When normal cells in the digestive tract are destroyed, vomiting and other severe digestive problems can result. Cell destruction can be life-threatening when the drugs attack immune cells in the bone marrow or cells in the heart muscle, leaving a person helpless against infections or prone to heart failure. Therefore, a chemotherapy dose high enough to curtail a spreading cancer is also often high enough to be severely disabling or fatal. If chemotherapy can be timed according to the rhythms in susceptibility of normal cells, treatment may be made more effective, less debilitating, or both.

A few research physicians are now giving chemotherapy on a circadian-timed basis, called chronotherapy, and comparing the results with untimed chemotherapy treatments. To date, people with kidney cancer, leukemia, and advanced cancers of the ovary, colon, and bladder have received chronotherapy. Of 63 women with ovarian cancer, all without chronotherapy died within three years, while half of those receiving chronotherapy lived at least five years.[19] Women who received timed therapy experienced less harm to the rest of the body, even while taking higher doses of the drugs (doxorubicin and cisplatin). Physicians achieved these results by timing the drugs to protect the digestive organs and bone marrow in order to attack the cancer with more powerful doses. They also calculated the kidneys' rhythms in ridding the body of poisons. All other chronotherapy studies show similarly promising results, although the approach might vary; for example, treating a kidney tumor with a constant infusion of drugs to ensure that the tumor cells are reached at their most vulnerable time.[20]

At least 15 commonly used anticancer drugs can be made more tolerable and perhaps more effective by proper timing, and further testing of these drugs on a variety of cancers is necessary. Ideally, physicians will eventually be able to time other anticancer therapies now being tested.

THE POSSIBLE FUTURE OF HEALTH CARE

Chinese physicians have known the importance of drug timing for more than 5000 years.[21] In China the type of treatment or drug dose a person receives can differ depending upon the time of day, day of the week, stage of the menstrual cycle, and the season. In Western medical tradition, Hippocrates noted in approximately 400 B.C. that the body's time structure must be taken into account. Presumably, health-care practitioners had recognized this fact long before any written records were made. Yet in Western medicine this perception did not take hold, and today the majority of physicians treat the body as though it were internally stationary.

This view of the body and of health care is slowly changing. Many physicians have begun to accept the principle that our bodies are rhythmically oscillating systems, as is all life. As more researchers study the time structure of life, called chronobiology, more of them will be teaching this concept in medical schools and including it in textbooks. Once physicians begin to redefine health through the study of rhythms, our future checkups and medical treatments may be quite different from those of today.

In the future, a physician may ask new questions, such as what time you go to bed and arise, and your usual mealtimes.

those who survive heart disease show a different pattern and timing of hourly ventricular ectopic beats than do those who die from the disease. If you planned to have surgery, you might prepare for it by rechecking your heart rate and blood pressure chronobiologically at home. Your surgery could be scheduled according to the time of day you can best withstand harm from general anesthesia, especially if you are older and therefore more vulnerable. If your surgery involved an organ transplant, it could be scheduled for a time in which your immune system is least likely to reject it. Studies show that the body rejects kidney transplants most frequently at multiples of seven to eight days; in other words, in weekly rhythms.[23] After any surgery, you and your health-care practitioners might be able to detect a potential infection with automatic body temperature monitoring at home or in the hospital. Some researchers think that core temperature taken chronobiologically can reveal the danger of infection before it takes hold and becomes obvious through fever.

In the future, breast biopsies may be timed according to the rhythms of the breast cells' sensitivity to the hormones estrogen and progesterone. This sensitivity is revealed in a cell's estrogen and progesterone receptors, which have daily, seasonal, and (before menopause) monthly rhythms. If the breast lump is malignant, the pathologist who analyzes the cancer would need to take these rhythms into account in order to provide correct information on the cancer. For premenopausal women in the future, biopsies or mastectomies may also be scheduled according to the possible effect of surgery timing on the spread of breast cancer, if such an effect is proved.

Our use of drugs may one day be profoundly influenced by chronobiology. Ideally, all drug labels would include information on proper timing along with the information already required by law. This means that when drug companies test their products for benefit and harm, they should be required to take timing into account, including the differences for age and sex. Already several European pharmaceutical companies are developing and selling drugs for asthma with regard to the day-night

The doctor might then show you how to take your own bl
pressure and offer you a self-monitoring instrument to take hor
This instrument would automatically record your temperat
and blood pressure several times during one day and night. E
newborns could be measured for vulnerability to high blood p
sure. Research shows that infants from families with a histor
high blood pressure have bigger daily swings in blood pres
than infants from families without such a history.[22]

Your physician might also record the rhythms of
immune system. In the future, changes in these rhythms
then be adjusted before you become unusually vulnerable t
fections or malignancies, and before disorders of the imm
system, such as rheumatoid arthritis, develop. Your imm
rhythms could also help you time the taking of drugs, from as
to chemotherapy. In some drugs the same dosage can e
stimulate or suppress immunity depending on the time of

If you are a woman, your physician might use sp
measuring devices and a computer to record seasonal rhyth
hormones such as prolactin, cortisol, aldosterone, estradio
sulin, and luteinizing hormone. You could also be asked
wish to wear a "chronobra" for a short while, a brassiere
with sensors to measure normal breast temperature rhythm
riodically, you might wear this bra to detect any chang
rhythm that could be signals of abnormal cells and breast c

Using these and other measurements, your physician
then draw up a chronogram, a diagram of your rhythms in h
Ideally, this diagram would reveal any early tendency tov
problem such as high blood pressure, heart disease, and p
even breast cancer and drug dependency. Some researchers
that we are born with the rhythms that predict our future l

If you become ill, your physician could use the
surements made during health as a comparison to help ass
problem. New measurements might help prevent or treat
example, if you had heart disease, your specialist could
24-hour electrocardiograph reading of your heart patter
analyze it to plan appropriate treatment. Over a five-year

differences in susceptibility to asthmatic attacks. Chronobiologists are in the process of examining several different types of medications in preparation for large medical trials on drug timing. These preparations include the study of meal timing and bright artificial light as ways of shifting certain rhythms, including those in the immune system and cell division. If circadian rhythms can be manipulated during medical treatment, it may become easier to time some drugs for the greatest benefit and the least harm.

Dealing with Current Medical Practice

By measuring your body's time structure, future physicians would acknowledge the uniqueness of your body while accepting the light-synchronized web of rhythms in us all. The study of each person's rhythms could encourage a more precise and individual approach to health care. Currently, however, very few physicians examine or treat their patients according to biological rhythms. Even when medical information becomes widely known among physicians, it can take years for the new knowledge to be accepted and put into practice, especially when it requires rethinking basic assumptions about the body and health care. Furthermore, the few doctors who are well versed in chronobiology may be impeded if they lack the computer systems and instruments required to record and correctly interpret a network of rhythms.

We can encourage change in our own medical care by informing ourselves and discussing chronobiological methods of health care with our physicians. The following suggestions may help:

1. If you take any drug included in the list under "Chronotherapy" earlier in this chapter, use the information in the list to help you decide when to take it. If your physician prescribed the drug, show her or him the list and discuss optimal timing.
2. If you are being treated for asthma, make sure your physician

is knowledgeable about treatment timing. This information is now widely available to professionals, and many already treat asthma chronobiologically. Find a specialist who does; or, if this is not possible, find one willing to help you obtain and read the three-part series on "Chronobiology and Asthma" in the *Journal of Asthma*.[24]

3. If you are undergoing chemotherapy for cancer, discuss the pertinent information in this chapter with your oncologist (cancer specialist). Ask him or her to consult with one of the researchers studying chemotherapy timing. (See the Resources section.) In general, keep in mind that chemotherapy does the least harm to the digestive system and urinary tract in the early evening hours. However, to protect the bone marrow and heart, the time of awakening (usually around 6:00 A.M.) is best.[25]

CHAPTER 8

Aging and Death

So Job died, being old and full of days.

JOB 42:17

OUR DAYS ARE numbered. But what is it that numbers them? How does the body know that it has to die, and what causes the gradual decline of old age? Like our nightly sleep, the physical changes that lead to the "great sleep" are still something of a mystery. Several theories attempt to clarify the body's passage to death, in which biological rhythms may play a part.

People of different cultures and different historical periods age differently. For example, some of those living in agrarian cultures may look quite old by middle age. Working in the sun ages their skin, and their teeth may have rotted through lack of dental care. Yet these same people may have stronger hearts, lungs, and bones, and better circulation than their sedentary, city-dwelling peers who look years younger. What we think of as inevitable signs of age are often the result of improper diet, stress, lack of exercise, and overexposure to the sun. However, it seems that no matter when and how healthfully we live, in late adulthood our bodies gradually lose resilience, fitness, and the capacity to function as they did when we were younger. In this chapter, the word "aging" will refer to this process.

The span of our lives appears to have an upper limit of 115 to 120 years,[1] and relatively few of us live even a full century. Although in the United States and several other countries the number of years we can expect to live has increased, the upper limit of human life remains unchanged. In evolutionary terms, members of each species are meant to live long enough to produce and raise offspring. As far as nature is concerned, what happens to us thereafter is unimportant. Aging and death are built into our bodies accordingly.

Although theories on aging vary, they all conclude that we age and die as a result of events that take place within cells. "Wear and tear" and "error" theories state that our bodies gradually lose their ability to repair damage from the environment or from within, and as a result eventually cease to function. For example, a cell's ability to repair its DNA, or genetic code, may decline with age. Cells may also begin to pass on erroneous genetic information to daughter cells. Unstable chemicals produced in the body, called oxygen free radicals, can damage cells. Such damage may accumulate over time, perhaps contributing to some diseases and to the general aging process.

Some researchers think that one or more "wear and tear" or "error" theories explain the process of aging and death. Others see them as part of a larger picture, which includes the "program" theories of aging. These theories suggest that our bodies have one or more internal clocks that time all or part of the life cycle: birth, growth, maturity, decline, and death. This set of theories brings aging and death within the realm of physical functions regulated by the 24-hour rhythm of light and darkness.

THE LIFE-CYCLE CLOCK

Scientists once believed that the body's cells could continue dividing forever. Given optimal conditions, they thought, cells, tissues, organs, and perhaps even human life could be immortal. Research has since shown that, ironically, the only known cells that can divide indefinitely are abnormal ones, such as cancer cells, also called immortalized cells.[2] Normal cells are mortal. In a laboratory, when normal cells are put into a dish, they will divide until the dish is engorged, then send and receive signals to stop dividing. Scientists do not know exactly why cells send the stop signal, but it is evidently a question of overpopulation: too little space and mobility. If the cells are then split into smaller groups and put in separate dishes, they will begin dividing again, and so on through repeated separations. After about 50 separations, however, the cells die no matter how much space and mobility are provided.

Because cells reproduce by dividing, they build families of identical twins. These families are called cell strains. Normal cell strains go through phases, including one of vigorous "youth" during rapid cell division. In the course of their divisions, cells age. They lose their capacity to build DNA; they accumulate color, or pigment, associated with age; and they go through many other changes associated with aging. Eventually they enter a phase in which their ability to divide is greatly reduced. Biologists call this the cell strain's *old age*.

Cells in a laboratory dish will divide at different rates, depending on the age of the person from whom they were taken. The older the person, the fewer times the cells divide before dying. In fact, research showing that rats and mice on a restricted diet live longer than their peers probably has nothing to do with any health benefits of cutting calories. Instead, "hungry" cells may divide more slowly, taking longer to reach old age and ultimate death. In Caucasian people, cells from the sun-exposed parts of the body divide fewer times than unexposed cells, showing the acceleration of the skin's aging process by ultraviolet light. This is one reason why people with the inherited sun protection of olive- or brown-toned skin tend to look younger than their lighter-skinned peers.

The timing of a cell strain's transition into old age and

death appears to be part of the genetic code within each cell's nucleus. Some researchers suspect that both the growth and the aging of cell strains are regulated by the same genes. These genes would then constitute the "ticking clock" of each cell strain's life span. In old age, as more and more cell strains die, the body's systems weaken, leaving us more vulnerable to diseases and to the breakdown of an organ's functioning. Some researchers think that the weakening of the immune system with age constitutes one of the major threats to life. However, even in ideal health, the heart muscle would eventually lose so many cells that it could no longer pulsate.

Aging and death may therefore be timed parts of the genetic code, just as growth, puberty, and menopause appear to be. Researchers now ask whether the timing of all these phases of life is centrally regulated. The very limitation of a cell strain's life span seems to require a biological clock that either counts cell divisions or measures recurring cellular events.[3] Some researchers think that cells must be controlled by a timing mechanism, a "life-cycle clock," which is able to switch various sets of genes on or off according to the phases of the life cycle. Such a clock would regulate the timing of all phases of our lives, from birth to death. Since the circadian system modulates cell division and influences growth, puberty, and menopause, it may be identical to or linked with a life-cycle clock. This idea is strengthened by the theory that the life-cycle clock sends its messages to cells through the hormonal system, and hormones also act among the circadian system's messengers. However, the immune system has also been proposed as the communicator.

If a life-cycle clock exists, it must act as a counting device or calendar, a means of recording the passage of time. The circadian system marks each time the sun rises by keeping its own approximate 24-hour rhythm, whether exposed to sunlight or not. Does it also have a "memory" for time? Some scientists think that each process of the circadian system has a predetermined memory. For example, in some animals the fetus has a memory for information on day length sent by the mother. Predetermined memory is still a subject of debate and may be true for some aspects of the system but not for others. If a critical part of the circadian system does record or memorize its own 24-hour rhythms, it may determine our allotted span of life by numbering our days.

Some chronobiologists speculate that science may eventually discover how to slow down the hypothetical life-cycle clock. Possibly a certain biological rhythm will be found that is "counted" as a way of measuring the genetically predetermined life span. This rhythm might then be lengthened through changes in living routine, light exposure, or drugs. One of humankind's oldest dreams is to prolong life. Yet, this dream also raises unanswered questions such as the quality of our extended years and the possibility of survival on a planet of limited space and resources.

THE RHYTHMS OF DEATH

Grim death took me without any warning;
I was well at night, and dead at nine in the
morning.

EPITAPH, SEVENOAKS, KENT, ENGLAND[4]

No matter how long we live, when death does come, it often has its preferred time, as does each event in the body's life cycle. Folk wisdom has it that death comes mainly at night, during the predawn hours. Statistics largely support this belief. Similar to birth, death favors the late dark hours, the dawn, or the morning. Seventy-eight percent of deaths from all causes occur between midnight and noon, with a peak at 7:00 A.M.[5] Moreover, 64 percent occur between 4:00 and 11:00 A.M. This same timing holds true for both sexes, irrespective of age or cause of death. Daily and seasonal rhythms of the body's susceptibility to the same infection, disease, surgical trauma, or environmental poison can tip the scale between survival and death.[6] These rhythms are evidently the primary cause of death's hourly and seasonal timing. Like the seasonal rhythms of birth, the seasonal rhythms of death

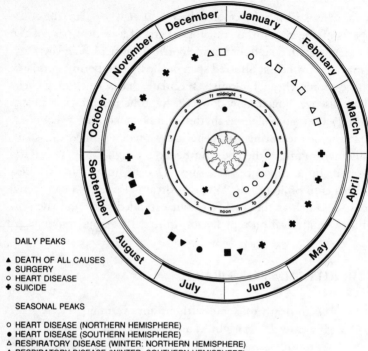

DAILY PEAKS

▲ DEATH OF ALL CAUSES
● SURGERY
○ HEART DISEASE
✦ SUICIDE

SEASONAL PEAKS

○ HEART DISEASE (NORTHERN HEMISPHERE)
● HEART DISEASE (SOUTHERN HEMISPHERE)
△ RESPIRATORY DISEASE (WINTER: NORTHERN HEMISPHERE)
▲ RESPIRATORY DISEASE (WINTER: SOUTHERN HEMISPHERE)
□ INFECTIOUS DISEASES (WINTER: NORTHERN HEMISPHERE)
■ INFECTIOUS DISEASES (WINTER: SOUTHERN HEMISPHERE)
✦ SUICIDE

Figure 15. *Clock of death.*

have evidently weakened over the years due to technology and our resulting remoteness from the influences of nature.

Related to the daily and seasonal rhythms come weekly rhythms in death. Sudden infant death syndrome in babies between 3 and 12 months of age occurs most often on weekends.[7] Men with no previous history of heart disease are most likely to have a fatal attack on a Monday.[8] These rhythms are evidently at least partly due to the body's weekly rhythms in sensitivity and resistance.

Death by suicide may also peak at certain times. Data from several countries show that suicide has a seasonal rhythm with a peak in the spring and, in some countries, a second peak in the fall.[9] Preliminary data also suggest a daily rhythm in suicide with a peak at 2:00 P.M. and a trough at 4:00 A.M.[10] This rhythm corresponds closely to rhythms in the hormone melatonin and may be related to melatonin's effects on other hormones that influence mood.

Death resulting from crime or suicide may also reflect lunar rhythms. A few studies show that such deaths cluster around the time of the full moon, reaching a peak on the day of the full moon.[11] The moon's strong gravitational pull during its full phase may affect the brain, encouraging emotional turbulence and aggression.

THE AGING OF BIOLOGICAL RHYTHMS

Because the circadian system is made up of cells, it changes with age, as do all of the body's systems. Biological rhythms play a crucial role in our physical and mental health, making any shift or weakening of the circadian system a cause of concern as we grow older. Researchers are now addressing this problem by probing the following questions:

- Do one or more of the pacemakers that coordinate rhythms change with age?
- Is there a shift in coordination between pacemakers?
- Do we become less sensitive to sunlight and other time cues with age?
- Does retirement from work outside the home or social isolation weaken the body's sense of time?
- In what ways can we alleviate or delay the above disruptions?

As we grow older, our biological rhythms become more individual, just as our personalities often do. In fact, a major characteristic of older people's rhythms appears to be their variability from one person to another, especially their rhythms of sleep. However, this in itself is a sign that with age we gradually loosen our ties to the 24-hour cycles of daylight and darkness. Some researchers consider the body's disorganization in time as a fundamental part of the aging process.

On entering middle age, we may notice a loss of circadian resilience if strenuous demands are put upon the body's rhythms. Some shift workers can tolerate their schedules for 15 or 20 years and then begin to suffer from them in their forties or fifties. Readjusting after an airplane trip across time zones may be slower, especially in old age.

There are other such signs. Sleep patterns are often manifestations of circadian health. Many people around age 65 or older say they go to sleep and awaken hours earlier than when they were younger. Some awaken between 3:00 and 5:00 A.M., unable to go back to sleep. This change in sleep timing suggests that with advancing age the circadian pacemaker often shifts forward relative to clock time. Apparently women are especially prone to this shift, and tend more toward age-related circadian changes than do men.

> Sometimes I sleep well and sometimes I don't. There are times when I wake up at one or two in the morning and think it's time to get up. And I get washed and get dressed. Then about an hour later I'm tired and think: "Well, I'll just lie down and cover myself up." And then I go back to bed again and sleep. But every night I pray: "Please God, let me sleep all night and not get up," and that helps.
>
> 79-YEAR-OLD WOMAN

Sleep also tends to become lighter in the elderly, who often awaken frequently, but this may have causes unrelated to circadian rhythms.

Although many biological rhythms persist unaltered in the older years, a complex array of chronobiologic changes occurs in our bodies with age, in some of us more strongly than in others. The pineal gland can calcify with age, although this tendency varies among countries. Melatonin's rhythms may weaken in our older years, possibly due to changes in the pineal. Animal research suggests that changes with age in the pineal gland and melatonin may alter our capacity to convert light signals into time-of-day information that is used to set the internal clock. [12]

In general our rhythms "flatten," or become less vigorous, with age. For example, the range of body temperature is 2 to 3 degrees in the young, but 1.0 to 1.5 degrees in the elderly. [13] The daily temperature cycle also becomes shorter and less stable, leading to a change in the relationship among temperature rhythm, the sleep-wake cycle, and sunlight or other time cues. These losses of circadian control reduce the body's ability to regulate and monitor its own temperature, making the elderly more vulnerable to both heat and cold. Our rhythm of heart rate may progressively flatten over the years, in men more than in women. Circadian rhythms of several hormones weaken or shift with age, including testosterone, cortisol, and growth hormone. Some hormones change with age throughout the life span.

As we grow older, we may also become less sensitive to sunlight and other time cues that normally keep biological rhythms in time with each other and with the 24-hour light-dark cycle. The pupil of the eye contracts differently in both light and darkness according to age. It is not yet known whether this affects the strength of light as a time cue. Some loss of hearing is very common in the elderly. Hearing loss and weakened eyesight or cataracts can partially shut out the sounds and light that remind the body of the time of day. In addition we may get little outdoor light because of curtailed activity. One small study showed the elderly spending an average of only one hour a day outdoors, with women getting less outdoor light than men. [14]

The older years often bring retirement from work outside the home, and children are grown and on their own. Although these can be liberating and joyful years, they can also bring social isolation, especially if ill health leads to a loss of regular activity, or death takes friends and loved ones. Social isolation can lead to further weakening of time cues if life becomes too unstructured and the cycles of light and dark, activity and sleep, lose their importance. Life in an institution such as a nursing home or hospital often further reduces the opportunities for social contact and for exposure to light of outdoor intensity.

> If somebody takes me outside during the day, I
> can go. They don't take me regularly, and I spend
> days without going outdoors at all. But I don't
> think about it, and I don't think it bothers me.
> I used not to be like this. I used to work. I was
> always out.
>
> 77-YEAR-OLD WOMAN IN A NURSING HOME

Those who live in nursing homes with no patios, porches, or sunrooms are likely to be exposed to only indoor lighting year round. This may encourage any tendency toward desynchronization, in which the body ceases to run according to the 24-hour cycles of light and darkness. In our older years we are more susceptible to desynchronization than the young.

Staying "in Time" in Our Older Years

Biological rhythms that are even slightly desynchronized can leave us more vulnerable to all challenges to the body. Therefore, as the circadian system weakens in old age, we are more than ever in need of sunlight and other powerful time cues to retain as much internal time structure and resilience as possible. Ironically, however, in this phase of life we are most likely to have less access to cues to the time of day. We and our health-care providers need to be aware of this pitfall and to think of ways of encouraging the body's rhythms to stay in harmony with each other and with the cycles of day and night. Some researchers think that the desynchrony of age can and should be corrected. Consider the following ways of encouraging healthful rhythms:

1. Keep your day as structured as possible, with regular bedtime and arising (whether or not you sleep) and regular activities, chores, and meals.

2. In your daily routine, include some exercise or activity outdoors during daylight hours.

3. If you are severely troubled by early-morning awakening or broken sleep, you may wish to try light therapy to improve the quality and timing of your sleep. (See chapter 3 for more information.)

4. Try measuring your blood pressure and heart rate regularly. You can use a blood pressure recorder, called a sphygmomanometer, available in manual and automatic styles at drugstores and medical supply stores. The instructions included with the device will explain how to record systolic and diastolic pressures. Some automatic blood pressure recorders also automatically measure your pulse. If your instrument does not record pulse, you can measure it yourself by counting the number of heartbeats at your wrist, neck (carotid artery), or chest, whichever is easiest, for one minute timed with a stopwatch.

   One study suggests that self-measurement several times a day can help a person maintain or even improve physical well-being over the years.[15] Measuring one's own rhythms probably leads to greater awareness of the body's pace and encourages regular physical activity to maintain health.

5. Some drugs can evidently resynchronize disturbed rhythms that may cause or exacerbate depression in the elderly. Consider drugs as a last resort, and take them only under supervision of a knowledgeable physician.

Researchers Look into the Future

AS WE BECOME more aware of the multiple effects of sunlight, we may begin to think about the health effects of spending the greater part of our days indoors. We drive or take public transportation to our jobs, often unable to enjoy the benefits of walking or cycling in the early-morning sun. We work indoors, spending most of our waking hours living by light from windows or lamps.[1] We may stay enclosed all day, frequently in windowless rooms, often not leaving work until after dark. Presumably, these patterns occur among people in many industrialized countries.

However, comparing our indoor way of life with the amount of time our distant ancestors spent outdoors can be misleading. Originally, we evolved with skin colors that helped protect us from the sun's harm—the very light-skinned living in cooler, cloudier areas such as Scandinavia and the British Isles, and the darker-skinned living in hotter, light-intense regions such as India and Africa. With the migrations of populations through the millennia, we do not necessarily live in areas appropriate to our skin color. This leads to conflicts between our bodies' need for sunlight and our tolerance of it. A Texan of Celtic ancestry, for example, can suffer severe skin damage from otherwise healthy outdoor activities.

Nonetheless, the fact remains that the time we spend outdoors in the brightness of daylight is radically different from the conditions in which humankind evolved. The intensity of daylight outdoors can reach more than 80,000 lux, varying according to latitude, time of day, season, and weather.[2] This differs drastically from the approximate 10 to 750 lux we are exposed to through home or office windows and by traditional artificial light. At the latitude of Boston, Massachusetts, dawn twilight (6 A.M.), possibly the most biologically effective light of the day, ranges from approximately 0.001 lux at the winter solstice to approximately 10,000 lux at the spring solstice.[3] Yet our indoor light through windows in the early morning rarely exceeds 750 lux at any season even when combined with artificial light.[4] Therefore, because of our indoor living habits, our experience of the intensity of light as well as its seasonal expansion is greatly reduced.

Two studies show that those who work indoors experience a daily average of only 1.5 hours of light stronger than 2000 lux.[5] This average includes those who work full-time in windowless offices, those who work within the home, and part-time workers. The studies showed much variation from one person to another, with part-time workers experiencing the most bright light, but some people spending more than 23 of their 24 hours in light of less than 1000 lux.[6] According to these studies, among the elderly, women spend less than one-third the time outdoors (20 minutes a day) compared to men (75 minutes).[7] These studies were done in the spring and late summer in San Diego, California. Those living in areas more cloud-covered, polluted, metropolitan, or northerly probably experience even less full daylight, especially in winter. This is particularly true of the ill, infirm, disabled, or imprisoned.

What these statistics mean to our health is still unknown, but some researchers think that living indoors as we do can deprive the body of optimal synchronization by sunlight, leaving us vulnerable to rhythm maladjustments.[8] Such potential maladjustments might reveal themselves most readily in those who are markedly light-sensitive. However, research on unusually bright lamps for general well-being is conflicting, with two studies showing improved mood and well-being, and one showing no change in mood.[9] Possibly these studies differ because those who experience stronger light-related changes in mood and behavior also respond more strongly and favorably to bright light.

> I don't think that workplaces are lighted correctly. I've heard that they can put bright lights in workplaces that can make you feel better. I guess employers don't think it's cost-effective. I think that it would be. I think that people would be tremendously more productive if they felt better, although I may be going too much by my own experience. Some people do seem to be oblivious.
>
> 42-YEAR-OLD-WOMAN WITH SEASONAL
> AFFECTIVE DISORDER

Those of us who think we could benefit from brighter light may improve our quality of life by increasing our time outdoors, using translucent window shades or curtains, working in sunny rooms, or installing lamps similar to those used in light therapy. Ideally, such lifestyle changes would be accompanied by appropriate concern and precautions for the eyes and skin.

The growing knowledge that light affects our health may

influence future architecture and city planning. Mental-health professionals, architects, and city planners have already formed the international Winter Cities Organization, meeting to discuss the effects of light in designing cities in the far north. American and Canadian researchers also gather with colleagues from the Soviet Union to discuss practical uses of bright lights during the long winter nights in polar towns and cities.

The relation of light to health and disease is likely to continue to hold our interest. Governments worldwide are now aware of the implications of damaging the ozone layer in the stratosphere, altering the potency of the sun's rays reaching the earth. The work of researchers such as those who form the Society for Research on Biological Rhythms, the International Society for Chronobiology, and the Society for Light Treatment and Biological Rhythms increasingly influences the study and practice of psychology and medicine. Furthermore, the space programs of the United States, the Soviet Union, and other countries are vitally interested in the effects of living without sunlight. Plans for further space travel and for permanent stations on other planets may eventually be fulfilled and surpassed. If so, future generations will learn through experience how the body changes over time without the daily, monthly, and seasonal cycles of light in which humankind evolved.

The following extracts on the future roles of light and biological rhythms were taken from taped interviews with researchers.

AWARENESS OF LIGHT AND BIOLOGICAL RHYTHMS

Charmane Eastman, Ph.D.
Associate Professor, Psychology Department
and Director of the Biological Rhythms Research Laboratory
Rush Presbyterian St. Luke's Medical Center
Chicago, Illinois

I remember when people didn't know that smoking was dangerous, and people didn't pay as much attention to their diets. I think that one of the next steps will be for people to realize that the amount of light they get and when they get sunlight is another important component to health. And people will watch when they get light just as they now watch their diets and the amount of exercise they get. That's the way I see the future, that [light exposure] will become something commonplace that people will take into account.

Robert E. McGrath, Ph.D.
Assistant Professor, Department of Psychology
Fairleigh Dickinson University
Teaneck, New Jersey

How should seasonality be considered as a general public health question? We have tended to ignore environment in dealing with public health issues in the past. I think that is partly a reflection of the nature of our society. We have become very technologically oriented, and there is an illusion that we are separate from the natural phenomena around us. But, in fact, the whole area of public health is very strongly influenced by environmental factors. And I think that one of the important ones is going to turn out to be seasonal issues. As a general public health issue I think that we are going to need to become more aware of the effects of light, and because of that, enhance our exposure to light in our day-to-day environment. I think that [our exposure to natural light] is something that does have public health consequences that we haven't thought about before.

Timothy H. Monk, Ph.D.
Associate Professor of Psychiatry
University of Pittsburgh School of Medicine
Pittsburgh, Pennsylvania

What I would like to see eventually is, as a first step, an awareness within people that they are not the same at one time of day [as they are at another, and] that there are certain times of day which are better for certain sorts of tasks. They should try and think in these terms.

Eventually, as a second step I would like this to be so engrained in people's self-awareness that they don't think twice about it but simply quite automatically schedule certain things in their lives at particular times of day. . . . If that happened, then a by-product of that, I think, would be that people would be much more aware of their own biological clocks, they would be less cavalier, less lax in their adherence to regular timings for bed, for meals, for exercise, and so on. And I think that regularity in one's life is, as far as I can see from a chronobiological point of view, inevitably going to lead to improvement in well-being and everything that arises from that.

USES OF LIGHT THERAPY

Carla Hellekson, M.D.
Insomnia Treatment and Research Program
Providence Medical Center
Seattle, Washington
(Formerly in private practice in Alaska at the Fairbanks
    Psychiatric and Neurological Clinic)

I think we have a problem with people reading popular books and then going out and buying a lightbox and using it, convinced that they have SAD. But maybe some other things are going on in their lives too. For example, when one patient told me what his budget for alcohol was each month, I said: "I'm not sure SAD is your primary problem." I think that a person should look at his or her whole situation together with a mental-health professional. Perhaps they will find that light therapy is appropriate, but perhaps also other approaches such as psychotherapy, family counseling, or a look at addictive behaviors may be equally important in terms of improving a person's overall well-being.

I think that people who have subsyndromal SAD [milder,

SAD-like feelings and behavior in the winter] can try light therapy as part of health hygiene and may not need mental-health supervision for that.

We also need to be very wary of all the different kinds of lighting products that are being manufactured right now and sift through them very carefully and track what organizations such as the Society for Light Treatment and Biological Rhythms are doing and what the Food and Drug Administration is investigating and approving in terms of determining which apparatuses are effective and safe.

I'm real concerned about the homemade, jerry-rigged kind of light fixtures some people are using because I really don't feel that we can guarantee the safety of those. For example, one man mounted two automobile headlamps in his home and his wife found them very effective. But I could not really say anything about the safety of that apparatus because I am not familiar with the characteristics of that kind of light.

Al Lewy, M.D., Ph.D.
Professor of Psychiatry
Director of Sleep Disorders Laboratory
Oregon Health Sciences University
Portland, Oregon

At the very least we can expect that light therapy will be the treatment of choice for a few types of disorders: winter depression, advanced sleep phase syndrome, and probably delayed sleep phase syndrome, and that light therapy can be used to help with jet lag and perhaps shift work.

With regard to types of depression other than the winter type, we are not sure whether light is going to be very useful. As an antidepressant by itself we are not convinced that it is going to be effective, but it is possible that it can be used in conjunction with other treatments for depression, providing there is some indication that there is a chronobiologic component. [For example], if there is a sleep disorder component to other types of depression, then light may be used to readjust sleep in those patients, just as it can be used in advanced and delayed sleep phase syndromes.

The number of people using light in the winter could increase quite dramatically if future data supports that there is a larger group of what we call subsyndromal patients with winter depression that would respond to light. And it might be shown even in very mildly subsyndromal people that a small amount of morning bright light in the winter will turn out to be a rather common use of adjusting one's light-dark cycle. This would be the maximum: that many, many people would get accustomed to thinking about their light-dark cycle in the winter and make some adjustments.

Norman E. Rosenthal, M.D.
Chief, Unit of Outpatient Services
Clinical Psychobiology Branch
National Institute of Mental Health
Bethesda, Maryland

I think that light should be studied in a variety of conditions. I don't think one should confine one's research necessarily only to seasonal people. I think that the full scope of the potential of light treatment should be explored and that one shouldn't put on restrictions until [this has been done].

Robert E. McGrath

Since the whole issue of light therapy was originally evaluated by psychologists and psychiatrists, there has been more of a tendency to see the primary light issue [as concerning] people who are at the extreme. But I think as time goes by we're going to see that a very large proportion of the population does show some effects from the changes of the seasons. So I do think that there are people for whom light is going to be a lifesaver when they've been severely depressed for many years or they've been drinking uncontrollably for many years. But for the majority of people who end up using lights, I think they're going to be people who find themselves during the winter feeling somewhat depressed, and finding that their alcohol intake is not out of control but beyond the point that they feel comfortable with.

SEASONAL AFFECTIVE DISORDER

Norman E. Rosenthal

[We are studying] the question of whether the visual processing of people with seasonal affective disorder may not be normal. [Our research suggests] that there is indeed some kind of abnormality in the processing of visual information, although of a more complex kind than we had presupposed. I think it's going to be worthwhile to investigate further the role of the eye and visual information processing in seasonal affective disorder in order to try and determine what the fundamental abnormality might be and how light may actually be working.

Then moving more centrally into the brain itself . . . a few studies suggest that the serotonin systems may be disturbed in seasonal affective disorder . . . and that some of the [disturbances] are normalized by light therapy. Clearly, the serotonin system needs to be probed further. Apart from the serotonin system, the dopamine system in the brain has been suggested to be abnormal in seasonal affective disorder. . . . [In addition] the secretion of ACTH (corticotrophin) by the pituitary is blunted in seasonal affective disorder patients, a finding that is not all that dissimilar to what nonseasonal depressives have shown. This blunting is normalized by bright light. It would seem as though some interesting secret may be revealed by pursuing the hypo-thalamo-pituitary-adrenal axis.

Another abnormality that we have shown is an immune abnormality, an abnormality of peripheral lymphocyte function-ing in seasonal affective disorder patients, that seems to be nor-malized by light. These are all angles that we are looking to pursue in the future.

LIGHT IN HIGH LATITUDES

Carla Hellekson

Over the past ten years of living and working in Alaska, I became aware that a large portion of the general population has a lot of the complaints of SAD although they don't have all the symptoms. [I found that] 8.9 percent of the Fairbanks population has SAD in winter and another 19 percent has subsyndromal SAD, [meaning] a lot of the complaints of winter depression but not the full-blown syndrome. That adds up to more than 25 percent of the population having a problem in the winter that might respond to changes in environmental lighting. This held a lot of interest for us because the public health implications are tremendous. If we design our work areas and our home areas so as to improve the lighting, we may effectively improve the well-being and productivity of people living in the far north.

An Alaska-Siberia medical exchange began several years ago. In 1988 we had the first exchange of scientists, where 10 scientists went to Novosibirsk, Siberia, USSR, followed by a return visit of 10 Siberian scientists [to Alaska]. The next round of visits is being planned.

The goal of this project is to find different kinds of research opportunities in which Siberians and Alaskans have similar interests and may collaborate in a productive way, and the area of SAD and light therapy is one of those areas. We are collecting information by questionnaire both in Siberia and Alaska. Our goal is first of all to look at the use of light therapy for SAD in high-latitude communities. We will also be looking at the uses of brighter lights within the home and working environment for those who have subsyndromal SAD.

Roger J. Cole, Ph.D.
Postdoctoral Fellow
University of California, San Diego

When people work in the Arctic or Antarctic during the winter, it's dark outside all the time, and they're never exposed to enough bright light to synchronize their biological rhythms. Therefore, they go into what is called a free-run; they go to bed an hour later and wake up an hour later every day. Their activities cycle around the clock. Bright light, if used once every 24 hours, could synchronize them . . . onto a 24-hour cycle. It could be helpful, especially when you have large groups of people working together and you want them all to be on the same schedule at the same time. You use bright light as the master synchronizer, just like sunrise/sunset is the master synchronizing agent for people in middle latitudes.

Richard G. Condon, Ph.D.
Professor of Anthropology and
Editor of *Arctic Anthropology*
University of Arkansas, Fayetteville

When you get to a region like the Arctic, where changes in temperature and light are so pronounced, it stands to reason that the more we understand about the influence of light on health, the more likely we are to implement better health programs for people who are living in the Arctic. And this is not just for the Inuit [Eskimo] themselves but for Arctic Indians and the white population, Americans and Canadians who have moved to the north. Let's understand first how human beings respond to dramatic changes in temperature and light. And then, once we understand that, we can start implementing better health programs, alter doctors' periodic visits to the smaller Arctic towns, alter the manner in which medication is given, to accommodate human bodily responses to extreme seasonal change.

We have to understand more, not just about physical diseases but also mental illnesses, which I don't think have been studied among the Inuit. I haven't seen any studies that deal with seasonal affective disorder, for example, among the Inuit.

CHILDBIRTH

Peter Nathaniels, M.D.
Director, Laboratory for Pregnancy and Newborn Research
Cornell University
Ithaca, New York

I think that the issue really is whether distress to the mother can actually modify the patterns of labor and delivery and to what extent that might be related to rhythms. I'm interested in the different stresses that can affect pregnancy and in how modifying the mother's rhythms during pregnancy may affect the fetus. We're beginning to learn how stress affects the uterus in its contractile patterns, blood flow to the uterus . . . those sorts of things may have a long-lasting effect on the baby. I think that if stress modifies the mother's rhythms during, say, 10, 20, 30 weeks of pregnancy, that could enormously [affect the fetus]. [For example,] a French group has looked into the epidemiology of premature birth, and there is evidence that the distress of changing your address, with all the problems of packing up your goods and chattels and moving across the country, produces a higher incidence of premature birth. Much, much more research needs to be done in this regard.

JET LAG

Roger J. Cole

There is no question that light will in the future be used to treat jet lag very effectively. The only question at this point is how and when to use the light. We know that bright light is needed, such as outdoor light or very bright indoor light with special light fixtures. But we don't know the exact timing of the use of the light. The big bugaboo in this area is that if the light is used at the right time it can rapidly eliminate jet lag. And if it's used at the wrong time it can make jet lag much worse. My prediction for the future is that there will be various lighting devices for treating jet lag available in airports, hotels, and commercially to put in people's bedrooms, and perhaps on airplanes.

Timothy Monk

We are a long way from having solutions to jet lag involving bright lights in airports. What we're left with in the jet lag situation is trying to at least help things along using common sense and a knowledge of chronobiology. For example, if I were flying to Paris for an important meeting and I knew I had to have the meeting the day after I arrived, it would be foolish of me to have that meeting at nine o'clock in the morning Paris time. That would be three o'clock in the morning Pittsburgh time. Much more sensible would be to schedule it for late afternoon Paris time, when it would be late morning Pittsburgh time, and I would be more able to cope with that meeting.

SHIFT WORK

Charmane Eastman

It won't be the case that there is *less* shift work in the future. So more and more people are liable to spend a lot of their time where they never see sunlight: they're sleeping during the day and working at night. It will be especially important for shift workers to think about when they get light. It is also important for them to think about eating right. They're prone to gastrointestinal problems.

I'm not sure how artificial light will be used to help shift workers. But it's possible that certain occupations that are sedentary will permit workers to sit near artificial light banks at certain times that have been proven by experiments to help them adapt to whatever shift they want to adapt to. We may see some companies that will install bright lights at work.

For shift workers, keeping light out can be just as important as letting light in. It may be important to block out sunlight at certain times to keep sunlight from shifting rhythms opposite to the way you want them to shift. Now we have a marketplace flooded with artificial light fixtures. In the future I expect there to be more special kinds of dark glasses that will be produced that shift workers can wear when they go outside and don't want the light at that time. It's not easy to make dark glasses that vary immediately with the light intensity so that they will be good when it's very bright and also when it's very dim, like at twilight.

One problem is that nobody agrees whether or not workers should really have their circadian rhythms adapt to the night shift or not. If they're adapted to the night shift, they're not adapted to the day shift. Even if we could use bright light to shift a person's internal body clock around enough to adjust a person's change in shift, we don't know what the long-run consequences would be. So, I think that the popular press has the idea that using bright light to help shift workers solve their problems is right around the corner; whereas I see this kind of work really in its infancy, with many years of research necessary.

Carla Hellekson

A potentially large interest of the Alaska-Siberia Medical Exchange research will be in the use of light for shift-work adaptation. In high-latitude communities typically you have work forces working under rather rigorous conditions. And that often involves rigorous shift schedules, such as in the oil industry on Alaska's north slope. And then the Soviets have a lot of workers at high latitudes, including their coal-mining operation at Spitsbergen in Norway, which is 86 degrees north. I think that when you have more than 25 percent of the population affected by the seasons, and a good number of those people working shifts, that group is going to be particularly at risk. The other thing we would like to see is whether we can help people adapt to their shifts without having to resort to medications and alcohol to help with sleep.

Timothy H. Monk

I think we have to recognize shift-work safety problems. And we're talking about things not necessarily as catastrophic and headline-catching as Three-Mile Island, but maybe something as unnewsworthy as someone running a red light on the way home from a graveyard shift [midnight to 8 A.M.] and causing a collision; somebody dropping a heavy piece of machinery on his foot; somebody reversing out of a loading bay without looking and causing an accident. Those things don't make the headlines, but it's quite possible and even probable that they result in more loss of life, misery, and cost than do the very dramatic ones that make the headlines.

As the baby boom gradually passes through middle age, I think we're going to find in the 1990s a significant problem of shift-work coping. We will have a huge bulge in population which is coming into their fifties, and we know that's the age where coping with shift work suddenly becomes a problem. And I think that we really do, as a society, have to begin to devote more resources to looking at shift-work strategies. If we don't do it now, I think in the late 1990s we will suddenly be presented with a major work-force crisis—when we find that we don't have enough people to man the shift-working positions that we need to keep society functioning. Rather than wait 10 years and then react to the crisis, I think it would be much better to address that crisis now, to find out what the aging effects are so that we can begin to rectify the situation before a crisis develops.

ALCOHOLISM

Robert E. McGrath

I don't see seasonality as being one of the two or three most important issues that are going on with alcoholics. But I do think that for a certain subgroup of people who have the potential to become problem drinkers, the seasons are going to prove to be a very important factor in the regulation of their drinking cycles.

It's been demonstrated, through recent research on how an alcoholic actually abuses alcohol, that there are natural peaks and valleys in the occurrence of abuse. We don't understand anything about that process at this point. And I think this is one of the first attempts to suggest that there are, in fact, environmental factors that are very important in the creation of those peaks and valleys.

Because of this, I think that, at least for a certain subgroup of people who have problems with alcohol, light can prove to be an important adjunct to treatment. This is our first year of actually using light to help people avoid drinking, so I don't have any results at this point. I can say, though, that during the past year we have identified at least 11 people who show a very clear pattern of losing control of their drinking in the fall and winter, most typically in the months of October and November. And I think it's a reasonable hypothesis that these people can be helped through using light.

[However], alcoholism is a multidimensional problem. So that whereas with depressives light in and of itself seems to be able to alleviate the problem, when we're talking about alcoholism I think it's important that light be seen as an adjunct to other treatment. Alcoholism is different from depression in that it's a behavioral response and it's actually a method of *coping* for these people. So [although] the people we're working with have what seems to be a biological propensity toward problems in the wintertime, I think [our work] needs to be done in the context of helping the person to develop better coping mechanisms—perhaps family therapy, individual therapy, Alcoholics Anonymous, whatever other services are able to help. I think that with alcoholism it's a much more complex problem than it is with the SAD patients. And I think it's very important to see light as just one portion of a multimodal method of dealing with drinking problems.

USES OF MELATONIN AS A DRUG

Al Lewy

We are interested in totally blind people who have free-running, 25-hour rhythms—who cannot be treated with light. Because they can't entrain to the 24-hour day, they have these four- and five-week cycles of insomnia and some mood problems. But we have evidence that melatonin acts on the body's clock. We have been able in preliminary studies to encapsulate melatonin and administer it orally to blind people to shift their rhythms forward. A dose of melatonin may act like a pulse of light, provided it is given at a certain time of day.

We also think melatonin might be used to help sighted people adjust the clock. It could be useful in treating certain types of depression, like winter depression, and certain types of sleep disorders. And there are researchers in other countries pursuing the jet lag aspect.

OZONE DEPLETION: THE CONSEQUENCES

Margaret Kripke, Ph.D.
Professor and Chairman, Department of Immunology
University of Texas M. D. Anderson Cancer Center
Houston, Texas

What the immune system is all about is protecting us from disease. We want to understand how exposing the skin to ultraviolet light causes changes in the immune system. We are also working on the immune response to infectious diseases. This is one of the main areas of concern in terms of ozone depletion. If there are really immunological effects of ultraviolet light in humans, then the question is whether these immunological changes will make people more susceptible to disease or will increase the severity of infectious diseases.

I think there is growing agreement that we are in fact experiencing depletion of stratospheric ozone and that we are likely to continue to do so for some time. One of the concerns is simply to monitor the situation and to find out what really is happening to ultraviolet light exposure levels.

The second issue is to be concerned with what the health effects of ultraviolet light radiation would be, specifically skin cancer, eye damage such as cataracts, and perhaps immunological effects. I think what we need to do is to worry about what our preventive measures might be to protect populations against increased exposure to ultraviolet light. We know that wearing protective clothing and avoiding the hours of the day when sunlight is the most intense are ways of reducing ultraviolet light exposure. We think we know that using sunscreens reduces sunburns, and we think that they are also protective in terms of preventing skin cancer. We don't know, however, whether sunscreens are going to protect against immunological damage. We also don't know whether pigment in the skin is protective against immunological damage.

In terms of immunological issues these are the questions that need to be addressed so that we will know what populations are at risk and how we might protect those populations against increased ultraviolet light.

I think we also need to educate people that ultraviolet light does cause cataracts. Certain kinds of cataracts are caused by the wavelengths of ultraviolet light that would be affected by ozone depletion. That may not be such a big problem in the United States, where most people can afford to wear sunglasses or to have cataract surgery. But certainly in [some Third World] countries that's a major problem—where cataracts are already a major health problem—that could get a lot worse if there is increased ultraviolet light in sunlight. I think that really is an issue: it's an education issue, it's an economic issue. We know how to prevent it, but the issue in preventing it is largely an economic one.

AGING

Erhard Haus, M.D., Ph.D.
Professor of Laboratory Medicine and Pathology
University of Minnesota Medical School
Minneapolis, Minnesota
Chairman of the Department of Anatomic
   and Clinical Pathology
St. Paul-Ramsay Medical Center
St. Paul, Minnesota

We are studying hormonal rhythms in people over the age of 60 and relating those rhythms to the functional state of the person. We find that circadian rhythms in aging remain very much intact when the person is healthy, but that there are some changes that may be characteristic for old age. And we are interested in seeing if there are any rhythm alterations or any changes, especially circadian but also circannual rhythms, when people are classified according to their functional state. We are using a number of functional tests, like the Activities in Daily Living Index and the Mental Status Index. Preliminary data show that there may be differences [that correlate] with hormonal changes in some people who function poorly, mentally and physically.

Al Lewy

We have a geriatrician in our group who is interested in insomnia in older people, and we plan to study the effects of light. Preliminary results suggest that older people respond to light in much the same way as younger people and can adjust their rhythms just as younger people can. And I would say that this is particularly important in older people, because avoiding one more medication [a "sleeping pill"] is very important given the complex interactions between multiple medications. The sleeping pill interacts with the blood pressure pill, heart pill, diuretic, and other medications that some of the elderly take on a continual basis. It is not likely that melatonin would interact in this way, but we are not yet giving melatonin to older people.

Timothy Monk

A lot of my present research is concerned with aging and how it affects sleep and the biological clock. And that's a very important issue because a lot of older people have sleep problems. A lot of them are using sleeping pills and a lot of them are having trouble with those sleeping pills. If we can help solve some of the sleeping problems of the elderly without having to resort to drugs, then I think that will make a dramatic impact on the well-being of a major sector of the population.

I am now looking at sleep and circadian rhythms in healthy 80-year-olds. It's a good project because it's not only of social relevance . . . it's also a model of circadian dysfunction. It's a situation where the circadian system is changing.

ON THE INTERPLAY OF RHYTHMS

Erhard Haus

We are now engaged in studying circadian, circaseptan, and circannual rhythms in children and in the elderly. Our purpose is to characterize their rhythms and to relate the rhythm parameters to growth and development in children, and to functional states of aging in the elderly.

We have followed up a cohort of elderly people essentially until time of death. We did find in this process very characteristic circadian, circaseptan, and circannual variations in mortality, especially from acute cardiac death, which showed a marked circadian rhythm but also circaseptan and circannual rhythms. The interesting aspect, especially in circaseptan [approximately seven-day] rhythms, is that this is in people who have no responsibilities essentially, live in a home for the aged, and for whom weekends and weekdays are relatively very similar. So it's not the stress of

Monday that hits these people, because they are not exposed to any stress like that.

Franz Halberg, M.D.
Professor of Laboratory Medicine and Pathology
University of Minnesota Medical School
Minneapolis, Minnesota

[In medicine] we find that the addition of circaseptan and circannual [rhythms] to the circadian component broadens our view and sharpens our tools. For example, a pacemaker [is a device that] makes the heart that has stopped start going again or maintains the heart that was about to fail. Now a chronobiologic pacemaker may be developed in Holland that can take into account not only the high-frequency, one-per-second heartbeat, but also the modulations of this heartbeat with a wide range of frequencies.

Whether we look at one end of the healing process, the cure, or whether we turn to prevention, it is much more important to examine the spectrum of intermodulating rhythms. To focus only on circadian, meritorious as it may be in comparison to doing nothing, is extremely shortsighted when one realizes that the addition of the entire spectrum, ultradian [shorter than 20 hours] as well as circadian, can reverse the outcomes—and the outcomes are what matter—of endeavors toward prevention or toward cure.

STAYING IN TIME IN SPACE

Roger J. Cole

With increasing jet travel and the advent of space travel, there are going to be more and more people exposed to circadian problems that can be treated by light. Light will have tremendous relevance for things such as space flight, where the light-dark cycle in a space shuttle orbiting the earth is about once every two hours; sunrise/sunset every two hours. Helping people synchronize their rhythms in space will be another application of light, an extension of jet-lag light treatment into space-lag.

Timothy Monk

NASA has a shuttle mission which is going to be devoted to such issues as sleep, biological rhythms, and performance, and a lot of the scientific community have submitted grant applications to be part of that. NASA is very interested in issues such as sleep and circadian rhythms in space.

Erhard Haus

In space medicine, chronobiology is something that is being followed because of space flights. If you shoot somebody into space, the environmental factors that have kept our circadian rhythmicity in step with the astronomical surroundings are abolished. But the organism can be kept in step or synchronized on the spacecraft by diet and a sufficiently regulated sleep-wake period. If this is not done and you let people go on their self-selected schedules, similar things would happen as in the isolation studies in bunkers and caves: the astronauts would be free-running on rhythms that are longer than 24 hours, and eventually desynchronize. In long space flights one has to keep a schedule that will maintain circadian rhythms to some extent.

Now we have the manned space stations from the Soviet Union . . . so under those conditions rhythms have to be kept in mind and can be used for optimum performance.

CHRONOBIOLOGY IN HEALTH CARE: FIVE ISSUES

The Medical Student

Erhard Haus

In medical school I think most students become aware of [biological] rhythms and that the system is rhythmic. But I don't think it's taught yet very widely, not in this country. I would say that Europe is way ahead of the U.S. in teaching chronobiology. But it's slowly coming here too.

Franz Halberg

What does a medical resident do today and what did he do in 1949–1950 when we started? Clearly the vast majority of medical residents as well as many professors of medicine, many professors of cardiology, say "blood pressure *is* . . . ," not realizing that the change in blood pressure each day can be of the order of 65 or more millimeters mercury on the average when the heart contracts, and 55 millimeters mercury on the average when the heart dilates in systolic and diastolic.

[But] there is one point to be made perhaps as compared to the late 1940s or early 1950s: the term *circadian* has entered the supplement to the *Oxford Medical Dictionary*. So most medical residents and most professors of medicine have heard of circadian and they have heard of rhythms, and what was once perhaps a foolish if not esoteric endeavor has become some sort of accepted—but still, in practice, ignored—medical science.

The Physician

Lawrence E. Scheving, Ph.D.
Rebsamen Professor of Anatomical Sciences
University of Arkansas for Medical Sciences
Little Rock, Arkansas

Physicians must become educated as to the potential of chronobiology. The findings of clinical research should be widely disseminated [in order to reach physicians] through the literature, seminars, etc. All of this is beginning to happen, and in my opinion the future looks very promising.

With time a patient should expect better management of treatment in certain medical conditions, such as respiratory problems, and when taking drugs that have potent side effects.

I think this is truly going to come about because industry has developed the pumps for delivering drugs in a chronobiological way. I think technology is going to make this very easy. Up until the time this technology develops, it is very difficult for the doctor. I don't expect that the average physician should be able to offer his patient timed treatment willy-nilly. I think that's unreasonable. But by the same token, he shouldn't dismiss lightly the whole field of chronobiology because he doesn't know anything about it. And that is very frequently done.

William J. M. Hrushesky, M.D.
Professor of Medicine, Immunobiology, and Microbiology
Albany Medical Center of Union University,
Albany, New York
Adjunct Professor of Chemical Engineering
Rensselaer Polytechnic Institute
Troy, New York

[When patients ask about timed treatment for cancer] they don't get positive responses, but they do get recognition that there is such a thing, which they didn't get five years ago. I get many calls from around the country from patients whose physicians are unwilling to further explore the possibilities of the timing of drugs. There is a tremendous reluctance on the part of physicians to change their practices in any way.

Mental Health

Norman E. Rosenthal

I think that chronobiology already has affected psychiatry. There are circadian theories of depression, of PMS, of seasonal affective disorder. . . . I think [chronobiology] has established itself as a legitimate area of study and of research in the field of psychiatry, and I see that trend continuing.

Erhard Haus

In psychiatry today you have a very wide recognition of rhythm disturbances in affective disorders—also in sleep research and treatment. So chronobiology is used fairly widely without necessarily calling it that. The whole dexamethasone suppression test—something used very widely in diagnostic workup of affective disorders in psychiatry—is based on chronobiologic changes.

Drug Timing

Lawrence E. Scheving

Exactly 10 years ago, the International Union Against Cancer sponsored a two-day meeting with a number of experts, including people from the Food and Drug Administration (FDA). The consensus at the end of this was that the FDA should include in their [drug testing] some guidelines for taking chronobiology into consideration. That was said to them, the guideline was published, and *nothing* has been done about it.

The FDA must include consideration of timing in their role as drug-testers. Congress may have to mandate this since it will involve changing many current practices.

Erhard Haus

I think chronopharmacology, the timing of drug treatment, is growing rapidly. I think that is an area which has a very large future, mainly where we are dealing with potent drugs that have significant side effects; seeing whether timing of treatment can lead to improved effectiveness and/or decrease in undesirable side effects.

William J. M. Hrushesky

It's pretty much impossible to deliver drugs at optimal times or in optimal patterns without technological innovation.

But physicians are not comfortable with high-tech products. So it's the job of the engineering firms to interface between the patients, physicians, and nurses who use the devices to make them comfortable with high technology that will allow optimal drug delivery.

There are now many devices available that provide physicians with the means of optimal drug timing. There are programmable systems that will deliver drugs at certain times automatically inside the patient's body; there are wearable programmable devices for drugs; and many other technologies to allow wearable delivery systems that can deliver drugs into an artery, vein, spinal canal, abdomen, chest, through the skin, or through the gut in a pulsed and timed way.

The devices are available, but physicians are just getting used to using devices that *don't* specify time. It's going to take intelligent interface between the user and the provider of the device in order for it to be used optimally. It's also going to take financial support for clinical research to discover how best to use all the drugs in terms of frequency, intervals, and circadian timing. We have information on a few drugs; we need information on *all* anticancer drugs and information on all *new* anticancer drugs as they come out.

Boundaries between Health and Disease

Erhard Haus

I think the recognition of the time factor in medicine advances quite rapidly. Whether people call it chronobiology and have all the concepts together is another question. But if you look into the different medical journals, you will find more and more that people are talking about time effects. In the *Journal of Clinical Endocrinology* there is hardly an issue where there is not some rhythm discussed. Chronobiology is hardly ever mentioned, but they are talking about episodic variations, circadian variations, seasonal variations—and all this, of course, is chronobiology.

In clinical medicine they now have feasible 24-hour monitoring of blood pressure and heartbeat, [and these have] led to an entirely new area in cardiology—and all this is chronobiology. Clinicians have become quite aware that physiologic functions vary periodically and have begun to study them and to treat accordingly.

I think that chronobiology as the human time structure is here. And the more we go into automated equipment that allows monitoring over time, the better we can handle output with computerized means, the more will chronobiology be applied.

The basic application I foresee in the future is in the diagnosis of disorders like high blood pressure; then risk-state detection—for example, the risk of developing coronary occlusion at certain circadian stages.

Lawrence E. Scheving

I think the future will bring many benefits in treatments, and prevention of disease. But most important perhaps, in my own mind, is utilizing [chronobiology] to get at the mechanism of action of many things we don't understand. As of 1989 we are very ignorant. We still do not know how a cell divides. What is the mechanism? We don't know this; we only know a bunch of steps it goes through. Now, if we can't come up with the mechanism of cell division in normal tissues, how are we ever going to understand it in abnormal tissues?

William J. M. Hrushesky

The implications for chronobiology in medicine are extremely broad. There are disease prevention, early diagnosis, and treatment implications of crhonobiology across all branches of medicine. For instance, in [the Pap smear for] cervical cancer screening, many results are incorrect, [showing abnormalities when there are none, called false positives; or not revealing abnormalities that are there, called false negatives]. We have data [showing] that the abnormalities associated with precancer and cancer of the cervix are not randomly distributed throughout the year. So there is a huge implication for mass screening: during which season should [Pap smears] be done to pick up the most true positives and the fewest false negatives?

In many screening programs for cervical cancer and breast cancer mammography, the stage of the menstrual cycle isn't considered either. It's clear that the [cells] within the vagina and the cervix of a cycling woman's body undergo major changes that would increase and decrease false negatives and false positives. Likewise, the changes in the breast of a cycling woman would affect the true ratio of correct and incorrect results in detection by mammography.

I think that the breadth of the importance of chrono-biology to optimal health care in the next century needs to be stressed. I think there's information in high-frequency rhythms about the boundaries between health and disease and about the state of health, not just the state of disease. And there is information across most frequency ranges that needs to be respected. We are not organisms that are invariant in time. We *have* menstrual cycles and seasonal changes in our physiology and in our chemistry. We *have* circadian changes in the way we handle drugs and respond to therapies. These things need to be taken seriously. And when they are, they open a whole new chapter in health care.

NOTES

INTRODUCTION

1. Sir James George Frazer, *The Golden Bough: A Study in Magic and Religion* (London: Macmillan & Co., Ltd., 1967), 103.
2. Ibid., 104.
3. Mircea Eliade, editor in chief, *Encyclopedia of Religion*, vol. 10 (New York: Macmillan Publishing Company, 1987), 86.
4. C. P. Thakur et al., "Relation between Full Moon and Medicolegal Deaths," *Indian Journal of Medical Research* 85 (March 1987), 316.
5. See W. J. M. Hrushesky, R. v. Roemeling, and R. B. Sothern's observations on Chinese medicine in "Preclinical and Clinical Cancer Chronotherapy," in J. Arendt, ed., *Biological Rhythms in Clinical Practice*, in press.

CHAPTER 1: Sunlight: The Giver of Time

1. Ovid, *Metamorphoses*, trans. Mary B. Innes (Harmondsworth, England: Penguin Books Ltd., 1955), 101.
2. Citing Jean Jacques Dortous de Mairan, translated from *Histoire de l'Academie Royale des Sciences* (Paris, 1729), as quoted in Alexander Borbély, *Secrets of Sleep* (New York: Basic Books, Inc., 1986), 177.
3. C. S. Pittendrigh, "The Photoperiodic Phenomena: Seasonal Modulations of the 'Day' Within," *Journal of Biological Rhythms*, in press.
4. Steven M. Reppert, "Maternal Entrainment of the Developing Circadian System," in Richard J. Wurtman, Michael J. Baum, and John T. Potts, Jr., eds., *The Medical and Biological Effects of Light*, Annals of the New York Academy of Sciences, vol. 453 (New York: New York Academy of Sciences, 1985), 164.
5. Simon Folkard, Peter Knauth, and Timothy H. Monk, "The Effect of Memory Load on the Circadian Variation in Performance Efficiency under a Rapidly Rotating Shift System," *Ergonomics* 19, no. 4 (1976): 21.
6. Timothy H. Monk et al., "Task Variables Determine Which Biological Clock Controls Circadian Rhythms in Human Performance," *Nature* 304, no. 5926 (11 August 1983): 543.
7. Associated Press article from the *Boston Globe*, 23 May 1989.
8. René Descartes, "The Passions of the Soul," in *The Philosophical Writings of Descartes*, vol. 1, trans. John Cottingham, Robert Stoothoff, and Dugald Murdoch (Cambridge: Cambridge University Press, 1985), 340–41.

9. Michael Terman et al., "Daylight Deprivation and Replenishment: A Psychobiological Problem with a Naturalistic Solution," in E. Bales and R. McCluney, eds., *Architecture and Natural Light* (Atlanta, Ga.: American Society of Heating, Refrigeration, and Air-Conditioning Engineers, in press). And Verena Lacoste and Anna Wirz-Justice, "Seasonal Variation in Normal Subjects: An Update of Variables Current in Depression Research" in N. E. Rosenthal and M. Blehar, eds., *Seasonal Affective Disorder and Phototherapy* (New York: Guilford Press, in press, cites Klinker et al., 1969 and 1972).

10. Descartes, "Treatise on Man" and "The Passions of the Soul," in *Philosophical Writings*, vol. 1, 106–7, 340–41.

11. Steven M. Reppert et al., "Putative Melatonin Receptors in a Human Biological Clock," *Science* 242 (7 October 1988): 78 (cites Sadun et al., 1984).

12. Barbara Zahorska-Markiewicz and Andrzej Markiewicz, "Circannual Rhythm of Exercise Metabolic Rate in Humans," *European Journal of Applied Physiology* 52 (1984): 329 (cites Ingemann-Hanssen, et al., 1982).

13. R. A. Wever, "Characteristics of Circadian Rhythms in Human Functions," *Journal of Neural Transmission* 21, suppl. (1986): 351; and Charles A. Czeisler et al., "Bright Light Induction of Strong (Type O) Resetting of the Human Circadian Pacemaker," in *Science* 244 (1989): 1328–33.

14. Charles A. Czeisler, "Biologic Rhythm Disorders, Depression, and Phototherapy: A New Hypothesis," *Psychiatric Clinics of North America* 10, no. 4 (December 1987): 699.

15. Bary W. Wilson, "Chronic Exposure to ELF Fields May Induce Depression," *Bioelectromagnetics* 9 (1988): 200 (cites seven studies).

16. C. F. Ehret, V. R. Potter, and K. W. Dobra, "Chronotypic Action of Theophylline and of Pentobarbital as Circadian Zeitgebers in the Rat," *Science* 188 (1975): 1212. See also Erhard Haus et al., "Reference Values for Chronopharmacology," in A. Reinberg, M. Smolensky, and G. Labrecque, eds., *Annual Review of Chronopharmacology*, vol. 4 (New York: Pergamon Press, 1988), 406.

17. D. S. Minors et al., "Irregularity of Rest and Activity: Studies on Circadian Rhythmicity in Man," *Journal of Physiology* (London) 381 (December 1986): 291.

18. Martin C. Moore-Ede, Frank M. Sulzman, and Charles A. Fuller, *The Clocks That Time Us* (Cambridge, Mass.: Harvard University Press, 1982), 339.

19. Ibid., 327.

20. Adapted from Timothy H. Monk, "Coping with the Stress of Jet-Lag," *Work & Stress* 1, no. 2 (1987): 165.

21. Timothy H. Monk and Lynne C. Aplin, "Spring and Autumn Daylight Saving Time Changes: Studies of Adjustment in Sleep Timings, Mood, and Efficiency," *Ergonomics* 23, no. 2 (1980): 168 (cites Monk and Folkard, 1976).

22. Moore-Ede, Sulzman, and Fuller, *Clocks*, 329 (cites J. Ruthenfranz, P. Knauth,

and W. P. Colquhoun, 1976; and Shift Work Committee, Japan Association of Industrial Health, 1979).

23. Martin C. Moore-Ede, "Jet Lag, Shift Work and Maladaption" *NIPS* 1 (October 1986), 159.

24. Moore-Ede, Sulzman, and Fuller, *Clocks*, 341 (cites R. F. Kraus and P. A. Buffler, "Sociocultural Stress and the American Native in Alaska: An Analysis of Changing Patterns of Psychiatric Illness and Alcohol Abuse among Alaskan Natives." *Culture, Medicine, and Psychiatry* 3 (1979): 111–151).

CHAPTER 2: Fertility and Childbirth

1. Pliny, *Natural History*, vol. 2, trans. H. Rackham, 1969, 549; and vol. 8, trans. W. H. S. Jones, 1975, 55, 57 (Cambridge, Mass.: Harvard University Press).

2. Erwin Buenning, *The Physiological Clock: Circadian Rhythms and Biological Chronometry* (London: English Universities Press Ltd., 1973), 183.

3. Dietrich Neumann, "Tidal and Lunar Rhythms," in Juergen Aschoff, ed., *Biological Rhythms*, vol. 4 of *Handbook of Behavioral Neurobiology* (New York: Plenum Press, 1981), 372.

4. Winnifred B. Cutler et al., "Lunar Influences on the Reproductive Cycle in Women," *Human Biology* 59, no. 6 (December 1987): 959 (cites five studies).

5. Ibid., 967–68.

6. P. H. Jongbloet, "Menses and Moon Phases, Ovulation and Seasons, Vitality and Month of Birth" (annotations) in *Developmental and Child Neurology* 25 (1983): 527; and Winnifred B. Cutler, "Lunar and Menstrual Phase Locking" *American Journal of Obstetrics and Gynecology* 134, no. 7 (August 1, 1980), 834 (cites four studies).

7. Jongbloet, "Menses," 527 (refers to five studies).

8. H. Hosemann, "Bestehen solare und lunare Einfluesse auf die Nativitaet und den Menstruationszyklus?" *Zeitschrift fuer Geburtshilfe und Gynaekologie* 133 (1950): 279 (cites Diepgen, "Die Frauenheilkunde der Alten Welt," in J. Veit, ed., *Handbuch der Gynaekologie* 12, Part 1 [Munich: Bergmann, 1937]: 160).

9. Ibid. (cites A. E. von Siebold, *Handbuch zur Erkenntnis und Heilung von Frauenzimmerkrankheiten* [Varrentrop, 1821]).

10. Michael J. Russell, Genevieve M. Switz, and Kate Thompson, "Olfactory Influences on the Human Menstrual Cycle," *Pharmacology, Biochemistry, and Behavior* 13 (1980): 737–38; Winnifred B. Cutler et al., "Sexual Behavior and Steroid Levels Among Gynecologically Mature Premenopausal Women," *Fertility and Sterility* 45, no. 4 (April 1986): 496–502; Winnifred B. Cutler et al., "Sexual Behavior Frequency and Biphasic Ovulatory Type Menstrual Cycles," *Physiology and Behavior* 34 (1985): 805–10; and Winnifred B. Cutler, Celso R. Garcia, and Abba H. Krieger, "Sexual Behavior Frequency and

Menstrual Cycle Length in Mature Premenopausal Women," *Psychoneuroendocrinology* 4 (1979): 297–309.

11. Martha K. McClintock, "Menstrual Synchrony and Suppression," *Nature* 229 (22 January 1971): 244–45.

12. E. M. Dewan, "On the Possibility of a Perfect Rhythm of Birth Control By Periodic Light Stimulation," *American Journal of Obstetrics and Gynecology* 99 (1967): 1016–19; and E. M. Dewan, M. F. Menkin, and J. Rock, "Effect of Photic Stimulation on the Human Menstrual Cycle," *Photochemistry and Photobiology* 27 (1978): 581–85.

13. Louise Lacey, *Lunaception* (New York: Coward, McCann & Geoghegan, Inc., 1974), 117.

14. Franz Waldhauser and Margot Dietzel, "Daily and Annual Rhythms in Human Melatonin Secretion: Role in Puberty Control," in Richard J. Wurtman, Michael J. Baum, and John T. Potts, Jr., eds., *The Medical and Biological Effects of Light, Annals of the New York Academy of Sciences*, vol. 453 (New York: New York Academy of Sciences, 1985): 212.

15. A Reinberg, "Éclairement et cycle menstruel de la Femme," in *La Photoregulation de la Reproduction Chez les Oiseaux et les Mammiferes*, Rapport au Collogue International du CRNS, Montpellier (1967): 529–30.

16. J. Valšík, "The Seasonal Rhythms of Menarche: A Review," *Human Biology* 37 (1965): 82.

17. Ibid.

18. Jiri Malek, J. Gleich, and V. Maly, "Characteristics of the Daily Rhythm of Menstruation and Labor," *Annals of the New York Academy of Sciences* 98 (30 October 1962): 1054.

19. Ibid.

20. B. L. Parry et al., "Melatonin and Phototherapy in Premenstrual Depression" (abstract), *Chronobiologia* 16, no. 2 (April–June 1989): 168.

21. Ernst Knobil, personal communication, 25 May 1988.

22. N. Sundararaj et al., "Seasonal Behavior of Human Menstrual Cycles: A Biometric Investigation," *Human Biology* 50, no. 1 (1978): 29.

23. F. A. Cook, "Some Physical Effects of Arctic Cold, Darkness, and Light," *Medical Record* 51 (1897): 835.

24. Veronica A. Ravnikar, Isaac Schiff, and Quentin R. Regestein, "Menopause and Sleep," in Herbert J. Buchsbaum, ed., *The Menopause* (New York: Springer-Verlag, 1983), 168–69.

25. Ibid., 169. Hormones such as estrogen and progestin taken during menopause can also cause serious health problems. See, for example, "Taking Hormones and Women's Health: Choices, Risks, Benefits," a 1989 paper by the National Women's Health Network, obtainable for $5 from the Boston Women's Health Book Collective, Box 192, West Somerville, MA 02144.

26. J. T. Eayrs, A. Glass, and H. H. Swenson, "The Ovary and Nervous System

in Relation to Behavior," in S. Zuckerman and B. J. Weir, eds., *The Ovary*, vol. 2 (New York: Academic Press, 1977), 430–31 (cites seven studies).

27. F. A. Cook, "Some Physical Effects," 835.

28. Richard G. Condon, *Inuit Behavior and Seasonal Change in the Canadian Arctic*, Studies in Cultural Anthropology no. 2 (Ann Arbor, Mich.: UMI Research Press, 1983), 154–55.

29. Alain Reinberg et al., "Circannual and Circadian Rhythms in Plasma Testosterone in Five Healthy Young Parisian Males," *Acta Endocrinologica* 80 (1975): 738–39 (cites five studies); and Alain Reinberg and Michel Lagoguey, "Circadian and Circannual Rhythms in Sexual Activity and Plasma Hormones (FSH, LH, Testosterone) of Five Human Males," *Archives of Sexual Behavior* 7, no. 1 (1978): 13.

30. Michael H. Smolensky, "Aspects of Human Chronopathology," in Alain Reinberg and Michael H. Smolensky, eds., *Biological Rhythms and Medicine* (New York: Springer Verlag, 1983), 138–39 (cites 13 studies).

31. Jongbloet, "Menses," 528.

32. P. Cohen, "Possible Relationship between Intergroup Variability in Circadian, Circamensual, and Circannual Rhythms in Man," *Chronobiologia* 16, no. 2 (April–June 1989): 123; and Jongbloet, "Menses," 528–29.

33. Smolensky, "Human Chronopathology," 140.

34. J. Elliott, "Finally: Some Details on In Vitro Fertilization," *Journal of the American Medical Association* 241 (1979): 868.

35. T. Roenneberg and J. Aschoff, "Annual Rhythm of Human Conception: The Role of Photoperiod and Ambient Temperature," *Proceedings of the Czechoslovakian Academy of Sciences*, in press.

36. Ellen W. Stern, Greer L. Alazer, and Nick Sanduleak, "Influence of the Full and New Moon on Onset of Labor and Spontaneous Rupture of Membranes," *Journal of Nurse-Midwifery* 33, no. 2 (March–April 1988): 57 (cites six studies).

37. Alain Reinberg, "Aspects of Circannual Rhythms in Man," in Eric T. Pengelley, ed., *Circannual Clocks: Annual Biological Rhythms* (New York: Academic Press, Inc., 1974), 459 (cites Smolensky et al., 1972).

38. Heinz Kirchhoff, "Unterliegt der Wehenbeginn kosmischen Einfluessen?" *Zentralblatt fuer Gynaekologie* 59, no. 3 (1935): 134–44.

39. E. Jenny, "Tagesperiodische Einfluesse auf Geburt und Tod," *Schweizerische Medizinische Wochenschrift* 14 (1933): 15; Michael Smolensky, Franz Halberg, and Frederick Sargent II, "Chronobiology of the Life Sequence," in S. Ito, K. Ogata, and H. Yoshimura, eds., *Advances in Climatic Physiology* (Tokyo: Igaku Shoin Ltd., 1972), 287; Eystein Glattae and Tor Bjerkedal, "The 24-Hour Rhythmicity of Birth," *Acta Obstetricia et Gynecologica Scandinavica* 62 (1983): 31–36; Malek, Gleich, and Maly, "Menstruation and Labor," 1047; and H. Kaiser and F. Halberg, "Circadian Aspects of Birth," *Annals of the New York Academy of Sciences* 98 (1962): 1057.

40. Alison Jolly, "Hour of Birth in Primates and Man," *Folia Primatologica* 18 (1972): 111 (cites Schlegel et al., 1966); and Malek, Gleich, and Maly, "Menstruation and Labor," 1049.

41. Kaiser and Halberg, "Circadian Aspects," 1063 (cites two studies); and Smolensky, "Human Chronopathology," 137 (cites Breart and Rumeau-Rouquette, 1979).

42. Reinberg, "Circannual Rhythms," 459.

43. *Childbirth Alternative Quarterly* 7, no. 3 (Spring 1986) (cites *World Population Data Sheet*, Washington, D.C., Population Reference Bureau, 1986).

CHAPTER 3: Sleeping and Waking

1. Charles A. Czeisler et al., "Human Sleep: Its Duration and Organization Depend on Its Circadian Phase," *Science* 210 (12 December 1980): 1264–65.

2. Alexander Borbély, *Secrets of Sleep* (New York: Basic Books, Inc., 1986) 193 (cites T. Åkerstedt and J. E. Fröberg, "Psychophysiological Circadian Rhythms in Women During 72 Hours of Sleep Deprivation," *Waking and Sleeping* 1 [1977]: 387–94).

3. Michael Terman, "On the Question of Mechanism in Phototherapy for Seasonal Affective Disorder: Considerations of Clinical Efficacy and Epidemiology," *Journal of Biological Rhythms*, in press.

4. Robert G. Skwerer, et al., "Neurobiology of Seasonal Affective Disorder and Phototherapy," *Journal of Biological Rhythms*, in press; and Verena Lacoste and Anna Wirz-Justice, "Seasonal Variation in Normal Subjects: An Update of Variables Current in Depression Research," in N. E. Rosenthal and M. Blehar, eds., *Seasonal Affective Disorder and Phototherapy* (New York: Guilford Press, in press).

5. Nathaniel Kleitman and Theodore G. Engelmann, "Sleep Characteristics of Infants," *Journal of Applied Physiology* 6 (1953): 269.

6. Michael E. Long, "What Is This Thing Called Sleep?" *National Geographic*, December 1987, 791.

7. Susan Wensley, "Shedding Light on Depression," in *P&S: The Journal of the College of Physicians and Surgeons of Columbia University* 6, no. 1 (Fall 1986): 18.

8. Borbély, *Secrets of Sleep*, 205–6.

9. Ibid., 43 (cites D. F. Kripke et al., "Short and Long Sleep and Sleeping Pills: Is Increased Mortality Associated?" *Archives of General Psychiatry* 36 (1979): 103–16).

10. R. A. Wever, "Characteristics of Human Circadian Rhythms," *Journal of Neural Transmission*, suppl. 21 (1986): 327; and Lacoste and Wirz-Justice, "Seasonal Variation," (cites A. Wirz-Justice, R. A. Wever, and J. Aschoff, "Seasonality in Freerunning Circadian Rhythms in Man," *Naturwissenschaften* 71 (1984); 316–19).

11. Lacoste and Wirz-Justice, "Seasonal Variation," (cites G. A. Kerkhof, "Interindividual Differences in the Human Circadian System: A Review," *Biological Psychiatry* 20 (1985): 83–112).

12. *International Journal of Chronobiology* 4 (1976): 100–103.

13. Charles A. Czeisler, Martin C. Moore-Ede, and Richard M. Coleman, "Resetting Circadian Clocks: Applications to Sleep Disorders Medicine and Occupational Health," in C. Guilleminault and E. Lugaresi, eds., *Sleep/Wake Disorders: Natural History, Epidemiology, and Long-Term Evolution* (New York: Raven Press, 1983), 247.

14. The most recent data (unpublished) as of 1989 from the National Ambulatory Medical Care Survey, National Center for Health Statistics, Public Health Service.

15. Martin C. Moore-Ede and Thomas A. Houpt, "Homeostatic Entrainment and Pacemaker Effects of Drugs That Regulate the Timing of Sleep and Wakefulness," reprint from NATO conference proceedings no. 415, *Biochemical Enhancement of Performance* (Neuilly-sur-Seine, France, n.d.), 9–5.

16. Czeisler, "Human Sleep," 1264.

17. Richard G. Condon, *Inuit Behavior and Seasonal Change in the Canadian Arctic*, *Studies in Cultural Anthropology*, no. 2 (Ann Arbor, Mich.: UMI Research Press, 1983), 142–43.

18. H. W. Simpson and J. G. Bohlen, "References in the North Polar Literature to Temporal Disorientation and Mental and Physical Changes Which Might Be Due to the Effects of the Arctic Light on the Circadian System," in J. N. Mills, ed., *Biological Aspects of Circadian Rhythms* (London: Plenum Press, 1973), 111–12.

19. Ibid., 114, citing from Dr. J. Lindhard's accounts of the Danish expedition to Greenland in "Contribution to the Physiology of Respiration under the Arctic Climate," *Meddelelser om Grønland* 41 (1913): 78–81.

20. D. Lingjaerde and T. Bratlid, "Triazolam (Halcion) Versus Flunitrazepam (Rohypnol) against Midwinter Insomnia in Northern Norway," *Acta Psychiatria Scandinavica* 64 (1981): 260.

21. Condon, *Inuit*, 134; and Richard G. Condon, personal communication, 15 June 1988.

22. Condon, *Inuit*, 134–35.

23. Frederick A. Cook, *Through the First Antarctic Night: 1898–1899* (Montreal: McGill-Queen's University Press, 1980), 303–4.

24. Simpson and Bohlen, "References," 113, quoting Dr. J. Lindhard's experiences.

25. "The Nature and Causes of Depression: Part II," *Harvard Medical School Mental Health Letter* 4, no. 8 (February 1988), 2.

26. Rolf M. Sinclair, "Moonlight and Circadian Rhythms," *Science* 235 (9 January 1987), 145, in response to Charles A. Czeisler et al., "Bright Light Resets

the Human Circadian Pacemaker Independent of the Timing of the Sleep-Wake Cycle,"*Science* 233 (8 August 1986), 667–71.

27. O. Lingjaerde, T. Bratlid, and T. Hansen, "Insomnia during the 'Dark Period' in Northern Norway," *Acta Psychiatrica Scandinavica* 71 (1985): 506.

CHAPTER 4: Eating and Drinking

1. See Martin C. Moore-Ede, Frank M. Sulzman, and Charles A. Fuller, *The Clocks That Time Us* (Cambridge, Mass.: Harvard University Press, 1982), 8–10 (cites observations of Swiss physician August Forel, 1910).

2. Juergen Aschoff et al., "Meal Timing in Humans during Isolation without Time Cues," *Journal of Biological Rhythms* 1, no. 2 (1986): 160; and Martin C. Moore-Ede and Charles A. Czeisler, eds., *Mathematical Models of the Circadian Sleep-Wake Cycle* (New York: Raven Press, 1984), 209.

3. J. E. Morley and A. S. Levine, "The Central Control of Appetite," *Lancet* 1 (19 Feb. 1983): 400.

4. Sarah Fryer Leibowitz, Gail Fogel Weiss, and Gail Shor-Posner, "Hypothalamic Serotonin: Pharmacological, Biochemical, and Behavorial Analyses of Its Feeding-Suppressive Action," *Clinical Neuropharmacology* 11, Suppl. 1, in press.

5. Ibid.

6. Ibid.

7. R. C. Graeber et al. *Human Eating Behavior: Preferences, Consumption Patterns, and Biorhythms*, Report for the Food Sciences Laboratory, U.S. Army (Natick, Mass.: Natick Research and Development Command, June 1987), 94.

8. T. Sasaki and F. Halberg, "Reproducibility during Decades and Individualization of Circannually Rhythmic Metabolic Rate in Japanese Men and Women," in A. Reinberg and F. Halberg, eds., *Chronopharmacology* (New York: Pergamon Press, 1978), 251.

9. Ibid., 247, 250.

10. T. Sasaki, "Geographical Distribution of Basal Metabolic Rate with Remarks to Biological Equator and Circannual Peak," *Chronobiologia* 14 (1987): 232.

11. Alain Reinberg, "Aspects of Circannual Rhythms in Man," in Eric T. Pengelley, ed., *Circannual Clocks: Annual Biological Rhythms* (New York: Academic Press, Inc., 1974), 475.

12. B. Zahorska-Markiewicz and A. Markiewicz, "Circannual Rhythm of Exercise Metabolic Rate in Humans," *European Journal of Applied Physiology* 52 (1984): 330; and F. Sargent II, "Season and the Metabolism of Fat and Carbohydrate: A Study of Vestigial Physiology," *Meteorological Monographs* 2, no. 8 (1954), 68 (cites three studies).

13. W. A. Van Staveren et al., "Seasonal Variation in Food Intake Pattern of Physical Activity and Change in Body Weight in a Group of Young Adult

Dutch Women Consuming Self-Selected Diet," *International Journal of Obesity* 10 (1986): 133.

14. S. M. Zifferblatt, C. S. Wilbur, and J. L. Pisky, "Understanding Food Habits," *Journal of the American Dietetic Association* 76 (1980): 11; Van Staveren et al., "Seasonal Variation," 138; and Reinberg, "Circannual Rhythms," 467.

15. Attarzadeh, "Seasonal Variation in Stature and Body Weight," *International Journal of Orthodontics* 21, no. 4 (1983): 8.

16. Michael Terman, "On the Question of Mechanism in Phototherapy for Seasonal Affective Disorder: Considerations of Clinical Efficacy and Epidemiology," *Journal of Biological Rhythms*, in press, (cites Terman et al., in preparation).

17. Van Staveren et al., "Seasonal Variation," 138–42.

18. J. Aschoff and H. Pohl, "Rhythmic Variations in Energy Metabolism," *Federation Proceedings* 29 (1970): 1550 (cites seven studies); and Zahorska-Markiewicz and Markiewicz, "Circannual Rhythm," 330.

19. Aschoff and Pohl, "Rhythmic Variations," 1550.

20. Graeber et al., *Human Eating*, 96.

21. E. Hirsch et al., "Body Weight Change During One Week on a Single Daily 2000-Calorie Meal Consumed as Breakfast (B) or Dinner (D)" (abstract), and H. Jacobs et al., "Relative Body Weight Loss on Limited Free-Choice Meal Consumed as Breakfast Than as Dinner" (abstract), *Chronobiologia* Suppl. 1 (1975): 31–32, 33; and J. Halberg, E. Halberg, and F. Halberg, "Nonobese Mammals Pair-Fed or on Free-Choice Diets May Be 'What They Eat' But Body Weight and Internal Circadian Timing Are Rhythmometrically Specifiable Functions of 'When They Eat,'" *Chronobiologia* 3 (1976): 77.

22. J. Halberg, E. Halberg, and F. Halberg, "Nonobese Mammals," 77–78.

23. A. H. Crisp and E. Stonehill, "Aspects of the Relationship between Sleep and Nutrition: A Study of 375 Psychiatric Outpatients," *British Journal of Psychiatry* 122 (1973): 393.

24. S. L. Smith and C. Sauder, "Food Cravings, Depression and Premenstrual Problems," *Psychosomatic Medicine* 31, no. 4 (1969): 281.

25. Madeline M. Gladis and B. Timothy Walsh, "Premenstrual Exacerbation of Binge Eating in Bulimia," *American Journal of Psychiatry* 144, no. 12 (December 1987): 1593.

26. Norman E. Rosenthal et al., "Seasonal Affective Disorder: Relevance for the Treatment and Research of Bulimia," in J. I. Hudson and H. G. Pope, eds., *Psychobiology of Bulimia* (Washington, D. C.: American Psychiatric Press, in press).

27. R. W. Morris, "Street Drug Interactions with Ethyl Alcohol, Circadian and Lunar Lethality Rhythms," *Life Sciences* 27 (1980): 2580.

28. V. P. Latenkov, "Circadian Rhythms of Adrenalin and Noradrenalin Excretion in Man under Normal Conditions and after Taking Alcohol," *Bulletin of Experimental Biology and Medicine* 99, no. 3 (1985): 346.

29. Ruth M. Guenther, "The Role of Nutritional Therapy in Alcoholism Treatment," *International Journal of Biosocial Research* 4, no. 1 (1983): 12.

30. R. Hermida et al., "Young Adult Women's Potential Endocrine Chronorisk of Alcoholism and Drug Addiction: Changes with Season in Kind and Timing," *Journal of the Minnesota Academy of Science* 48, no. 3 (1982/83): 20.

31. See R. P. Sturtevant et al., "Chronopharmacokinetics of Ethanol. III: Variation in Rate of Ethanolemia Decay in Human Subjects," *International Journal of Clinical Pharmacology* 16 (1978): 594–99; D. W. Minors and J. M. Waterhouse, "Aspects of Chronopharmacokinetics and Chronergy of Ethanol in Healthy Man," *Chronobiologia* 7, no. 4 (1980): 465–80; and R. Wilson, E. Newman, and H. Newman, "Diurnal Variation in Rate of Alcohol Metabolism," *Journal of Applied Physiology* 8 (1956): 557.

32. Alain Reinberg, "Chronobiology and Nutrition," in Alain Reinberg and Michael H. Smolensky, eds., *Biological Rhythms and Medicine* (New York: Springer Verlag, 1983), 225.

33. John Brick, "Circadian Variations in Behavioral and Biological Sensitivity to Ethanol," *Alcoholism: Clinical and Experimental Research* 8, no. 2 (March–April 1984): 210; and Reinberg, "Chronobiology," 236–37.

34. Morris, "Street Drug," 2578.

35. G. Schechter, P. White and F. Halberg, "Cosinor-Quantified Circannual Differences in Schizophrenic, Anxiety, and Alcohol Abuse Disorders," *Chronobiologia* 14 (1987): 232; and Ruthann P. Sturtevant, personal communication, 16 January 1989.

36. Robert E. McGrath, "A Preliminary Report on Seasonal Alcohol Abuse and Dependence," paper presented at the annual meeting of the Society for Light Treatment and Biological Rhythms, Bethesda, Md., 21 June 1989 (cites A. B. Goff et al., 1988; and M. R. Eastwood et al. 1978).

37. Ibid.

CHAPTER 5: Mood and Behavior

1. British Broadcasting Corporation, world service broadcast, 22 October 1987.

2. Norman E. Rosenthal et al., "Seasonal Affective Disorder: Relevance for the Treatment and Research of Bulimia," Figure 2, in J. I. Hudson and H. G. Pope, Jr., eds., *Psychobiology of Bulimia* (Washington, D.C.: American Psychiatric Press, in press).

3. Siegfried Kasper et al., "Psychological Effects of Light Therapy in Normals," *Journal of Biological Rhythms*, in press.

4. Michael Terman, "On the Question of Mechanism in Phototherapy for Seasonal Affective Disorder: Considerations of Clinical Efficacy and Epidemiology," *Journal of Biological Rhythms*, in press (cites Terman et al., in preparation).

5. Ibid.

6. Frederick A. Cook, *Through the First Antarctic Night: 1898–1899* (Montreal: McGill-Queen's University Press, 1980), 300.

7. J. Lindhard, "Contribution to the Physiology of Respiration under the Arctic Climate," *Meddelelser om Grønland* 41 (1913): 78–81, as cited in H. W. Simpson and J. G. Bohlen, "References in the North Polar Literature to Temporal Disorientation and Mental and Physical Changes Which Might Be Due to the Effects of the Arctic Light on the Circadian System," in J. N. Mills, ed., *Biological Aspects of Circadian Rhythms* (London: Plenum Press, 1973), 113.

8. Cook, *Antarctic Night*, 301.

9. Ibid., 304, 319.

10. Thomas A. Wehr, David A. Sack, and Norman E. Rosenthal, "Seasonal Affective Disorder with Summer Depression and Winter Hypomania," *American Journal of Psychiatry* 144, no. 12 (December 1987): 1602 (cites S. W. Jackson, *Melancholia and Depression from Hippocratic Times to Modern Times* (New Haven: Yale University Press, 1986).

11. Daniel F. Kripke, "Therapeutic Effects of Bright Light in Depressed Patients," in Richard J. Wurtman, Michael J. Baum, and John T. Potts, Jr., eds., *The Medical and Biological Effects of Light*, Annals of the New York Academy of Sciences, vol. 453 (New York: New York Academy of Sciences, 1985), 270 (cites F. Halberg, "Physiologic Considerations Underlying Rhythmometry, with Special Reference to Emotional Illness," in J. DeAjuriaguerra, ed., *Symposium Bel-Air III: Cycles Biologique et Psychiatrie* [Paris: Masson & Cie, 1967], 73–126).

12. Terman, "On the Question," (cites C. J. Hellekson, "Phenomenology of Seasonal Affective Disorder," in N. E. Rosenthal and M. Blehar, eds., *Seasonal Affective Disorder and Phototherapy* (New York: Guilford Press, in press).

13. Ibid.

14. Latitude is relative. For example, moving to Massachusetts from Colorado can bring on SAD; moving to Massachusetts from Alaska can alleviate it.

15. F. H. Humphris, *Artificial Sunlight and Its Therapeutic Uses* (Oxford: Humphrey Milford Oxford University Press, 1924), 221–23, as quoted in Anna Wirz-Justice, "Light Therapy for Depression: Present Status, Problems, and Perspectives," in P. Berner and E. Gabriel, eds., *Psychopathology* 19, suppl. 2 (1986): 140.

16. Michael Terman et al., "Light Therapy for Seasonal Affective Disorder: A Review of Efficacy," *Neuropsychopharmacology*, in press.

17. Michael Terman et al., "Dawn and Dusk Simulation as a Therapeutic Intervention," *Biological Psychiatry* 25 (1989): 966–70.

18. Thomas A. Wehr et al., "Eye- Versus Skin-Phototherapy of Seasonal Affective Disorder," *American Journal of Psychiatry* 144 (1987): 753–57; and Dan A. Oren et al., "Effects of Different Light Wavelengths in SAD" (abstract), Annual Meeting of the Society for Light Treatment and Biological Rhythms, 21 June 1989, 26.

19. Robert G. Skwerer et al., "Neurobiology of Seasonal Affective Disorder and

Phototherapy," *Journal of Biological Rhythms* 3, no. 2 (1988): 142; and Dan A. Oren, Jean R. Joseph-Vanderpool, and Norman E. Rosenthal, "Supersensitivity of SAD Patients to Dim Light" (abstract), Annual Meeting of the Society for Light Treatment and Biological Rhythms, 21 June 1989, 7.

20. Wirz-Justice, "Light Therapy," 138; and Rosenthal et al., "Seasonal Affective Disorder: Relevance," 7.

21. Betsey M. Sutherland et al., "Photoreactivation and Other Ultraviolet/Visible Light Effects on DNA in Human Skin," in Wurtman, Baum, and Potts, eds., *Effects of Light*, 73–79.

22. "Airs, Waters, Places," in *Hippocrates*, vol. 1, trans. W. H. S. Jones (New York: G. P. Putnam's Sons, 1923), 105.

23. Eiji Takahashi, "Seasonal Variation of Conception and Suicide," *Tohoku Journal of Experimental Medicine* 84 (1964): 215–226; and E. Souetre et al., "Seasonality of Suicides: Environmental, Sociological, and Biological Covariations," *Journal of Affective Disorders* 13 (1987): 215.

24. Martin C. Moore-Ede, Frank M. Sulzman, and Charles A. Fuller, *The Clocks That Time Us* (Cambridge, Mass.: Harvard University Press, 1982), 370 (cites Wehr, 1979).

25. Ibid. (cites Morgan and Cheadle, 1976).

26. D. Borsook et al., "Gamma-Aminobutyric Acid and the Neural Basis of Circadian Timekeeping: Implications for Pathophysiology and Psychopharmacotherapy of Circadian Based Disorders," in A. Reinberg, M. Smolensky, and G. Labrecque, eds., *Annual Review of Chronopharmacology*, vol. 1 (New York: Pergamon Press, 1984), 53; and Philip W. Gold, Frederick K. Goodwin, and George P. Chrousos, "Clinical and Biochemical Manifestations of Depression: Relation to the Neurobiology of Stress (Part II)," *New England Journal of Medicine* 319, no. 7 (18 August 1988), 416.

27. D. F. Kripke et al., "Phototherapy for Nonseasonal Major Depressive Disorders," in N. E. Rosenthal and M. Blehar, eds., *Seasonal Affective Disorder and Phototherapy* (New York: Guilford Press, in press); and Terman and Wirz-Justice, in preparation.

CHAPTER 6: Skin and Bones

1. Vitamin D is actually a hormone, not a vitamin as was originally thought. See D. M . Davies, "Calcium Metabolism in Healthy Men Deprived of Sunlight," in Richard J. Wurtman, Michael J. Baum, and John T. Potts, Jr., eds., *The Medical and Biological Effects of Light*, Annals of the New York Academy of Sciences, vol. 453 (New York: New York Academy of Sciences, 1985), 25 (cites Kodicek, "The Story of Vitamin D: From Vitamin to Hormone," 1974). Vitamin D obtained through light-chemical reaction is called vitamin D_3, but that obtained through food or diet supplements is called vitamin D_2. In this chapter both types are referred to simply as vitamin D.

2. Michael F. Holick, "The Photobiology of Vitamin D and Its Consequences for Humans," in Wurtman, Baum, and Potts, eds., *Effects of Light*, 5.

3. Barbara Gilchrest, personal communication, 18 January 1989; and Holick, "Photobiology," 5.

4. Holick, "Photobiology," 11.

5. David H. Sliney, "Physical Factors in Cataractogenesis: Ambient Ultraviolet Radiation and Temperature," *Investigative Ophthalmology and Visual Science* 27 (May 1986): 782.

6. Robert M. Neer, "Environmental Light: Effects of Vitamin D Synthesis and Calcium Metabolism in Humans," in Wurtman, Baum, and Potts., eds., *Effects of Light*, 15.

7. A. R. Webb, L. Kline, and M. F. Holick, "Influence of Season and Latitude on the Cutaneous Synthesis of Vitamin D: Exposure to Winter Sunlight in Boston and Edmonton Will Not Promote Vitamin D Synthesis in Human Skin," *Journal of Clinical Endocrinology and Metabolism* 67, no. 2 (1988): 376–77.

8. Ibid.

9. J. M. Aitken, J. B. Anderson, and P. W. Horton, "Seasonal Variations in Bone Mineral Content after the Menopause," *Nature* 241 (5 January 1973): 60.

10. Holick, "Photobiology," 1.

11. Neer, "Environmental Light," 19; and Michael F. Holick, "Vitamin D Requirements for the Elderly," *Clinical Nutrition* 5, no. 3 (May–June 1986): 125 (cites Doppelt et al., 1983).

12. Davies, "Calcium Metabolism," 26.

13. Joseph Wechsberg, "Mørketiden," *New Yorker*, (18 March 1972), 113.

14. Ultraviolet light on the skin may alleviate depression in a minority of those with seasonal affective disorder, but this is still under debate. See chapter 5.

15. Seymour Zigman, "Recent Research on Near-UV Radiation and the Eye," in Frederick Urbach and Richard W. Gange, eds., *The Biological Effects of UVA Radiation* (New York: Praeger Publishers, 1986), 253–54.

16. See Hugh R. Taylor et al., "Effect of Ultraviolet Radiation on Cataract Formation," *New England Journal of Medicine* 319 (1 December 1988): 1429–33; and Zigman, "Recent Research," 252–62.

17. British Broadcasting Corporation broadcast; and *New York Times*, 17 April 1988.

18. Margaret A. Tucker et al., "Sunlight Exposure as Risk Factor for Intraocular Malignant Melanoma," *New England Journal of Medicine* 313, no. 13 (26 September 1985): 789.

19. Erik Thorud, Ole Petter Fraas Clausen, and Ole Didrik Laerum, "Circadian Rhythms in Cell Population Kinetics of Self-Renewing Mammalian Tissues," in Leland N. Edmunds, Jr., ed., *Cell Cycle Clocks* (New York: Marcel Dekker, Inc., 1984), 116.

20. Irene E. Kochevar, Madhu A. Pathak, and John A. Parrish, "Photophysics, Photochemistry, and Photobiology," in Thomas B. Fitzpatrick et al., *Dermatology in General Medicine* 3rd ed. (New York: McGraw-Hill Book Company, 1987), 1453.

21. Adapted from John A. Parrish, H. A. D. White, and Madhu A. Pathak, "Photomedicine," in Thomas B. Fitzpatrick et al., eds., *Dermatology in General Medicine*, 2d ed. (New York: McGraw-Hill, 1979), 984.

22. C. Cole et al., "Effect of Indoor Lighting on Normal Skin," in Wurtman, Baum, and Potts, eds., *Effects of Light*, 315.

23. Barbara A. Gilchrest, "Geriatric Skin Problems," *Hospital Practice*, 30 September 1986, 55.

24. Barbara A. Gilchrest, "Overview of Skin Aging," *Journal of Cutaneous Aging and Cosmetic Dermatology* 1, no. 1 (1988): 2.

25. Vincent A. DeLeo, "Prevention of Skin Cancer," *Journal of Dermatologic Surgery and Oncology* 14, no. 8 (August 1988): 903 (cites S. Chew et al., 1988).

26. C. D'Arcy J. Holman, Bruce K. Armstrong, and Peter J. Heenan, "A Theory of the Etiology and Pathogenesis of Human Cutaneous Malignant Melanoma," *Journal of the National Cancer Institute* 71, no. 4 (October 1983): 651–56; and Robert A. Lew et al., "Sun Exposure Habits in Patients with Cutaneous Melanoma: A Case Control Study," *Journal of Dermatologic Surgery and Oncology* 9 (12 December 1983): 981–86.

27. Margaret L. Kripke, "Health Effects of Stratospheric Ozone Depletion: An Overview," in T. Schneider et al., eds., *Atmospheric Ozone Research and Its Policy Implications* (Amsterdam: Elsevier Science Publishers B.V., 1989), 797–98 (cites Romerdahl et al., in press).

28. B. A. Gilchrest, "Impact of Age and Environment on Cutaneous Function," *Giornale Italiano di Chirurgia Dermatologica ed Oncologia* 2, no. 3–4 (1987): 185 (cites two studies).

29. Margaret L. Kripke, "Potential Effects of Increased UVB Radiation on the Immune System," U.S. Senate Committee on Environment and Public Works Hearing on Stratospheric Ozone Depletion, 12 May 1987, 4; Peter Hersey et al., "Immunological Effects of Solarium Exposure," *The Lancet*, 12 March 1983, 545; and Peter Hersey et al., "Alteration of T Cell Subsets and Induction of Suppressor T Cell Activity in Normal Subjects After Exposure to Sunlight," *The Journal of Immunology* 131, no. 1 (July 1983): 171–74.

30. Daphne A. Roe, "Photodegradation of Carotenoids in Human Subjects," *Federation Proceedings* 46, no. 5 (April 1987): 1986.

31. Hersey et al., "Immunological Effects," 545; Gilchrest, "Impact of Age," 189 (cites O'Dell et al., 1980); and Edward C. De Fabo and Frances P. Noonan, "Mechanism of Immune Suppression by Ultraviolet Irradiation in Vivo," *Journal of Experimental Medicine* 157 (July 1983): 95.

32. Report of the Ozone Trends Panel, NASA, March 1988, as cited in M. Kripke, "Health Effects," 795.

33. John S. Hoffman, ed., *An Assessment of the Risks of Stratospheric Modification*, U.S. Environmental Protection Agency, March 1987, as cited in M. Kripke, "Health Effects," 797, 799.

34. Margaret L. Kripke, "Potential Effects of Increased UVB Radiation on the Immune System," U.S. Senate Committee on Environment and Public Works Hearing on Stratospheric Ozone Depletion, 12 May 1987, 5 (cites human and animal studies).

35. Lois Y. Matsuoka et al., "Sunscreens Suppress Cutaneous Vitamin D Synthesis," *Journal of Clinical Endocrinology and Metabolism* 64, no. 6 (1987): 1166–67; and Barbara Gilchrest, personal communication, 18 January 1989, referring to study by Michael F. Holick.

36. Holick, "Vitamin D," 128–29.

37. Neer, "Environmental Light," 18 (refers to Neer et al., 1971).

38. *Health Facts* XIII, no. 115 (December 1988): 2 (cites study by John Trevithick et al., and population studies by Tufts USDA Human Research Center on Aging).

39. Homer S. Black, "Photocarcinogenesis and Diet," *Federation Proceedings* 46, no. 5 (April 1987): 1901–5.

CHAPTER 7: Wellness and Disease

1. Quotation adapted from Franz Halberg, *Chronobiology of Human Blood Pressure*, 2d ed., (Minneapolis: Medtronic Continuing Medical Education Seminars, August 1986), 97.

2. Frederick A. Cook, *Through the First Antarctic Night: 1898–1899* (Montreal: McGill-Queen's University Press, 1980), 292.

3. From *The Art of Prolonging Life* (London: J. Bell, 1797).

4. Alain Reinberg, "Aspects of Circannual Rhythms in Man," in Eric T. Pengelley, ed., *Circannual Clocks: Annual Biological Rhythms* (New York: Academic Press, Inc., 1974), 476–77.

5. Danielle Pansu et al., "Circannual and Circa-Semiannual Rhythms of Basal and Stimulated Gastric Secretion in Conscious Cats," *Chronobiology International* 4, no. 1 (1987): 59.

6. *Chronobiology: A Science in Tune with the Rhythms of Life*, brochure produced by Earl Bakken (Minneapolis: 1986), 12 (cites J. E. Muller, P. H. Stone, and Z. G. Turi, "Circadian Variation in the Frequency of Onset of Acute Myocardial Infarction," *New England Journal of Medicine* 313 (21 November 1985): 1315–22.

7. Michael H. Smolensky, "Aspects of Human Chronopathology," in Alain Reinberg and Michael H. Smolensky, eds., *Biological Rhythms and Medicine* (New York: Springer Verlag, 1983), 168.

8. Ibid., 178.

9. G. Fernandes, F. Halberg, and R. A. Good, "Circadian Rhythm in T. B.

and Natural Killer Cells," in M. H. Smolensky et al., eds., *Recent Advances in the Chronobiology of Allergy and Immunology* (New York: Pergamon Press, 1980), 292.

10. Richard G. Condon, *Inuit Behavior and Seasonal Change in the Canadian Arctic*, Studies in Cultural Anthropology no. 2, (Ann Arbor, Mich.: UMI Research Press, 1983), 145.

11. F. Halberg, E. Halberg, and F. Carandente, "Chronobiology and Metabolism in the Broader Context of Timely Intervention and Timed Treatment," *Diabetes Research Today* Symposia Medica Hoechst, vol. 12 (Capri) (New York: F. K. Schattauer Verlag, 1976), 46 (cites Virey, 1814, quotation translated by Hyman).

12. The information is from the following sources: (aspirin) J. G. Moore and R. H. Goo, "Day and Night Aspirin-Induced Gastric Mucosal Damage and Protection by Ranitidene in Man," *Chronobiology International* 4, no. 1 (1987): 111; (sleeping pills) Alain Reinberg, "Clinical Chronopharmacology: An Experimental Basis for Chronotherapy," in Alain Reinberg and Michael H. Smolensky, eds., *Biological Rhythms and Medicine* (New York: Springer Verlag, 1983), 239 (cites five studies); (antihistamines) ibid. (cites two studies); (bronchodilator) William J. Hrushesky, personal communication, 10 January 1989; (steroids) ibid.; (indomethacin) Reinberg, "Clinical Chronopharmacology," 238–39 (cites Job et al., 1981).

13. Robert R. Klevecz et al., "Circadian Gating of S Phase in Human Ovarian Cancer," *Cancer Research* 47 (1 December, 1987): 6267.

14. R. C. Graeber et al., *Human Eating Behavior: Preferences, Consumption Patterns, and Biorhythms*, Report for the Food Sciences Laboratory, U.S. Army (Natick, Mass.: Natick Research and Development Command, June 1987), 94 (cites four studies).

15. P. Cohen, Y. Wax, and B. Modan, "Seasonality in the Occurrence of Breast Cancer," *Cancer Research* 43 (1983): 892; and H. I. Jacobson and D. T. Janerich, "Is Seasonality in Human Reproduction Related to Seasonality in Tissue Levels of Estrogen Receptor?" in *Functional Correlates of Hormone Receptors in Reproduction* (New York: Elsevier Science Publishing Co. Inc., 1980), 579.

16. Jacobson and Janerich, "Seasonality," 574.

17. A. Bluming et al., "Timing of Breast Cancer Surgery Relative to Menses Determines Outcome" (abstract), annual meeting of the American Society of Clinical Oncology, 21–23 May 1989; and H. V. Ratajczak, R. B. Sothern, and W. J. M. Hrushesky, "Estrous Influence on Surgical Cure of a Mouse Breast Cancer," *Journal of Experimental Medicine* 168 (July 1988): 78.

18. *Chronobiology: A Science in Tune with the Rhythms of Life* 13–14 (refers to studies by Halberg, 1977, in collaboration with Gupta and Deka, 1975).

19. W. J. M. Hrushesky, R. V. Roemeling, and R. B. Sothern, "Preclinical and Clinical Cancer Chronotherapy," in J. Arendt, ed., *Biological Rhythms in Clinical Practice*, in press.

20. William J. M. Hrushesky et al., "Circadian-Based Infusional Chrono-Chemotherapy Controls Progressive Metastatic Renal Cell Carcinoma," *Seminars in Surgical Oncology* 4 (1988): 110; and Reinhard von Roemeling et al., "Progressive Metastatic Renal Cell Carcinoma Controlled by Continous 5-Fluoro-2-Deoxyuridine Infusion," *Journal of Urology* 139 (1988): 259.

21. Hrushesky, Roemeling, and Sothern, "Preclinical," 2.

22. Halberg, *Chronobiology of Human Blood Pressure*, 173.

23. Fernandes, Halberg, and Good, "Circadian Rhythm," 291.

24. M. H. Smolensky et al., "Chronobiology and Asthma. I. Day-Night Differences in Bronchial Patency and Dyspnea and Circadian Rhythm Dependencies" *Journal of Asthma* 23, no. 6 (1986): 321–43; Smolensky et al., "Chronobiology and Asthma. II. Body-Time-Dependent Differences in the Kinetics and Effects of Bronchodilator Medications," *Journal of Asthma* 24, no. 2 (1987): 91–134; and A. Reinberg et al., "Chronobiology and Asthma. III. Timing Corticotherapy to Biological Rhythms to Optimize Treatment Goals," *Journal of Asthma* 25, no. 4 (1988): 219–48.

25. John Moore and Lawrence Scheving, personal communications, 6 September 1988; and William J. M. Hrushesky, personal communication, 10 January 1989.

CHAPTER 8: Aging and Death

1. National Institute of Aging, personal communication, 9 January 1989.

2. Glenn A. Zorn and Bonnie Smith, "Cell Clocks and Cellular Aging," in Leland N. Edmunds, Jr., ed., *Cell Cycle Clocks* (New York: Marcel Dekker, Inc., 1984), 557.

3. Leland N. Edmunds, Jr., "Clocked Cell Cycle Clocks: Implications toward Chronopharmacology and Aging," in Harvey V. Samis, Jr., and Salvatore Capobianco, eds., *Aging and Biological Rhythms* (New York: Plenum Press, 1978), 170.

4. Peter Bogaty and David D. Waters, "Circadian Patterns in Coronary Disease: The Mournfulness of Morning," *The Canadian Journal of Cardiology* 4, no. 1 (January–February 1988), 9.

5. Michael Smolensky, Franz Halberg, and Frederick Sargent II, "Chronobiology of the Life Sequence," in S. Ito, K. Ogata, and H. Yoshimura, eds., *Advances in Climatic Physiology* (Tokyo: Igaku Shoin Ltd., 1972), 294, 295 (cites statistics from 53 studies of 433,000 deaths).

6. F. Halberg, E. Halberg, and F. Carandente, "Chronobiologic Optimization in Surgery," *Chronobiologia* 8, no. 3 (July–September 1981), 288.

7. Erhard Haus, et al., "Reference Values for Chronopharmacology," in A. Reinberg, M. Smolensky, and G. Labrecque, eds., *Annual Review of Chronopharmacology*, vol. 4, (New York: Pergamon Press, 1988), 378 (cites Murphy et al., 1986).

8. Simon W. Rabkin, Francis A. L. Mathewson, and Robert B. Tate, "Chronobiology of Cardiac Sudden Death in Men," *Journal of the American Medical Association* 244, no. 12 (19 September 1980), 1357.

9. See E. Souetre et al., "Seasonality of Suicides: Environmental, Sociological, and Biological Covariations," *Journal of Affective Disorders* 13 (1987): 215–25.

10. Paul A. Kettl, Tracy Collins, and Edward O. Bixler, "Melatonin and Hour of Suicide" (abstract), American Psychiatric Association meeting, San Francisco, 6–12 May 1989.

11. C. P. Thakur et al., "Relation between Full Moon and Medicolegal Deaths," *Indian Journal of Medical Research* 85 (March 1987): 318 (cites three studies).

12. K. A. Dawson, "Temporal Effects of Pinealectomy, Melatonin, and Photocycle Reversal on Age-Related Behavioral Changes" (abstract), *Chronobiologia* 16, no. 2 (April–June 1989), 126.

13. Daniel R. Wagner, "Sleep," *Generations* (Winter 1984), 34.

14. Scott S. Campbell et al., "Exposure to Light in Healthy Elderly Subjects and Alzheimer's Patients," *Physiology and Behavior* 42 (1988): 142.

15. H. Levine et al., "Rhythm-Referred Changes Gauge Optimization of Life Quality for Elderly and Other Ages," *Chronobiologia* 8, no. 2 (April–June 1981), 189.

EPILOGUE

1. Daniel F. Kripke and Lois Watanabe Gregg, "Circadian Effects of Varying Environmental Light," in L. Miles and R. Braughton, eds., *Clinical Evaluation and Physiological Monitoring in the Home and Work Environment* (New York: Raven Press, in press).

2. Approximate measurement at noon on June 21, 38 degrees north latitude (central United States, southern Europe), in John E. Kaufman and Jack F. Christensen, *The IES Lighting Handbook* (New York: Illuminating Engineering Society, 1972), figure 7–8, p. 7–5.

3. Michael Terman and David S. Schlager, "Twilight Therapeutics, Winter Depression, Melatonin, and Sleep," *Sleep and Biological Rhythms*, in press.

4. Ibid.

5. Thomas J. Savides et al., "Natural Light Exposure of Young Adults," *Physiology and Behavior* 38 (1986): 572; and N. Okudaira, D. F. Kripke, and J. B. Webster, "Naturalistic Studies of Human Light Exposure," *American Journal of Physiology: Regulatory Integrative and Comparative Physiology* 14, no. 4 (October 1983): R613.

6. Okudaira, Kripke, and Webster, "Naturalistic Studies," R614.

7. Richard J. Wurtman and Judith J. Wurtman, "Carbohydrates and Depression," *Scientific American* (January 1989), 75 (cites Daniel Kripke).

8. Savides et al., "Natural Light," 572; Okudaira, Kripke, and Webster, "Nat-

uralistic Studies," R615; and Michael Terman, "Daylight Deprivation and Replenishment: A Psychobiological Problem With a Naturalistic Solution," in E. Bales and I. R. McCluney, eds., *Architecture and Natural Light* (Atlanta: American Society of Heating, Refrigeration, and Air-Conditioning Engineers, in press).

9. Siegfried Kasper, "The Effects of Phototherapy in Normals with and without Reported Seasonal Changes of Mood and Behavior," *Archives of General Psychiatry*, in press (cites Wirz-Justice et al., 1986; Dietzel et al., 1986; and Rosenthal et al., 1987).

Because of the nature of this book, it was not possible to include all notes originally intended. The author wishes to acknowledge the researchers whose studies contributed to the following chapters but are not included in the chapters' notes.

Chapter 1
J. G. Bohlen, Richard G. Condon, Nancy P. Gordon, Lois Watanabe Gregg, Kenneth R. Groh, Gerard A. Groos, Franz Halberg, Fritz Hollwich, Ronald Konopka, Daniel F. Kripke, Mary C. Lobban, Johanna H. Meijer, John C. Meinert, Dan A. Oren, Russel J. Reiter, C. P. Richter, Benjamin Rusak, H. W. Simpson, and Michael Young.

Chapter 2
Frank A. Brown, Jr., Bruce Chabner, A. Chavarria, J. L. Cloudsley-Thompson, Michael Cohen, Michael Cooperstock, Ursula Cowgill, Michael G. Dube, Jackie E. England, H. Munro Fox, Rose E. Frisch, Effie Graham, R. Iglesias, H. I. Jacobson, D. T. Janerich, Joseph T. Keohan, F. Leidenberger, Marc Lippmann, Joseph Majzoub, A. Menaker, W. Menaker, Steven M. Reppert, N. Sasakawa, Machelle M. Seibel, Martha Stuart, E. Takahashi, A. Terrés, L. Michael Trapasso, T. Uehata, Penny Ward, David R. Weaver, Wilse B. Webb, G. E. Webley, Robert A. Wolfe, and Mark J. Yurchisin.

Chapter 3
Domien Beersma, D. Borsook, Serge Daan, Alfred J. Lewy, Charles S. Mullin, Jr., and Patricia N. Prinz.

Chapter 4
K. J. Acheson, Kursheed Asghar, J. P. Flatt, Margaret M. Heffernan, Ancel Keys, Verena Lacoste, J. H. Mendelson, C. P. Richter, D. M. W. Salmon, F. Sargent II, Lawrence E. Scheving, Albert J. Stunkard, Anna Wirz-Justice, J. J. Wurtman, and R. J. Wurtman.

Chapter 5
George P. Chrousos, Philip W. Gold, Frederick K. Goodwin, N. Mrosovsky, Gordon Parker, C. P. Richter, and Stephen Walter.

Chapter 6
Israel Abramov, Karunyan Arulananthem, Derek J. Cripps, Robert M. Greenstein, L. C. Harber, Lester F. Libow, Mary Rudolf, Sara Scheide, and Luke Thorington.

Chapter 7
Peter Bogaty, Devendra P. Dubey, Erhard Haus, M. Krzanowski, David M. Lakatua, John D. Palmer, H. W. Simpson, Andrew Smith, David D. Waters, and Edmund J. Yunis.

Chapter 8
Donald L. Bliwise, Bruce Chabner, Michael Cohen, Gerhard Dirlich, Devendra P. Dubey, Charles F. Ehret, S. Fujimaki, Kenneth R. Groh, E. Jenny, Marc Lippman, John C. Meinert, Walter Nelson, Jorge A. Romero, Elliot D. Weitzman, R. A. Wever, and Edmund J. Yunis.

GLOSSARY

Biological rhythms. Recurrent, predictable changes in the body's functions. Biological rhythms can repeat themselves every 24 hours, or have longer or shorter cycles. Examples are circadian, circalunar, and circannual rhythms (see below). Biological rhythms often reflect the planetary rotations of the earth and moon in relation to each other and to the sun.

Chronobiology. The study of the time structures of life, such as biological rhythms.

Chronotherapy. Medical treatment timed according to the rhythms of the body's tissues or organs in order to increase a treatment's desired effects and/or reduce its undesired effects.

Circadian rhythm. A biological rhythm recurring in approximate 24-hour cycles.

Circadian system. A network of rhythms in the body's cells, tissues, and fluids, usually synchronized by sunlight in order to function in time with each 24-hour cycle of day and night.

Circalunar rhythm. A biological rhythm recurring in approximate 29.5-day cycles, like the cycles of the moon.

Circannual rhythm. A biological rhythm recurring in approximate yearly cycles, also called a seasonal rhythm.

Circaseptan rhythm. A biological rhythm recurring in cycles of approximately one week. Researchers debate whether this rhythm is built into the body or imposed on the body by our calendar.

Desynchronization. The state of two or more normally synchronized rhythms in the body's functions that have changed their timing in relation to one another. Rhythms can break away from one another if a person is deprived of all time cues, such as sunlight, over a long period of time.

Free-running. The approximate 25-hour cycle of the body's innate circadian system. This is the "approximate day" to which the body's rhythms are synchronized unless they are set by sunlight or other time cues to the 24-hour day-night cycle. When the body is deprived of all time cues, it first free-runs, then desynchronizes.

Lux. A unit of illumination equal to the direct light of a candle on a surface one meter away. Lux cannot be translated into watts, but as a point of reference, 2500 lux = the light from six to eight 40-watt lamps, at a distance of two to three feet.

Pacemaker. Clusters of nerve cells in the brain that receive light signals from the eye and/or transmit these signals to other cells. Also called a biological clock or oscillator.

Ultradian rhythm. A biological rhythm recurring in cycles of less than 20 hours.

Zeitgeber. A time cue, such as sunlight, that sets the body's network of rhythms according to an appropriate time scale such as 24 hours. From the German, meaning time-cue, or, literally "giver of time."

RESOURCES

W. J. M. Hrushesky, M.D.
Albany Veterans Administration Medical Center
Division of Oncology 111-C
113 Holland Avenue
Albany, N.Y. 12208
(518) 445-5297, or (518) 462-3311
Runs medical trials testing optimal timing of a variety of cancer treatments
including surgery, radiation, chemotherapy, biological response modifiers,
and human growth factors.

Light Therapy Information Service
New York Psychiatric Institute
(212) 960-5714
Provides information on light therapy for seasonal affective disorder, sleep
scheduling disorders, and the use of bright light in alleviating jet lag and
adjusting to shift work. Directs callers to research programs or private
practitioners nationwide and in Europe. Also has names of companies
making lamps used in treatment, and information on safety recommen-
dations and insurance reimbursement for such lamps.

NOSAD
P.O. Box 40133
Washington, D.C. 20016
Washington, D.C.–based organization for seasonal affective disorder. Sends
information on SAD through its quarterly newsletter, and organizes support
groups in the Washington area. Has information on support groups across
the country and offers guidelines on forming new groups. For a membership
application write to the address above.

Society for Light Treatment and Biological Rhythms
722 West 168th Street
Box 50
New York, N.Y. 10032
Sends newsletter with information on research, book reviews, and notices

of meetings. Membership open to the general public as well as to researchers, students pursuing an advanced degree related to bright light treatment or biological rhythms, and corporations (manufacturers of lightboxes and related equipment, pharmaceutical companies, publishers). For a membership application write to the address above, or to the European membership office:

Anna Wirz-Justice, Ph.D.
Psychiatrische Universitaetsklinik
University of Basel
Wilhelm Klein-Strasse 27
Ch-4025 Basel
Switzerland

INDEX

About the Author

Jane Wegscheider Hyman is a medical writer and consultant to the Boston Women's Health Book Collective. She is a coauthor of *The New Our Bodies, Ourselves*, and *Ourselves, Growing Older*. Born in the the United States, she spent her early adulthood in Vienna, Austria, and now lives in Newton, Massachusetts.